DUKE UNIVERSITY PUBLICATIONS

ITURBIDE *of* MEXICO

THE PLAZA DE ARMAS, MEXICO CITY

From an engraving made in 1810 by Louis Bouquet for Alexander von Humboldt's *Vues des cordillères et monumens des peuples indigènes de l'Amérique*

ITURBIDE
of MEXICO

WILLIAM SPENCE ROBERTSON
Professor of History, Emeritus
University of Illinois

GREENWOOD PRESS, PUBLISHERS
NEW YORK   1968

Preface

AS A GRADUATE student investigating the picturesque career of Francisco de Miranda in the old Library of Yale University, I came across a bundle of manuscripts concerning a Mexican named Agustín de Yturbide or Iturbide. Rumor had it that these papers had been brought to the United States by a soldier who had fought in Mexico. As the spectacular career of Iturbide interested me, from that time forth, more or less in connection with my other historical studies, I undertook to gather material concerning the Mexican revolutionary who was largely instrumental in separating his native land from the rule of Spain and who also became the first Emperor of Mexico. In recent years the trail led me to Spain, Mexico, Texas, and California.

A great deal of rare printed and manuscript material has been found in libraries and archives, especially in our Hispanic Southwest. Many persons facilitated my use of that material. Miss Helen Bruner, the Librarian of the Sutro Branch of the California State Library, was of inestimable service to me when I delved into the uncatalogued part of the Sutro Collection. Mr. Gabriel A. Martins of Austin, Texas, kindly allowed me to examine in his law office a useful collection of manuscripts from Mexico. The writer also appreciated the helpfulness of Mrs. Eleanor Bancroft, the assistant to the Director of the Bancroft Library at the University of California. Mr. Donald Coney, as the Librarian of the University of Texas and later as the Librarian of the University of California, was very helpful to me during my sojourn in Austin and in Berkeley. Worthy of special mention was the generous fashion in which the University of Texas made available to me the rich treasures of books, periodicals, and original manuscripts which in recent years have been added to its Library and its Archives Collection.

Mention should not be omitted of some other persons who in one way or another aided me in my long-sustained quest. Dr. Constantine E. McGuire of Washington, D. C., was instrumental in securing for me a copy of the famous Plan signed by Iturbide at Iguala on February 24, 1821, which is owned by Mrs. Louise de Yturbide. Dr. Solon J. Buck, the Director of the Manuscript Division of the Library of Congress, was of assistance to me in checking my citations of the Iturbide Papers which had been dislocated by the rearrangement of those manuscripts after I had first used them. Father William J. Coleman of Maryknoll Junior College obliged me by searching for material for my biography in the Archives of the Vatican and in the Achives of the Spanish Embassy at Rome.

Dr. Robin A. Humphreys of University College, London, facilitated certain research of mine in the Public Record Office, London. Dr. Carlos E. Castañeda and the late Dr. Charles W. Hackett of the University of Texas gave me helpful suggestions concerning my investigations. Both Dr. Herbert E. Bolton and Dr. James F. King of the University of California also gave me aid and advice. Director Dorothy W. Knepper of the San Jacinto Museum of History was of service in furnishing me with copies of documents and photographs of portraits preserved in that museum. The one-time director of the national archives of Mexico, Lic. Julio Jiménez Rueda, aided me by securing from the archives of Morelia certain data about the marriage of Iturbide. Dr. Silvio Zavala, a leading Mexican historian, secured for me copies of rare documents concerning the father of Agustín de Iturbide and also furnished me with photographs of portraits from the gallery in the Museo Nacional de Historia in the Castle of Chapultepec. My late lamented friend, Sr. Rómulo Zabala, helped me by securing from the Archivo del Museo Mitre in Buenos Aires some useful data regarding the visit of the Argentina Liberator, José de San Martín, to London, where in 1824 he had a mysterious interview with the Liberator of Mexico.

To the staff of the University of Illinois Library I am indebted for frequent service. In particular, I should mention those members of the staff who served me at the reference desk. The Editor of Duke University Press made helpful suggestions about the book. My wife aided me by copying documents, criticizing the text, and reading the proof.

W. S. R.

Urbana, Illinois
May 29, 1951

Contents

List of Illustrations

[ix]

ITURBIDE *of* MEXICO

CHAPTER I

Youth In Valladolid

AGUSTÍN DE ITURBIDE, the Liberator of Mexico, sprang from a noble family which was seated in the one-time Kingdom of Navarre. A branch of that family had flourished in the valley of Baztán, which was not far from the place in the province of Guipúzcoa where Ignacio Loyola was born.[1] The *casa solariega* or ancestral home of Basque forefathers of the Mexican Liberator may indeed have stood in that valley. Little is known of the life of the Iturbides in Old Spain. From the mists of the western Pyrenees, however, there emerges the dim figure of José de Iturbide, a native of the Spanish portion of the former Kingdom, who in the second quarter of the eighteenth century was living in a region lying south of the ancestral home. It is clear that he espoused María Josefa de Areguí or Arreguí. At present the early career of their son, José Joaquín de Iturbide y Arreguí, is obscure. According to a rare manuscript, that child was baptized on February 6, 1739, in the parochial church of San Juan Evangelista in the town of Peralta.[2] Printed sources confirm the view that José Joaquín de Iturbide, the father of Agustín, was born in 1739 in that part of Old Spain where people cherished memories of the defense of their homeland by liberty-loving Basques at the Pass of Roncesvalles.

It was in all likelihood during his early manhood that José Joaquín de Iturbide emigrated from Navarre with that fructifying stream of hardy and enterprising Basques who proceeded from Biscayan provinces of Spain to various parts of the Spanish Indies. Perhaps because a relative was emigrating to central Mexico, José Joaquín chose to

[1] García Caraffa, *Diccionario heráldico y genealógico de apellidos españoles y americanos*, XLVI, 130-133.

[2] Copy, Extractos de varias diligencias practicados en España y en Valladolid á pedimento de D. José Joaquín de Iturbide con las que calificó pertenecerle los apellidos de Iturbide, Areguí, Alvarez de Eulate y Gastelu . . . , f. 1, MSS, L.M.C. (The titles of MSS cited in the footnotes retain the spelling of the original documents.) In 1823 Agustín de Iturbide declared that his father was eighty-five years of age (Bustamante, *El Honor y patriotismo del general D. Nicolas Bravo*, p. 68); in a proclamation issued by Iturbide in May, 1821, he declared "no ignorais que tengo un Padre Europeo . . ." (*El Mejicano Independiente*, June 9, 1821, pp. 2-3).

settle in the city of Valladolid, the capital of the province bearing that name as well as the seat of the important bishopric of Michoacán.[3] A news item published in a gazette of the City of Mexico recorded in 1786 that one "Don Joseph Iturvide," evidently the father of Agustín de Iturbide, was a member of the cabildo or municipal council of Valladolid and the owner of an hacienda at Quirio, which was a short distance from that city.[4] As membership in a cabildo was an object of ambition to Creoles—persons of Spanish descent born in the Indies—it appears that long before the end of the eighteenth century the emigrant from Spain had gained distinction in central Mexico.

The coat of arms of his family was quartered. The first quarter was a blue field bearing three diagonal bands of silver; the second was a red field adorned with two lions rampant in gold; the third was also red with two golden lions; and the fourth was a blue field bearing three horizontal bands of silver.[5] In the city of his adoption José Joaquín de Iturbide married María Josefa Arámburu, a daughter of Sebastian Arámburu and Micaela Carrillo Arámburu. From this union there sprang five children: Agustín, Mariano, Francisco, Josefa, and Nicolasa or, as she was sometimes called, María Nicolasa.[6]

Upon one occasion Agustín de Iturbide declared that on all sides his lineage was both Biscayan and Navarrese.[7] It is clear that his mother was of Basque descent. In a funeral address made at her grave José García de Torres declared that she had been born in the bishopric of Michoacán of distinguished and pious parents. This orator explained that they had entrusted their daughter at an early age to the care of two maiden aunts who lived in a convent in the picturesque town of Pátzcuaro.[8] Scarcely any contemporary documents have come to hand concerning the brothers and sisters of Agustín or the married

---

[3] In a sketch entitled "Mexico, an Empire," which was published in the *Aurora* on June 21, 1822, the assertion was made that José Joaquín de Iturbide emigrated from Old Spain to Mexico in 1763 at the age of twenty-three; Iturbide, "Don Agustín de Iturbide," *Records of the American Catholic Historical Society of Philadelphia*, XXVI, 289, gives the date of the emigration of José Joaquín as 1766. When the Provisional Junta of Mexico granted José Joaquín de Iturbide a pension in 1821, it mentioned "el dilatado tiempo de su radicacion en este Reino . . ." (*Gaceta imperial de México*, November 17, 1821, p. 178). Cf. Cuevas, *El Libertador*, pp. 18-19.

[4] *Gazeta de Mexico*, August 22, 1786, p. 194.

[5] Ortega y Pérez Gallardo, *Historia genealógica de las familias mas antiguas de México*, vol. III, part II, p. 1 of the section pertaining to the Iturbide family, plate preceding p. 1, also p. 14.

[6] *Ibid.*, p. 2 of the section pertaining to the Iturbide family.

[7] Bustamante, *Cuadro historico de la revolucion mexicana*, V, 135.

[8] García de Torres, *Oración fúnebre de la Señora Doña María Josefa de Arámburu, Carrillo y Figuera, Villaseñor y Cervantes*, pp. 6-8.

HOUSE OF JOSÉ JOAQUÍN DE ITURBIDE IN VALLADOLID
(MORELIA), MEXICO
From Julio Zárate, *La Guerra de Independencia*

life of his parents. Upon receiving news of the death of his mother many years later, he wrote to a close friend that his spirit was greatly depressed, for that "virtuous and prudent woman" was the person whom he loved the most.[9]

The home of the Iturbide family in Valladolid (now called Morelia) was a stone house of one story which still stands in a street near the spacious cathedral. Agustín was born on September 27, 1783, the same year in which Simón Bolívar, the Liberator of northern South America, was born at Caracas. The eldest son of José Joaquín de Iturbide was baptized in the cathedral of San Agustín. Mexican writers have plausibly explained the names given to the child as being due to a conjunction of peculiar circumstances. One circumstance was that September 27 happened to be the saints' day of San Damian and San Cosme. Another circumstance was mentioned in the tradition that the safe delivery of the child was accomplished after three days of travail only by the miraculous intercession of Diego Baselenque, one of the venerated founders of the province of Augustinians in central Mexico, an apostle whose mummified body had been preserved in the cathedral of Valladolid.[10] In any event, it cannot be gainsaid that on October 1, 1783, José de Arreguí, a canon of the cathedral, christened the baby as Agustín Cosme Damian. A tale which has been told in our own time that Agustín was a mestizo, that is, an offspring of the union of a Spaniard and an Indian, should be belied by the fact that the certificate of baptism designated the baby as "a Spanish child."[11]

Among other traditions concerning him was that as a boy he had cut off the toes of chickens so that he might have the strange pleasure of watching them trip on their stumps. It seems possible, however, that this story told by Vicente Rocafuerte, a bitter enemy of Iturbide who, after serving the republic of Mexico, became a liberal statesman of Ecuador, resulted from the Mexican's ruthless conduct while serving as a royalist officer. Rocafuerte also asserted that José Joaquín de Iturbide sent his eldest son to an academy in Valladolid, where the lad did not complete the course of study but became notorious because of his idle and vicious conduct.[12]

[9] Iturbide to Juan Gómez de Navarrete, December 15, 1820, in I. MSS, box 16.
[10] Alamán, *Historia de Mexico*, V, 46-47.   [11] *Ibid.*, p. 733.
[12] *Bosquejo ligerísimo de la revolución de Mégico*, p. 7. This booklet contains useful documents, but the author's comments are at times prejudiced and misleading. In 1832 an anonymous writer described it as a "rapsodia de inepcias contra la persona del Sr. Iturbide" (*Un Regalo de año nuevo para el Señor Rocafuerte ó consideraciones sobre sus consideraciones*, p. 6). See also Alamán, *op. cit.*, V, 80 n. 51.

The truth of the matter appears to be that education in Mexico—
as indeed throughout colonial Spanish America—was, to say the least,
unsystematic. Hence, as judged by present standards, Agustín's formal
education was defective. Yet he grew up in a city which, as the seat
of a bishopric, had become an intellectual center. In the year of
Iturbide's birth Miguel Hidalgo, who later became a revolutionary,
was teaching philosophy there in the College of San Nicolás. A
theological seminary had also opened its doors at Valladolid to aspiring
young men. By the time Agustín de Iturbide entered its spacious
patio, learned friars were giving instruction in Latin, rhetoric, philosophy, theology, and the Sacred Scriptures. The little Latin which he
learned evidently made some impression upon his mind, because more
than a quarter of a century later, when engaged in a campaign against
the insurgents, he wrote to the Viceroy concerning an unfortunate
cleric who had joined them, *Neseitis quid petatis*.[13] Roman Catholic
writers who have studied the obscure annals of the Valladolid Theological Seminary have stated that Iturbide's name stood high on the roll
of its students who became distinguished ecclesiastics, publicists, or
revolutionaries.[14]

Within its cloistered walls Agustín was doubtless much influenced
by the prevailing religious atmosphere. Undoubtedly the lad was also
affected by the devout sentiments of his family. In later years he
proudly avowed that his pious parents had taught him to recite the
rosary at an early age.[15] Among the volumes in his possession shortly
before his death was a treatise mentioned in a list of his father's books
which concerned the art of commending oneself to God.[16] It is to such
circumstances that one should ascribe the fidelity that Agustín displayed throughout life to the Church of Rome.

Aside from family and educational influences, the youth must have
been affected by the imposing structure of the church establishment.
With its own government, law, magistrates, and precedents, the Roman
Catholic Church had become an influential power in the State. Largely
by virtue of bequests and gifts, much credit, land, and specie had
passed into the possession of the dead hand. Ecclesiastics enjoyed
special privileges, such as exemption from the jurisdiction of civil
courts. In Mexico City alone there were more than a score of mon-

[13] Iturbide, *Correspondencia y diario militar*, III, 421.
[14] Buitrón, *El Seminario de Michoacán*, p. 8; Torre, "Datos históricos de Morelia,"
El Tiempo Ilustrado, October 2, 1904, pp. 646-656.
[15] Iturbide to F. M. Calleja, August 14, 1816, f. 8-8 *verso*, in I. MSS, 5.
[16] Iturbide, *La Correspondencia de . . . después de la proclamación del Plan de
Iguala*, II, 231.

asteries and nunneries which sheltered some two thousand nuns and monks.[17]

If Agustín actually succeeded in completing a course of study in the theological seminary, it appears that he did not carry his formal education much further. Many years later, in a bitter criticism of Iturbide's military conduct, Dr. Antonio de Labarrieta, the senior curate of the city of Guanajuato, wrote thus approvingly of his early life: "I have known him since he was a youth, for our families were on intimate terms. In him a good education was given to a fine intellect. He had pleasing manners and lastly a happy combination of estimable social and religious qualities which gained for him the esteem of our native province." Whatever tomes the young man may have used in the seminary, in his father's house he undoubtedly browsed in a choice and varied collection of books on historical, literary, and religious subjects. Among divers works which José Joaquín de Iturbide listed as having been stolen from him by the rebels in 1810, he mentioned treatises concerning the annals of Navarre, a history of Spain, a biography of Cicero, *La Araucana, Las Viages de Pons, Las Poesías de Gerardo Lobo, El Seminario de agricultura, La Arte de encomendarse á Dios, Gil Blas,* and *Don Quixote.*[18] Moreover, the youth evidently had access to other libraries in his native city.

José Joaquín de Iturbide had prospered in the province of Valladolid which in 1786, like other provinces of Mexico, had by royal ordinance been designated an *intendencia* (intendancy).[19] There fertile plains had been carved into haciendas which were held by thriving landlords and tilled by a vassal peasantry. In a legal document drawn up many years later by the widow of Angel de Iturbide, who was a son of Agustín de Iturbide, she stated that José Joaquín de Iturbide had owned two houses in the city of Valladolid with their furnishings and also a hacienda at Quirio. She estimated that his possessions and his wife's had been worth more than one hundred thousand pesos.[20] "At fifteen years of age," said Lucas Alamán in his *Historia*

[17] Humboldt, *Essai politique sur le royaume de la Nouvelle-Espagne,* II, 173-174.

[18] The quotation is from *Informe del Dr. Don Antonio de Labarrieta,* p. 3; Nota de los libros que en el saqueo de mi casa de Valladolid me robaron los insurgentes, in MSS, Y.U.

[19] In spite of the royal ordinance of 1786, introducing the intendancies, the term *province* was still occasionally applied to territorial divisions in Mexico.

[20] Alice Green de Iturbide, Testimonio de la protocolización de la cuenta de división y partición de los bienes que quedaron por fallecimiento de Sr. General Libertador Dn. Agustín de Yturbide expedido para la señora albacea Doña Alicia Green de Yturbide en su carácter de tutora legítima de su único hijo el menor D. Agustín de Yturbide y Green, June 12, 1880, in A.H.I.N.A.H., legajo 48—expediente 45.

de Mexico, Agustín "was managing an hacienda belonging to his father."[21] Active in agricultural and pastoral pursuits, the young Creole developed a strong constitution which was seasoned by outdoor life.

During his youth the armed forces in Mexico were composed of militia and a small force of regular soldiers. As the militia had declined, Viceroy Branciforte undertook to re-establish it. Accordingly during the last decade of the eighteenth century, Count Casa Rul organized the infantry regiment of the intendancy of Valladolid. At a review of that regiment held by the Viceroy in May, 1798, there were present some eight hundred men.[22]

Shortly before that date, Agustín de Iturbide had been drawn to the profession of arms. Like other Creoles of the upper class, he began his public career as a minor officer. The earliest certificate of his military service drawn up near the end of December, 1800, and countersigned by Casa Rul, shows that on October 16, 1797, by a provisional appointment Iturbide became a second lieutenant of the infantry regiment of his native province. This record further stated that the young soldier was of noble lineage, that his health and conduct were good, and that he was considered valiant.[23] An official report of his military service which was prepared four years later simply recorded that his capacity and application were both normal.[24] During Iturbide's youth a provincial regiment of militia in Mexico ordinarily included a small number of veteran soldiers who received regular pay. The other members of such a regiment, who were mostly Creoles, were paid only on account of their attendance at the annual review, which ordinarily lasted about a month.[25]

Agustín was an athletic and sprightly cadet. Presumably he was attired in the costume prescribed by a royal order of January 10, 1790, for provincial infantry. This uniform included coat and trousers of an indigo color. White braid bordered the collar of the coat, while

---

[21] Alamán, *Historia,* V, 47.

[22] Branciforte to Sr. Álbarez, July 20, 1797, in A.G.N., Correspondencia de Virreyes, Branciforte, vol. 4; *Instrucciones que los virreyes de Nueva España dejaron a sus sucesores,* pp. 135, 146, 148.

[23] Hoja de servicio del regimiento provincial de infantería de Valladolid de Michoacán, December, 1800, in A.G.S., Guerra, legajo 7276.

[24] Hoja de servicio de Iturbide, December, 1804, in A.G.N., Yndiferente de Guerra, vol. 1804.

[25] "El ejército de Nueva España a fines del siglo XVIII," *Boletin del archivo general de la nacion,* vol. IX, no. 2, pp. 236-275.

its shoulders were adorned by yellow galloons. The helmet bore the insignia of the regiment.[26]

Eighteen hundred and five was an important year in the young militiaman's life. While a student in the seminary he had become enamored of Ana María Huarte, the daughter of Isidro Huarte, the provincial intendant who was in charge of justice, industry, financial matters, and military affairs in his district. On February 27 the archdeacon of the cathedral of Valladolid administered the sacrament which united Agustín de Iturbide in the bonds of holy matrimony with Ana María. She was described in the marriage certificate as being nineteen years of age. Her mother was the deceased Ana María Muñiz Huarte. The brother of Ana María and a sister of Agustín attended the young couple. The ceremony was witnessed by the bride's father as well as by a relative of Iturbide named Domingo Malo, who belonged to the same regiment as the groom. On the following day a nuptial Mass was celebrated in the oratorio at the home of the newly married pair.[27]

Isidro Huarte was a descendant of a well-known Spanish family.[28] His daughter was not only a beauty but also an heiress. Tradition has it that Ana María was educated at the Academy of Santa Rosa María, which was near the Valladolid Theological Seminary. As her father was in prosperous circumstances, he was, according to a legal document, able to bestow upon his daughter a substantial dowry which included precious jewels. In addition, from time to time he gave to Ana María and Agustín various sums of money. Many years later, the widow of Angel de Iturbide stated that, according to an account prepared by Isidro Huarte in August, 1821, he had by that time presented to Ana María and her husband more than 30,000 pesos.[29]

Soon after his marriage the young officer was ordered to leave Valladolid with his regiment. He next served in the garrison of Mexico City, the capital of the Viceroyalty. At that time the capital had a population of some 130,000. Located in a valley subject to inundation and with streamlets trickling through narrow streets, the city had been embellished by successive viceroys, who had provided parks and boulevards. The fortress-palace of Chapultepec had been

[26] Zúñiga y Ontiveros, *Calendario manual y guía de forasteros en México*, 1821, p. 190.

[27] Partida de matrimonio, in A.P.C., Libro de matrimonios, vol. XV.

[28] Alamán, *op. cit.*, V, 47.

[29] Alice Green de Iturbide, Testimonio de la protocolización . . . , June 12, 1880, in A.H.I.N.A.H., 48-25.

erected upon the summit of a crag from which potable water was brought to the city by an aqueduct. An institution known as the Academy of San Carlos had become a school of fine arts. The Plaza de Armas (later called the Zócalo), the most important square in the metropolis, was bordered on the east by the extensive palace of the viceroys and dominated on the north by a cathedral with twin towers, the largest religious temple in the New World.[30]

Iturbide doubtless enjoyed to the full an opportunity of becoming well acquainted with the capital city. After a short sojourn there, his regiment was ordered to proceed to Jalapa, where the militia of his native province was to be quartered for military training. Evidently he performed his duties to the satisfaction of his superior officers; for on October 29, 1806, he was brevetted first lieutenant, an appointment which was confirmed six months later by a royal order.[31] It is to be presumed that he was in a military camp when in March, 1807, Viceroy Lizanza y Beaumont inspected the soldiers who were stationed at Córdoba, Jalapa, Orizaba, and Perote.[32] The total armed force in the Viceroyalty at this time numbered some 32,000.[33]

Meanwhile a series of events was taking place in Europe which affected the Spanish Indies profoundly. Napoleon's attempt to extend his sway over the Iberian Peninsula led him to seize fortresses in northern Spain. A tumult at Aranjuez in March, 1808, induced the inept King Charles IV to relinquish his right to the Spanish throne in favor of his eldest son Ferdinand, who was promptly proclaimed the monarch. Two months later Ferdinand VII was forced by Napoleon to renounce his right to the crown. At Bayonne on June 6, 1808, the French Emperor announced that his brother Joseph was King of Spain and the Indies. As if by magic, there sprang up in Spain juntas or local councils, which not only denounced French usurpations but also assumed political authority. When news of the startling changes in Spain reached the Indies, it seemed as though a spark had been dropped into the tinder that lay scattered about the Spanish dominions.[34]

[30] Humboldt, *Essai politique*, II, 14. A school of painting, sculpture, and architecture had been founded in the city of Mexico in 1781. On December 25, 1783, King Charles III issued a *cédula* approving the establishment of the academy and giving it the name Academia de San Carlos de Nueva España (Gonzáles Obregón, *México viejo*, pp. 520-521).

[31] Hoja de servicio of Iturbide, December, 1814, in I. MSS, 5.

[32] *Gazeta de Mexico*, April 18, 1807, p. 262.

[33] Humboldt, *op. cit.*, V, 55.

[34] Robertson, "The Juntas of 1808 and the Spanish Colonies," *English Historical Review*, XXI, 575-578, 584.

General José de Iturrigaray, an elderly scion of a noble Navarrese family, was at that time serving as the Viceroy of New Spain. By virtue of his position he was the alter ego of the Spanish King. On July 19 the cabildo of Mexico City urged the Viceroy to refuse to acknowledge French domination. He issued a proclamation announcing that a local junta had resolved to recognize no other sovereign than Ferdinand VII. He exhorted the people to rally to the support of their deposed monarch.[35] Meanwhile a friar named Melchor Talamantes was planning a national congress of New Spain to consider the fate of Middle America.[36] This was indicative of an undercurrent favoring a radical change.

The irresolute Viceroy summoned to the capital city certain regiments which he considered loyal. A rich landowner named Gabriel de Yermo, who resided there, soon placed himself at the head of disaffected citizens. During the night of September 15 they deposed Iturrigaray.[37] Early the next morning, certain members of a judicial and administrative council known as the audiencia, the Archbishop of Mexico, and other officials met in the episcopal palace. They decided to disregard the royal instructions specifying the name of Iturrigaray's successor. On their own authority they selected Pedro Garibay, who held the rank of Marshal, to serve as Viceroy.[38]

Many civil magistrates and military officers promptly displayed their intention to support the new regime. In the words of the *Gazeta de Mexico*, the official organ of the government and the chief vehicle for the dissemination of news, they manifested their desire to be employed in "the royal service and to shed the last drop of their blood" in defense of Roman Catholicism, of Ferdinand VII, and of the motherland.[39] Among the first officers to step forward was Félix María Calleja, who had fought for several years under the Spanish banner in the Old World, had in 1789 sailed to New Spain, and had by 1808 become the commander of a brigade in the viceregal army.[40]

Lieutenant Iturbide, perchance because of legal business concerning the purchase of an hacienda, happened at this critical moment to be in Mexico City. Whatever may have been his motive, perhaps

---

[35] Lafuente Ferrari, *El Virrey Iturrigaray y los orígenes de la independencia de Méjico*, pp. 24-25, 201-204.

[36] *Ibid.*, p. 179; García, *Documentos historicos mexicanos*, VII, 419-436.

[37] Lafuente Ferrari, *op. cit.*, pp. 255, 395.

[38] *Gazeta extraordinaria de Mexico*, September 16, 1808, pp. 675-680.

[39] September 21, 1808, pp. 701-702.

[40] Camacho, "Don Félix Ma. Calleja, Virrey de Nueva España," *Boletín del instituto de estudios americanistas de Sevilla*, vol. I, no. 1, p. 51.

because of expediency, he promptly followed Calleja's example.[41] The name of Agustín de Iturbide was accordingly published in the official gazette on September 21, 1808, near the head of a list of persons who had just pledged their service to Acting Viceroy Garibay. Realizing keenly the need of financial aid, that magistrate soon wrote to Iturbide's father asking him to make as large a contribution as possible to a subscription which would be opened for the succor of the Spanish patriots who were at war with the French. Near the end of his letter Garibay expressed the hope that he would soon be advised of a gift, dictated by piety and patriotism, from José Joaquín de Iturbide.[42]

On October 28 the Acting Viceroy wrote a letter thanking that correspondent for his generous offer to contribute to the needs of the motherland until Ferdinand VII was restored to his throne. Garibay styled this pledge a proof of the donor's fidelity.[43] In a list of gifts from inhabitants of the Viceroyalty to the Spanish cause which was published in the *Gazeta extraordinaria de Mexico* on November 11, 1808, there was mentioned an immediate contribution from the head of the Iturbide family of one thousand pesos and also the promise of an annual contribution of five hundred pesos during the war of Spain with France. On October 23, 1809, José Joaquín de Iturbide notified Archbishop Francisco Javier Lizanza y Beaumont, who had been appointed Viceroy of Mexico by the Central Junta which had been set up in Spain, that on that day he had redeemed his pledge by paying the promised contributions into the royal treasury.[44] Four days later the Viceroy wrote a letter to the donor expressing his appreciation of the generous sentiment of patriotism which had animated him.[45] The Iturbides of Valladolid thus became the supporters of a provisional regime which gave a new face to Mexican politics.

That the finances of this family were in good condition was also shown by the fact that in December, 1808, Lieutenant Iturbide purchased the hacienda of San José de Apeo, located near Maravatio in his native province. The value of the estate was indicated by the judgment of the audiencia of Mexico in March, 1809, that the young officer should pay eight thousand pesos for its crops and fruits.[46] As finally determined by that tribunal, the price of the Apeo farm was

[41] Alamán, *Historia*, V, 47 and n. 4.
[42] Garibay to J. J. de Iturbide, October 3, 1808, in MSS, Y.U.
[43] *Idem* to *idem*, October 28, 1808, *ibid*.
[44] J. J. de Iturbide to Lizanza y Beaumont, October 23, 1809, *ibid*.
[45] Lizanza y Beaumont to J. de Iturbide, October 27, 1809, *ibid*.
[46] Alice Green de Iturbide, Testimonio de la protocolización . . . , June 12, 1880, in A.H.I.N.A.H., 48-25.

ninety-three thousand pesos. The transaction was made possible by the aid of funds derived from the Huarte family. In his last testament Iturbide stated that in the purchase of this property he had used some thirty thousand pesos of his wife's dowry.[47]

His attitude toward revolutionary discontent was tested by a plot formed in central Mexico. In September, 1808, because of the disbanding of soldiers who had been quartered at Jalapa, Lieutenant José Mariano de Michelena returned to Valladolid, his native city. There he soon became the center of a coterie of young Creoles belonging to prominent families of the neighborhood. In this circle, besides his brother José Nicolás, there were Captain José García Obeso, a lawyer named Manuel Ruíz de Chaves, and Vicente de Santa María, a Franciscan friar. According to an account composed by its leader, the ostensible purpose of the plotters was to crystallize public sentiment concerning the policy which, in view of the deposition of Ferdinand VII, the Mexicans should adopt with respect to the motherland. The machinations were not confined to Valladolid, for agents were dispatched to adjacent towns and cities. Plans were laid to start a rebellion on December 21, 1809—a rebellion which evidently was to aim at the establishment of Mexican independence. Shortly before that date, however, a person who became aware of the conspiracy denounced it to the authorities. In consequence the chief conspirators were thrust into prison or sent into exile.[48]

Mexican writers have not infrequently discussed the relations between Iturbide and the conspirators. In his account of the incident the arch-conspirator declared that the informer was a Creole with whom the plotters had had dealings, a person who thus greatly injured them, but one who later decisively aided the cause of independence.[49] A partisan of the revolution named Carlos María de Bustamante, who printed many historical documents, later alleged that it was Lieutenant Iturbide who betrayed the plotters because they did not favor making him a general.[50] Julio Zárate, a well-known Mexican historian, not only asserted that the Creole mentioned by Michelena was actually that lieutenant, but also that the Viceroy sent him a letter of thanks

[47] Castillo Negrete, *Mexico en el siglo xix*, IV, 453.

[48] Hernández y Dávalos, *Coleccion de documentos para la historia de la guerra de independencia de Mexico de 1808 a 1821*, II, 5-6.

[49] On Iturbide's share in the conspiracy, see further Arriaga, "¿Traicionó Iturbide a los Conspiradores de Valladolid?," *Universidad michoacana*, vol. II, nos. 8 and 9, pp. 22-23.

[50] Manuscrito, manifiesto de Iturbide, comentada por Carlos M. de Bustamante con letra de el mismo, Hernández y Dávalos Collection, 17-8-4255, in MSS, U.T.

for his aid in thwarting the conspiracy.[51]   In an undated autobiographical sketch Iturbide mentioned the role which he had played as a
militia officer:

"I do not claim credit for my presence at the assemblies, camps,
and reviews that I attended in which the infantry regiment of Valladolid took part. Neither do I desire credit for executing various commissions entrusted to me before 1809 because of the confidence and
esteem of my military commander. Nor do I wish recognition on
account of the arrest of one of the first conspirators against the rights
of the King—an arrest which I secured personally at the expense of
labor and special pains and not without some peril."[52]

According to his own story, therefore, Iturbide actually arrested
one of the ringleaders of the rebellious conspirators.

There is no doubt that both in his father's house and in the theological seminary pains were taken to instruct him in the doctrines of
Roman Catholicism. As the son of a prosperous landed proprietor in
a region where broad haciendas largely determined the life of the
intendancy and as an overseer of family estates, the aspiring young
lieutenant naturally took a keen interest in the conservation of the
existing social and economic system. As a discerning Mexican writer
has aptly said, this young man naturally felt that it was his duty to
cherish the environmental conditions under which he had grown up—
a heritage which included the domination of the King, of the Spanish
bureaucracy, and of the Roman Catholic Church.

[51] Zárate, *La Guerra de independencia*, p. 75 n.
[52] Undated, Apuntes interesantes pa. el. M., f. 1, in I. MSS, 5.

CHAPTER II

Struggles for Mexican Independence

IN MAY, 1810, the Regency to which the Central Junta of Spain had transferred its authority relieved Archbishop Lizanza y Beaumont of his onerous viceregal duties. Soon afterward the Regency appointed as his successor Francisco Xavier de Venegas, an energetic general who had fought bravely against the French invaders of Spain. Disembarking at Vera Cruz in August, 1810, he made his way leisurely to Mexico City. On September 14 he set foot in the viceregal palace.[1]

Two days later the discovery of a revolutionary plot in the central plateau of Mexico caused its leaders to precipitate an uprising. Warned that they had been denounced to colonial authorities, the curate of Dolores, Miguel Hidalgo, who was the soul of the conspiracy, started a revolt against the existing regime. It is the purpose of this chapter to describe the role of Iturbide in the complicated series of events which ensued.

Iturbide's earliest account of his reaction to the opening struggle ran as follows:

"When the insurrection began, I was at the hacienda of Apeo on an indefinite furlough from military service which had been granted to me by Señor Lizanza in order that I might recover from a serious illness from which I was suffering. On September 20 I received news of the outbreak of the rebellion. At once I planned to proceed to the capital city. Upon arriving there, I presented myself to his Excellency Señor Venegas. I made known to him my desire to engage actively in the royal service. Honorable, talented, and influential persons gave him good reports about me. In consequence he directed me to capture the rebels Luna and Carrasco, who had attacked the town of Acámbaro. . . ."[2]

After consulting with a junta in the city of Valladolid, however, Iturbide decided to march first to Maravatio. Upon reaching that town, he found that his small force was greatly outnumbered by the

[1] *Gazeta del gobierno de Mexico*, September 14, 1810, p. 745.
[2] Undated, Apuntes interesantes pa. el M., f. 1, in I. MSS, 5.

malcontents. Hence he decided to withdraw his men. He returned to the capital, where he explained his cautious operations to the Viceroy. According to an official report, on October 12, 1810, with thirty-five soldiers, he prevented the entrance into Maravatio of some five or six hundred rebels. He thus saved the surrounding district with its arms and munitions for the royalist cause.[3]

As Hidalgo marched from Dolores to Celaya, and thence to Guanajuato, which his soldiers pillaged on September 28, his motley following steadily increased in numbers. The commanding military officers of the city of Valladolid were seized by revolutionaries. Prominent ecclesiastics and civilians forsook the city. Before dawn on October 5, 1810, José Joaquín de Iturbide, accompanied by the family of his eldest son, fled from the paternal home. After visiting the hacienda of Apeo, they proceeded to Mexico City.[4] The views which Lieutenant Iturbide formed concerning the insurgents were partly due to his knowledge of the devastation wrought by their army, which was largely composed of Indians and mestizos.

In the intendancy of Valladolid the insurgents wrought much havoc. Writing to a friend a few years later, the head of the Iturbide family complained that his residence, as well as his hacienda at Quirio, was completely sacked. "You will understand," he said, "to what an unhappy situation I have been reduced by these misfortunes."[5] He recorded that rebels carried off some cherished books from his library.[6]

Agustín de Iturbide stated in an early account of his dealings with the rebels that when he was in command of a small force of royalists at the town of San Felipe del Obraje, which was only a few leagues from the revolutionary soldiers, the daring curate of Dolores in vain made him certain attractive proposals: "The pardon of my father and the protection of my entire family. Hidalgo even carried his seductive offer so far as to promise me all these favors, not in order that I should follow his partisans and work actively in his support, but merely so that I should desert the King's party. One can imagine the strife in my heart, which was torn by such feelings as love for my family and loyalty to the King."[7]

---

[3] Hoja de servicio of Iturbide, December, 1814, *ibid*.

[4] J. J. de Iturbide, Relación sucinta de mi viage desde Vallad'd. á esta capl. en el año de 1810, y en el de 1813 á Querétaro, in MSS, Y.U.

[5] J. J. de Iturbide to I. Aguirrevengea, July 8, 1814, *ibid*.

[6] *Idem*, Nota de los libros que en el saqueo de mi casa de Valladolid me robaron los insurgentes, *ibid*.

[7] Apuntes interesantes pa. el M., f. 8, in I. MSS, 5. Iturbide later asserted that

On October 19, 1810, Viceroy Venegas directed Iturbide to proceed with his detachment to join Torcuato Trujillo, a ruthless colonel who had accompanied him from Spain and who had been placed in charge of a small force of regular soldiers.[8] In the meantime Hildalgo had marched from Valladolid toward the valley of Mexico. The Viceroy instructed Colonel Trujillo to pursue the insurgents. Iturbide, who had sent word to that officer about Hidalgo's movements, joined the royalist force at Toluca.[9] Trujillo stationed his soldiers on the Monte de las Cruces, a lofty peak near the crest of the mountain range which encircled Mexico City. He thus blocked the road to the capital. Within sight of its spires and domes, a fierce conflict took place on October 30 between his soldiers and the revolutionists. Though the royalists were compelled to withdraw before overwhelming numbers, this engagement had for them some of the effects of a victory.[10] From Chapultepec on November 6, 1810, Trujillo sent a report to the Viceroy praising the conduct of his soldiers at Las Cruces: "I recommend to your Excellency all the soldiers of every class who took part in this glorious action," he wrote. "Lieutenant Don Agustín de Iturbide, who was under my orders, fulfilled with skill and honor whatever I desired. He did not leave my side during the entire retreat."[11] As a reward for his loyal service, on November 17, 1810, the Viceroy appointed Iturbide a captain of fusiliers, an appointment which was soon superseded by a captaincy in the regiment of Tula.[12] Yet that officer expressed his dissatisfaction at the scant recognition accorded to the provincial militia of Valladolid.[13]

Unlike some dissatisfied Spanish colonists in South America, Hidalgo's followers did not promptly form a junta to direct political and military activities. Early Mexican revolutionists mentioned their purpose, however, in their battle cries. Not only did they declare

---

Hidalgo offered to make him a general; see *Carrera militar y politica de Don Agustin de Iturbide ó sea memoria que escribió en Liorna*, pp. 4-5. Though this story was believed by Alamán, *Historia de Mexico*, V, 48, it was derided by Bustamante. See his Manuscrito, manifiesto de Iturbide, comentado por Carlos M. de Bustamante con letra de el mismo, Hernández y Dávalos Collection, 17-8-4255, in MSS, U.T. Cf. Castillo Ledón, *Hidalgo*, II, 84.

[8] Iturbide, *Correspondencia y diario militar*, I, 5.

[9] Trujillo to Venegas, October 25, 1810, in A.G.N., Historia de Operaciones, Riaño y Trujillo, 1.

[10] Bustamante, *Cuadro historico de la revolucion mexicana*, I, 81 n.

[11] Trujillo to Venegas, November 6, 1810, in A.G.N., Historia de Operaciones, Riaño y Trujillo, 1; in part in Bustamante, *op. cit.*, I, 81 n.

[12] Hoja de servicio de Iturbide, December, 1814, in I. MSS, 5.

[13] Iturbide, *Correspondencia y diario militar*, I, 7-8.

themselves in favor of the Roman Catholic religion and the rule of Ferdinand VII, but they denounced the evils of the viceregal government. At times they even threatened Peninsular Spaniards with death.[14] When in September, 1810, the warrior-priest summoned the city of Guanajuato to surrender, he mentioned certain projects which he had conceived. Among these was a proclamation declaring that the Mexican nation was free and independent. Hidalgo asserted that he did not view the Spaniards residing in Mexico as enemies but merely as obstacles to his success, whose property would be confiscated as a war measure.[15] During the following month, after the city of Guadalajara, the seat of a minor audiencia, had fallen into his hands, he appointed an agent to proceed to the United States in order to negotiate treaties with her government.[16] Even earlier than in South America, leading insurgents in Mexico began to discard the mask of allegiance to Ferdinand VII.

The curate of Dolores soon issued decrees which aimed at social and economic reforms, such as the abolition of slavery.[17] The closest approach he made to the formulation of a political program was a proclamation issued at Valladolid in December, 1810, which made known his intention to convoke a congress of representatives of all the cities, towns, and villages of Mexico. This Congress was to maintain Roman Catholicism and to enact good laws.[18] But the lack of a definite politico-military plan which might have won Hidalgo support from conservative classes, the excesses committed by his undisciplined followers, and his ignorance of strategy and tactics greatly hindered the progress of the revolt. Nevertheless, he has been styled "the Father of Mexican Independence."

After some spectacular successes, his army was decisively checked on January 17, 1811, by viceregal soldiers under General Calleja at a bridge over the river Calderón. Shortly afterward Hidalgo was betrayed to the royalists, stripped of his clerical garments, and executed.[19]

Aside from minor engagements with insurgents in 1811, Captain Iturbide became involved in a discussion with viceregal officials about the transportation of military supplies. This exchange of views took

---

[14] Alamán, *Historia*, I, 335.

[15] Bustamante, *op. cit.*, I, 28; Hernández y Dávalos, *Coleccion de documentos para la historia de la guerra de independencia de Mexico de 1808 a 1821*, II, 116-117.

[16] García, *Documentos historicos mexicanos*, VI, 27, 33.

[17] Fuente, *Hidalgo intimo*, pp. 496-497.

[18] Hernández y Dávalos, *op. cit.*, II, 303.

[19] Robertson, *Rise of the Spanish-American Republics*, pp. 97-106. Castillo Ledón, *Hidalgo*, II, *passim*.

place because of the impressment by a royalist official of mules belonging to haciendas of his family. In a petition to Viceroy Venegas the captain stated that a number of those mules employed in the royalist transport service had been killed in an engagement with insurgents, some had been stolen while on the road, and others were being used by rebels to transport grain to a stronghold. The petitioner complained that he had been injured to the extent of some three thousand pesos for which he had not presented a claim but had left an adjustment to the judgment of the Viceroy.[20] A little later Venegas thanked him for having waived in favor of the royal treasury his right to the payment of fourteen hundred pesos for mules which had been lost in a clash with revolutionists at Zitácuaro.[21]

At that place in August, 1811, leading revolutionists set up a council of three men styled the supreme governmental junta. Its first president was Ignacio Rayón. It agreed, for the time being, to profess loyalty to Ferdinand VII. In the following March, Dr. José M. Cos, an insurgent journalist who had studied at the University of Guadalajara, addressed a manifesto to the Spaniards in Mexico in which he suggested that they relinquish their claim to supreme authority to a Mexican congress which should be independent of Spain but should represent Ferdinand VII.[22] Early in the following month, however, the Viceroy ordered that, with other seditious documents, this plan for reconciliation with the motherland should be burned by the hangman in the great square of the capital.[23]

Iturbide's military diary shows that during 1812, at the head of soldiers from Tula, he marched some fifteen hundred leagues as an officer in the Army of the Center commanded by General Diego García Conde,[24] one of two brothers who were serving as royalist commanders. Among others, Iturbide met during this year two Spanish officers, namely, Félix María Calleja and Pedro Celestino Negrete,[25] whose careers were destined to be intertwined with his own. In large part his campaign took place in an extensive and fertile plain designated the Bajío, which stretched from Querétaro to the city of Guanajuato. Iturbide had several brushes with mounted followers of Albino García, an Indian contraband trader.[26] Using primitive, Arab-

[20] Iturbide, *Correspondencia y diario militar*, I, 9. See further "Las Mulas de Iturbide," *Boletín del archivo general de la nación*, vol. II, no. 1, pp. 71-93.
[21] Venegas to Iturbide, August 7, 1811, Gates Collection, no. 214, in MSS, T.U.
[22] *Ilustrador Americano*, June 10, 1812, in García, *op. cit.*, vol. III.
[23] Miquel i Vergés, *La Independencia mexicana y la prensa insurgente*, p. 62 and n. 5.
[24] Iturbide, *op. cit.*, I, 139.   [25] *Ibid.*, pp. 98, 103, 110.
[26] On Albino García, see Osorno Castro, *El Insurgente Albino García*, pp. 24-31.

like tactics, at times making fierce charges, now concentrating with savage rapidity, and then vanishing into their dens, they were difficult to capture, to rout, or to destroy.

During 1812 General Diego García Conde accordingly planned to capture the rebel bandit. After the entire division of that general had tried in vain to outwit him, on the evening of June 4, 1812, with 170 men Iturbide marched stealthily from Salamanca to Valle de Santiago. Early the next morning they penetrated into that town, surrounded the house of Albino García, and captured him. In addition, his brother, a large number of horses and mules, as well as arms and munitions, were seized.[27]

"I am not able to calculate with accuracy the number of insurgents who lost their lives," Iturbide informed his commander. "This is very difficult, for they were scattered in various streets, houses, and plazas; but I believe that, including more than one hundred and fifty whom I ordered to be shot, they numbered over three hundred." He expressed poignant regret at the death of one of his soldiers as well as at the necessity of executing so many miserable persons, without the consolation of religion. He wrote that, though this slaughter had been very fortunate for the public welfare, yet it had much depressed his spirits,[28] a remark which was denounced by a revolutionary as "a mixture of barbarism and hypocrisy."[29]

Though harassed by guerrillas, Iturbide proceeded safely to his headquarters. On June 5 he made the following entry in his diary: "I arrived at Celaya at half-past five in the afternoon with the prisoners after traveling for twenty-one hours without alighting from my horse."[30] At that place Albino García, with other rebels, was summarily executed.[31] On June 6, 1812, the jubilant officer was brevetted lieutenant colonel.[32]

Colonel Iturbide soon undertook another expedition into the enemy's country. During the evening of July 23 he led his regiment by forced marches from the hacienda of San Nicolás to Valle de Santiago. Though an insurgent leader named José Liceaga had fled from that place before the royalists arrived, a large band of guerrillas had gathered there. During the forenoon of July 24 they stubbornly opposed the attacking party.

[27] *Ibid.*, pp. 228-234; hoja de servicio of Iturbide, December, 1814, in I. MSS, 5.
[28] *Gaceta extraordinaria del gobierno de Mexico*, June 18, 1812, pp. 641, 643.
[29] Mier, *Historia de la revolución de Nueva España*, II, 141.
[30] Iturbide, *Correspondencia y diario militar*, I, 113.
[31] *Gaceta extraordinaria del gobierno de Mexico*, June 18, 1812, p. 644.
[32] Hoja de servicio of Iturbide, December, 1814, in I. MSS, 5.

"Seldom," recorded Iturbide, "have I seen the insurgents so tenacious in a campaign, . . . but they paid dearly for their temerity."[33] In a report to his commander, after describing the slaughter of rebels and the capture of military supplies, he sanctimoniously mentioned other effects of the engagement upon his regiment: "How much the protection of the God of Hosts blesses and gives it grace without ceasing. . . . I believe that one hundred men worthy of the name of soldiers can now march through Valle de Santiago without danger of being attacked."[34] Two days later General García Conde notified the Viceroy that he was forwarding Colonel Iturbide's report concerning "the glorious action which he fought against the insurgents at Valle de Santiago." The general added "again I recommend to you such a worthy officer who constantly demonstrates to me his valor, prudence, and military skill. . . ."[35] And, as if to voice a desire for advancement, on August 31, 1812, Iturbide drew up representations to Venegas in which he proposed the formation of a regiment of provincial dragoons, stressed his long years of military service, and stated that he had kept on the road at his own expense some of his servitors for use in the mail service and also as spies.[36]

Iturbide next undertook to circumvent Liceaga, who had withdrawn to Lake Yuriria. There two islands had been linked together by a causeway and fortified so strongly that they were supposed to be impregnable. To this fortification the rebel gave his family name. Within its bristling walls arrangements were made for the founding of cannon and the manufacture of gunpowder.[37] Though General Diego García Conde held it to be unnecessary and dangerous to attack Fort Liceaga, Iturbide undertook to make an assault. He began by driving bands of rebel guerrillas from the surrounding region. By October 20 he had reached a point on the shores of the lake opposite the fort. There he brought canoes and built rafts upon which to transport his men. Under date of Sunday, November 1, 1812, he wrote in his diary as follows: "At two o'clock in the morning the notorious Liceaga Isle was captured by surprise without the loss of a single one of our soldiers or the escape of a single rebel. Blessed be the Lord Almighty!"[38] He felt that for King and country he had risked his happiness and his fortune by undertaking such a hazardous

[33] Iturbide, *op. cit.*, I, 118.
[34] Copy, Iturbide to Diego García Conde, July 27, 1812, in A.G.N., Historia de Operaciones, Diego García Conde, 1811-1821, vol. 4.
[35] Diego García Conde to Venegas, July 29, 1812, *ibid.*
[36] Iturbide, *Correspondencia y diario militar*, I, 12-13.
[37] Alamán, *Historia*, III, 267.   [38] Iturbide, *op. cit.*, I, 131.

exploit. In his official report of the destruction of rebels during the assault he thus denounced them: "Miserable men, they will have realized their error in that terrible place where they will not be able to mend their ways."[39]

Upon the death of the commander of a detachment of soldiers on the frontier belonging to forces under José de la Cruz, who was stationed at Guadalajara, that sanguinary Spanish general strongly urged Viceroy Venegas to appoint Colonel Iturbide to the vacant post. The general said that this officer had taken part in more than forty military engagements. He mentioned Iturbide's "activity, talent, fitness for command, proved patriotism, military skill, knowledge of the service, and experience in an independent command." To these qualities Cruz added "the loans made to the royal treasury, the voluntary gifts, the loss of the major part or almost all of his fortune, the relinquishment of his family, and the other merits which he possesses."[40] Nevertheless, the recommendation of the royalist general was not carried out.

Soon afterward Colonel Iturbide engaged in an action similar to that which had resulted in the fall of Fort Liceaga. In his native province near the town of Zacapú was an island which the rebels had strongly fortified. After careful preparations at Valladolid, Iturbide proceeded to that place. Though harassed by roving bands of insurgents, his soldiers constructed batteries with which they bombarded the fort. After the besieged opened fire upon their foes, the royalist commander recorded that, because of "the favor of Heaven, which guides us as if by hand, and because of the protection of our batteries, . . . we had only two soldiers wounded. . . ."[41] To prevent the insurgents from destroying their supplies and shooting their prisoners, on February 28 he ordered a general assault, which met with success. On the day following the operation his victorious soldiers began to destroy the rebel stronghold. An insurgent journal mockingly remarked that Iturbide's mother had compared him with Scipio.[42]

During 1813 he continued to harass his antagonists. While in command of a division of the Army of the North, he drove into flight some rebels led by one Najar, who had attacked him near the fortified island of Xauxilla. He soon captured that island, from which

[39] *Gaceta del gobierno de Mexico*, January 7, 1813, p. 27.
[40] Cruz to Venegas, January 24, 1813, in A.G.N., Historia de Operaciones, José Cruz, 1813, vol. 10.
[41] Iturbide, *Correspondencia y diario militar*, I, 148.
[42] *Ilustrador Americano*, April 17, 1813, in García, *Documentos historicos mexicanos*, vol. III.

the besieged were forced to flee without their arms and munitions. He encountered another band of revolutionists led by two inveterate rebels known as the Rayón brothers on April 16, routed them, and captured their arms and artillery in an engagement at the bridge of Salvatierra. To General José de la Cruz, Iturbide reported that his soldiers after much heavy firing had made a triumphal entry into that town on Holy Friday. "It is not easy," he wrote, "to calculate the number of miserable, excommunicated persons who as the result of yesterday's action tumbled into the deep abyss; but in view of reports of the commanders of detachments at various points and because of the number of corpses which I have seen, I infer that about three hundred and fifty rebels were slain."[43]

This statement, which implied that he had put to death many prisoners in cold blood, was criticized by Carlos María de Bustamante, who wrote an account of the Mexican fight for independence. Bustamante asserted that only eighteen rebels were executed at Salvatierra and that the royalist officer had intentionally conveyed a false impression in order to curry favor with the Spaniards.[44] Long afterward Iturbide evidently admitted to a confidant that his vainglorious dispatch had been composed by a clerical scribe, that, contrary to his custom, he had signed the draft without reading it, and that, after it had been published in the official gazette, he had endured in silence the criticism directed against himself.[45]

Early in 1813, by an order of the Spanish Regency, General Calleja, who had served as the ruthless commander of the Army of the Center, became the Viceroy. Upon learning of the engagement at Salvatierra, Calleja provisionally appointed Iturbide colonel of the newly organized infantry regiment of Celaya, which was eventually to be composed of eight companies aggregating twelve hundred men recruited in the Bajío. The Viceroy directed the colonel to solicit the people of the region around Celaya and Querétaro to make contributions for the equipment of his regiment. Calleja also placed Iturbide in command of the royalist forces in the intendancy of Guanajuato.[46]

The Viceroy prepared instructions to guide Iturbide in the command of those forces. The colonel was directed to keep a diary in

[43] *Gaceta del gobierno de Mexico*, April 29, 1813, p. 440.

[44] Bustamante, *Cuadro historico*, II, 278.

[45] Malo, *Apuntes historicos sobre el destierro, vuelta al territorio mexicano y muerte del libertador, D. Agustin de Iturbide*, pp. 20-21. See further Alamán, *op. cit.*, III, 339 n. 9.

[46] Calleja to Iturbide, April 27, 1813, in I. MSS, 7; Iturbide, *Correspondencia y diario militar*, I, 42.

which to record important events. He was to send Calleja reports concerning his military activities, to clear the roads of rebels, to escort convoys of livestock, merchandise, or silver, and to keep his men in a good state of discipline. He was to dispense to soldiers and civilians alike prompt and equitable justice. At least a part of the merchandise or other property seized in military engagements was to be distributed among the soldiers who had taken part in the capture. Rebels falling into the hands of the royalists were to be treated in accordance with a proclamation issued by Viceroy Venegas. Agriculture, commerce, and mining were to be fostered.[47]

Iturbide understood the responsibility, as well as the honor, involved in his promotion. Yet in a letter to his father he declared that, although he counted upon divine protection for happiness, he would appreciate seeing his country become tranquil so that he might retire from military service in order to enjoy the pleasures of family life and to devote himself to the education of his children. "Because neither the galloons, nor the decorations, nor the adulation with which fate has somewhat flattered me," wrote the colonel, "have banished those pleasures from my mind. . . ."[48]

After a retired royalist officer named Pedro de Otero had complained of a visitation to his hacienda by some of Iturbide's soldiers, Calleja chided the royalist commander and urged him to become reconciled with that officer.[49] A lengthy defense of his conduct was not prepared by the colonel until weeks had elapsed. He then explained that whatever ravages had been made by his soldiers in the hacienda were due to the attitude of a padre in charge of it who stubbornly refused to furnish any fodder for the cavalry horses.[50] In response the Viceroy informed Iturbide that he was satisfied with his punctiliousness and honorable conduct in the affair. "I have made known," added Calleja, "that I esteem you, and that I appreciate these qualities. Your spirit should be soothed by the assurance that I recognize merit wherever I happen to find it."[51]

Indeed, even before he penned this justification, the Viceroy had solicited from the Spanish Minister of War a sanction of the important appointment which he had accorded the colonel. Calleja warmly praised his military successes as well as his loyalty to the Spanish

[47] Instrucciones para la división de la provincia de Guanajuato, April 27, 1813, in A.G.N., Iturbide, vol. 1.
[48] Iturbide to J. J. de Iturbide, May 2, 1813, in MSS, Y.U.
[49] Calleja to Iturbide, September 1, 1813, in A.G.N., Iturbide, 1.
[50] Iturbide to Calleja, October 24, 1813, ibid.
[51] Calleja to Iturbide, November 15, 1813, ibid.

FÉLIX MARÍA CALLEJA, VICEROY OF NEW SPAIN, 1813-1816
From a portrait in the Museo Nacional de Historia, Castillo de Chapultepec

cause. He stated that Iturbide had valuable properties and trade in the region under his charge. In particular, he lauded the role of that officer in the engagement at the bridge of Salvatierra. He not only mentioned a concession which Iturbide had just made of sixteen thousand pesos which the royal treasury owed him for the transportation service of one hundred and eighty mules furnished for the use of the Army of the North but also expressed regret that it had not been possible to liquidate this account nor that "of various loans of consequence" which the colonel had made.[52] On his part, Iturbide expressed regret that he could not do more to aid the royalist cause. He wrote a letter to Calleja on September 1, 1813, which contained this explanatory paragraph:

"Señor Excellency, I would enjoy making another contribution in specie to the royalist cause, but the expense of a numerous and honorable family, the fact that my haciendas have been in the possession of the bandits since the beginning of the deplorable insurrection in which we are involved, and that my hands have been worthily occupied by the baton and the sword, which means that I have been deprived of the liberty to dedicate myself to any of the interests that particularly affect me—all of these circumstances limit and hinder the execution of my desire to promote the welfare of my country. There is no action in its favor which might with propriety be called a sacrifice."[53]

On September 5, 1813, Calleja decided to reform the military administration of the Viceroyalty. Hence he divided an extensive region which had been under the control of General José de la Cruz into two parts. He put the intendancy of Valladolid in charge of General Diego García Conde. The intendancy of Guanajuato he placed in charge of Colonel Iturbide. Each of these commanders was to be directly responsible to Calleja.[54] By virtue of that appointment, the colonel was given the command of an important district which included the Bajío.

In the meantime the insurrection had found a new leader in the remarkable curate José María Morelos, a native of the city of Valla-

---

[52] Calleja to the Minister of War, August 30, 1813, in A.G.N., Correspondencia de Virreyes, Calleja, 1813, vol. $\frac{2}{255}$.

[53] "Las Mulas de Iturbide," Boletin del archivo general de la nacion, vol. II, no. 1, pp. 71-72.

[54] Calleja to the Minister of War, September 5, 1813, in A.G.N., Correspondencia de Virreyes, 1813-1818, $\frac{16}{268}$.

dolid. Morelos soon gave fresh spirit to the movement by virtue of his military activity and political initiative. As early as November 16, 1810, in a letter to Hidalgo, Morelos sketched a revolutionary program in which he proposed that slaves were to be set at liberty and that the government should be entrusted to Creoles. He also expressed himself in favor of partitioning the large haciendas so that small plots of land could be distributed among the laboring classes. He even declared that nobles, wealthy people, and important office-holders, whether Spaniards or Creoles, should be considered as the enemies of the Mexican people. This program contained the germs of a social revolution.[55]

In 1813 Morelos convoked a Congress at the town of Chilpancingo. In an address to its members he maintained that sovereignty originally resided in the people, that they were free to alter their government, and that Mexico should become absolutely independent.[56] On November 6, 1813, the Congress, which was composed of only seven members, adopted a Declaration of Independence from Spain. The Declaration announced that all Mexicans who opposed the independence of their country were to be considered as traitors. Only the Roman Catholic religion should be tolerated. The new government was to protect that faith and to preserve the purity of its doctrines. Among the powers which this act vested in the legislature, besides the authority to make laws concerning domestic affairs, was the power to negotiate with the Holy See for the regulation of the Mexican Church.[57]

The Chilpancingo Congress recognized Morelos as the military commander of the revolutionary forces. It also appointed him the chief executive of the projected state. He soon decided to organize his forces for an attack upon those royalists who were entrenched in the city of Valladolid.[58] Suspecting his intention, the vigilant Viceroy not only ordered General Ciriaco de Llano to direct its defense but also placed him in command of the Army of the North.

Morelos stationed several thousand men on Santa María Hill, which overlooked Valladolid. Acting under the orders of General Llano, Iturbide marched against the insurgents. Breaking through a fringe of soldiers that guarded the rebel camp, he reached the tent of Morelos, who narrowly escaped capture. According to the com-

[55] Copy, Hernández y Dávalos Collection, 2-28-15 and 16, in MSS, U.T. On the political ideas of Morelos, see further Zavala, "Mexico: La Revolución, la Independencia, la Constitución de 1824" (Levene, Historia de América, VII, 49-51), where Zavala expresses doubt concerning the socio-political views attributed to Morelos.
[56] Hernández y Dávalos, Coleccion de documentos, V, 165-166.
[57] Ibid., V, 214.   [58] Ibid., V, 159-166.

manding officer's report to Calleja, an attack on December 25, 1813, forced the enemy to flee from the field. Llano praised Iturbide, the second in command, who had carried out his orders satisfactorily.[59] In his official report Iturbide reasoned that the most important result of this exploit was the indisputable proof that Morelos was not invincible.[60] He wrote to a friend that thanks should be given to Almighty God for the victory because it would promote the peace and tranquillity of his native land. He expressed hope that the "disastrous, unjust, and tumultuous rebellion" would come to an end in the very intendancy where it had originated.[61]

Though Iturbide had not infrequently been praised by his superior officers, and though he had been promoted to a colonelcy, yet he felt that his service had not been adequately recognized. Several days after his arrival in Mexico City in February, 1814, he addressed to Calleja a lengthy petition to urge that the Spanish Regency should elect him a member of the National Order of San Fernando, which had been created by a decree of the Cortes.[62] The act provided that, in recognition of outstanding service, the government of Spain could issue a diploma of that order to any qualified member of the armed forces.[63]

Naïvely asserting that it took an effort on his part to overcome the natural repugnance which all honorable men felt upon being compelled to compose their own eulogies, Iturbide directed attention to certain of his military engagements that resembled those actions mentioned in the decree which founded the new order as prerequisite to membership therein. He based his claim to that distinction upon certain feats of arms: the capture of Albino García, the rout of the insurgents at Calpulalpan, the reduction of the fort on Liceaga Island, the capture of Fort Zacapú, the battle at the bridge of Salvatierra, and the check given to the rebels at Valladolid. "I well know," wrote Iturbide in his comment concerning the discomfiture of Morelos, "that everything has depended upon the most special protection given to our arms by the God of Hosts; but, having served as an instrument,

[59] Llano to Calleja, January 3, 1814, in A.G.N., Historia de Operaciones, Llano, vol. 18.

[60] Iturbide to Calleja, February 24, 1814, in I. MSS, 5.

[61] To Count Pérez Gálvez, December 29, 1813, in MSS, S.J.M.H., accession no. 53776.

[62] Iturbide to Calleja, February 24, 1814, f. 5-5v, in I. MSS, 5; Calleja to Iturbide, February 28, 1822, in A.G.N., Iturbide, 3.

[63] *Colección de los decretos y ordenes que han expedido las cortes generales y extraordinarias*, I, 198-212.

I cannot do less than to present the matter such as it is. . . ." The Creole asked that he should be conceded the pension, the salute, and the insignia cited in the legislative decree as a reward to generals for six distinguished exploits. He explained that he was animated in part by a desire to make known the right of "a son of this country, who has striven to serve the just cause, to so honorable a decoration."[64] Though his plea, accompanied by testimonials regarding his military conduct, was forwarded to Llano, and though that commander wrote the Viceroy on June 28, 1814, transmitting information and documents about the candidate,[65] yet the Cross of the Order of San Fernando was not pinned upon the ambitious Creole's breast.

During the very time when the Mexican Congress guarded by Morelos was fleeing before royalist soldiers, the despicable King Ferdinand VII, who was blindly admired by some Spaniards, was restored to the Spanish throne. He soon issued a decree announcing his intention to disregard the liberal Constitution adopted in 1812 as well as other acts of the Cortes.

From his headquarters at Irapuato on October 15, 1814, Iturbide published news of the restoration of the Spanish King. He soon made arrangements to celebrate the significant event. Church bells were rung, a triple salute of artillery was fired, and soldiers and towns-people alike shouted *Viva el Rey*. In the tent of the military commander a portrait of Ferdinand VII was hung under a rich canopy which bore the royal coat of arms. A solemn Mass was celebrated in the village church. During the afternoon of October 17 the soldiers marched to an open field where they staged a representation of the royalist victory at the bridge of Calderón.[66] A contemporary historian later alleged that to climax the celebration some fifty rebels who had been captured by the royalists were executed.[67]

Meantime, in other parts of the Viceroyalty the cause of independence had fluctuated. Early in 1814 Mariano Matamoros, a curate who had left his parishioners at Jantetelco and distinguished himself as a lieutenant of Morelos, was captured by the royalists and executed. A few months later Iturbide, who was in charge of an expeditionary force, failed to intercept Morelos, who was convoying the fugitive Congress.[68] Asserting that it held the sovereignty originally vested in

[64] Iturbide to Calleja, February 24, 1814, f. 5-5v, in I. MSS, 5.
[65] Llano to Calleja, June 28, 1814, *ibid*.
[66] Iturbide, *Correspondencia y diario militar*, II, 272-274.
[67] Bustamante, *Cuadro histórico*, IV, 296.
[68] *Gaceta del gobierno de México*, June 15, 1815, pp. 609-610.

the people, at Apatzingán on October 22, 1814, that assembly adopted a "Constitutional Decree for the Liberty of Mexican America." The act declared that Roman Catholicism was the religion of the State. It provided for an executive composed of three magistrates, a congress of elected delegates, and a judiciary of five persons who, like the executive power, were to be chosen by the legislature. It declared that all persons born in New Spain were equal.[69] Notable on account of its democratic character, because of the distracted condition of the country the fundamental law was not put into operation.

Seven days after the Constitution had been promulgated, from the hacienda of Villachuato, Iturbide issued an order which became notorious in Mexican military annals. He announced that to prevent the spread of the rebellious spirit he had decided to separate the insurgents in his district from its loyal inhabitants. In an arbitrary fashion he directed that, after the lapse of three days, the followers, the wives, and the children of malcontents of whatever stripe were to be meted out the same harsh treatment as that accorded to rebel soldiers bearing arms.[70] Asserting that he respected both the merit and the important service of Iturbide, on January 6, 1815, the curate Antonio de Labarrieta sent a protest to the Viceroy against the inhumanity of an order which menaced women and children with imprisonment. Labarrieta maintained that Spanish piety and generosity would not sanction such a horrible policy. "Holy God," he exclaimed, "what times have come upon us!"[71]

In reply the Viceroy asserted that he had sent advice to Iturbide concerning his conduct. He declared, however, that, because of the barbarous acts of rebels who were ravaging the country, it was necessary for the royalists to be rigorous.[72] In fact during a controversy in which he later became involved with the bishop of Puebla, who had denounced the cruelty of royalist commanders, Calleja sprang to their defense. He acknowledged that he wished to promote the pacification of Mexico by any means in his power.[73]

A report signed by Colonel Iturbide at San Miguel el Grande in September, 1814, showed that the third division of the Army of the North, which was then under his command, was composed of 46

[69] Hernández y Dávalos, *Colección de documentos*, V, 720-722.

[70] García, *Documentos historicos mexicanos*, V, 430-431.

[71] "Notable carta del cura de Guanajuato, Dr. D. Antonio Lavarrieta," *Boletin del archivo general de la nacion*, vol. I, no. 1, p. 92.

[72] *Ibid.*, pp. 96-97.

[73] "Controversia entre el obispo de Puebla y el virrey Calleja," *ibid.*, vol. IV, no. 5, p. 656.

artillerymen, 758 cavalry, and 1,136 infantry.[74] During that year no small part of his time was spent in the protection of convoys transporting goods between towns in the interior of the country or between the provinces and Mexico City. In a letter to the Viceroy on October 8 he described the protection which he had given to a long train of wagons that was returning from Querétaro to the province of San Luis Potosí. He also mentioned his clashes with the bandits who had stolen many cattle from haciendas.[75] He informed Calleja on the next day that a recent convoy had brought him quicksilver and tobacco. Further, he explained that the proceeds from their sale in conjunction with income from the *alcabala* tax had enabled him to meet in part the expenses of his division of the army.[76]

Early in November, 1814, at his order, Colonel Castañon attacked the town of Purandiro, surprised the insurgents, and killed their leader, a notorious rebel named Villalongín. When he reported this action to the Viceroy, Iturbide stated that in less than two months his command had killed or captured some nine hundred insurgents. In lamenting that he had to put to death among others a priest named Saenz, he wrote thus: "Such is the strait in which we are placed by the extreme malice of some miserable ecclesiastics who are imitators of Judas. Oh, what would we gain if they realized their dignity and acted accordingly! What evils could be avoided!"[77]

During the next month Iturbide informed Calleja that the task of pacifying the intendancy of Guanajuato was being accomplished.[78] The Viceroy reported to Madrid that the spread of the insurrection in the central portion of Mexico had been checked. He explained that this success was due in no small part to Iturbide's bravery and military skill.[79]

So provoked was that officer by the ravages of insurgents in various haciendas throughout his district, however, that he proposed to issue a proclamation in his own name threatening them with condign punishment. He undertook to announce that he would put to death one tenth of the imprisoned wives of those guerrillas. He also proposed

[74] Copy, Exército de Operacs. del Norte, tercera división, September 1, 1814, Gates Collection, no. 219, in MSS, T.U.

[75] Iturbide to Calleja, October 8, 1814, Gates Collection, no. 266, *ibid.*

[76] *Idem* to *idem*, October 9, 1814, Gates Collection, no. 271, *ibid.*

[77] *Gaceta del gobierno de Mexico*, January 12, 1815, p. 36.

[78] *Ibid.*, pp. 38-39.

[79] Calleja to M. Lardizabal, December 31, 1814, in A.G.N., Correspondencia de Virreyes, $\frac{18}{268}$.

that in case a royalist soldier or courier should be murdered, all of the imprisoned wives should be executed. If these inhumane measures did not cause the rebels to desist, he further proposed that various towns which harbored them should be razed.[80] After mature consideration, however, even the cruel Viceroy declined to allow Iturbide to post a proclamation threatening such barbarous punishments.[81]

A little later, Calleja instructed General Llano to prepare for an attack on Cóporo, a hill in the intendancy of Valladolid which had been strongly fortified by Ramón Rayón. This stronghold furnished a convenient rendezvous for the insurgent cavalry that preyed upon convoys. The Viceroy directed that Llano's army should be re-enforced by soldiers from the province of Guanajuato led by Iturbide, who was appointed the second in command.[82] In January, 1815, the expeditionary force laid siege to Fort Cóporo. At a meeting of royalist officers held on February 4, almost all of them voted in favor of an immediate attack. Colonel Iturbide, however, maintained that the difficulties and obstacles confronting the besiegers were too great. He advised that instead some royalist troops should be cautiously withdrawn to adjacent towns while the remainder of the investing force continued the siege. Nevertheless, he expressed his willingness to lead an attack should the officers decide in favor of such action.[83]

Early in March, Llano ordered him to assault the fort. The general stated that Iturbide could select the officers and soldiers whom he wished to have in his force. Praising his "skill, military talents, and warlike spirit," as well as his zeal and patriotism, Llano voiced the hope that his soldiers would contribute by their success to the conservation of religion, peace, and the rights of the King.[84]

When he undertook this task, Iturbide expressed the opinion that success could be secured only by surprising the defenders. An attack at dawn on March 4, however, was repulsed with heavy loss.[85] A council of war decided unanimously that it would be unwise to renew the assault. In a dispatch to the Minister of the Indies concerning the siege, the Viceroy reported that the royalist troops had conducted them-

---

[80] Iturbide to Calleja, December 30, 1814, and enclosure, in A.G.N., Iturbide, 5.

[81] Calleja to Iturbide, December 11, 1815, in A.G.N., Historia, Operaciones de Guerra, 5.

[82] In A.G.N., Correspondencia de Virreyes, $\frac{18}{268}$

[83] Bustamante, Cuadro historico, III, 104-108. A plan of Mount Cóporo is furnished by H. H. Bancroft (History of Mexico, IV, 609).

[84] Bustamante, op. cit., III, 109.

[85] Iturbide, Correspondencia y diario militar, III, 98-99.

selves with praiseworthy serenity and valor.[86] Iturbide promptly
returned to the intendancy of Guanajuato, where he soon dispersed a
band of insurgents. In a letter to Madrid Calleja stated that this
officer had been instrumental in pacifying that region.[87]

Iturbide was still dissatisfied with the recognition which he had
been accorded. It seems probable that this feeling was not disconnected
with a desire to visit Europe. Furthermore, he had not relinquished
his ambition to become a knight. In June, 1815, he petitioned the
Viceroy for a royal license to proceed to Spain, where he wished to
reside for two years. When he transmitted the request to Madrid,
Calleja expressed hope that the Minister of the Indies would induce
the King to sanction a request which he recommended should be
granted because of the important service performed by the petitioner
during the rebellion.[88] Nevertheless, the aspiring colonel was not
allowed to start on a transatlantic journey.

News which he received on September 25, 1815, of his appointment
as the commandant of the Army of the North and of the intendancies
of Guanajuato and Valladolid dimmed his vision of a journey to
Spain. Although he demurred at this appointment, asserting that
another officer could be found who was better suited than himself to
fill the difficult post,[89] yet on October 21 he received through General
Llano an order from the Viceroy that he should undertake the duties
of his new position.[90] Not only was Colonel Iturbide thus advanced
to the independent command of a royalist army which numbered some
4,000 men,[91] but he was also placed in charge of two important
intendancies. He was soon instructed to place the intendancy of
Guanajuato under the direct control of Colonel Orrantia. More than
an inkling of his activity during a part of his public career may be
gathered from statistical entries in his diary which record that, during
the years 1813, 1814, and 1815, he had marched in pursuit of the
rebels some five thousand leagues over rugged mountains, across
barren plateaus, and through hot, humid lowlands.[92]

[86] Calleja to the Minister of the Indies, April 6, 1815, in A.G.N., Correspondencia
de Virreyes, Calleja, 1813-1816, $\frac{18}{268}$.

[87] Idem to idem, June 30, 1815 (no. 29), ibid.

[88] Calleja to the Minister of the Indies, June 30, 1815 (no. 40), in A.G.N., Correspondencia de Virreyes, Calleja, 1815, $\cdot\frac{10}{263}$

[89] Iturbide, Correspondencia y diario militar, III, 392.

[90] Ibid., p. 265.

[91] Torrente, Historia de la revolucion hispano-americana, II, 288.

[92] Iturbide, op. cit., III, 297.

In an account of his public life which he composed years later Iturbide wrote concerning his career as a royalist officer that victory had always rewarded the forces which he commanded. "I did not lose a single engagement," he asserted. "I fought whatever enemies confronted me. Many times my forces were inferior to those of the enemy in the proportion of one to ten or of eight to twenty."[93] Though he qualified that boastful statement by a footnote in which he explained his failure to capture Fort Cóporo, he omitted to mention his unsuccessful attempt to capture Morelos.[94] Near the end of that year, however, while guarding the flight of Congress, that insurgent leader was captured by another royalist officer. Stripped of priestly robes, after a most expeditious trial, he was sentenced to be shot in the back as a traitor to the King. He was executed on December 22, 1815. The star of the Mexican revolution seemed to have set.

Notwithstanding the successful campaigns which he had waged against partisans of independence and the high esteem which he had gained with prominent viceregal officials, at times Iturbide lamented the carnage. On rare occasions, according to Lucas Alamán, a contemporary publicist who later wrote a useful *Historia de Mexico*, Iturbide actually entertained dreams of Mexican independence. In March, 1815, after the sanguinary and fruitless attack on Fort Cóporo, in a conversation with Captain Vicente Filisola, an Italian who had entered the royal service in Spain, Iturbide not only voiced regret at the useless bloodshed but also expressed the opinion that independence could be easily attained if the soldiers of Mexico who were serving under the Spanish banner would join their rebellious countrymen. Yet, because of the undisciplined condition of the insurgent partisans and the atrocious political and social system which they had proposed, he felt that it was necessary to finish with them before forming a plan for the establishment of an independent regime. When Filisola admitted that he agreed with these views, the colonel said that perhaps the day would come when he could remind his comrade of their dialogue.[95] Though it is possible that in recording the incident in a history written many years after the revolution led by Iturbide had ended in triumph, Alamán might have been influenced by that suc-

[93] Iturbide, *Carrera militar y politica*, p. 7. On the authenticity of this account, see W. S. Robertson, "The Memorabilia of Agustín de Iturbide," *Hispanic American Historical Review*, XXVII, 454.
[94] Iturbide, *Carrera militar y politica*, p. 7 n. 7.
[95] Alamán, *Historia*, V, 50.

cess, yet his evidence is re-enforced by views expressed upon more than one occasión by the revolutionist himself.[96]

With regard to his vindictive cruelty toward the rebels, it is not sufficient to ascribe this, as a Mexican biographer has done, simply to the intolerant spirit of youth. No less influential was the fact that Iturbide was carrying out the designs of relentless masters like Viceroy Calleja and King Ferdinand VII. Furthermore, he pursued this policy in company with other royalist commanders who were also sanguinary. A contemporary likened the cruelties of Calleja to the proscriptions of Robespierre.[97] Properly to judge Iturbide, one must consider his acts in view of his environment and of the customs of his age. Sometimes he even considered himself as an instrument of God.

Moreover, as a Mexican historian has stated, at times a revolutionary leader showed heartless cruelty in the civil war. Such a spirit was provocative of retaliation. Occasionally Iturbide's prejudice affected his policy. During his activity as a royalist officer former friendship signified little or nothing to him when it did not accord with his duty to Ferdinand VII. A tale told of him was that upon capturing a rebel friar whom he had known in his youth, Iturbide received him graciously, conversed with him in a familiar manner, treated him to a cup of chocolate, and then casually informed him that within two hours he should be prepared to meet his Maker.[98] This cruel military commander could be all things to all men.

Iturbide later explained that he took up arms against the insurgents, not to make war upon the Mexicans, but against rebel bands which were harassing the country, for their object was not to secure the liberty and independence of Mexico but "to exterminate the Europeans, to destroy property, to commit excesses, to flout the laws of war and humane customs, and even to disregard religious practices."[99] Whatever may be the exact amount of truth in this allegation, there is no doubt that by 1816 he had become discontented. Although in a certain letter Iturbide addressed Viceroy Calleja as his "most revered

[96] An address attributed to Iturbide on the day of his coronation began thus: "Cuando en noviembre de 20 salí de esta Capital para el Sur con objeto, de ejecutar el plan que años antes meditaba, . . . ," *Gaceta del gobierno imperial de Mexico*, August 3, 1822, p. 582. See also "Las Mulas de Iturbide," *Boletin del archivo general de la nacion*, vol. II, no. 1, p. 93.

[97] Santa Anna, *Muerte del Señor Concha*. With regard to the cruelty and venality of royalist commanders, see further Toro, *Compendio de historia de Mexico*, pp. 163, 195, 213, 225, 262-263.

[98] Rocafuerte, *Bosquejo ligerísimo de la revolución de Mégico*, pp. 12-13.

[99] Iturbide, *Carrera militar y politica*, pp. 5-6 n. 5.

General and most beloved protector,"[100] yet he was displeased with the government because it had grudgingly granted him scant recognition for his valuable military service. Upon more than one occasion, perhaps because he was a Creole, his advancement had been retarded or blocked completely. In his heart he was well aware that whatever attitude he might assume with respect to the government, he had gained a detailed knowledge of strategic Mexican terrain, a high prestige as a military commander, and an extensive acquaintance with influential royalist officers.

[100] Iturbide to Calleja, July 27, 1814, in A.G.N., Iturbide, 3.

CHAPTER III

Interlude

THE YEARS from 1816 to 1820 form an interlude between two periods in Iturbide's life: the period when he fought to restore the rule of Ferdinand VII in Mexico, and the period when he undertook to separate his country from Spain. Though the military correspondence and the diary of the royalist officer which were published by the Mexican government record some of his activities, they do not bring into relief the fact that his conduct was at times criticized severely.

A letter from Iturbide to Juan Gómez de Navarrete, a well-educated lawyer of the intendancy of Valladolid who was acquainted with his family, shows that as early as April, 1815, he was aware that complaints were being lodged against him. Mentioning certain criticisms of his management, the colonel explained that he had treated them with philosophic serenity because he had hoped for opportunities to expose calumnies and to reveal the truth. He declared that the government had not brought any accusation against him and that a viceregal official named Bernardo Villamil had informed him that it was satisfied with his conduct. "This assurance," continued Iturbide, "and the distinctions conferred upon me by the Viceroy have tied my hands. I know that his Excellency asked for secret reports about my conduct, and allow me to say that in them I have been justly treated." Nevertheless, he voiced a wish that his behavior should be scrutinized in order that he could be accorded the satisfaction befitting his position. He asserted that he was so disgusted with the situation that he would rather be a farm hand than to hold his command. "I would have asked for my retirement some time ago," he added, "but such a step would not become my character."[1]

Early in 1816 he was informed by Calleja that inhabitants of the intendancy of Guanajuato were making frequent complaints that their towns, their haciendas, and their commerce were being ruined by the depredations of rebels.[2] Villamil informed him that many criticisms

[1] Draft, April 3, 1815, in I. MSS, 16.
[2] Calleja to Iturbide, no. 103 (undated), in A.G.N., Iturbide, 7.

were being made of his conduct, but that he should carry out his just intentions and embrace every opportunity to make known that the accusations were false.[3] Iturbide could therefore not have been much surprised when on April 10, 1816, he received a confidential letter from the Viceroy directing him to proceed at once to the capital city in order to answer charges which various individuals had lodged against him. The accused officer was instructed to transfer to Colonel José de Castro the command of the Army of the North.[4]

Iturbide acted promptly. On that very day he addressed a circular to officers of his army in the intendancies of Guanajuato and Valladolid to notify them that, having been directed by the Viceroy to proceed to Mexico City because of matters concerning the royal service, he had relinquished to Colonel Castro his functions as the commandant of those districts and of the Army of the North.[5] After Iturbide arrived in the capital, he spent some time attending to family affairs. In May, 1816, at the end of a lengthy rebuttal of accusations made by two colonels concerning his military conduct, Iturbide declared that he could have no greater glory than to shed his blood in defense of a holy religion, a just king, and a beloved country.[6]

His enforced retirement from the military service of Spain took place at a significant time. In 1816 it seemed as though the struggles for the independence of the Spanish Indies had ceased. In the ancient Empire of the Incas a general revolutionary movement had indeed scarcely begun. A Spanish commander named Pablo Morillo had subjugated Venezuela and New Granada. Royalists had conquered the insurgents in Chile. Although José de San Martín was recruiting the Army of the Andes, yet none of the provinces of the vast Viceroyalty of La Plata had yet framed a declaration of independence from Spain. As Calleja had almost crushed the rebel guerrillas in Mexico, he undertook to consider the incriminatory reports which were being widely circulated about the deposed commander of Guanajuato and Valladolid.

On June 24, 1816, the Viceroy solicited information from important organizations and individuals of the intendancy of Guanajuato con-

[3] B. Villamil to Iturbide, January 30, 1816, in I. MSS., 9.

[4] Calleja to Iturbide, April 4, 1816, in A.G.N., Historia de Operaciones, Iturbide, 9; Iturbide, Correspondencia y diario militar, III, 338.

[5] Circular á los comtes. de divisnes. y secciones del exto. y en pueblos organizados de las provs. de Guanaxto. y Valladolid, in I. MSS., 4.

[6] Cuevas, El Libertador, pp. 124-167. Like some of the other documents published by Cuevas, the document here cited was secured by him from the Iturbide Papers in the Library of Congress.

cerning the conduct of Iturbide. Alamán, who was a native of that region, stated that, apprehensive of the vengeance of the accused colonel, certain persons made misleading replies in his favor, others purposely expressed themselves in ambiguous terms, while still others omitted mention of anything which might offend him.[7]

Some comments about Calleja's inquiry by contemporaries of the accused commander were found among the papers preserved by his family. Among others, José Solano of Silao belittled the critics. He made the philosophic reflection that Providence had willed this ordeal for that officer so that his vindicated honor would be rendered more pure, and so that he would learn who were his friends and who were his emulators.[8] Basilio Peralta wrote to the colonel from the city of Valladolid to express indignation that a soldier who had risked his health and his life in the royalist cause should have been attacked by inconsiderate and malignant persons.[9] Antonio de Soto sent a letter from León to inform Iturbide of the inquiry. "Who can obscure the fact, which is clearer than the sun at midday," asked this friend, "that you have not aspired to anything more than the extermination of our enemies without meddling in other affairs?"[10]

Not of least interest were the views expressed by Colonel Manuel Iruela, the commandant of Salamanca, who was an intimate friend of the accused colonel. He replied to the Viceroy on July 7, 1816, in part, by this defense:

"I say to your Excellency that, during all the time that I have been under Iturbide's orders, I have seen nothing unworthy of the honor pertaining to the important posts which he has occupied. I have beheld in him much disinterestedness and integrity. He was steadfast in his decisions; his behavior was generally humane. He was as benign toward well-behaved persons as he was inexorable toward evildoers. There was not an hour during the day or the night that demanded his attention which he dedicated to repose. He was always prompt to sally forth either against the bands of rebels concerning whom he had been warned or to give aid to persons who asked for it. . . . A lover of our august sovereign, he was an upright defender of the rights of his Majesty, intrepid on the fields of Mars, unwearied in his labors, and constant in his vigils. . . . I affirm that never have I received an order to protect solely any article of his commerce; nor have I known of such an order being given to anyone else. . . .

[7] Alamán, *Historia de Mexico*, IV, 347.
[8] Solano to Calleja, July 3, 1816, in I. MSS, 9.
[9] Peralta to Iturbide, July 4, 1816, *ibid*.   [10] Soto to Iturbide, July 5, 1816, *ibid*.

Lastly, most esteemed Sir, I have seen in church his religious disposition. In his house he is a Christian; and on various occasions I have beheld him liberal in charity."[11]

The outstanding criticism of Iturbide was made by Dr. Antonio de Labarrieta. That curate had been early attracted by revolutionary doctrines, but long before 1816 he had taken an oath of loyalty to the Spanish government, had preached with zeal in favor of the loyalist cause, and had even donated silver from the church coffers for the support of the viceregal army.[12] Though he was apprehensive that the discredited colonel might be restored to his command, on July 8, 1816, he dared to write a denunciation of that officer which more than offset Iruela's laudatory letter. After warmly praising the valiant actions of Iturbide during his early career, Labarrieta severely criticized his conduct after his talent had been signally recognized by the viceregal government. The accuser alleged that he had punished people unjustly, that he had cast into prison men and women against whom no complaints had been brought, and that he had cruelly treated the wives and children of insurgents. He charged that, disregarding the Viceroy's instructions, instead of promoting agriculture, trade, and mining, Iturbide had injured or destroyed those industries.

"He has set fire to haciendas, thus furnishing an evil example to the rebels. By seizing livestock belonging to farms, he has rendered their cultivation impossible. . . . He has destroyed commerce, because as a commander he has not only made himself a merchant but also a monopolist of trade. . . . It has been generally reported that in order to convoy sugar, wool, oil, and cigars belonging to himself, he has pretended to send out expeditions in the royal service. . . . It is impossible, your Excellency, for me to describe in detail all the facts which justify my complaint. To do so it would be necessary to write a volume. . . . In fine, Iturbide has made himself a sovereign. . . . His enemies call him the 'Pygmalion of America!'

"With respect to his conduct as a military officer, it is notorious that his soldiers are neither well disciplined nor properly subordinated and that, despite the fact that he has drawn from the royal treasury alone about one million three hundred thousand pesos, his forces are not well organized. . . . Iturbide cannot have a sound basis of Chris-

[11] Iruela to Calleja, July 7, 1816, *ibid*.

[12] Hernández y Dávalos, *Coleccion de documentos para la historia de la guerra de independencia de Mexico*, II, 371-372; copy, Testimonio of Manuel Espiñosa, October 19, 1811, Hernández y Dávalos Collection, 10-3-720, in MSS, U.T.; copy, Calleja to Venegas, October 23, 1811, Hernández y Dávalos Collection, 10-3-717, *ibid*.

tian faith; for that is incompatible with the inhumanity and other excesses which I have mentioned in detail."[13]

Shortly after reaching the capital city, Iturbide had resigned his dual post. Still, he remained the colonel of the regiment of Celaya. As a copy of Labarrieta's arraignment came into his hands, on August 14 he addressed a justificatory letter to Calleja. He declared that he could not believe that either the Viceroy or Miguel Bataller, the military judge, would give the least credit to the accusations, for their author was not entitled to any esteem because of his corrupt life, his troublesome disposition, and his poor judgment in political matters. Iturbide also mentioned the accuser's reputation as a one-time rebel. He declared that, in discussing the last part of the accused's career, Labarrieta had suddenly metamorphosed "a man of distinguished principles and education into an evil monster."

Denying that he had acted despotically, Iturbide expressed his willingness to submit documents to the Viceroy to disprove that accusation. In regard to his alleged cruelty, he explained that it had not been his intention to impose special punishments upon women but to guard them securely in order to prevent crimes by their relatives and to bring those culprits to reason. He stated that of one hundred and eighty women who had been incarcerated, only eighty still remained in prison. He declared that the charge brought against him of having destroyed agriculture was false. Categorically did he allege that not a single hacienda had been sacked at his instance. In defense of his actions he asserted:

"I have not issued a single proclamation or taken a step of any importance without reporting to your Excellency immediately. Convinced of this truth by uninterrupted experience, you do not need any other evidence concerning Labarrieta's accusation that I freely imposed laws by a species of sovereignty. . . . With respect to expenditures, you well know that the troops under my command are among those which have been most economically handled. . . . When convenient I shall make known the large economies that I have assured to the royal treasury. These economies were very important because of the great scarcity of funds for the subsistence of the troops needed to preserve order and to promote the pacification of the country."

Discussing Labarrieta's charge that he was irreligious, the colonel remonstrated thus, ". . . he reproaches me impiously, because I recite

[13] Labarrieta, *Informe del Dr. Don Antonio Labarrieta, cura de la ciudad de Guanajuato, sobre la conducta que observó Iturbide siendo comandante general del Bajío*, pp. 5-8.

the rosary and attend Mass." Commenting on another part of the curate's denunciation, Iturbide asserted that it was marked by "the suspicious perversity, corruption, and malice of its author." Not only did he intimate that his impudent calumnies might be due to a criminal intent, but he also declared that he was well enough acquainted with the laws of the Viceroyalty to demand a suitable vindication.[14] In sum, the accused officer attacked the character of his clerical critic, countered some of the charges brought against himself, alleged that the Viceroy had been duly informed of his administrative measures, and maintained that his conduct could be fully justified.

Friends of Iturbide again rallied to his support. On August 14 Pedro Yandiola addressed him from Querétaro to criticize Labarrieta's "malicious, hypocritical, and scandalous report."[15] After reading the curate's denunciation, Colonel Iruela addressed another long letter to the Viceroy protesting against this false and insolent defamation of Iturbide. Iruela reasoned that it was peculiar that no other person or organization had deplored the lack of discipline in the Army of the North. He declared that the rebels in Valle de Santiago had not only acclaimed the curate's libel but had posted it in public places.[16]

A change in the government of the Viceroyalty was meanwhile impending. Early in March, 1816, the Spanish Minister of State notified the Council of the Indies that, because of the merit of Juan Ruíz de Apodaca, Ferdinand VII had selected him to act as the Viceroy of Mexico during his royal pleasure.[17] On March 16 the King signed a formal notification of that appointment. Apodaca, a lieutenant general in the Spanish navy who had served as the ambassador to the Court of London and as the Captain General of Cuba, was not inappropriately characterized by a Spanish writer as an old-fashioned Castilian cavalier, loyal and trustful.[18] The new Viceroy reached Mexico City on September 20, 1816.[19] As the result of an interview with him, the retired colonel felt that he had refuted the charges which had been brought against himself.[20]

Labarrieta's reply to Iturbide's counterblast of August 14 was laid

---

[14] Cuevas, El Libertador, pp. 115-124.

[15] Yandiola to Iturbide, August 14, 1816, in I. MSS, 9.

[16] Iruela to Calleja, September 21, 1816, ibid.

[17] P. Cevallos to the Council of the Indies, March 2, 1816, in A.G.I., Audiencia de México, estante 85—cajón 5—legajo 14.

[18] Endorsed "Fecha en Palacio á 16 de Marzo de 1816," ibid.; on Apodaca, see Navarro y Rodrigo, Iturbide, p. 49.

[19] Gaceta del gobierno de Mexico, September 24, 1816, pp. 931-932.

[20] Iturbide, Correspondencia privada, p. 111.

before Apodaca. The cleric complained that, exhausting all the acrimonious and insulting expressions in the Spanish language, the accused had grossly outraged his honor. He reasoned that Iturbide's reply was not merely a refutation of the charges which had been filed but also a personal attack upon himself. He denied that he was a disciple of Hidalgo. He neither favored the rebellion nor was he influenced by fear. It was strange, he reasoned, that during this period no such repeated charges had been brought against any other of the royalist commanders as had been brought against Iturbide. Labarrieta reiterated his charges concerning the accused officer's cruelty and arbitrariness. He added that Iturbide had subjected prisoners to torture.

The curate also asserted that, before the rebellion broke out, Iturbide did not possess more than the hacienda at Quirio, another farm which he had bought in the vicinity of Maravatio, and a house in his native city. In contrast he now had a fine house in Irapuato and another in Querétaro. Moreover, although he complained of poverty, the colonel had in concealment at least three hundred thousand pesos. These funds had not been derived from his salary but from booty or from commercial transactions. Iturbide's trade was so public and so scandalous that everyone in the city of Guanajuato knew his store where oil, sugar, and tallow were being sold. As an aid in solving the deplorable situation, the clerical accuser suggested that the Viceroy should send an agent incognito to study conditions in the Bajío.[21]

A note written by a viceregal official on the margin of this vindication recommended it to the Viceroy's attention because it proposed a feasible means of settling the controversy.[22] There is nothing to show, however, that an agent was ever sent to the Bajío to make an investigation. Upon hearing of the fresh complaint from Guanajuato, a priest named José López, who had been born in the bishopric of Michoacán, addressing Iturbide as a beloved friend and protector, denounced Labarrieta as "arrogant, daring, and turbulent."[23]

Behind the scenes Calleja had meanwhile addressed a confidential report concerning his administration to Marquis Campo Sagrado, the Spanish Minister of War. After a brief account of the condition of the intendancies of Guanajuato and Valladolid and the state of the Army of the North, he added an explanation:

[21] Vindicación hecha por el Dor. D. Antonio Lavarrieta, cura del Guanajuato, con motivo de la impugnación que en 12 de Agto. de 1816 hizó el coronel Dn. Agustín de Iturbide al informe dado en 8 de Julio del mismo año, undated, Genaro García Collection, in MSS, U.T. Library.

[22] Ibid.

[23] López to Iturbide, November 12, 1816, in I. MSS, 9.

"I should not omit mentioning to your Excellency in this dispatch that the complaints and representations which were sent to me against Colonel Don Agustín de Iturbide, who was in command of those two provinces and of that army, obliged me some four months ago to direct him to come to this capital to reply to charges presented in certain papers which have been filed here. The officers who at present hold military positions are very much provoked with those commanders against whom complaints have not been made. Because, if one had to act upon such accusations, none of those officers would be in posts which they today occupy and the government would be left without officials who could be used. I have repeatedly informed you of my views on this matter. I have asked for some military commanders, who, possessing the required virtues, would have relieved me from the bitterness and the compromises which I have endured because of the fact that an officer, who by his valor and intelligence is fitted to command a division in a campaign, often lacks the talent required for civil and political administration or engages in his former mercantile occupation. It is not possible to prevent this commercial activity entirely, for that would plunge such an officer into misery and deprive the State of his service. Besides, such a policy would provoke suspicion and would incite accusations against the government which neither could nor should entrust the fate of military operations to inexperienced hands."[24]

This significant exposé was written at the very time when Iturbide's case was being seriously considered by Calleja, who as Captain General was in charge of military justice in the Viceroyalty. Miguel Bataller, the *auditor de guerra*, was acting as the legal adviser to the chief magistrate. Rocafuerte mentioned that Bataller was of opinion that the charges brought by Labarrieta against the accused officer could not be considered valid because he was a member of the militia and, according to the spirit of its regulations, was at liberty to carry on trade.[25] At a later time another contemporary stated that the military judge had said that the accused colonel deserved to be punished, but that he had to be treated "with indulgence because he had put to death many insurgents."[26] During the revolution against

[24] Calleja to Campo Sagrado, September 6, 1816, Iturbide, *Correspondencia privada*, p. xv; the original is in A.G.N., Correspondencia de Virreyes, Calleja, 1813-1816, $\frac{18}{268}$.

[25] Rocafuerte, *Bosquejo ligerísimo de la revolución de Mégico*, p. 259; Alamán, *Historia*, IV, 349 and n.

[26] Manuscrito, manifiesto de Iturbide, comentada por Carlos M. de Bustamante con letra de el mismo, Hernández y Dávalos Collection, 17-8-4255, in MSS, U.T.

Spanish rule in continental America it was evidently the custom of some Mexican officials to wink at the profitable commerce which was carried on by indispensable royalist commanders. Indeed it appears that the Viceroy himself was aware of Iturbide's more or less irregular mercantile transactions.

The colonel was not satisfied with the evidence in his case which was being presented to Bataller. Presumably to be used in the further justification of his conduct, on September 7, 1816, Iturbide prepared an account of his military activities with special attention to the last years of his service. Supplementing an official report that had been lodged in the military archives, the officer mentioned certain reforms which he asserted had been introduced at his instance in reconquered towns and cities. Lastly, he again emphasized the aid which he had furnished the viceregal government by supplying many mules for the transport service of the royalist forces.[27]

Five days later, a précis by Viceroy Calleja concerning the Iturbide case was published in the official gazette. This report stated that the complaints against him had been examined, that his answer had been heard, and that the military judge had decided that the accusations were without justification. Hence Calleja declared that there was no warrant for summoning Iturbide to appear before a judge. The statement was even made that the accused was free "to return to the command of the Army of the North." Yet, with seeming inconsistency, the qualification was added that as certain persons had "formally presented themselves as his accusers," their complaints would also have to be considered. An explanation was furnished that because of the notoriety of the case, this tentative decision was made public for "the information of the people by order of the government and at the request of the said commander."[28] Under the circumstances, the verdict seems like a lame attempt to vindicate Iturbide's arbitrary and corrupt conduct by officials who were privy to them. On September 20, 1816, Apodaca arrived in Mexico City, where he was received as the Viceroy.

The accused officer did not consider the case closed. For a week later in a letter to Iruela, Iturbide stated that he would not assume the command of his army unless he was at least morally certain that the new Viceroy entertained a just opinion of his intentions.[29] Though

[27] Relación de los servos. hechos pr. el corl. Dn. Agn. de Yturbide y qe. no constan en su oja de servos. qe. existe en la subinspon. gral., in I. MSS, 5.
[28] *Gaceta del gobierno de Mexico*, September 12, 1816, p. 892.
[29] Iturbide, *Correspondencia privada*, p. 112.

no final judgment was ever made public in this case, on October 24, 1816, Apodaca ordered Iturbide to transfer promptly his correspondence and papers as commander of the Army of the North to Colonel Francisco Orrantia, who was also placed in charge of the intendancy of Guanajuato.[30] Even then Colonel Iturbide—for he still retained the nominal command of the regiment of Celaya—did not despair of a favorable verdict. In a letter to a friend he expressed hope that the affair would soon be concluded justly so that Labarrieta's accusations, which contained atrocious calumnies, would injure no one but their author.[31] According to Alamán, after Viceroy Calleja had removed Iturbide from his command, certain influential mercantile houses of the Bajío ceased to protest against the conduct of the former commandant.[32] Among papers sedulously preserved by the Iturbide family was an unsigned criticism of a fresh arraignment which had been circulated by Labarrieta. This brief vigorously defended the accused colonel and roundly denounced the daring and insistent curate.[33]

On November 14 the retired officer was notified that Colonel Cristóbal Ordoñez had been appointed the commander of the intendancy of Guanajuato.[34] About two weeks later Iturbide addressed a letter to Viceroy Apodaca stating that he had received news that since his recall conditions had become much worse in that region, for the insurgents had increased their power and influence. Further, he declared that his critics were inventing malicious tales about his conduct, which he considered a proof that there was collusion between his enemies and certain revolutionists designed to hinder or to prevent his return to the army. He enclosed a copy of a letter from Padre Torres, a revolutionary chieftain, to a correspondent stating that several complaints about Iturbide's acts as a royalist commander had been framed by confidants of the rebels. He asserted that he had resigned his command three times, but that he did not feel inclined to leave Mexico City until he had been accorded a public justification of his conduct. Alleging that military command had no attraction for him,

---

[30] Apodaca to Iturbide, October 24, 1816, in I. MSS, 7.

[31] Iturbide, op. cit., p. 113.

[32] Alamán, op. cit., IV, 349 and n. Bancroft (History of Mexico, IV, 646 n. 1) states that Iturbide was "readily absolved" and that he refused "to return to his command."

[33] Examen analytico del memorial que el Dr. Dn. Antonio Labarrieta, cura de Guanajuato, dirigió al exmo. Sor. Virrey contra la conducta, acciones y persona del Sor. coronel Dn. Agustín de Iturbide, año de 1816, in I. MSS, 5.

[34] Apodaca to Iturbide, November 14, 1816, in A.G.N., Historia de Operaciones, Iturbide, 9.

he stated that he still desired to support the cause of Ferdinand VII. He avowed that not even the vexations which he had suffered during his sojourn in the capital city could alter his belief in "the great and noble cause" for which he had fought.[35] When he acknowledged the receipt of this letter, Apodaca expressed hope that the colonel would transmit to him any additional information about the controversy which might reach him.[36] In January, 1817, Iturbide's wife and three children settled down with him in a house in the capital city.[37] Though he was no longer in active service, his name was still printed in the list of viceregal officials as the colonel of the regiment of provincial infantry of Celaya.[38]

It is plain that he had another string to his bow. In April, 1815, Iturbide had addressed a letter to Juan Gómez de Navarrete expressing a wish that he would accompany the Iturbide family to Spain.[39] Not until the autumn of 1816, however, did Marquis Campo Sagrado write to the viceregal government to inform it that the King had granted Iturbide permission to visit the motherland on affairs of great importance pertaining to his family. Apodaca wrote a tardy endorsement on this note on May 1, 1817, to the effect that the petitioner was to be informed of the decision.[40] Two months passed before the Viceroy notified the retired colonel that, under the circumstances, in the opinion of the subinspector of the army, it was not convenient to release him from the command of the regiment of Celaya. "This officer," the subinspector explained, "has, in addition to valor and military talent, a practical knowledge of the region where his regiment is stationed—qualities which make him very useful to the service."[41]

Perhaps the colonel had anticipated that he would not be completely exonerated. For in June, 1817, he signed a power of attorney which authorized José Antonio López, who had occasionally served as a curate, to act on his behalf in Spain.[42] What Iturbide wished to secure is indicated by a letter which he received from the agent several months later. López stated that, without the support of influential persons, his progress at the Court of Madrid was slow. He complained

[35] Iturbide, *Correspondencia y diario militar*, III, 576.
[36] *Ibid.*, p. 577.
[37] Iturbide, *Correspondencia privada*, p. 132.
[38] Zúñiga y Ontiveros, *Calendario manual y guía de forasteros en México*, 1817, p. 187.
[39] Iturbide to Gómez de Navarrete, April 3, 1815, in I. MSS, 16.
[40] Campo Sagrado to Apodaca, September 15, 1816, in A.G.N., Reales Cédulas, vol. 214.
[41] Iturbide, *Correspondencia y diario militar*, III, 578.
[42] Copy, June 11, 1817, in I. MSS, 5.

that he had not received certain certificates concerning his master's affairs, such as records of his military service and accounts of the gifts and loans which he had made to the viceregal government. These documents were necessary, said López, in order that by their means a royal order could be obtained declaring that Iturbide was innocent of the calumnious accusations which his enemies had spread throughout the realm. Other papers were needed to support his claim to the grade, the office, and the decoration to which he aspired. It probably did not soothe the creole officer's feelings to learn that, after arriving in Spain, Calleja had been decorated not only by the cross of the Order of San Hermenegildo but also by the insignia of the Order of Isabella the Catholic.[43]

On November 25 López wrote that Iturbide's desire to be rewarded by the cross of the Order of Isabella the Catholic ought to be approved by the provincial deputation of Mexico.[44] Early in the following January the agent stated that he had decided to send to King Ferdinand VII an account of the latest steps taken in the affair and that the King should also be informed of a report made by Calleja. López hoped that the monarch would then issue a statement to the effect that he was satisfied with Iturbide's services and merit and also that the colonel was innocent of the accusations which had been filed against him in Mexico.[45] No such justification has been found.

Notice should be taken that the facts adduced and the explanations set forth contemporaneously by the retired colonel concerning the charges against him do not agree with views which he expressed in an autobiographical sketch composed in 1823. In a footnote to that sketch Iturbide stated that in 1816 certain influential persons residing in Guanajuato and Querétaro complained about him to the Viceroy but that they submitted no proof of their accusations. Not only did he gloss his actions but he summarized the judgment in terms favorable to himself.

"Viceroys Calleja and Apodaca knew about this affair. After making inquiries of *ayuntamientos*, curates, and the best-informed political chiefs of the provinces and of the army, who justified me, they declared their agreement with the decision of their auditor and of two superior judges, namely, that the accusation was calumnious throughout, that there remained open to me an action for damages against my calumniators, and that I might resume the exercise of the offices

[43] López to Iturbide, September 23, 1817, *ibid.*, p. 10.
[44] *Idem* to *idem*, November 25, 1817, *ibid.*
[45] *Idem* to *idem*, January 23, 1818, *ibid.*

which I had held. I did not wish either to re-assume command or to profit by my legal rights, and I relinquished the salary which I had enjoyed."[46]

Iturbide further explained that he gave up his military command because of delicacy, and, because of his natural inclination, betook himself to the cultivation of haciendas belonging to his family. Evidently it was the resulting financial needs that on November 21, 1816, led to his borrowing from Diego Fernández de Cevallos twenty thousand pesos which were to bear interest at 6 per cent per annum, a sum which had evidently been advanced to an employee on his estate. As late as 1855, that loan had not been liquidated.[47]

Meantime Iturbide was searching for a residence for his parents and himself as well as managing the family estates.[48] He finally secured the use of a farm which had occasionally been leased by the viceregal government on easy terms as a favor to a person who had become dissatisfied with his place in society. Located near Chalco in the valley of Mexico, this estate had at one time belonged to the Company of Jesus and hence was often designated as the "Hacienda Compañia." In 1818 he took up his residence on that hacienda, where he spent much time until the latter part of the year 1820. Presumably because of this venture, he experienced financial difficulties.[49] A letter which he wrote in March, 1818, concerning monetary affairs shows that he had drawn upon his father-in-law for some five hundred pesos.[50]

It appears that the acrimonious and protracted discussion concerning his activities in the Bajío had affected Iturbide's morale. Mentioning his case in a letter to María Nicolasa de Iturbide, a friend of the family named José Gallegas wrote that the controversy had so much affected Agustín that his very countenance displayed his distress. "This is not strange," declared Gallegas, "for I know his punctilious honor and certainly dread a worse turn in his health. After that, what will happen?"[51]

A bitter enemy alleged that during this trying period Iturbide became so enamored of María Rodríguez y Velasco, a seductive beauty called "La Güera" who figured prominently in the creole society of

[46] Iturbide, Carrera militar y politica de Don Agustin de Iturbide, ó sea memoria que escribió en Liorna, p. 8 n. 8.
[47] H. Lozano y Ormenta to M. Diaz de Bonilla, July 6, 1855, in A.G.R.E., 1559-11.
[48] Iturbide to J. J. and María de Iturbide, April 30, 1817, in MSS, Y.U.
[49] Iturbide to Juan Gómez de Navarrete, July 20, 1817, in I. MSS, 16.
[50] Iturbide to I. Huarte, March 11, 1818, Gates Collection, no. 221, in MSS, T.U.
[51] April 2, 1818, in MSS, Y.U.

the capital city, that he falsely accused his wife of infidelity and had her incarcerated in a convent where she had to subsist on a miserable pittance. "During this residence in Mexico City," that critic added, "he squandered all the ill-gotten riches which he had accumulated in Guanajuato and was reduced to such a decadent condition that he was miraculously transformed from a sanguinary royalist into an ardent patriot."[52] A Mexican contemporary said of the retired commander's conduct during this interlude:

"In the flower of his age, with a fine presence, refined and pleasing manners, gracious and insinuating in conversation, and well received in society, Iturbide indulged without restraint in the dissipations of the capital city. . . . Having spent in a lavish manner the wealth which he had accumulated by his mercantile transactions in the Bajío, he found that his fortune was much reduced at the very time when the re-establishment of the Constitution of 1812 and the results of that event opened a new prospect to his quest for glory, honor, and riches."[53]

If we may trust the recollections of certain contemporaries, during his retirement the one-time royalist commander was entertaining curious thoughts. A lawyer named José Manuel Bermúdez Zozaya later declared that Iturbide had remarked to him that, when the war to exterminate the partisans of independence had terminated, it would be convenient to advocate that cause, purged of its viciousness. Iturbide reasoned that properly to accomplish its object, however, the project of independence would have to be reformed and set forth in a new plan so that it would focus public opinion and unify all interests.[54] It appears that these recollections, which are re-enforced by other sources, were more than the afterthoughts of one who had himself become a champion of independence. Manuel Gómez Pedraza, an intimate friend, declared that, chagrined at the manner in which he had been treated, in 1820 Iturbide became convinced of the justice of the separatist cause.[55] Moreover, in view of the attacks made upon him, it seems that he was also convinced that he could no longer expect to have a brilliant career in the Spanish military service and that therefore he should seek a new avenue for his ambition.

---

[52] Rocafuerte, *Bosquejo ligerísimo*, pp. 21-22; the quotation is from *ibid.*, p. 261. Pi y Margall, *Historia de España en el siglo xix*, II, 646, ascribes Iturbide's change of heart to the influence of his mother's relatives, "who were ardent patriots."

[53] Alamán, *Historia*, V, 49.

[54] Zozaya, *Oración cívica pronunciada en la Alameda el 27 de Octubre de 1841*, p. 7.

[55] *Manifiesto que Manuel Gómez Pedraza, ciudadano de la república de Méjico, dedica á sus compatriotas*, p. 7. See further, Alamán, *op. cit.*, V, 49-50.

Whatever may have been the motives of viceregal officials in postponing a final decision with regard to the accusations concerning Iturbide's conduct as a military commander, it appears that the charges had injured his *amour-propre*. This took place in spite of the fact that during campaigns against the insurgents, he had been lining his private purse. On the other side, evidence has been found to show that the colonel had not been fully recompensed for the contributions which he had made to the King's cause while he was a royalist officer.[56] Furthermore, it is plain that during his retirement a difference had arisen between him and the Viceroy concerning the work of arranging his voluminous military correspondence. In November, 1820, Count Venadito refused to reimburse Iturbide fully for alleged expenditures he had incurred in that task which amounted to six thousand pesos.[57]

Thus it appears that, during a critical period in the history of Mexico, certain real or fancied wrongs were rankling in the mind of an able and ambitious creole commander who at times had been stricken with remorse at the sanguinary role which he had played during the insurrection. Evidently he had dreamed of becoming the Liberator of his native land but with a radically different program than that which had been more or less vaguely formulated by either Hidalgo or Morelos. It was perhaps more than a tradition which a Mexican author preserved when he wrote that upon leaving Mexico, Calleja had remarked that the only person capable of separating that country from Spain was Agustín de Iturbide.[58] How much would we not have gained, exclaimed a Spanish writer many years later, if Calleja and Bataller had performed their duty and transported Iturbide to Spain bearing the fetters of a convict!

[56] Iturbide to Apodaca, April 24, 1818, asked that he be sent 1,000 pesos as well as his current pay, I. MSS, 15.

[57] Venadito to Iturbide, November 17, 1820, in A.G.N., Historia, Operaciones de Guerra, Iturbide, 9. A valiant Spaniard named Francisco X. Mina with a few daring companions left England in May, 1816, for Texas to aid the Mexican insurgents. He led some of his filibusters into the intendancy of Guanajuato. On October 27, 1817, at a hacienda called Venadito near Silao he was surprised by royalists, captured, and put to death. Hence King Ferdinand VII conferred upon Apodaca the title of "Conde del Venadito."

[58] Cuevas Gonzaga, *Porvenir de México*, p. 30.

CHAPTER IV

The Plan of Iguala

KALEIDOSCOPIC changes in Spain during 1820 profoundly affected her far-flung dominions. On January 1 Rafael Riego, the commander of a battalion of Asturian soldiers stationed near Cadiz, proclaimed the liberal Constitution which had been formed by the Cortes in 1812. A revolutionary spirit soon spread over the Peninsula. On March 7 King Ferdinand VII stated that he intended to support the organic law. He soon accepted liberal statesmen as his advisers. News of the restoration of constitutional rule in the motherland reached Mexico near the end of April. On May 31, 1820, Viceroy Venadito, other viceregal officials, and important magistrates of Mexico City took an oath to support the Constitution of Spain.[1] Venadito directed officials throughout the Viceroyalty to take an oath to maintain the Constitution. A royal order was circulated in which the King not only hypocritically praised the constitutional regime but also asked the Spanish-American revolutionists to lay down their arms.[2] In accordance with the organic law, deputations composed of leading officials and elected members were revived in Mexican provinces.

A junta of Liberals in Madrid acting in conjunction with the Council of State had meantime drawn up a memorandum concerning the policy to be adopted toward the Spanish Indies. Those publicists recommended that colonial officials in New Granada, Peru, and Venezuela should urge the revolutionists to adopt the Constitution of 1812 and to send deputies to the Cortes. Hostilities by land and sea were to be temporarily suspended. Insurgents were to be informed that the Spanish government had decided to send commissioners to hear their complaints and to make provisional adjustments with them. Spanish officials in the Indies were to be assured that the King desired a reconciliation which would "consolidate the monarchy and maintain its splendor." As the peninsular authorities were ignorant of the actual condition of affairs in Mexico, but were convinced that the revolutionaries there did not have a general government, the junta decided

[1] *Gaceta del gobierno de Mexico*, June 1, 1820, p. 529.
[2] *La Constitución de 1812 en la Nueva España*, II, 172-183.

that the Mexican Viceroy should be instructed to act cautiously until he discovered the real plans of the rebels. He was to offer rewards to such persons as would promote a reconciliation between them and the motherland.[3]

In April, 1820, Venadito published in a broadside the terms of a general pardon which had been granted by the Spanish King.[4] Moreover, when the Council of State appointed commissioners to proceed to Chile, La Plata, New Granada, Peru, and Venezuela to propose to the insurgents an adjustment of their differences with Spain, it decided that no agents were to be sent to Mexico because that country was considered relatively tranquil. Nevertheless, the council directed that a copy of its memorandum should be sent to the Mexican Viceroy so that, in case need should arise, he could be guided by it.[5]

Important results followed the promulgation of the Spanish Constitution in Mexico. The first issue of a new periodical entitled the *Semanario Político y Literario de México*, which appeared on July 20, declared that the nation was now free from tyrannical restrictions. It praised the Constitution as being based upon the rights of man. In September, 1820, deputies were selected to represent Mexico in the Cortes. Electors in the intendancy of Valladolid selected Juan Gómez de Navarrete, an intimate friend of Agustín de Iturbide, as a deputy. Manuel Gómez Pedraza, who was chosen to represent the intendancy of Mexico, later asserted that at this time he discussed with Iturbide a plan for the independence of their native land and that they even devised a cipher for use in their correspondence.[6]

The Cortes took steps that grievously displeased Roman Catholics. On August 17, 1820, it adopted a decree suppressing the Society of Jesus. It resolved that in certain cases clerics should be subject to the jurisdiction of civil courts and that real property should not be acquired by the Church. Moreover, on October 1 it passed an act which provided that certain religious orders should be suppressed, that other orders should have no more than one community in a particular district, and that no new convents or monasteries should be erected.[7]

---

[3] "Muy reservado," to "Excelentísimo Señor," April 11, 1820, in A.G.I., Indiferente General, 146-1-15.

[4] April 17, 1820.

[5] Ligeros apuntes en el expediente sobre remitir á las provincias disidentes de Ultramar comisionados que tratan de establecer la paz por medios de conciliación, in A.G.I., Indiferente General, 146-1-15.

[6] *Manifiesto que Manuel Gómez Pedraza, ciudadano de la república de Méjico, dedica á sus compatriotas*, pp. 8-9; *Manifiesto del ciudadano Manuel Gómez Pedraza*, p. 3.

[7] *Decretos del rey Don Fernando VII*, VI, 43-44, 141-142, 155-159.

Some ecclesiastics were much disturbed at the prospective results of such iconoclastic measures upon the Mexican hierarchy.

Among intelligent laymen various ideas were entertained. If one glanced over all classes of society, said a member of the audiencia of Mexico, one saw "fears in some people, jealousies among other people, and in most people hopes of a favorable change."[8] At Puebla on November 30, 1820, there was published the first number of *La Abeja Poblana*, a journal which praised the altered attitude of European governments toward the making of laws. It appears that certain Mexicans favored a monarchical form of government, others wished a centralized republic, while still others desired a federal organization.

By April, 1820, thousands of Mexican revolutionists had accepted the pardon offered by the Spanish government. A measure of tranquillity had been restored to some parts of the Viceroyalty.[9] The Viceroy expected soon to reconquer other sections. The most important of these was the region lying between Acapulco and the capital city. There the rebel guerrillas were led by an Indian named Pedro Asencio and by his indomitable compatriot, the brave but illiterate Vicente Guerrero, who had been fighting the royalists for almost a decade. As the royalist commander, Colonel José Gabriel Armijo, did not succeed in executing Venadito's instructions to destroy the insurgents, in August a padre named José Epigmenio de la Piedra was entrusted with the hazardous mission of ascertaining what were Guerrero's intentions. Though the friar disclaimed a purpose to offer a royal pardon and explained that his intention was to propose a reconciliation with Spain based upon peace, union, and the Roman Catholic religion, all he secured from the rebel chieftain was a disdainful remark that this proposal harmonized with his own ideas.[10]

Soon after hearing of the failure of this mission, Venadito's dissatisfaction reached a climax. On October 27 he wrote to Colonel Armijo to express the hope that his zeal would remove any obstacle which prevented the pacification of the district under his command.[11] In a letter to the Minister of the Colonies the Viceroy explained that, as the colonel had asked several times to be relieved of his post because of ill health, he had finally released him. Venadito then selected a Spanish veteran named Melchor Álvarez for the vacant post, but as

---

[8] Alamán, *Historia de Mexico*, V, 40.

[9] Venadito to M. Moreno, April 9, 1820, Heartman MSS, in MSS, T.U.

[10] Relación que hace al Virey el Sr. de la Piedra de los incidentes habidos en su comisión cerca del Gral. Guerrero, 2 de Agosto á 7 de Octubre de 1820, Hernández y Dávalos Collection, 13-4-1278, in MSS, U.T.

[11] Zárate, *La Guerra de independencia*, p. 660.

that officer demurred at accepting this position because of illness, he turned next to Colonel Agustín de Iturbide, whom he later described to the Court of Madrid as one "who from the beginning of the insurrection had labored with efficiency and good results in favor of the cause of the King and the nation."[12] On November 9, 1820, the Viceroy appointed Colonel Iturbide the commander of the military district of the South which stretched from the mining town of Taxco to the port of Acapulco. Iturbide promptly responded that though the climate of the tropical lowlands had almost proved fatal to his health upon two occasions, he would accept the appointment on condition that, when the campaign was over, he would be relieved of the command.[13] Alamán explained that the selection of the retired colonel for this important post was due to the advice given Venadito by Miguel Badillo, a colonel who was temporarily in charge of the military affairs of the Viceroyalty. Apparently Venadito gave the new commander oral instructions that he should induce both Asencio and Guerrero to accept the proffered pardon and that, so far as possible, he should avoid the shedding of blood.[14]

Colonel Iturbide soon undertook to set his house in order. He drew up detailed instructions concerning such matters as the sowing of barley and the planting of corn in the tilled fields of the hacienda near Chalco.[15] On November 9, declaring that he needed money for the support of his family and claiming that the government still owed him some thirteen thousand pesos on account of certain financial transactions, Iturbide asked that the Viceroy should direct the royal treasury to pay him six thousand pesos.[16] On November 17 Venadito ordered a fiscal agent to pay the creditor a small monthly sum and notified him that it was impossible to pay at once the entire amount which he had demanded.[17] Two days later, on the eve of his departure from the capital city at the head of the expedition, Iturbide again requested that the government should pay him six thousand pesos which his family urgently needed because of his impending departure on military service.[18] From his camp at Teloloapan—in the present state of

---

[12] *Diario de las actas y discusiones de las cortes, legislatura de los años de 1820 y 1821*, vol. XX, no. 5, p. 33.

[13] Bustamante, *Cuadro historico de la revolucion mexicana*, V, 93.

[14] Alamán, *Historia*, V, 57-58.

[15] Instrucción pa. gobierno de D. Franco. Narvaez pa. el manejo de esta hazda. en la proxima estación, November 12, 1820, in I. MSS, 17.

[16] Iturbide to Venadito, November 9, 1820, in A.G.N., Historia, Operaciones de Guerra, Iturbide, 9.

[17] Venadito to Iturbide, November 17, 1820, *ibid.*

[18] Iturbide to Venadito, November 19, 1820, *ibid.*

Guerrero—on November 26 the new commander of royalist troops in the South repeated this request in a different form.[19] There is nothing to show that he ever was paid the six thousand pesos.

There seems to be no doubt that, in addition to dissatisfaction cause he had not been publicly exonerated of the charges against him, Iturbide now had additional reasons for being disgusted with viceregal rule. It is not without significance that in a letter which he sent to a correspondent on November 14, he intimated that he stood at the threshold of important events.[20] Five days after he had marched out of the capital at the head of a small expeditionary force, the re-installed royalist officer addressed a letter to Gómez de Navarrete in which he discussed the effects of the promulgation of the Constitution of 1812 in Mexico.

"Because of the advantages which it offers, the Constitution has many true supporters. Other individuals fear it because of the heterogeneity of the Kingdom. Some people believe that it will be the means of assuring the permanent union of Spanish America with the Spanish Peninsula. Not a few persons love the Constitution because they believe it to be the most certain means by which independence may be attained."[21]

It appears that no suspicion of his loyalty had entered the minds of royalist officials. In an address which Colonel Armijo made to his soldiers, he declared that the moral virtue, the sound judgment, and the military skill of his successor would crown the task of pacification with success.[22] Shortly after starting his campaign, Iturbide sent a letter to Venadito to ask that as many soldiers as he desired should be placed at his disposal. He avowed that his purpose was not to enhance his reputation but to restore order to his country and to ensure the glory which the Viceroy would soon enjoy of seeing Mexico completely pacified.[23] On December 15 Venadito expressed satisfaction with the measures which the newly appointed commander had taken. He reminded Iturbide that, because of "his activity, zeal, and love" for their adored King, he expected him to do everything in his power to secure the pacification of the region under his charge.[24]

Several days before the Viceroy wrote this letter, at Teloloapan, the headquarters of the military district of the South, Armijo had

[19] *Idem* to *idem*, November 26, 1820, *ibid*.
[20] *Idem* to J. M. Malo, November 14, 1820, in MSS, L.
[21] November 25, 1820, in I. MSS, 16.
[22] *Suplemento al Noticioso General*, January 1, 1821, p. 2.
[23] Bustamante, *Cuadro historico*, V, 93-94.
[24] Venadito to Iturbide, December 15, 1820, in A.G.N., Iturbide, 4.

transferred to the new commander the soldiers under his charge who numbered some eighteen hundred men.[25] Encamped at that place, on December 14 Iturbide gave a cordial greeting to his one-time regiment of Celaya composed of about five hundred and fifty men, which he had requested should be placed under his orders. He declared that they had reached the only part of Mexico which still harbored in its ravines the remainder of those partisans who would not recognize the government of Ferdinand VII. In no modest tones did he remind his former command that while its members had served under his orders they had always entered the camp of the enemy as victors. He asserted that, should the rebels persist in their intentions, they would learn to their cost the temper of his soldiers. "There will not be lacking persons who will descant about our cruelty," he added; "that does not matter; we well know that the father who punishes a bad child is not cruel, nor is the physician cruel who operates upon gangrene with fire and steel. . . ."[26]

Conflicting accounts mention the ensuing activities of his forces that now numbered some twenty-five hundred men.[27] One fact, however, stands out in relief. The new royalist commander did not succeed in subjugating the rebels by force of arms. Indeed there is no doubt that his soldiers were discomfited or actually defeated more than once. On December 28 his rear guard fell into an ambuscade laid by Pedro Asencio near Atalatlaya.[28] In a letter to a relative early in 1821, Colonel Iturbide confessed that he was constantly in a perturbed state of mind.[29] Declaring that he was in bed because of a fever, on January 18 he addressed Venadito from Teloloapan to state that, as a result of his measures, he believed that Guerrero would be inclined to accept the pardon offered by the Spanish government.[30] Yet shortly afterward he reported that royalist soldiers under Colonel Berdejo had defeated that partisan near a place called the Cueva del Diablo.[31] In the light of subsequent events, it appears that the royalist colonel was

[25] Copy, Rumbo de Acapulco, estado q. manifesta la fuerza q. hoy día de la fha. existe en dho. rumbo para conocimto. del Señor coronel Dn. Agustín de Iturbide, quien en la misma toma por supor. orn. de 14 del corriente el mando gl. del expdo. rumbo, December 3, 1820, *ibid.*

[26] Al reximto. de Celaya, su coronel, December 14, 1820, in I. MSS, 15.

[27] Alamán, *Historia*, V, 65.

[28] Iturbide to Venadito, December 31, 1820, in A.G.N., Historia, Operaciones de Guerra, Iturbide, 4.

[29] *Idem* to D. Malo, January 9, 1821, in MSS, Y.U.

[30] In A.G.N., Iturbide, 4.

[31] *Gaceta del gobierno de Mexico*, February 22, 1821, p. 179.

not keeping Venadito fully informed concerning the politico-military situation at the front.

Early in his campaign Iturbide lauded the measures which the Viceroy had taken for the subjugation of the rebels. He expressed hope that the pacification of the Viceroyalty might be accomplished before the end of February. On New Year's Day he reported that Bishop Juan Ruíz de Cabañas, who had accepted the mitre of Guada-lajara in 1796, had advanced him twenty-five thousand pesos for the support of the army. Because of such representations, Venadito not only furnished Iturbide with additional munitions but also directed treasury officials to place twelve thousand pesos at his disposal.[32]

In a dispatch to Madrid the Viceroy explained that the persistence of the rebels in the district south of the capital city was due to its mountainous terrain and unhealthful climate.[33] After the fashion of his predecessor, on January 19 he urged Iturbide "to exterminate" the insurgents.[34] Shortly afterward he made suggestions which he thought might lead to their "total destruction."[35] On February 3 he expressed confidence not only that the royalist commander would take steps to crush the rebels but also that he would adopt measures to convoy a precious shipment of silver destined for Acapulco.[36] Thir-teen days later, he stated that in all he had directed that some thirty thousand pesos should be forwarded to that commander.[37]

There is ample evidence to show that while he was operating against Guerrero and writing dissemblingly to the Viceroy, the roy-alist commander was meditating about an ingenious step. Further, he had unfolded his plan to various persons outside of his camp, especially to ecclesiastical dignitaries and military officers. Among other emis-saries, he had dispatched Captain Francisco Quintanilla to interview influential persons.[38] As early as November 25, 1820, in a letter to Gómez de Navarrete, Iturbide mentioned a correspondence which he was carrying on with Pedro C. Negrete, who, after serving the Spanish King on the high seas, had turned up in New Spain, where he even-tually fought against the insurgents near the Pacific coast. In this letter Iturbide mentioned his project in these words:

[32] Bustamante, *Cuadro historico*, V, 95-96.
[33] Venadito to A. Porcel, January 10, 1821, in A.G.I., Audiencia de México, 90-2-16.
[34] *Idem* to Iturbide, January 19, 1821, in A.G.N., Iturbide, 4.
[35] Iturbide, *Correspondencia y diario militar*, III, 629.
[36] *Ibid.*   [37] *Ibid.,* III, 655.
[38] Quintanilla to Alamán, October 1, 1850, Alamán, Archivo relativo a su historia de México, Genaro García Collection, in MSS, U.T. See further, Alamán, *Historia*, V, 72.

"Today I have written from this place to that friend [Negrete] proposing that we have an interview as soon as possible; for, if he enters into an agreement with me, I do not doubt that my plan of pacification will be completed in happiness, and that perhaps in January we shall gather the laurels in Mexico City. My desire only includes the honor of arranging the combination; afterward I wish to return to the wheat and the corn of the Hacienda Compañía."[39] In another letter to Gómez de Navarrete on December 7, 1820, Iturbide made known that he was spreading information about his politico-military ideas.

"Leaders and officials who are here show me that they are favorably disposed for the task. Though only two of them are aware of the comprehensiveness of my project, many of them earnestly offer to be employed at the most important points, which is very praiseworthy. There is much need of time in order to strengthen the plan more and more. I say to strengthen it more and more, because wherever my forces advance, I wish to avoid shedding the blood of soldiers and also the blood of unfortunate, wasted persons whose lives are demanded by humanity and whose labor is needed for the welfare of the country. . . ."[40]

A little later in another letter to the same correspondent Iturbide wrote:

"People have assured me that in the province of Guanajuato the inhabitants wish independence, that many persons in San Luis Potosí also desire it, that even among provincial soldiers and peninsular troops they speak with much freedom in favor of independence, and that, if there was a leader with ideas who would place himself at the head of a movement, they would follow him blindly. This makes me apprehensive, for a tumultuous uprising would bring a thousand evils upon us which might cause the complete ruin of our unfortunate country. I regret to say that in the last mail I have not received a single letter either from you or from any other of my itinerant friends."[41]

On January 25 he wrote an important letter from Teloloapan to a legal friend named Juan José Espinosa de los Monteros of Mexico City and enclosed certain confidential papers concerning his program for action. Among the documents were drafts of a plan and of a proclamation. Iturbide stated that these projects were concerned with an

---

[39] In I. MSS, 16.
[40] *Ibid.* Zamacois, *Historia de Méjico*, vol. X, pt. I, p. 578, asserts that about this time Iturbide showed Quintanilla a copy of the plan later proclaimed at Iguala.
[41] December 15, 1820, in I. MSS, 16.

event which would occur early in the following month. Confiding in his correspondent's friendship and patriotism, he not only asked him to read the papers at the earliest opportunity but also to offer suggestions regarding the mode of making public the reasons which impelled him to take action:

"Be so good as to correct or to modify freely according to your wishes the proclamation which is marked number 1 and the articles of the plan marked number 2. Add, omit, or embellish as your experience or knowledge may suggest. You will agree with me that both the proclamation and the plan should be most concise. Accordingly you will at once undertake the task of composing a manifesto which strikes the keynote of each one of the articles of the plan according to the ideas expressed in document number 3. In addition write another proclamation according to the principles formulated in number 4."

Above all, Espinosa de los Monteros was urged to make haste in correcting the enclosed papers. In a postscript he was told that Iturbide also needed proclamations concerning peace and union, manifestos on certain subjects which required explanation, and projects for a junta, a cortes, and an army.[42] Although there is no evidence to show that this correspondent returned the papers with corrections or modifications, the letter is significant because it indicates that Iturbide's scheme for the pacification of Mexico was revolutionary in character, that it had been given a concrete form, and that he was ready to employ his friends in drafting documents which would implement his plan for independence.

On the same day he wrote in a similar strain to Negrete. Asserting that he entertained no doubt concerning the outcome of his plan, for it was just, mature, and very important, he stated that it had been read by some friends distinguished by talent, firmness, and character who had approved it without proposing any alterations. After naming certain persons who he presumed would co-operate with him in his design, he stated that at the right moment proclamations would be issued which would destroy jealousy and preserve order. Measures had also been taken, Iturbide said, to ensure that the soldiers who supported the project would be properly treated. "The time is very short, the project is vast," he added, "and the laborers are few."[43]

Shortly afterward Iturbide wrote to Negrete again to state that this correspondent had probably noticed proposals in the scheme which did

[42] Zárate, La Guerra de independencia, p. 674 n. 2.
[43] Bustamante, Cuadro historico, V, 141.

not exactly agree with his ideas. He explained that neither did some proposals please him, but that they were necessary in order to gain the adherence of certain persons. He asserted that he had already gathered seven hundred thousand pesos for the execution of the project and that, if necessary, interested parties would contribute more funds. "My plan is so well formed and has such extensive ramifications," continued Iturbide, "that it cannot fail to bring about peace in a short time and without any bloodshed in the entire region under my charge. At present I calculate upon securing all the aid which is necessary from the capital, from adjacent points, and even from places at a distance. . . ."[44] Perhaps because he considered the plan defective, Negrete did not agree to support it. Colonel Anastasio Bustamante, who had fought the rebels under Hidalgo, was also loath to favor it; for he wrote to Iturbide to express regret that he could not accompany him in his "glorious marches and fatigues."[45]

In the middle of February, 1821, Colonel Iturbide addressed a letter from Chilpancingo to an officer named Domingo E. Luaces, who was the military commander of the city of Querétaro. Enclosing copies of a plan for the independence of Mexico, Iturbide made a further disclosure of his intentions. He declared that he counted upon securing arms, money, soldiers, and military officers; for without such aid no one could undertake an enterprise so important to present and future generations. He expressed the confident belief that the country had at Querétaro a commander who was both brave and illustrious, one who would know how to co-operate effectively "with his talent and his sword in the re-establishment of peace and in the union of all the inhabitants of this country. . . ." Iturbide reasoned that the attitude of that city would much affect the outcome of the movement. "Be so good as to tell me all that occurs to you about the plan . . . ," he implored. Soliciting the co-operation of Luaces in his project for Mexican independence, he declared that its military leader should be elected by the soldiers supporting the movement, whom he styled "the Army of the Three Guarantees." He said that he desired nothing for himself, except the honor of contributing to the happiness of his country.[46] Four days later he wrote to Bishop Cabañas, to solicit support for his project from a prince of the Church. Iturbide avowed that it was necessary to protect Roman Catholicism.

"On the one hand, I shall carry out my intention of maintaining the

[44] *Ibid.*, pp. 141-143.
[45] February 6, 1821, A.M.C., D/481.3/1846.
[46] Iturbide to Luaces, February 17, 1821, in A.M.C., D/481.3/1831.

Roman Catholic religion and of becoming a mediator between European Catholics and Mexican Catholics, or, on the other hand, I shall perish in the attempt. If I succeed, I shall consider myself happy. . . . Under this date I shall write to our mutual friend Señor José de la Cruz about the matter. I am sending him a copy of the letter which I have directed to his Excellency the Viceroy as a preliminary to my plan. Although I believe that he will not fail to make it known to you, Most Illustrious Sir, I enclose another copy of it so that you can meditate about the support upon which I count for so important a decision, and so that you can favor a holy, just, and convenient plan. . . ."[47]

Enclosing a copy of the letter which he had written to Cabañas, Iturbide soon sent an epistle to Pedro José de Fonte, a native of Spain who in 1816 had been consecrated as the Archbishop of Mexico. The propagandist described the object of his plan as grand, convenient, and necessary. He declared that the influence of the Archbishop, who was at the fountainhead, would contribute in no small degree to its success. He ventured the opinion that the prelate would actively support it.[48] In this case, however, as the sequel will show, the effort was almost fruitless. Iturbide also addressed a note to Miguel Bataller in which he justified his change of attitude toward the viceregal government. He asserted that, if the mine which had been laid in Mexico should explode, neither the Viceroy, nor that judge, nor himself, nor the three of them together, could remedy the evil. Iturbide reasoned that it would be easier to confine the immense waters of the ocean in one shell than to guide an unbridled people in the proper use of reason.[49]

So far had his negotiations progressed by February 18, 1821, that he had addressed a letter to the Viceroy alleging that Guerrero had placed himself under his orders with a following of twelve hundred men. The royalist commander admitted, however, that as yet he had not inspired the insurgent chieftain with sufficient confidence so that he would converse with him. But Guerrero had sent an agent named José Figueroa with authority to draw up an agreement which was to include a statement that Guerrero's followers were not to be considered as offenders who had been pardoned. Iturbide expressed hope that

[47] *Católicos sentimientos del Sr. Generalísimo Don Agustín de Iturbide expresados en su carta al Señor obispo de Guadalajara.*

[48] Bustamante, *op. cit.*, V, 134.

[49] *Ibid.*, pp. 136-137. Alamán (*Historia*, V, 103) stated that letters written by Iturbide to various personages about his project which were printed in the *Cuadro histórico* were taken by Bustamante from the archives of the Ministry of War.

partisans of other insurgent leaders, who numbered thirty-five hundred men, would also join him. Several days later, Venadito made reply to Iturbide to express satisfaction at the news but to state that any agreement with Guerrero must conform to his wishes, to the royal dispositions, and to the latest decisions of the Cortes. Further, he declared that that rebellious leader and his followers should start on their new course by taking publicly the oath prescribed by the Spanish Constitution and by agreeing to a formal armistice.[50]

In a letter to Pedro Negrete the colonel enclosed a copy of an important epistle explaining his project which he had outlined for the Viceroy. He did not send this letter to Venadito, however, until February 24. Iturbide declared that the motherland had cleared the way for his plan. He asked the magistrate to avert the horrible catastrophe which threatened the Viceroyalty, to make his name immortal, and to obtain the favor of the Almighty. The writer reasoned that circumstances favored the insurrection because the Viceroy could not secure troops with which to oppose the movement; while the execution of the plan would prevent the shedding of blood. If Ferdinand VII or a prince of the Spanish dynasty would proceed to Mexico, he could take possession of the country. Iturbide declared that his plan offered the true solution for the dilemma which confronted his native land. He asked that the Viceroy should place himself at the head of a governmental junta composed of ten persons named in the plan. He maintained that by the aid of that junta he could check any tumult which might arise. In conclusion the sponsor of the project made this avowal concerning his motives:

"I am neither a European nor an American. I am a Christian, a man, and a partisan of reason. I know the nature of the evils which threaten us. I am convinced that there is no other way of avoiding them than that which I have proposed to your Excellency. I realize that in your superior hand is the pen which may write either confusion, bloodshed, and desolation for northern Spanish America or religion, peace, and happiness."

Annexed to this letter was a note of explanation in which Iturbide called upon the Lord Almighty to witness that he was not animated by thoughts of ambition or of personal aggrandizement. Further, he stated that, if his program was carried out, he would return to the bosom of his family and again devote himself to the idyllic life of a farmer. His heart would remain satisfied without seeking for tinsel, he affirmed, because his eyes had never been dazzled by false splendor.

[50] *Gaceta extraordinaria del gobierno de Mexico*, February 23, 1821, pp. 187-188.

Shrewdly did he reason that, if his new scheme of government was approved by the Viceroy, it would reconcile discordant political factions and would prevent a fresh revolutionary conflagration, because each faction would believe that it had gained much at little cost.[51] Iturbide entrusted those communications to Antonio Mier and José Epigmenio de la Piedra.[52]

The crux of the politico-military situation lay in the relations between Iturbide and Vicente Guerrero. As early as January 10, 1821, the royalist commander had begun to correspond with the insurgent leader about the future of Mexico. Affirming that he wrote frankly, and as one interested in the welfare of his country, Iturbide declared:

"You are in a position to contribute to this in a special manner by ceasing hostilities and by submitting with your troops to the orders of the government with the understanding that I shall allow you to remain in command of your force and shall even secure for you some provision for its support. This measure is proposed in view of the fact that, animated by the grandest ideas of patriotism and liberality, our representatives have started for the Spanish Cortes. There they will energetically present our needs. Among other matters they will propose that, without exception, all the sons of Mexico should enjoy the same privileges as the citizens of Spain. Now that his Majesty Ferdinand VII cannot become our sovereign, perhaps his august brother Señor Don Carlos or Don Francisco de Paula will proceed to Mexico. If this should prove to be impossible, you may be certain that the deputies will omit nothing which will conduce to the complete happiness of our native land. But, if contrary to our expectations, we should not be granted justice, I shall be the first person to aid with my sword, with my fortune, and with my ability in the defense of our rights. I swear this to you and to all the world on my word of honor which you can trust; for never has it been broken, and never will it be broken."[53]

Iturbide expressed the hope that, as liberal ideas now prevailed in Spain, Mexico could scarcely fail to secure justice at court. Besides, he suggested that, if the insurgent leader would send an agent to confer with him, he would guarantee such a person safe conduct

---

[51] Bustamante, *Cuadro historico*, V, 123-124.

[52] Alamán, *Historia*, V, 103-104; *Apuntes biográficos del señor prebendado de la santa iglesia metropolitana de México*, pp. 6-7.

[53] Bustamante, *Cuadro historico*, V, 100. The text of this letter found in the book published in Mexico in 1846, which is the edition regularly cited in this biography, is almost identical with the version found in that volume which was printed in 1827 (see carta quinta, p. 18).

through his lines. Evidently the royalist colonel wished to sound the views of the renowned patriot guerrilla.

Guerrero replied on January 20 in a letter which, though probably composed by a scribe, furnishes a clue to his character. He began by explaining the principles of the revolution. Reminding his correspondent of his role as a royalist commander who had left nothing undone to subjugate the patriots, he reasoned that Iturbide ought to undertake an enterprise more worthy of his reputation than that which he had suggested. The patriot leader urged that commander to occupy himself at once with the true welfare of his country instead of awaiting the outcome of the efforts of the Mexican deputies to the Cortes. Moreover, Guerrero pointedly declared that he would never accept pardon from the Spanish government. His motto was independence or death. He disclaimed any intention to dictate to his comrades in arms or to tyrannize over them. "You should decide for the true interests of the nation," he advised, "and then you will have the satisfaction of beholding me serve in the army under your orders. You will become acquainted with a man without ambition or self-interest, who only aspires to free himself from oppression, a man who does not wish to elevate himself upon the ruins of his compatriots."[54]

Mexican historians have not been in agreement about the first meeting between the two leaders. Lucas Alamán, who at this time was on his way to Spain, on good authority later maintained that no conference took place between the two correspondents before the new revolutionary plan was proclaimed.[55] On the other hand, Rocafuerte, as well as other contemporaries, insisted that an interview was actually held.[56] The Mexican historian Julio Zárate believed that the tradition that such an event actually occurred was based upon the recollections of persons who had witnessed that meeting.[57] A plaque attached to the walls of the one-time *convento* of San Rafael in Taxco, which is a short distance from Iguala, states that in that building in 1821 local patriots learned of the plan for independence, that they sent it to Guerrero, and that consequently he met Iturbide. This inscription presumably embodied a tradition, for in reality it was not carved until 1842.[58]

[54] Rocafuerte, *Bosquejo ligerísimo de la revolución de Mégico*, p. 57.
[55] Alamán, *Historia*, V, 76 and n. 46. See further, *infra*, p. 76.
[56] Rocafuerte, *op. cit.*, pp. 62-63.
[57] Zárate, *La Guerra de independencia*, pp. 675-676. See further Gallo, *Hombres ilustres mexicanos*, IV, 322, where J. J. Lafragua ascribed this view to Manuel Gómez Pedraza, who had made a statement to that effect.
[58] Valle, "Iturbide no es Autor Único y Exclusivo del Plan de Iguala," *Excelsior*, September 27, 1942. In the article Valle did not quote the inscription in full. The

The interview was reputed to have occurred at a place called Acatempan, which was a short distance from Iturbide's headquarters. According to a contemporary publicist and historian named Lorenzo de Zavala, who claimed to have secured the details from Guerrero himself, the two personages embraced each other tearfully. Iturbide disclosed his plan for the independence of their native land. Guerrero then announced to his escort that he recognized the former royalist commander as the first chief of the national armies.[59] Other Mexicans have depicted the meeting as one of the most picturesque and significant scenes in their history.[60]

Yet in none of the available explanations which Guerrero gave of his attitude toward the Plan of Iguala has any mention whatever been found of this alleged interview with Iturbide or of the supposed embrace at Acatempan. After Iturbide had fallen from power, Guerrero described his accession to the revolutionary plan, which was objectionable to him in some particulars, as due to the conviction that it was the least perilous manner of establishing the independence of Mexico.[61] Furthermore, as will be shown later in this chapter, there is evidence which indicates that the former royalist commander did not meet Guerrero until after the revolutionary plan had been approved by its author's soldiers. In sum, the writer does not accept the story that Iturbide and the patriot commander embraced each other at Acatempan before the revolutionary plan was proclaimed.

Early in February, 1821, Iturbide had entrusted Miguel Cavaleri, one of his confidants who was reputed to be a gamester, with a special

---

plaque bears the following inscription, which the writer copied in October, 1941:

"En ese atrio que veis ahí se juntaron,
Iturvide y León Leal y convenieron
Con Gómez y otros libres que asistieron
A oir leer el nuevo plan que concertaron;
Este plan al fiel Guerrero lo mandaron,
Y en Acatempan allí se unieron
Estos dos héroes que nos dieron
Libertad en la patria que salvaron.
27 de setiembre 1842.
El autor Pbro. Manuel Eleuterio Gómez.
El H. Ayuntamiento de 1921. Septbre. 27."

[59] Zavala, *Ensayo histórico de las revoluciones de México*, I, 76-77.

[60] Salgado, *El Abrazo de Acatempan*, pp. 9-26; Pérez, "El memorable abrazo de Acatempan," *Excelsior*, September 27, 1921. A picture of the embrace as represented in a painting in the national museum is shown in Cuevas (*El Libertador*, p. 31).

[61] Guerrero, *Manifiesto del ciudadano . . . á sus compatriotas*. See further Sprague, *Vicente Guerrero*, pp. 42-43, where the alleged interview between Iturbide and Guerrero at Acatempan is mentioned only in p. 140 n. 41. Cf. Cotner, *The Military and Political Career of José Joaquín de Herrera*, p. 34.

mission to the capital city. The agent evidently conferred with various persons there about the project of independence.[62] Thence he proceeded to the city of Puebla, where by the aid of Padre Joaquín Furlong he had Iturbide's plan as well as an accompanying proclamation set up secretly on a small printing press. He returned with the printed documents to the town of Iguala.[63]

Meantime the activities of Iturbide had become meshed with the proceedings of the Spanish Cortes. Among some thirty Mexican deputies chosen to that legislature were the liberal thinkers Juan Gómez de Navarrete, Manuel Gómez Pedraza, José Mariano de Michelena, Miguel Ramos Arizpe, and Lucas Alamán. Near the end of 1820 they proceeded to the eastern coast of Mexico, where they were to take ship for Spain.

Juan Gómez de Navarrete wrote to Iturbide from the city of Vera Cruz. There he had met a deputy who had assured him that public opinion favored a union between Mexico and Spain, a constitutional monarchy, and a national congress. Gómez de Navarrete asked his correspondent to send news of everything that happened in Mexico in duplicate letters addressed to him at Habana and Madrid.[64] On January 5 he assured Iturbide that certain deputies had agreed that, in the confidence that their countrymen would succor their families, they would champion the rights of Mexico in the Cortes.[65] A scheme of Gómez de Navarrete pertaining to this period preserved in the Iturbide Papers is the undated draft of a project providing for the independence of the Mexican Empire from Spain, a project which in some particulars bears a strong resemblance to the plan that Iturbide actually proclaimed.[66]

Alamán, who was a deputy from the intendancy of Guanajuato, recorded that during secret meetings in a monastery at Vera Cruz the deputies were told of Iturbide's revolutionary project. Gómez de Navarrete proposed to them that they should delay their departure for Spain and that, as soon as the movement for independence began, they should install a congress. According to Alamán, various views were expressed concerning the project for independence. Certain deputies lacked confidence in its author; others favored a republic instead of a monarchy, while many were averse to making a political

---

[62] Cavaleri's letter of April 18, 1822, printed in *El Sol*, April 20, 1822, p. 174. On Cavaleri, see Alamán, *Historia*, V, 77.

[63] Bustamante, *Cuadro historico*, V, 106-109; Miquel i Vergés, *La Independencia mexicana y la prensa insurgente*, pp. 249-250.

[64] December 22, 1820, in I. MSS, 16.

[65] *Idem* to *idem*, January 5, 1821, *ibid.*   [66] Proyecto de C., *ibid.*

decision at that time.[67] The upshot was that, without reaching a final decision, Gómez de Navarrete and other deputies embarked for Spain less than two weeks before Iturbide proclaimed at Iguala the provisions of his revolutionary scheme.[68]

The genesis of that famous plan has been variously explained. There is a tradition accepted by some Mexican historians that the project had its origin within the walls of a church in which, after his recall from military service, Iturbide had engaged in spiritual exercises. This church, then commonly known as La Casa Profesa or merely La Profesa, was the former Jesuit temple of San Felipe Neri in the capital city. The story is that, profoundly dissatisfied with Spain's policy concerning religious matters, early in 1820 a group of ecclesiastics hatched a conspiracy in the oratorio of that temple. A ringleader in the plot was Matías Monteagudo, the rector of the University of Mexico, who was also a canon of the metropolitan cathedral. The clerical conspirators schemed to separate their country from the motherland by the aid of Iturbide.[69] For that purpose, asserted Vicente Rocafuerte, they drew up a scheme which in essence was the same as the plan proclaimed at Iguala.[70] This writer also asserted that, influenced by the advice of his inamorata, "La Güera," the creole champion decided not to proclaim the plan as framed in La Profesa, but to modify it in certain essentials.[71] From that workshop, said a royalist colonel, there stepped forth the chosen leader, Agustín de Iturbide, who was destined to tear the veil from those conspirators.[72] An anonymous analyst of the Mexican revolution, whose account was preserved in the national archives of Mexico, recorded a variation of the story. For he alleged that "the exact text of the plan for the consummation of independence" was placed in Iturbide's hands by Antonio Joaquín Pérez, an ecclesiastic who had served as a deputy to the Cortes which framed the liberal Constitution of 1812.[73]

On the other hand, many years later José Malo, a relative of Iturbide who claimed to have made a fair copy of the Plan of Iguala for

[67] Alamán, Historia, V, 72-73. See further Alamán, Apuntes para la biografía del excmo. Sr. D. Lucas Alamán, p. 12. Valadés, Alamán, pp. 101-109.

[68] Gaceta del gobierno de Mexico, March 22, 1821, p. 285.

[69] Alamán, Historia, V, 45-46, 98; Banegas Galván, Historia de Mexico, I, 449 and n. 3.

[70] Rocafuerte, Bosquejo ligerísimo, p. 5.

[71] Ibid., pp. 41-42.

[72] Cuevas, Historia de la iglesia en Mexico, V, 101.

[73] Copias de documentos relativos á la consumación de la Independencia de México é Imperio de Iturbide, in A.G.R.E., 40-16-153. On Pérez, see Alamán, op. cit., IV, 111-112.

his uncle,[74] recorded different impressions concerning its provenance. Rejecting the view that the project proclaimed at Iguala was formed in the oratorio of *La Profesa*, Malo stated plausibly that at Teloloapan, Iturbide dictated the project to Antonio de Mier, who took it to Mexico City with a letter to Espinosa de los Monteros directing that this correspondent should make such changes in it as he might deem suitable, and that he should then transmit it to the rector of the University of Mexico. Monteagudo, continued Malo, "made no modification in the plan; Señor Espinosa made some changes. Because of the lack of caution displayed by Mier, he was placed under arrest, and the manuscript remained in the hands of Espinosa."[75]

An account of the provenance of the Plan of Iguala presented in Alamán's *Historia de Mexico* re-enforces Malo's explanation at important points. The historian asserted that the copy of the project which Iturbide sent from Teloloapan to Espinosa de los Monteros was still in the possession of that lawyer's children. "This copy," added Alamán, "is in the handwriting of Mier, a follower of Iturbide, with corrections and additions in the hand of Iturbide himself."[76] In criticizing an assertion of Manuel Gómez Pedraza that he aided in formulating the revolutionary plan, another Mexican writer asserted that "Iturbide formed his plan for independence with the aid and co-operation of various persons. . . ."[77] Gómez Pedraza mentioned a rumor that even Viceroy Venadito was aware of Iturbide's project for the emancipation of Mexico.[78]

These explanations support the view that Iturbide was at least in part the author of the much-discussed plan. This view is borne out by a statement of Carlos María de Bustamante, who had access to materials which apparently are now absent from the national archives of Mexico. In a manifesto read to the Mexican Congress in April, 1823, this chronicler asserted that before marching from Mexico City against Guerrero, Iturbide had sketched the revolutionary project.[79] In his *Historical Picture* Bustamante wrote that, if Iturbide did not actually compose all parts of the plan, at least he modified it. "I

[74] Malo, *Funestos recuerdos del libertador de México*, p. 16.

[75] *Idem, Apuntes historicos sobre el destierro, vuelta al territorio mexicano y muerte del libertador*, p. 52 n.

[76] Alamán, *Historia*, V, 98 n.

[77] Nepomuzeno Cabrera, *Notas al manifiesto publicado en Nueva-Orleans por el general D. Manuel Gómez Pedraza*, p. 5.

[78] Gómez Pedraza, *Manifiesto que . . . dedica á sus compatriotas*, p. 10. See also F. Quintanilla to Alamán, November 17, 1850, Alamán, Archivo relativo a su historia de México, in MSS, U.T.

[79] *Manifiesto histórico a las naciones y pueblos del Anáhuac*, pp. 5-6.

have seen and held in my hands," he declared, "the original corrected in his own handwriting."[80] Among annotations which he made on a manuscript copy of Iturbide's autobiography, Bustamante likened the plan to Irish cheese manufactured out of various kinds of milk. He further declared that certain persons attributed it to Iturbide, while other persons ascribed it to Espinosa de los Monteros. Further, making additions to the list of candidates for the honor of its authorship, he asserted that this person declared that the licentiate Juan de Azcárate was its author, that person maintained that its author was José Bermúdez Zozaya, while another person held that its author was Juan Gómez de Navarrete. "I believe," concluded Bustamante by way of summary, "that each of these persons retouched that plan."[81]

In any case it is clear that early in 1821 Iturbide had virtually decided upon the program which he would employ in an attempt to remedy the evils of his native land. Marching from Teloloapan, he traversed the northern part of the district under his command in order to visit detachments of royalist soldiers and to harry the insurgents. On February 23 he reached the town of Cocula, which was a short distance southeast of his headquarters. From that place he addressed a letter to the cabildo of Acapulco. After mentioning the existing menace to the rule of Ferdinand VII, to the Roman Catholic religion, and to Spanish and Mexican soldiers in the Viceroyalty, he revealed his politico-military project in a passage which furnishes a significant link in the study of his revolutionary activity:

"All the necessary measures have been taken; all the resources and the perils have been calculated; the interests of Europeans and of Mexicans have been coalesced; opinions and rivalries have been reconciled; great evils have been prevented or banished by the plan, presented to the Chief of the Kingdom and to the protecting army, designated that of the Three Guarantees, that is, the conservation of the Roman Catholic Apostolic religion, without the toleration of any other faith; the absolute independence of Mexico; and the intimate union of Europeans and Mexicans. This plan is finished. God, reason, and moral as well as physical force are on our side. For you there remains only the task of rectifying public opinion and of checking any slight movement which seditious persons may incite. An extract from the plan accompanies this letter."[82]

[80] *Cuadro historico*, V, 108.

[81] Manuscrito, manifiesto de Iturbide, comentado por Carlos M. de Bustamante con letra de el mismo, Hernández y Dávalos Collection, 17-8-4255, in MSS, U.T.

[82] No. 1°, signed by Iturbide at Cocula and addressed to the *ayuntamiento* of Acapulco, February 23, 1821, in MSS, S.J.M.H., accession no. 5749. In this letter Iturbide anticipated coming events.

The "extract" was composed of twenty-three articles. These were concerned with such matters as religion, independence, the union of classes, the form of government, the prerogatives of the clergy, and the Army of the Three Guarantees. In fact a comparison of this document with the primitive text of the plan proclaimed at Iguala demonstrates that by February 23, 1821, Iturbide had formulated every one of its articles and had arranged them in the same order as that in which they were originally made known to his comrades in arms. With the exception of such matters as capitalization, punctuation, and choice of words, the only important difference between the so-called extract from the plan which was sent to Acapulco and the primitive text of the Plan of Iguala was that the extract was not prefaced by a species of preamble.[83]

On the following day, at Iguala, a village located several miles northeast of Cocula, Iturbide took a most important step. He signed a plan composed of twenty-three articles which embraced all the provisions included in the document sent to the cabildo of Acapulco. This project was preceded by a proclamation. It bears a postscript directing that it should be filed in the archives. It is written on Spanish stamped paper which bears the dates 1820 and 1821. This text of the Plan, which has been preserved by the Iturbide family until the present day, shows no trace of corrections. But the first folio of that document bears an endorsement by a circular die which mentions the advent of the liberal constitutional regime. Upon the face of that stamp Iturbide wrote a phrase which recorded that the use of such stamped paper had been authorized for "the era of independence."[84] This primitive text has never been published.

To the writer it appears that Agustín de Iturbide has as good a claim to the authorship of the Plan of Iguala as President Washington (who was efficiently aided by Alexander Hamilton and James Madison) has to the authorship of the famous "Farewell Address." It appears likely that the royalist colonel had incorporated into the text which he made public whatever suggestions or emendations had seemed to him appropriate. Such as this unique plan was, Iturbide made it known to the world.

He consistently maintained that the plan by which he aimed to loosen the knot that bound Mexico to Spain was his own work. In

[83] N. 2. Extracto del plan, February 23, 1821, a copy certified by Francisco de Rivas y Lazumbe, March 18, 1824, *ibid.*, accession no. 5750. Cf. *infra*, pp. 72-74, where the Plan of Iguala is described.

[84] Plan of Iguala bearing the signature of Iturbide, Iguala, February 24, 1821, in MSS, Y.

FACSIMILE OF A PART OF THE LAST FOLIO OF THE PLAN SIGNED BY
AGUSTÍN DE ITURBIDE AT IGUALA ON FEBRUARY 24, 1821
Courtesy of Mrs. Louise de Yturbide, Washington, D. C.

his memoirs he drew the long bow thus: "I formed my plan known as that of Iguala. I call it my plan because I alone conceived it, elaborated it, published it, and carried it out."[85] In a footnote to an authentic Spanish text of that autobiography, without mentioning the aid given by his collaborators, he made a similar explanation: "A pamphleteer has asserted that the project was the work of a club of Serviles who held their meetings in *La Profesa*. . . . Any person who has read the plan will be convinced from its contents alone that it could not have been dictated by Servilism. . . . After the plan . . . had been drawn up, I consulted about it with distinguished individuals of the different parties. Not one person withheld his approval. It was not modified in any manner; nothing was added or erased."[86]

In more than one contemporary document emanating directly from Iturbide himself after the Plan of Iguala was formulated, he also spoke of the pronouncement as his plan. In a letter to General José M. Dávila, the governor of the province of Vera Cruz, on February 24, 1821—the very day when he proclaimed the project—Iturbide reasoned thus: "The object of my plan is to ensure the preservation of the holy religion that we profess and which we have sworn to support; to make the Empire of Mexico independent of any power; to conserve it for King Ferdinand VII, if he should deign to establish his throne in its capital under regulations which I have specified; to cause to disappear the odious and sinister rivalry of provincialism; and to unite by a just equality the interests of all the inhabitants of this Empire."[87]

With regard to the provision in the plan for a monarchical government, Iturbide explained that he had decided upon this principle not merely because he felt that a monarchy was the form of government which most honored a society, but because a moderate constitutional system was the best for his country. A little later he expressed the opinion that only such a political system would suit the imperfec-

[85] Iturbide, *Carrera militar y política de Don Agustin de Iturbide, ó sea memoria que escribió en Liorna*, p. 11.

[86] *Ibid.*, n. 9.

[87] Cuevas, *El Libertador*, p. 185. Joel R. Poinsett, who had served as the American agent in Mexico while Iturbide was the Emperor, wrote in a letter of March 20, 1823, to Charles S. Todd concerning Iturbide thus: "He was the agent of the higher order of Clergy who were desirous of preserving the Kingdom of Mexico in all the purity of despotism as a refuge for the beloved Ferdinand from the Constitution, the liberals and the descansados but especially to prevent the execution of the decrees of Cortes which went to deprive them of their worldly wealth. Under their auspices the plan of Iguala was adopted." MSS. P., copy.

tions and the passions of men. "Only in that manner," he said, "could there be avoided frequent and ruinous conflicts in which the people would struggle for their liberty, the nobles and the great men would struggle for power, and the monarch for arbitrary dominion."[88] The champion of the Iguala Plan must have known that his professions of fidelity to the King of Spain would attract some of the ultra-loyalists known as Serviles who were blindly devoted to Ferdinand VII. He could scarcely have been unaware that by advocating the establishment of an imperial regime in Mexico he was conjuring up memories of the Aztec Empire.

Whatever may have been the understanding reached by Guerrero and Iturbide, the former royalist commander soon emerged as the leader of a fresh revolution. At Iguala he proclaimed its program in a plan composed of twenty-three articles. Article I declared that the Mexican nation was independent. Article II stipulated that the religion of the country should be Roman Catholicism. Article III provided that the inhabitants of Mexico should be united, without any distinction between Mexicans and Europeans.

Other articles provided that the government was to be a constitutional monarchy under Ferdinand VII. In case he refused to occupy the throne, Prince Carlos or Prince Francisco de Paula should be invited to become the monarch. If no one of those princes would accept the invitation, the Congress of Mexico could then offer the crown to a member of another reigning European dynasty. Mexico was meanwhile to be governed by a junta headed by the Viceroy. It was to frame regulations for the election of deputies to Congress. The legislature was to form a constitution which the monarch was to swear to observe before he entered the country. Caste distinctions were to be abolished. All the inhabitants were declared to be free and equal. A military force designated the Army of the Three Guarantees was to be formed for the preservation of Roman Catholicism, union, and independence.

Essentials of this program agree with certain proposals made in Iturbide's letters to Guerrero, Negrete, and the cabildo of Acapulco. In style the original plan resembled the language used in Iturbide's letters to Guerrero. The program was not always logical or consistent. In places its provisions were tentative, for the author was evidently attempting to formulate a plan which would please all classes of Mexican society. Its dominant idea was that Mexico should have an independent government and yet remain attached to Spain.

[88] Iturbide, *Breve manifiesto del que subscribe.*

A study of successive printings of the plan—for it was republished on several occasions after its first publication—proves that from time to time it was modified. For example, Article IV of the text found in the military correspondence of Iturbide in the *Archivo General de la Nación* in Mexico City (which was not published until 1930) contains a clause declaring that a European prince should be invited to rule over Mexico in order to prevent the fatal effects of ambition. This explanation has not been found in other published editions. No trace of Article XIX of the plan printed by order of the Regency in October, 1821, was found in this archival text.[89] Furthermore, in some editions certain features of the Plan of Iguala were emphasized. Then, too, the punctuation, the spelling, and the language of the document were altered with the passage of time. In fine, the texts of the famous plan which have been published by certain Mexican writers are not identical with the official text which Iturbide ordered to be preserved in the archives. It appears not unlikely that he had on hand variant copies of the Iguala Plan some of which eventually found their way into print.[90] Moreover, persons who have translated the plan into English have occasionally taken liberties with the text. Some foreign as well as Mexican writers have printed the program for Mexican independence without the proclamation that accompanied it when made public early in 1821.

This proclamation was a species of preamble written in the grandiloquent style often affected by Mexican leaders of this period. Designating as "Americans" the inhabitants of the Viceroyalty, whether born in America or in another continent, Iturbide stated that Mexico had been for three hundred years under the tutelage of a nation, most Catholic and pious, heroic and magnanimous. Spain had established there opulent cities, provinces, and kingdoms. The branch of the

[89] *Correspondencia y diario militar de Don Agustin de Iturbide,* III, 663-665. Among texts which the writer has seen, the version published by Bustamante, *Cuadro historico de la revolucion mexicana,* V, 116-119, most closely resembles the text in the A.G.N. On October 5, 1821, the Regency of the new Empire ordered that the text of the Plan of Iguala should be published. What might therefore be considered as the official text of the plan was printed in the *Gaceta imperial de México,* October 20 and 23, 1821, pp. 81 *et seq.* That text, however, does not reproduce exactly the original document signed by Iturbide at Iguala on February 24, 1821. Neither does the version of the plan printed by Valle (*Iturbide,* pp. 58-62), who asserted in a note (p. 62) that a comparison of his version with the text printed in the *Correspondencia* cited above shows the modifications which Espinosa de los Monteros and others made in Iturbide's original plan. It is, of course, possible that Iturbide authorized changes to be made from time to time in the text.

[90] A copy of the Plan of Iguala, dated February 24, 1821, published in the "imprenta imperial" does not conform exactly to the archival version.

tree was now equal to the trunk. Public opinion in the colony favored absolute independence from Spain and from all other nations. The author of this manifesto reasoned that the only measure which would prevent the evils resulting from the rebellion was a general union of Mexicans, Europeans, and Indians:

"European Spaniards! Mexico is your country, for you live there. In it are your beloved wives and your tender children, your haciendas, your commerce, and your other possessions. Mexicans! who among you can say that you are not of Spanish descent? Behold the delicate chain which unites us; consider the other bonds of friendship, education, language, interdependence of interests, and harmony of sentiment, and you will realize that they are so intimate and so strong that the general happiness of the Kingdom requires that all its people should be united in one opinion and in one voice. The time has arrived when you should show a uniformity of sentiment and should make known that our union is the powerful hand which emancipates Mexico from foreign rule. At the head of a valiant and resolute army, I have proclaimed Mexican independence."[91]

The proclamation of independence made known by Iturbide at Iguala was unique. Instead of denouncing Spain and the Spaniards, it praised them. In other particulars it differed with earlier declarations by Mexicans of their desire to separate from the motherland. Hidalgo never published a formal act proclaiming independence. The Declaration of Mexican Independence adopted at Chilpancingo on November 6, 1813, contained only some rudimentary provisions concerning the powers to be vested in Congress. The Plan of Iguala not only made a reassertion of the independence of Mexico, but, unlike the Declaration of Independence of the Thirteen Colonies of North America, it outlined a provisional scheme of government. This system was to be based upon a reformed society and implemented by an army pledged to support its political and social guarantees. In contrast with the designs of early Mexican insurgents, Iturbide's plan aimed to preserve the rights and privileges of the upper classes. None of the formal Mexican declarations of independence echoed the political philosophy of the immortal act of July 4, 1776, even so faintly as did the Act of Independence adopted by Venezuela in 1811 or that which was adopted in 1819 by the United Provinces of La Plata.

A contemporary account printed in El Mejicano Independiente, a

[91] Bustamante, op. cit., V, 116. This translation was made in view of the fact that Mexicans of that period sometimes used the term "América," when they meant Mexico, "Americanos" when they meant Mexicans.

periodical published by the revolutionaries shortly after the Plan of Iguala was proclaimed, records that, although signed by Iturbide at Iguala on February 24, 1821, the program was not formally approved by his staff until March 1. On that day the leading officers of the army assembled in the military headquarters. There Iturbide told them that the independence of Mexico was necessary because that was the general wish and also because a renewal of the long and sanguinary war was imminent. He declared that the only remedy was a project which would conform to the prevailing opinion. When the Plan of Iguala was read and the membership of the proposed junta announced, the officers greeted the proposals with enthusiasm. They expressed a desire to have their colonel proclaimed as their general. On the next day, with the sun glancing on the epaulets of his uniform as a royalist colonel, placing one hand on the hilt of his sword and the other on the Holy Scriptures, Iturbide took an oath to support the independence of the Mexican Empire, to maintain the Roman Catholic Apostolic religion, and to preserve the peace and union of Europeans and Mexicans. Indeed, independence, religion, and union were often mentioned by his compatriots as the three guarantees of the Plan. Iturbide also pledged himself to obey King Ferdinand VII in case he swore to accept the Constitution which was to be framed by the Cortes of Mexico.

Other officers of the one-time royalist Army of the South followed this example. A *Te Deum* was chanted in the village church. Salutes were fired by three regiments. During the afternoon of March 2 the privates took the same oath which had been sworn by their officers. Then, declaring that religion, union, and country deserved his first attention, Colonel Iturbide said that he would neither accept the post of general nor would he retain the insignia of his rank as colonel, insignia which he dramatically tore from his sleeves. A contemporary put the following words into his mouth: "I will not abandon you in the enterprise which you have undertaken; and, if necessary, my blood will seal my fidelity." This chronicler added that "the army responded with *vivas* to the First Chief—acclamations which did not die away until the soldiers had ceased marching before him."[92] An order was soon issued that, instead of *España*, the password should be *Independencia*.[93]

[92] *El Mejicano Independiente*, March 10, 1821, pp. 1-12, printed an account of these proceedings by Agustín Bustillos. A briefer account is the following: M.M., *Acta celebrada en Iguala el primero de Marzo y juramento que al día siguiente prestó el Sr. Iturbide con la oficialidad y tropa de su mando.*

[93] Zamacois, *Historia de Méjico*, vol. X, part 11, apéndice, p. 47.

Guerrero's tattered soldiers, who perhaps numbered one thousand, did not take part in the acclamation of the one-time royalist colonel as the leader of a new insurrectionary movement. On March 9 the leader of the rebel guerrillas wrote to Iturbide from his camp a letter—later printed in a rare issue of *El Mejicano Independiente*—which implied that he was about to meet that leader for the first time.

"I cannot describe my joy upon receiving your last letter dated the sixth of this month and with it the proclamation of the Viceroy whose language reiterates his opposition to the beneficent plan of independence and at the same time displays his fear because of the humility with which he addresses the people. Doubtless he knows their decided opinions. I consider all this to be in our favor and I believe our triumph to be certain. Divine Providence will protect justice. The valiant arms of the Three Guarantees will by the aid of good intentions assure forever the august destiny of Anáhuac.

"Without fail, I shall march from this place very early tomorrow morning for Ixcatepec. In a short time you will see a part of the Army of the Three Guarantees of which I shall have the honor to be a member. I shall present myself to you as a subordinate soldier with the band of deserving men whom I lead. . . . This letter will be the most pertinent proof to confirm what I have offered you. It will inform you that my delay has been indispensably necessary in order to arrange certain affairs. . . . I reserve for our meeting an expression of my great pleasure and a demonstration of my favorable disposition."[94]

Another significant bit of contemporary evidence concerning the first meeting of Guerrero and Iturbide was found by the writer in the Mexican national archives. From Taxco a royalist officer named Tomás de Cagigal sent word to his commander that on March 14, 1821, Guerrero with some of his soldiers had joined the Army of the Three Guarantees at Teloloapan. There, continued Cagigal, they took an oath to support independence, Roman Catholicism, the union of Americans and Europeans, and the constitutional King. According to that officer, the one-time royalist army was viewed with suspicion by Guerrero's followers. On March 16 they proceeded toward Tetola, while Iturbide divulged that he would proceed to Valladolid.[95] Nothing was said either in the dispatch of the royalist officer or in the letter of Guerrero about a meeting at Acatempan with the protagonist of the drama.

[94] *El Mejicano Independiente*, March 24, 1821, pp. 38-39, quoted in part in Alamán, *Historia*, V, 119.
[95] Cagigal to Armijo, March 18, 1821, in A.G.N., Historia de Operaciones, Armijo, 1812-1821, vol. 21.

José Servando Teresa de Mier, an iconoclastic Dominican friar who had long dreamed of Mexican independence, asserted that the Iguala Plan was formed by Iturbide in conjunction with Venadito.[96] In fact, however, the situation was quite otherwise. If, as has been alleged, Apodaca had upon an earlier occasion actually proposed to Ferdinand VII that he should proceed to Mexico,[97] it is clear that by the time that Iturbide had proclaimed his plan, the Viceroy had changed his views. Indeed his reactions in 1821 were similar to those which he had expressed in 1809 when, as the Spanish minister in London, he had protested to the English government against the revolutionary intrigues of Francisco de Miranda, who was planning to separate Venezuela from the motherland.

In a proclamation dated March 3, 1821, the Viceroy denounced Iturbide as "an ungrateful military commander whom the nation and the government had distinguished and rewarded in a generous fashion." Venadito stigmatized the Plan of Iguala as unjust from every standpoint and inconsistent with an article of the Spanish Constitution which the Mexicans had just sworn to support. "Though Iturbide presented the plan to us adorned with pompous phrases in order to conceal his sinister designs," added the Viceroy, "those plans do not conform to the fidelity that we should owe to the King; . . . they are inimical to public tranquillity, and, in sum, are intended only to promote the special designs which he has proposed." Venadito exhorted the inhabitants of Mexico that, if papers of a revolutionary character were sent to them, they should neither peruse them nor listen to the reading of them, for such documents were contrary to the solemn oath which they had taken to observe the Spanish Constitution, to be faithful to Ferdinand VII, and to obey the laws.[98]

A legend that the Viceroy favored the Plan of Iguala is further belied by his correspondence.[99] In a dispatch to Madrid he thus described the proceedings of Iturbide:

"This perfidious and ungrateful commander, forgetting his duty and abusing in the most unprecedented manner the confidence which I had placed in him, has under specious pretexts raised the standard of a new rebellion. He has made known some chimerical plans that are irreconcilable with the dignity, the decorum, and the interests of both the nation and the King. . . . He has made common cause

[96] Mier, *Memoria política-instructiva enviada desde Filadelfia en Agosto de 1821 á los gefes independientes del Anáhuac*, p. 36.
[97] Villanueva, *La Monarquía en América: Ferdinand VII y los nuevos estados*, p. 56.
[98] Copy, March 3, 1821, in A.H.I.N.A.H., 40-1.
[99] Zamacois, *op. cit.*, vol. X, part 1, pp. 583-584, discusses the legend.

with the insurgents. . . . He has had the audacity to direct his evil suggestions to the authorities of this capital and of the provinces. And, finally, he has had the temerity to assume a threatening and insulting attitude; for he has resolved to resist the legitimate government in order, if possible, to establish the new system which he has conceived in his inflamed imagination. . . . Because of his knowledge as a native of the country, because of the numerous military expeditions which he led in the time of my predecessors, and because of his skill in military strategy, this new chieftain is a terrible enemy."[100]

An extract from a letter by a person who subscribed himself as José Antonio told how the news of Iturbide's project was received in the capital:

"We find ourselves perhaps in the greatest distress that could occur in this country. On February 27 the Viceroy received some papers from Colonel Iturbide proclaiming the independence of Mexico. . . . His Excellency with his accustomed dexterity at once convoked a junta of generals who decided to pursue the traitor. At once there began to assemble in Mexico City both cavalry and infantry. In command of them were the most distinguished military leaders, such as Morán, Concha, Llano, and General Liñán. Some persons estimate the number of these troops as high as 10,000."[101]

According to Carlos María de Bustamante, when the chief magistrate became aware of the proposal that he should join hands with Iturbide to support the plan for Mexican independence, he exclaimed indignantly, "Jesus Christ! How could I make use of that man against whom there are such grave accusations?"[102] It is clear that Venadito wrote to Iturbide on February 27 to declare that his correspondent could gather from the fact that he had not opened his letter what he thought of the "unconstitutional project of independence." The Viceroy asked that the recreant commander should at once relinquish his project, should be faithful to the King and the Constitution, and should continue to guard a convoy destined for Acapulco in order to execute the orders designed to secure the complete pacification of his military district.[103]

[100] Diario de las actas y discusiones de las cortes, legislatura de los años de 1820 y 1821, XX, 33-34. Zerecero, Memorias para la historia de las revoluciones en México, pp. 349-351, prints a letter alleged to have been written by Ferdinand VII to the Mexican Viceroy on December 24, 1820, in which the King denounced the Spanish Liberals and stated that he would consider making his escape to Mexico.

[101] "Jose Anto." to Gómez de Navarrete (?), March 7, 1821, in I. MSS, 6. Cf. the account in El Mejicano Independiente, April 2, 1821, p. 79.

[102] Manuscrito, manifiesto de Iturbide, comentada por Carlos M. de Bustamante con letra de el mismo, Hernández y Dávalos Collection, 17-8-4255, in MSS, U.T.

[103] El Mejicano Independiente, April 28, 1821, p. 77.

When his plan had matured, Iturbide felt an urgent need of resources with which to execute it. He knew that a convoy of silver
valued at 525,000 pesos was due to leave the capital city to pay for
the cargo of a galleon which had recently reached Acapulco from
Manila.[104] Fears were entertained by royalists that the valuable shipment might be captured by rebels while in transit. In view of the
circumstances, Iturbide ordered that the treasure should be detained
by his forces. In a letter to its owners on February 24, he justified
the seizure because of military necessity. He promised that, if the
Viceroy approved his plan, their specie would be stored in Acapulco
or wherever they desired; but that, if Venadito was not pleased with
the project, some of the silver would perforce have to be used to
meet the military expenses of his campaign. He assured the con-
signors, however, that in the latter case the Mexican nation would
reimburse them with interest.[105] According to a contemporary, Iturbide not only kept the specie which was in transit but also secured
additional aid by the sale of the galleon's cargo. In an undated manifesto which praised that leader as the father of his country, Guerrero
declared that the funds which had been sequestrated would be repaid
to the merchants by the Mexican nation.[106] About a month later the
agent of the *consulado* or mercantile tribunal of Manila denounced the
detention of the convoy as arbitrary. He wrote to Venadito that by
seizing the specie entrusted to his custody, Iturbide had "cast all good
Spaniards into consternation."[107]

The Viceroy's suspicions had meantime been confirmed. He sent
a secret order to Colonel Armijo directing him to assume charge of
the military district of the South as soon as he became aware of any
innovation in its management.[108] He warned Colonel Mateo Guilty,
who commanded a detachment of royalist soldiers in that district, not
to obey any order of Iturbide which was contrary to his duty to the
King and the Constitution.[109]

Venadito soon took another significant step. He issued a broadside which not only denounced the subversive plans of an officer whom

[104] Bustamante, *Cuadro historico*, V, 107 and n.
[105] See further Mier's undated account which begins thus, "La inquisición . . . ,"
Correspondencia de Fr. Servando Teresa de Mier, 1821-1823, Genaro García Collection,
in MSS, U.T.
[106] Guerrero, *Manifiesto patriótico que hizó siendo comandante general de la división
del ejército de las Tres Garantías*, p. 2.
[107] Copy, F. A. Terán to Venadito, March 22, 1821, in I. MSS, 17.
[108] Venadito to Armijo, February 27, 1821, in A.G.N., Historia de Operaciones,
Armijo, 1812-1821, vol. 21.
[109] Copy, *idem* to Guilty, February 27, 1821, in A.H.I.N.A.H., 50-R-33.

the government had liberally rewarded but also exhorted the people of Mexico to disregard them and to remain faithful to the existing regime.[110] A junta entrusted with censorship announced that the Iguala Plan was seditious. It ordered that all copies of the project should be delivered to the proper authorities within twenty-four hours.[111] On March 14 the chief magistrate issued another proclamation in which he declared that pride, hypocrisy, avarice, and ingratitude had animated the perfidious Iturbide, who, deaf to the supplications of an octogenarian and honorable father and ignoring the wishes of a virtuous wife and seven innocent children, had placed himself under the orders of Guerrero.[112] Venadito announced in another broadside that, as the former royalist commander had refused an offer of pardon, he had lost the rights of a Spanish citizen and was outside the pale of law.[113] When, at the instance of the Viceroy, Archbishop Fonte distributed this proclamation among the clergy of his diocese, he stressed their obligation to obey the legitimate civil authorities. The priests were directed to exhort their faithful communicants to obey the viceregal government.[114]

Nine days later the Viceroy published a third broadside directing that government officials should allow no one to travel through the provinces unless furnished with a passport.[115] In a proclamation dated April 5, asking the people to support the existing regime, he bitterly denounced Iturbide as well as several inveterate revolutionists who, like Asencio and Guerrero, had accepted the Plan of Iguala.[116] Early in June, Venadito issued a fresh broadsheet providing for the conscription of able-bodied men between sixteen and fifty years of age who were to be designated the "Defenders of the Integrity of the Two Spains."[117]

Iturbide had meantime started to distribute proclamations concerning his designs. In a journal printed in his camp the conduct of the Viceroy was sharply criticized because he had denounced the champion of independence without deigning to write a single line in response to his communications.[118] On his own behalf, in a letter to

[110] March 3, 1821.

[111] *Noticioso General*, March 12, 1821, p. 4.

[112] *Gaceta del gobierno de Mexico*, March 15, 1821, pp. 265-266.

[113] March 23, 1821.

[114] March 19, 1821. Fonte's response to the Viceroy on March 16 is quoted in the *Noticioso General*, April 2, 1821, p. 1.

[115] March 23, 1821.

[116] *Gaceta del gobierno de Mexico*, April 7, 1821, pp. 347-349.

[117] June 7, 1821.

[118] *El Mejicano Independiente*, April 28, 1821.

Bishop Cabañas, who wished him to examine Iturbide's proposals, Venadito explained that neither the law nor his honor would allow him to treat with the new insurgent commander, who had disturbed the peace of the Viceroyalty, had seized the Manila convoy as well as revenues of the Church, and had merely wished to gain time to consummate his crimes and to make himself "the despot of this hemisphere."[119]

Iturbide's views with respect to the effects of this revolutionary movement upon his own fortunes deserve a passing glance. On July 29, 1821, in reply to a warning that royalist troops had been detailed to ravage his haciendas, he expressed indifference at the damage which they might wreak upon his property. "From the moment when I dedicated myself to the service of my country," he explained, "I renounced everything for such a sacred purpose."[120] A few months later he described his motives in leading a fresh insurrection. He asserted that even before 1820 he had been watching for a favorable moment to secure for his countrymen liberty without peril. Rightly did he link the insurrection in New Spain with that in Old Spain:

"Finally the last revolution in the Spanish Peninsula took place, a revolution caused by the excessive oppression of which its inhabitants complained. Obviously the principles by which the legitimacy of that uprising was supported were applicable to our political circumstances which demanded from day to day with increasing vigor the same reforms that had been adopted in the motherland, reforms which would not be practicable here so long as the seat of authority was located two thousand leagues away. Such was the general opinion. The minds of men were agitated. A thousand ominous signs presaged local uprisings which would have disrupted the country into a thousand fragments. In this situation I obtained the military command of the South. I promulgated my plan, united all parties, and reconciled divergent interests. Although popular support promised the most brilliant and rapid success, the inflexible tenacity of some persons threatened the cause with perils which could only be met by force."[121]

A discerning contemporary noticed some of the weaknesses of the plan. Padre Mier held that Ferdinand VII would not desire to voyage to Mexico. Above all, this critic expressed the opinion that the revolutionary Congress which was destined to assemble in the capital

---

[119] Venadito to Cabañas, May 22, 1821, W. B. Stephens Collection, no. 1828, in MSS, U.T.
[120] Iturbide to J. Oscoy, July 29, 1821, in A.M.C., D/481.3/193.
[121] *Gaceta imperial de México*, October 18, 1821, pp. 73-74.

city would not favor the founding of a monarchical regime.[122] That the new champion of independence glossed over the efforts of such men as Morelos was little noticed at the time. It was not strange, however, that although Iturbide had summoned his countrymen to found a new nation, he made early pariots like Ignacio Rayón seem like pariahs,[123] for he had led royalists against rebels for almost six years. Dr. Silvio Zavala, a leading Mexican historian of our own day, rightly takes the view that Iturbide's project lacked the extreme nationalistic sentiment which had marked previous creole insurrections.[124]

Despite its defects, the plan proclaimed by Iturbide at Iguala did much to regenerate the patriot cause. In his project he had formulated doctrines which appealed to many persons in the diverse and dissentient classes of Mexico, both monarchists and republicans, poor peasants and prosperous landowners. As Rocafuerte for once aptly said, it was necessary to temporize with this group and with that group; it was advisable that the Liberals should not be openly exasperated nor should the Serviles be deprived of all hope.[125] Dissatisfied with the ecclesiastical policy recently adopted by the Spanish government, influential members of the clergy, who had not favored the uprising led by Hidalgo, were attracted by assurances offered them in the Plan of Iguala concerning the conservation of their property, their privileges, and their religion. Prominent officers who had fought against the insurgents were drawn to the cause of independence not only because they were personally acquainted with its new champion but also because of the prestige which he had won as a royalist commander. At the same time, the acceptance of Iturbide's plan by Guerrero insured its support by many partisans of the rebellion.

Assurances in Iturbide's plan concerning the preservation of property rights and the retention of public offices pleased landowners and officeholders who had been antagonized by the doctrines and the practices of earlier revolutionists. Unlike Morelos, Iturbide expressed no views that one could properly designate as communistic. Moreover, the Plan of Iguala, the earliest political plan proclaimed for the Mexican nation, not only declared that she was independent but also sketched a provisional frame of government. That a monarchy was proposed did not at first blush seem objectionable to some Mexicans who had been nurtured under a monarchical regime. Indeed Itur-

[122] Undated, Mier, Obras y Cartas, Genaro García Collection, in MSS, U.T.
[123] Santibañez, El Plan de Iguala, pp. 87-88.
[124] Zavala, "México: La Revolución, la Independencia, la Constitución de 1824," in R. Levene, Historia de América, VII, 81.
[125] Rocafuerte, Bosquejo ligerísimo, p. 42.

AGUSTÍN DE ITURBIDE DEPICTED AS DISPLAYING THE PLAN OF IGUALA
A Mexican portrait in the San Jacinto Museum of History, San Jacinto
Monument, Texas

bide's project appeared less objectionable to them than the scheme of Colonel Nicola at the end of the American Revolution to crown Washington as king seemed to some patriots in the United States. Upon publishing a translation of the Plan of Iguala, the *Aurora* of Philadelphia not inappropriately said that "it contains something to please everybody."[126]

Colonel Iturbide had not lost sight of possible support for his monarchical scheme by Mexican deputies at the Court of Madrid. On March 17 he addressed a letter to Gómez de Navarrete concerning his project. In this letter he enclosed representations intended for transmissal to Ferdinand VII and to the Cortes in which he described the precarious condition of Mexico, mentioned the unfavorable attitude of Viceroy Venadito toward the Iguala Plan, and solicited its sanction by the motherland. In another letter addressed to the Cortes he declared that the separation of Mexico from Spain was inevitable.[127]

[126] June 9, 1821.
[127] Olagaray, *Coleccion de documentos historicos mexicanos*, II, 47-62, 75.

CHAPTER V

Campaign of Liberation

THE PLAN of Iguala was not everywhere favorably received. As early as March 4, 1821, an infantry regiment quartered in the capital city declared through its colonel that all its members were anxious to furnish unequivocal proof of their loyalty to the King.[1] At Querétaro on the following day Colonel Luaces exhorted his troops to prefer a glorious death to the acceptance of infamous proposals made by enemies of their happiness.[2] The cabildo of that city issued a proclamation to its inhabitants declaring that Iturbide wished to renew the evils of civil war, to enslave his brothers, and to shackle them by a heavy chain. On March 6 the ecclesiastical cabildo of Puebla informed General Ciriaco de Llano that the astounding events in the South would not induce it to renounce its love for peace or its obedience to the legitimate authorities.[3] The military commander of Iturbide's native city posted a proclamation which denounced the project of independence as criminal.[4]

An illustration of the sentiments of liberal Mexicans is furnished by the experience of Padre José Izquierdo, who had been sent by the viceregal government on a mission of pacification. This agent wrote to Iturbide early in 1821 to declare that he anticipated with pleasure hearing about his views.[5] Upon learning of the Plan of Iguala, Izquierdo informed its author that he had become an adherent of the independent cause.[6] Writing to Venadito on the same day, the friar praised the plan for independence in extravagant words:

"I cannot explain to you the extraordinary joy that filled my soul when I learned of a project which agreed so well with my own ideas, a project so legal in its provisions, one that puts into practice a measure which all the inhabitants of Mexico have meditated for eleven

[1] *Gaceta del gobierno de Mexico*, March 10, 1821, pp. 242-243.
[2] *Manifiesto*, March 5, 1821.
[3] *Gaceta del gobierno de Mexico*, March 10, 1821, p. 240.
[4] *Ibid.*, March 13, 1821, pp. 246-247.
[5] Izquierdo to Iturbide, March 2, 1821, in A.M.C., D/481.3/1840.
[6] *Idem* to Iturbide, March 27, 1821, *ibid.*

years. In it I saw the dénouement of an event which could not have otherwise been achieved without horror, bloodshed, and disaster. I beheld in it peace, harmony, mildness, fraternity, consolation, and all the benefits which mortals can hope to enjoy on earth."[7]

Certain Mexicans undertook to keep Deputy Gómez de Navarrete informed of the progress of events. A merchant of Vera Cruz named Pedro del Paso y Troncoso wrote him a letter to state that he was much astonished to learn about the Plan of Iguala because Iturbide must have known of a project for the emancipation of his country which the Mexican deputies contemplated proposing to the Cortes. The correspondent mentioned the agitated condition of the capital city in the following passage: "When the news spread that the government was preparing a defense, people breathed again; they took heart; and those men who did not belong to the national militia enrolled in that force, satisfied that Iturbide's plan would not succeed or that, if accepted, it would be with clauses which were more rational and which would harmonize with the Spanish Constitution until another constitution was adopted. . . . Because of the fatal results which the equality of castes would entail, all good citizens have viewed the ill-considered Article XII of the Plan of Iguala with fear."[8]

When, in the course of his picturesque career, Mier escaped from a Cuban prison and arrived in the United States in the autumn of 1821, he felt that there was in that country a general disapproval of Iturbide's plan. "Without making reply in the newspapers," he continued, "Don Manuel Torres, the minister of Colombia, and I found no other mode of tipping the scales in favor of Mexico than to take the view that absolute independence was the object and the basis of the plan, and that the remainder of it was an impracticable political strategem due to circumstances."[9] An English traveler, Captain Basil Hall, who visited the Pacific shores of Mexico in 1822, commented more favorably. He declared that the Plan of Iguala had dexterously involved all classes, especially those persons who had the most to lose, the clergy and the Spaniards: the latter class, which possessed "nearly all the active capital in the country"; and the former class, which had gained a great "influence over men's minds."[10]

When the Iguala Plan was proclaimed, the royalist forces in New

[7] Copy, ibid.
[8] April 3, 1821, ibid.
[9] Mier, *Memoria política-instructiva enviada desde Filadelfia en Agosto de 1821 á los gefes independientes del Anáhuac*, pp. 37-38.
[10] Hall, *Extracts from a Journal Written on the Coasts of Chili, Peru, and Mexico in the Years 1820, 1821, 1822*, II, 269-270.

Spain were stationed at special posts or in city garrisons. General Pedro Negrete was located in a region known as Nueva Galicia. Brigadier Diego García Conde was in command of the city of Durango. His brother Alejo, who had been born in Ceuta, was in command of certain frontier provinces in the northwest, while northeastern frontier provinces were in charge of Brigadier Joaquín de Arredondo, who had fought under the Spanish flag in the Peninsula. Colonel Luaces, whom Iturbide had in vain tried to win over to his cause, still commanded the royalist forces in the city of Querétaro. The city of Valladolid was in charge of Colonel Luis Quintanar. A native of the intendancy of San Luis Potosí named Miguel Barragán headed a detachment of troops at Ario. Various contingents of royalist soldiers guarded the city of Puebla. A member of the colonial nobility, José Morán, the Marquis of Vivanco, was stationed in the region near Mount Orizaba. A Spanish Marshal, José Dávila, was the governor of Vera Cruz City. The coast near that port was in charge of the ambitious creole lieutenant, Antonio López de Santa Anna, a native of Jalapa in the intendancy of Vera Cruz.

When the Viceroy became aware of the fresh revolutionary movement, he directed Pascual de Liñán, the subinspector of viceregal troops, to take charge of the Army of the South. Upon being notified of reappointment to his former command, Colonel Armijo undertook to join Liñán.[11] A contemporary estimated that the royalist forces stationed near the capital city numbered 6,000. He expressed the opinion that, if these soldiers had been led against Iturbide at once, he could have been put to rout, but that persons who favored independence persuaded the viceregal government to adopt a dilatory policy.[12]

Among the instructions prepared for commanders of the insurgent army was an article directing them to treat the inhabitants with moderation and urbanity.[13] Iturbide, whose total force after the accession of Guerrero was about eighteen hundred men, soon took steps to attract his countrymen to the cause of independence. In an undated address to royalist soldiers of the frontier, he expressed satisfaction at the report that they had abandoned the military service of the Viceroy. He asked them to aid him in the establishment of Mexican liberty with its accompanying benefits to the country and to the Roman Catholic religion. "Come then," he implored, "to succor me

[11] *Gaceta del gobierno de Mexico*, March 15, 1821, p. 265.
[12] Rocafuerte, *Bosquejo ligerísimo de la revolución de Mégico*, pp. 71-72.
[13] Olagaray, *Coleccion de documentos historicos mexicanos*, II, 116.

in the tasks necessary to secure such interesting objects. You know me well. Never have I deceived you; and if I have in fact led you many times to places where you have earned laurels and a distinguished name, you may hope that, should you follow the footsteps of this army in which are enrolled thousands of your former comrades in arms, you will again be rewarded by victory."[14]

On March 22, 1821, the Commander in Chief issued a general order to the Army of the Three Guarantees promising rewards to soldiers who enrolled under his banner. Mexicans who enlisted in his army within six months after March 2 were to be presented with two oxen and a piece of farming land. Europeans who joined the revolutionists but who wished eventually to leave Mexico were to be rewarded by an equivalent recompense in money. Soldiers who deserted the vice-regal forces to join the liberating army were to be cordially received as well as properly remunerated for their horses and military equipment. Civilians who served the cause of independence were not only to be protected but also to be recommended to the new government.[15]

A few weeks after the Plan of Iguala was publicly proclaimed, Iturbide started a propaganda campaign. To make his purpose widely known, he addressed a circular to Mexicans of all classes. "The independence of this country," he declared, "is the aim that has induced me to leave the Spanish party, which I had previously defended, and to lead those persons who wish to follow me." He set forth the need of separation from Spain by a series of inquiries. Among other questions he asked the following:

Had the despotism of the audiencia, the Viceroy, or the military commanders in Mexico ceased? Had the Mexicans seen such favors accorded to mining or to any other industry as would offset the exactions levied upon industries? Had certain proposed commercial reforms been carried out? Had authors been allowed to write as freely in Mexico as in Spain? Had persons who had spoken truthfully about the evil acts of Calleja and Trujillo been thrown into prison? Had the Cortes of Spain conceded to her American colonists the proper supplementary representation in its hall? Had the people noticed the scorn with which mulattoes in Mexico were deprived of those rights of citizenship that were accorded them in the motherland?[16]

Lieutenants of Iturbide soon sent him reports of the progress of

---

[14] Soldados del heroico cuerpo de frontera, in A.M.C., D/481.3/204.

[15] El Mejicano Independiente, April 7, 1821.

[16] Abitantes de América, March 25, 1821, in A.G.N., Operaciones Realistas, Acevedo, 1810-1821, vol. 20.

their arms. On March 14 Celso de Iruela reported that he had stationed himself at the hacienda of Molino with a small force in order to besiege a fort at Perote which occupied a strong position on a tableland west of Jalapa. Iruela added that though the local cabildo had urged the royalist commander of the fort at Perote to proclaim the Plan of Iguala, he had not yielded. However, José Joaquín de Herrera, who after rising to the rank of lieutenant colonel in the viceregal army, had withdrawn from military service and become a pharmacist, had accepted the plan.[17]   On March 18 Herrera wrote to Iturbide from San Juan de los Llanos. He stated that not a single day passed without deserters from the royalist ranks joining him. "The entire province," said Herrera, "displays the greatest interest in our enterprise. All the people acclaim us. All persons wish to be armed in defense of their rights." After receiving these reports, the Generalissimo was convinced that near Perote a large number of partisans of independence had been mustered. He therefore accorded to both Herrera and Iruela the title of lieutenant colonel "in the name of the nation."[18]

A curate named José Martínez proclaimed independence at Actopan. At Orizaba on March 23 in company wtih Francisco Miranda this cleric summoned Antonio Santa Anna to surrender. A few days later that wily royalist officer capitulated to Herrera.[19]   Another royalist officer wrote to the Viceroy from Jalapa that the adjacent region was in a ferment and that a desire for independence prevailed among all classes.[20]   The city of Córdoba surrendered to Herrera on April 1. Nevertheless, a sanguinary struggle ensued for the possession of that city between his soldiers and royalists under the command of Colonel Francisco Hevia. After this colonel was killed during an assault, bitter house-to-house fighting occurred. On May 17 the besieged were inspirited by the arrival of re-inforcements led by Antonio Santa Anna, who had seized the town of Alvarado and joined the revolutionists. Leaving Córdoba in ruins, on May 21 the royalists raised the siege.[21] The new champion of independence then besieged Jalapa, which soon capitulated. The insurgents thus gained important places in the region near the city of Vera Cruz. Santa Anna issued a pompous proclamation declaring that, upon the very spot where the banner of

[17] Cotner, *The Military and Political Career of José Joaquín de Herrera*, pp. 1-36.

[18] *El Mejicano Independiente*, April 7, 1821, p. 57.

[19] Bustamante, *Cuadro historico de la revolucion mexicana*, V, 186-187.

[20] J. A. Horbegosa to Venadito, March 27, 1821, in A.G.N., Operaciones Realistas, 1820-1821, vol. H.

[21] Bustamante, *op. cit.*, V, 187-198.

Castile was first flung to the breeze in the New World, his soldiers were about to display "the eagle of the Mexican Empire."[22]

Iturbide's thoughts naturally turned to the Bajío. He sent Captains Quintanilla and La Madrid to the intendancies of Guanajuato and Valladolid to prepare the way for a change in the political order. At the head of a detachment of dragoons at Silao, on March 16, 1821, Luis de Cortazar, a royalist colonel, declared in favor of the revolutionary plan. Colonel Anastasio Bustamante now took sides with the partisans of independence.[23] He wrote to Iturbide that forces under the command of Cortazar and himself had overpowered the royalist garrison in Celaya. Even before Bustamante had reached the city of Guanajuato, its garrison had declared for the independent cause. Accepting the statements of Alamán concerning the resources thus gained, Hubert Howe Bancroft represented the accession of Bustamante's soldiers as one of the turning points of the revolution.[24] Late in March the military commander of San Miguel el Grande led the royalist soldiers out of the city, which soon went over to the independents.[25] At Zitácuaro Captain Vicente Filisola proclaimed his adherence to the Plan of Iguala.[26] In a letter to Iturbide, Colonel Cortazar soon boastfully reported that the entire intendancy of Guanajuato had declared in favor of independence without "the shedding of a single drop of blood."[27]

At Zitácuaro on April 12 a revolutionist under Iturbide's direction wrote a sanguine account of the progress of the campaign. The chronicler recorded that in the intendancy of Valladolid only the capital had refrained from announcing its support of "a just liberty." A part of Nueva Galicia had declared in favor of the insurrection. The entire intendancies of Zacatecas and San Luis Potosí had been won over to the revolutionary cause. "National troops" had made progress in the intendancies of Mexico, Puebla, and Vera Cruz. Only their capitals still offered resistance to the supporters of the Iguala Plan. The annalist continued thus:

"At this moment we have 25,000 men under arms. These forces include the most experienced and enthusiastic battalions, officers, and commanders. . . . Very soon a national congress should be estab-

[22] Ibid., p. 200.

[23] Olagaray, Coleccion de documentos historicos mexicanos, II, 82-84.

[24] Bustamante to Iturbide, March 21, 1821, A.M.C., D/481.3/1846. Alamán (Historia de Mexico, V, 124) estimates Bustamante's forces at 6,000, which Bancroft accepts (History of Mexico, IV, 714).

[25] Gaceta del gobierno de Mexico, April 5, 1821, p. 341.

[26] Alamán, Historia, V, 121, 751.   [27] Olagaray, op. cit., II, 84.

lished. This is much desired by the First Chief of the Army of the Three Guarantees, for he wishes only the happiness of the country which he will establish without fail. Not a single drop of blood has been shed during these great successes; nor is any disorder known to have taken place anywhere."

The author of this account further stated that the policy of all the military commanders had been "not to use forcible measures with anyone; nor to injure the interests of any citizen—not even of those persons who have opposed the liberal system—and to furnish passports and escorts to such persons as wished to change their residence. In case of certain commanders and officials, their assistants have even been allowed to accompany them. . . . All the independent divisions and bands, without excepting the smallest of those that originally belonged to the viceregal regime, are entirely subordinated to the Commander in Chief of the army."[28]

In explaining the remarkable success of the insurrectionary movement, Rocafuerte admitted that even the inhabitants of the Bajío, forgetting the injuries and insults which they had suffered, received the one-time royalist commandant with enthusiasm and obeyed his orders.[29] Even after conflicts had taken place between his adherents and the royalists, the patriot Generalissimo did not despair of persuading the Viceroy to adopt his plan. Expressing chagrin that, instead of welcoming his ideas, Venadito had publicly denounced them and had stigmatized his religious sentiments as hypocrisy, his disinterestedness as ambition, his patriotism as ingratitude, and his philanthropy as treason, on April 28 Iturbide wrote to him in part:

"I concede that your Excellency is responsible to Spain for the Spanish-American Continent, but you will not deny that you are also responsible to Heaven for all the evils which will be precipitated by a bitter war that can be avoided. . . . If you view the matter from the standpoint of politics, let me ask what can you expect from the Court of Madrid? What aid can the distracted Peninsula give you in the turbulent epoch of its great disorder and misery? On the other side, what could not the Apodaca family become in extensive and rich Mexico, a domain free and grateful?"[30]

Venadito's reaction was voiced in a letter to Bishop Cabañas, who, in conjunction with two viceregal military officers, had urged him to

[28] Noticias para México, April 12, 1821, Miscelanea de documentos relativos al excmo. Sr. D. Agustín de Iturbide, no. 9, in MSS, B.N.M.

[29] Rocafuerte, Bosquejo ligerísimo, p. 93.

[30] Triunfo de la libertad de la imprenta, no. 7, p. 2.

examine the proposals of Iturbide. The Viceroy emphatically declared that he would not open any epistle sent him by the perfidious colonel. He explained that his honor and the laws did not permit him to treat with the recreant who had robbed convoys and seized church revenues—a recreant who designed to make himself the despot of the western hemisphere.[31]

Meanwhile, disquieting rumors about his policy toward Europeans had reached Iturbide. Hence from León on May 1 he issued a proclamation which denounced as "a monstrous calumny" the report that his campaign would culminate in a Sicilian Vespers directed against Peninsular Spaniards. Boasting that he had been making sacrifices for eleven years in order that they might be shielded from harm, he tried to console them by declaring that his own father was a native of Spain.[32]

The patriot leader undertook to induce General José de la Cruz, the commander of Nueva Galicia, to accept his plan. As the result of arrangements made by General Negrete, on May 8, 1821, at the hacienda of San Antonio, Cruz and Iturbide held an interview. The latter solicited the royalist officer, who was sympathetically inclined, to induce Venadito to listen to his proposal concerning the pacification of Mexico.[33] Though this fresh attempt to interest the Viceroy in his project was futile, Iturbide felt that the journey of thirty leagues which Cruz had made from his headquarters to the meeting would demonstrate to the entire country that the partisans of independence deserved serious attention.[34]

They next marched against the city of Valladolid, which was protected by two lines of fortifications. From his camp on May 12 Iturbide issued a manifesto asking his fellow-citizens whether it was necessary to fertilize the tree of liberty with more Mexican blood. "Do you wish," he inquired, "that I should forcibly invade the city in which I first saw the light of day, a city for whose preservation I risked my life?" He reminded them of the memorable occasion in December, 1813, when he saved their homes from being pillaged by insurgents under Morelos.[35] On the same day he wrote to the cabildo

[31] May 22, 1821, W. B. Stephens Collection, no. 1828, in MSS, U.T.

[32] El Mejicano Independiente, June 9, 1821, pp. 1-2.

[33] Ibid., pp. 2-4; Triunfo de la libertad de la imprenta, no. 3. In colonial days the term "Nueva Galicia" was applied to a vast region extending northeast from the Pacific Ocean to the intendancy of San Luis Potosí (Priestley, José de Gálvez, map opposite p. 48). During the struggles for independence the term was applied to the southern part of the intendancy of Guadalajara.

[34] Iturbide to C. Camacho, May 19, 1821, in A.H.I.N.A.H., 50-1-7.

[35] El Primer gefe de ejército imperial mejicano de las Tres Garantías a los hijos y habitantes de la ciudad de Valladolid.

of Valladolid and to Colonel Luis Quintanar, the commander of that city, to ask that they should avoid the horrors of war by agreeing to a reconciliation with his followers.[36] After the royalist commander declined to fall in with this proposal as being inconsistent with his duty, Iturbide drafted generous terms of surrender.[37]

Shortly after agents of the cabildo had visited Iturbide, Quintanar sent two officers to learn the terms of capitulation. Though these proposals were at first inacceptable, after the besiegers had pierced the outer line of the fortifications, and in view of the increasing desertions from the royalist ranks, Quintanar went over to the camp of the investing army.[38] Almost immediately his successor, Colonel Manuel Rodríguez de Cela, informed Iturbide that he would surrender. On May 20 articles of capitulation were signed. They provided that the garrison was to proceed to Mexico City accompanied by any citizens who might desire to leave. No person was to be molested because of his political opinions. Mules were to be furnished for the transportation of luggage belonging to royalist soldiers. During the evacuation the besieging army was to remain in the lines which it had already occupied.[39] The garrison soon marched out of the fortifications with the honors of war. After *Te Deum* had been chanted in the conventual church of San Diego, Iturbide led a military procession into his native city, where he was acclaimed with joy.[40]

The manner in which the victorious commander inspirited his followers and coadjutors in the movement for independence is indicated in a letter which he wrote to Guerrero, who, as the commander of a division of the Army of the Three Guarantees, had failed to capture Acapulco. "Let us," said Iturbide, "rescue from misery many unhappy persons. . . . We have good friends in considerable numbers and well endowed. A society like that cannot fail to prosper."[41]

There seems no reason to doubt the statement made in an official survey of the progress of the Iturbidista revolution that, after the capitulation of Valladolid, the Army of the Three Guarantees was considerably increased by bands of insurgents, by recruits under Colonel Anastasio Bustamante, and by deserters from the royalist forces.[42]

[36] Bustamante, *Cuadro historico*, V, 154-156.
[37] *Contestaciones que precedieron á la capitulación de la ciudad de Valladolid*, p. 11.
[38] Iturbide to Camacho, May 19, 1821, in A.H.I.N.A.H., 50-1-7.
[39] *Capitulación hecha entre el Señor Don Agustín de Iturbide, . . . y el comandante de la plaza de Valladolid, Don Manuel Rodríguez de Cela.*
[40] Bustamante, *op. cit.*, V, 158.
[41] May 29, 1821, in A.H.I.N.A.H., 50-1-7.
[42] *Triunfo de la libertad mejicana ó sea resumen oficial de los progresos de la independencia de Nueva España*, p. 4.

Here and there ecclesiastics went over to the independents. Manuel de la Bárcena, the Spanish archdeacon of the bishopric of Michoacán, who was acquainted with European political philosophy, published a notable manifesto with a subtitle concerning *The Justice and the Necessity of the Independence of New Spain.* In reasoning like that used in Tom Paine's iconoclastic pamphlet entitled *Common Sense,* which had spurred the patriots of the Thirteen Colonies, Bárcena argued that the announcement of Mexican independence could be considered either as that of a subjugated people who had recovered their liberty and sovereignty or as that of a colony which, having come of age, had freed herself from the motherland. Maintaining that it was unjust to tie New Spain to Old Spain, he declared that every colony contained the seed of independence, which, if nourished, would develop into a sturdy tree.[43]

Iturbide soon marched from Valladolid toward the intendancy of Guanajuato. Early in June he had reached Acámbaro. By that time he felt the pressing need of funds for the support of his soldiers. He accordingly issued a broadside announcing that every inhabitant of the towns and villages which favored independence should contribute to the support of the army by a voluntary gift proportioned to his respective capital. In a copy of the notice addressed to a curate Iturbide declared that he counted upon that cleric's well-known zeal for a just cause to bring the need for such contributions forcibly to the attention of his parishioners and to make clear to them the happy consequences which should flow from such opportune aid to their country.[44] This appeal indicated that, in contrast with conditions during the early Mexican struggles for independence, in 1821 some influential ecclesiastics more or less openly favored the revolution. Writing about desertions from the King's cause, Alamán asserted that at the portals of their convents nuns presented disaffected soldiers with medals, money, and scapularies just as though they were inciting new champions of the faith to join an army raised to defend the Roman Catholic religion.[45] On the other hand, when he heard of certain Carmelites in San Luis Potosí who did not favor independence, Iturbide sternly ordered that, if they persisted in this attitude, they should be deported from the city. Furthermore, the prior of their monastery was to bring those friars to a realization of the religious and political conduct which they should observe.[46]

[43] *Manifiesto al mundo,* p. 8.
[44] June 1, 1821, addressed to D. Yanki, Gates Collection, no. 222, in MSS, T.U.
[45] Alamán, *Historia,* V, 190.
[46] Iturbide to A. Echávarri, July 11, 1821, in A.M.C., D/481.3/1852.

Shortly afterward the Mexican patriot known as Guadalupe Victoria, who had just emerged from a cave in the mountains of the intendancy of Vera Cruz in which he had taken refuge after the death of Morelos, proposed to Iturbide that, instead of a Spanish prince, one of the leaders of the early Mexican revolution should be selected to occupy a throne in Mexico under a system of limited monarchy.[47] Peculiar though it may seem, Iturbide did not favor such a change in his plan. In explaining his viewpoint he was reported to have said that the Mexicans had already decided to support whatever their prospective Congress determined should be done. "So that if Congress should declare that something is white," he added, "though I believe it to be black, I shall agree that it is white!"[48] If one may judge by this alleged expression of sentiment, Iturbide was willing to make genuine concessions to avoid a difference with Congress, which he at this time acknowledged would be the supreme authority in the State. In a similar spirit, upon the death of Pedro Asencio, when directing that the soldiers of the deceased commander were to serve under Guerrero, Iturbide altruistically said: "To promote the welfare of the country it is necessary that we relinquish any personal designs and that we sacrifice whatever is necessary to gain that end."[49]

The fate of the citizens of Guadalajara, the capital of the intendancy bearing that name, was largely determined by the actions of General Pedro Negrete, who, upon reaching the village of San Pedro, finally proclaimed himself in favor of Iturbide's plan. An announcement by Negrete on June 13 that the municipal officials had decided for immediate independence or death and that his soldiers would at once advance against the city of Guadalajara, forced the hand of General Cruz. On that day Negrete issued a circular to the people in which he declared that their emancipation had just been made known in Guadalajara. "The soldiers have sworn to the Lord Almighty," he announced, "to sustain with their blood independence, union, the rights of the King, and the holy religion of our fathers."[50]

The religious factor in the Iturbidista revolution was strongly stressed in a notable sermon. On June 25 in the cathedral of Guadalajara, Dr. San Martín preached from a text in the First Epistle of St. Peter, "Love fraternity. Fear God. Honor the King." The priest justified the movement for independence because he viewed the

[47] Alamán, *op. cit.*, V, 172-173.
[48] Rocafuerte, *Bosquejo ligerísimo*, p. 74.
[49] Iturbide to F. Martínez, June 13, 1821, in A.M.C., D/481.3/1834.
[50] Bustamante, *Cuadro historico*, V, 160.

Spanish conquest of Mexico as illegitimate. Further, he denounced certain decrees of the Cortes concerning ecclesiastical affairs. On the other hand, he praised the revolutionary program:

"Iguala, Iguala, your name will not be insignificant among the peoples of our America! In your breast the seed of independence was sown in order to preserve our sacred religion! . . . The war for our independence is a religious war. All persons should be soldiers, the ecclesiastic and the layman, the noble and the common man, the rich and the poor, the old and the young. All of us should take up arms, we should range ourselves beside our military leaders and resolve to die on the field of honor and of religion! . . ."[51]

Religious sentiment was supplemented by wise conduct. Not only was Iturbide generous and humane in the terms granted to royalist troops that gave up their arms, but he directed his lieutenants to treat the soldiers who capitulated to them in a similar fashion. In a letter addressed on June 22, 1821, to Anastasio Bustamante and Colonel José Echávarri, a native of northern Spain who had forsaken the royalist cause in New Spain, he directed that, in quartering soldiers in towns and villages, they should consider the welfare of the people and the garrisons in such places. He also insisted that the swords and other equipment of royalist officers who had surrendered should be at once returned to them. Further, with certain reservations, he ordered that they should be allowed to select the towns or villages in which they wished to live. Knapsacks were to be returned to private soldiers, who were to be assured that the patriot Commander in Chief would very soon have the satisfaction of allowing them to join the party that suited them best.[52] At this time certain leaders in the revolutionary movement even contemplated dispatching an agent to the President of the United States with instructions to solicit aid and also to propose that a provisional treaty of commerce should be arranged between Mexico and that country.[53]

From Acámbaro the army of liberation marched to the town of San Juan del Río, which was the key to the important city of Querétaro. Early in June that town capitulated to Iturbide.[54] Shortly afterward a sally made by the Querétaro garrison was checked. Partly

[51] Alamán, *Historia*, V, 16.
[52] In A.M.C., D/481.3/1846.
[53] Copy, Exposicion de los principales sucesos de la segunda revolución hecha al Sor. Presidente de los Estados Unidos . . . que no se remitió, June 22, 1821, Documentos relativos al Imperio de Iturbide, 1821-1824, f. 5-10, Genaro García Collection, in MSS, U.T. Library.
[54] Bustamante, *op. cit.*, V, 162-163.

because of the activity of patriot emissaries and partly because of propaganda by partisans of independence, Colonel Luaces lost many soldiers by desertion. When summoned to surrender, he replied that though he preferred to die with honor rather than to live in infamy, he would not fruitlessly sacrifice the small force which remained faithful to Spain.[55]

Giving up all hope of succor, Luaces soon decided to surrender.[56] Articles of capitulation drawn up on June 28 by commissioners of both parties provided that the royalist soldiers were to march out of the city with the honors of war on condition that they should not again take up arms against Mexican independence. Further, as soon as possible, they were to embark for Habana.[57] Iturbide announced that for the time being he abolished certain extraordinary imposts by which the viceregal government had oppressed the Mexicans. He reduced the *alcabala* tax to 6 per cent.[58] A bulletin published by the victorious army declared that a tablet commemorative of the promulgation of the Spanish Constitution which had been torn down during the struggles for independence should be restored. The Generalissimo announced that the organic law should remain in force so far as it was in harmony with the independence of Mexico until her representatives adopted new institutions. From Aguascalientes on July 6 Negrete sent word to Iturbide that not a single town or ranch in that vicinity had failed to acclaim the Plan of Iguala. During the same month various towns in the frontier provinces of the East also declared in favor of that plan.[59]

At a military camp on the road to the capital city Iturbide addressed a broadside to his countrymen. After mentioning the victories won for the cause of independence, he announced that he would exhaust every other resource before he caused the mountains encircling that city to echo the sound of cannon. The object of his campaign, he avowed, was to elevate Mexico to the ranks of the great, free, and independent nations. His correspondence shows that he was striving to avoid a military reverse which might delay or hinder the advance of his army. He warned a certain commander not to advance at once upon Huehuetoca, still less to make an attack upon the enemy.

[55] *Ibid.*, p. 176.

[56] Luaces to Iturbide, June 28, 1821, in A.M.C., D/481.3/1831.

[57] Bustamante, *op. cit.*, V, 177-178.

[58] *Gaceta imperial de México*, October 13, 1821, pp. 47-50.

[59] *Ejército imperial mexicano de las Tres Garantías, papel volante*, July 5, 1821; Iturbide, *La correspondencia de . . . después de la proclamación de Plan de Iguala*, II, 97-102, 103, 106, 138, 152.

"We are not in a position to make a move which does not assure us a favorable result," he advised, "neither can we expose ourselves to suffer the terrible consequences which the least misfortune would entail."[60] A week later one of his officers expressed poignant regret because Iturbide did not favor a proposal to name a battalion of soldiers after himself. Although anxious that the revolution should spread, the Commander in Chief was not always intent upon presenting himself at the front of the stage. Near the end of July he addressed a letter to the bishop of Oaxaca asking him to use his influence to promote the adoption of the Iguala Plan in that place.[61]

Other revolutionary leaders had meanwhile been active in the region between the city of Puebla and the Gulf of Mexico. Early in 1821, after an imprisonment lasting three years, the undaunted and magnanimous insurgent, Nicolás Bravo, who after fighting under Morelos had been captured by the royalists and thrust into a dungeon, was set free by the Viceroy. One of the last acts of Iturbide as a royalist officer was to direct viceregal officials to transfer to the released prisoner certain lands of his family near Chilpancingo which had been sequestrated.[62] After an interview with that commander, who made him a colonel, Bravo undertook to recruit men for the independent cause. He soon joined Captain José Joaquín Herrera, who had taken possession of Córdoba and Orizaba, against the royalist leader Colonel Francisco Hevia. Puebla was invested by soldiers under the command of Bravo and Herrera. The city was defended by the Spanish General Ciriaco de Llano with the Marquis of Vivanco second in command. Neither the dispatch of reinforcements from Mexico City nor a sally by the beleaguered garrison sufficed to relieve the besieged city. Meantime Iturbide's army had reached the Holy City of Anáhuac. While soldiers of the revolution were encamped in the shadow of the great pyramid of Cholula, an armistice was negotiated with the defenders of Puebla.

The truce provided that hostilities should cease, that a line of demarcation should be drawn between the contending forces, and that the royalist commander should select commissioners to confer with the Generalissimo.[63] Articles of capitulation which were signed on July 28, 1821, provided that the city was soon to be evacuated, that the victors were to aid the vanquished garrison to transport their

[60] Cuevas, *El Libertador*, p. 237.
[61] J. Oviedo to Iturbide, July 21, 1821, A.M.C., D/481.3/1842; Iturbide, *La Correspondencia de . . . después de la proclamación del Plan de Iguala*, II, 151.
[62] Iturbide to C. Moya, December 5, 1820, in I. MSS, 11.
[63] Bustamante, *op. cit.*, V, 207-213.

belongings, that the Spanish soldiers were to embark for Habana as soon as possible, and that meanwhile they were to refrain from hostilities against the partisans of independence. Officers and regular soldiers who did not wish to follow the garrison might proceed elsewhere under the protection of the liberating army. Members of the local militia were to remain in their homes "without incurring any prejudice because of their political opinions or because of the military service" which they might have furnished the royalists since the opening of hostilities.[64] The same humane policy was to be followed with respect to civilians. What a striking contrast these provisions furnish compared to the treatment meted out by Iturbide to patriot soldiers who surrendered to him during his career as a royalist commander! It seemed as though the leopard had changed his spots.

At Puebla a new actor came upon the crowded stage. This was the influential opportunist, Antonio Joaquín Pérez, who in May, 1814, had become an adulator of Ferdinand VII, had been appointed the bishop of Puebla, and had become an ardent supporter of the revolution in Mexico.[65] Indeed Iturbide had left his wife and children in the care of that bishop during the campaign of liberation. Upon receiving from the Generalissimo a request for money with which to promote the cause of the Three Guarantees, Pérez responded that there was not a single real in the cathedral coffers, but that he had collected from his friends twenty-five thousand pesos which he placed at the disposal of the victorious commander. "I wish that circumstances were otherwise," he explained, "so that I could furnish whatever aid is necessary for the sake of our friendship and the just cause."[66] The entrance of Iturbide into the ecclesiastical stronghold took place amidst popular rejoicings. In a letter congratulating him upon that triumph, Pérez hailed him as "El Libertador."[67] From Tlaltinapan a lieutenant of the Generalissimo lauded him as "the Liberator of the independent Mexican Empire."[68]

Lodged in the episcopal palace, Iturbide was frequently compelled to appear on its balcony to greet an applauding public. On August 5 an oath to support independence was taken in the stately cathedral.

[64] Capitulación acordada para la evacuación de la ciudad de Puebla. . . . In a letter to Felipe Martínez, Iturbide instructed him to grant a pardon to persons near Cuernavaca who had been induced to serve in the viceregal forces, July 29, 1821 (in A.M.C., D/481.3/1834).
[65] Navarro y Rodrigo, Iturbide, pp. 101-102; Alamán, Historia, V, 23-24.
[66] Olagaray, Coleccion de documentos historicos mexicanos, II, 86.
[67] August 3, 1821, in A.M.C., D/481.3/1834.
[68] F. Martínez to Iturbide, August 3, 1821, ibid.

ITURBIDE AS AN IMPERIAL MILITARY COMMANDER
A Mexican painting in the San Jacinto Museum of History

Preaching on a text from the Psalms, Bishop Pérez likened Mexico to a youth who had just been freed from parental tutelage. In commenting upon the Plan of Iguala he expressed the opinion that under the conditions existing in Spain nothing could be so agreeable to Spanish princes as the loyal offer of an empire in Mexico. With regard to the union of Mexicans, he urged that this guarantee should be observed. In a eulogistic strain he declared that one of the most valiant caudillos who a short time ago had persecuted the independent cause was now purifying it. "Carry on your enterprise, son of fortune and of victory," he exclaimed. "Yield with docility to the high purpose for which Divine Providence has designed you! . . ."[69] A contemporary later alleged that in the episcopal palace of Puebla a decision was reached that the victorious military commander should be elevated to the throne of Mexico.[70]

The bishop soon submitted to Iturbide a list of nominations to chaplaincies in the armed forces which he wished to have approved. In August that commander not only named an ecclesiastic as the chaplain of a certain regiment but also asked Pérez to clothe that person with the requisite spiritual authority.[71] In this manner Iturbide undertook to handle in a minor case the delicate problem of the *Patronato Real*. Evidently he assumed that the right to nominate candidates to ecclesiastical vacancies had passed from the King of Spain to the head of the revolutionary movement.

Among the persons who made known an alteration in their attitude toward Iturbide was José Joaquín Fernández de Lizardi, an alumnus of the University of Mexico who had served the early revolutionists with both pen and sword. The editor of a periodical called *El Pensador Mexicano*, he was later given that sobriquet.[72] In March, 1821, in a dialogue entitled *Chamorro y Dominiquin* he maintained that the true solution for Mexican ills was union among the contending factions. Possibly in response to an appeal from Iturbide, in July, 1821, Fernández de Lizardi left Mexico City to join the insurgents.[73] After he was placed in charge of their press at Tepotzotlan, he directed the publication of pamphlets favoring their cause. On August 4, 1821, he published a tract addressed to those Spaniards who favored inde-

[69] Alamán, *Historia*, V, 202.

[70] *Diario de las sesiones del congreso constituyente de la Federación Mexicana*, p. 42. Cf. Bustamante, *Manifiesto histórico á las naciones y pueblos del Anáhuac*, p. 8.

[71] Pérez to Iturbide, August 20, 1821, in A.M.C., D/481.3/1844.

[72] González Obregón, *Don José Joaquin Fernández de Lizardi*, pp. 11-17, 73-76.

[73] Fernández de Lizardi, *Oración de los crillos hecha por un Gachupin*, pp. 10-11.

pendence as well as to certain Mexicans whom he considered traitors to their country.[74]

Meanwhile, in consultation with leading viceregal officials, Venadito had apparently resolved to resist the revolution to his last breath.[75] On June 1 he summoned all able-bodied male citizens between seventeen and forty years of age to join battalions to be composed of "defenders of the integrity of the Two Spains."[76] Four days later he declared that he would serve as a colonel of that army and would participate in the fatigues which it was destined to suffer.[77] By broadsides he sought to secure arms and horses for his soldiers.[78] One of his last official acts was to issue a proclamation dated July 5, 1821, in which he stated that persons spreading false reports would incur heavy penalties, that anyone harboring deserters would be punished by imprisonment, and that the penalty for inducing soldiers to desert the King's cause would be death.[79]

On that very day an uprising of soldiers in the capital city induced Venadito to relinquish his authority. He signed a paper declaring that he entrusted the military and political command of the Viceroyalty to Marshal Francisco Novella on condition that the safety of himself and his family would be assured and that he would be furnished with an escort to the port of Vera Cruz.[80] The act of insubordination which caused him to resign was explained by a citizen of the United States as being due to the bribery of royalist officers by merchants of the capital.[81] Upon returning to the Peninsula, certain Spanish officials alleged, however, that the Viceroy had welcomed the uprising because it had furnished him with a bridge of silver by which he made his escape from a perilous situation.[82]

Marshal Novella, who had been serving as the subinspector of artillery, soon published a circular announcing that, as the Viceroy of New Spain, he would set up a junta headed by himself which would administer the affairs of state. The *Gazette* reported that on July 8, in the reception hall of the viceregal palace, during an audience with

[74] González Obregón, *op. cit.*, p. 78.
[75] Venadito, *Apuntes para la historia.*
[76] Gates, *The William Gates Collection*, item 420.
[77] June 5, 1821, Gates Collection, no. 421, in MSS, T.U.
[78] June 16, 1821.
[79] Gates Collection, no. 186, in MSS, T.U.
[80] Iturbide, *La Correspondencia de . . . después de la proclamación del Plan de Iguala*, I, 150. Cf. Bancroft (*History*, IV, 717-718).
[81] Manning, *Diplomatic Correspondence of the United States concerning the Independence of the Latin-American Nations*, III, 1607.
[82] Navarro y Rodrigo, *Iturbide*, p. 98 and n.

viceregal officials and with the Archbishop of Mexico by his side, Novella promised to maintain the rights of the constitutional King, the honor of Spain, and the security of her citizens. He took an oath to do so with his hand upon the hilt of his sword, in the presence of the Holy Scriptures and of an image of the crucified Christ.[83] The new Viceroy, as he styled himself, soon issued a proclamation announcing that he would fight to the end to maintain the unity of the Spanish Empire. By a series of fervent exhortations he sought to rally the Mexicans around the flag of the defenders of the integrity of both Spains.[84]

When the change of rulers was announced to the soldiers of independence, it was stated that the Viceroy, who had retired to Guadalupe, had been seized at midnight on July 5, that Mexico City was in a state of anarchy, and that the commander of the imperial army had consequently been compelled to accelerate his advance upon the capital.[85] One of Iturbide's lieutenants named Castro, however, wrote to Venadito to inform him that he should not be alarmed at the sight of imperial soldiers who were to serve as his escort because they remained faithful to the beloved Ferdinand VII.[86] Though approving the sympathetic tone of this note, Iturbide, who was busily preparing to besiege the capital, informed Castro that he would prefer that the former Viceroy did not accept the offer because of the danger that enemies of independence would consider it a confirmation of the rumor that Venadito had favored his design to liberate Mexico. For the time being, advised the Generalissimo, the former magistrate would have to remain a prisoner of the partisans of independence.[87] To Negrete, Iturbide wrote that he could die content with the thought that his children were to enjoy "the inestimable gift of a just liberty, the most precious gift which the Almighty has conceded to mankind."[88] A bulletin of the Army of the Three Guarantees announced that the people could now take refuge in the shade of the sturdy tree of liberty.[89]

The last titular Viceroy of Mexico was deposed by a mutiny of his own troops. One after another, royalist commanders as well as patriot chieftains had undertaken to espouse the Iguala Plan. With

[83] *Gaceta del gobierno de Mexico*, July 10, 1821, pp. 715-718.
[84] See the *bandos* published in *ibid.*, July 7–August 14, 1821, and in the *Noticioso General* on July 18–August 15, 1821.
[85] *Aviso al público*, July 12, 1821.
[86] A. Castro to Venadito, July 8, 1821, in A.M.C., D/481.3/184.
[87] July 15, 1821, *ibid.*   [88] Iturbide, *op. cit.*, II, 125.
[89] *Ejército imperial mexicano de las Tres Guarantías, papel volante*, July 13, 1821.

respect to the form of the new government, at Cuernavaca on July 23 Iturbide explained that the Spanish Constitution would be in force so far as it was in harmony with the system of independence until a congress of deputies from the Mexican provinces should adopt the system most conducive to their happiness.[90] As the result of a series of engagements with viceregal forces, the soldiers of Iturbide had come into possession of important towns and cities throughout the Viceroyalty. Influential ecclesiastics had become champions of independence. By the end of July, 1821, the patriot army was in control of all the important strategic places with the exception of Acapulco, Mexico City, Fort San Carlos at Perote, the port of Vera Cruz, and the castle of San Juan de Ulúa. During that very month General José de San Martín, who had heroically carried the flag of Argentine independence over the lofty Andes to Chile and thence by sea to the ancient Empire of the Incas, had proclaimed Peruvian independence at Lima.

A most remarkable feature of the last campaign for Mexican independence was the conduct which Iturbide adopted toward his antagonists. Instead of waging a cruel and relentless war upon the royalists who opposed his revolutionary movement, he followed a policy of mildness and conciliation. It is difficult to determine whether this was done because he had so long served the royalist cause that he could not be implacable toward his former comrades or because he calculated thus to win support for his politico-military plans. Probably both of these motives were influential. Capitulations were drawn up between patriots and loyalists as the result of negotiations instead of at the point of the sword. Generous terms were conceded to vanquished royalists. Iturbide's public utterances breathed an air of humanity and reconciliation.

Consul Wilcocks wrote to the government at Washington in high praise of the Iturbidista revolution. He expressed the opinion that it had not been accomplished "by means of unbridled passions, cruelty, rancor, or revenge, but, on the contrary," had from its beginning been accompanied by "brotherly love, patriotism, disinterestedness, truth, and good faith. . . ." He even mentioned Iturbide in the same breath with Washington.[91] In sharp contrast with this favorable view of the Liberator of Mexico were the satirical queries of a South American who had forsaken the valley of Mexico for the banks of the Potomac. Among other questions, Rocafuerte asked how Iturbide could suddenly transform himself from a sanguinary leader into a humane one, "from an enthusiastic defender of Spanish tyranny into an enemy of that

[90] *Op. cit.*, II, 142.
[91] Manning, *Diplomatic Correspondence of the United States*, III, 1613.

domination, and finally from the stalwart enemy of the liberty of his native land into its most devoted protector?"[92] Whatever view is taken of the conduct of the victorious military commander, from March to August, 1821, the Iturbidista rebellion had spread over a large part of Mexico. This rapid success with comparatively little bloodshed was doubtless partly due to the fact that the way had been cleared by the labors and the sacrifices of earlier insurgents. It was also promoted by the dissatisfaction which prevailed, especially among ecclesiastics, with Spanish policy and with the viceregal regime. Furthermore, the victorious military commander had displayed his intention to reform the Mexican administrative system. The triumph of the Plan of Iguala was due in large measure to the fact that the support of ragged, insurgent soldiers as well as of sanguinary, royalist commanders had been won. Then, too, the conciliatory and humane attitude which Iturbide uniformly followed toward royalist soldiers and commanders greatly aided the cause of the Three Guarantees. The incidence of the plan upon diverse classes and interests won wide support. All of which is to say that the leader and the occasion had met. Iturbide was the man of the hour, who brought a fratricidal civil war to an end in less than seven months after his plan was proclaimed.

Although evidently neither the Cortes nor King Ferdinand VII deigned to respond to representations which Iturbide addressed to them concerning his plan,[93] it naturally attracted attention in Spain. Early in June, 1821, a dispatch from Venadito that discussed the Plan of Iguala was laid before the Cortes in which Mexican deputies had taken their seats. José Mariano de Michelena declared that the plan had "great moral force" and that the Spanish government ought to make a decision concerning it within a few days. He advised that a ship should be held ready to weigh anchor in order that a report of the action taken could be promptly sent to Mexico.[94] Gómez de Navarrete proposed that the government should equip a vessel to transmit the news that the legislature was considering a reform in the administration of the Indies. He maintained that the viceregal government should inform the revolutionists of this prospect. "I have known Colonel Iturbide personally for many years," he exclaimed, "and I am fully convinced that, if my proposal is carried out,

---

[92] *Bosquejo ligerísimo*, p. 82. On the humane treatment accorded by the patriot commander to his antagonists, see further Iturbide, *La Correspondencia de . . . después de la proclamación del Plan de Iguala*, I, 69, 170-171.

[93] Navarro y Rodrigo, *Iturbide*, pp. 75-76.

[94] *Diario de las actas y discusiones de las cortes, legislatura de los años de 1820 y 1821*, vol. XX, no. 5, pp. 37-38.

hostilities will be suspended and bloodshed prevented! For this I will answer to the Cortes with my head!"[95]

He was followed by Gómez Pedraza, who urged that the government should instruct Venadito to make clear to Iturbide that the Cortes was considering Mexican affairs and that, if he would peacefully await the decision of the Spanish government, the Viceroy would suspend hostilities.[96] Instead of favoring action which might have resulted in a compromise with the insurgents, however, the legislature adopted a resolution to the effect that, in view of the conditions existing in New Spain, the Minister of the Colonies should propose the measures which he judged suitable for the pacification of that kingdom.[97] A few days later, when the Council of State again considered the Mexican uprising, it decided that the policy which had been pursued by the Viceroy should be approved.[98]

Unaware that Spanish legislators had allowed a fine opportunity for reconciliation with the Mexican insurgents to slip, the ardent republican Mier wrote in part as follows to General José de San Martín about the progress of the continental movement for independence: "All America would now be free, if it had not been for the madness of Iturbide in the Kingdom of Mexico where he undertook to revive the ancient Mexican Empire with Ferdinand VII or one of the princes of Spain or of Austria to serve as Emperor. . . ."[99] Viewing the transformation from a different standpoint, Basilio Arrillaga, the learned Provincial of the Society of Jesus in New Spain, rejoiced at the birth of the Mexican nation:

"This event, of which we may well be proud, was rather the work of the Lord Almighty than of men. . . . Hostilities were carried on with so much celerity, prudence, and good fortune that they could scarcely be called a war. In seven months . . . a powerful army was formed, the strongest fortresses were captured, and many thousands of enemies were either overcome by military force or more frequently were obliged by prudence or by dint of circumstances to relinquish the struggle. . . . How many difficulties and civil wars have not the founding of a new republic or the establishment of a new system of government ordinarily caused! With respect to political organization, as the very name of Empire indicates, we have selected the monarchical form but have nevertheless limited its power."[100]

[95] *Ibid.*, pp. 42-43.   [96] *Ibid.*, p. 38.
[97] *Ibid.*, p. 45. See further *American State Papers, Foreign Relations*, IV, 827-828.
[98] June 8, 1821, in A.H.N., Actas del Concejo, legajo 23d.
[99] Unfinished letter, November, 1821, Correspondencia de Mier, 1821-1823, Genaro García Collection, in MSS, U.T.
[100] Decorme, *Historia de la Compañía de Jesús en la República Mexicana*, I, 218.

CHAPTER VI

The Treaty of Córdoba

ON JUNE 8, 1821, the *Gaceta de Madrid* printed the following item of news from Cadiz dated May 31: "Yesterday there sailed for Terra Firma and Vera Cruz the warship *Asia* commanded by Captain Josef Primo de Ribera. On board was his Excellency Don Juan O'Donojú, the Captain General of New Spain."

Juan O'Donojú, who was of Irish lineage, had a spectacular career in the service of Spain. While fighting under General Blake against the French invaders, he was severely wounded. He had served in both the ministries of state and of war during the captivity of Ferdinand VII. His name was inscribed on the long list of Friends of the Constitution who shortly after the restoration of that monarch were cast into dungeons by Francisco Eguía, the governor of Castile.[1] O'Donojú remained incarcerated until October, 1817, when the governor formally declared that he was absolved from a charge which had been brought against him while he was the Minister of War. As a salve to his wounded feelings, Eguía declared that the accusation which had been lodged against him "ought not to affect the honor and the good reputation which he deserved." The torture to which he had been subjected, however, had left scars. Assertions that he had held a high rank in the Masonic Order furnish another clue to his liberal sentiments.[2]

Unsettled political conditions existing in Spain under the constitutional regime naturally affected the policy adopted toward the colonies. On January 16, 1821, Ferdinand VII informed Ramón Feliú, the Minister of Justice, that in view of the merit and the services of General O'Donojú, he had named him Captain General of New Spain "with all the privileges and distinctions which the viceroys of that Kingdom had enjoyed."[3] Several days later a royal decree was

[1] Señora Josefa O'Donojú to Count Toreno, undated, *El Sol*, May 22, 1822, p. 213.

[2] The quotation is from Eguía to Apodaca, October 22, 1817, in A.G.N., Reales Cédulas, 217; Liceaga, *Adiciones y rectificaciones a la historia de Mexico que escribió D. Lucas Alamán*, p. 499.

[3] Cayetano Valdés to García Herreros, January 16, 1821, in A.G.I., Audiencia de México, 88-3-14.

framed which declared that O'Donojú had been appointed the Superior Political Chief of the Viceroyalty with the honors, prerogatives, and faculties pertaining to that position in accordance with the Constitution of 1812 and with due regard to the decrees of the Cortes and the Laws of the Indies.[4] Though a committee of the Council of State objected to the terms used in making the appointment,[5] acting on behalf of the King, on March 28, 1821, the Council nevertheless decided that the Captain General of New Spain should be accorded the title of Superior Political Chief.[6] If we may trust Alamán's summary of a royal order concerning the appointment, the King had proposed that the new magistrate should be paid a salary of 70,000 pesos annually.[7]

Formal instructions to O'Donojú directed him to enforce the Constitution and the reform decrees. The government of the Mexican provinces was to conform to the fundamental law. Only organizations and assemblies permitted by the Constitution were to be allowed to function. Agriculture, commerce, and mining were to be promoted. Mexicans and Spaniards were to alternate in holding public offices. The sanguinary strife between them was to be brought to an end so that tranquillity might be restored to the Viceroyalty. Offices, honors, and other rewards were to be promised to leaders of the rebellion if they agreed to lay down their arms. Otherwise, they were to be persecuted rigorously and punished. "These principles indicate sufficiently," said the Minister of the Colonies, "that the intention of the government is to prefer mild measures to attract and conciliate instead of acts of force and bloodshed. . . ."[8]

The government next considered what persons were to accompany the new magistrate. Tomás Moreno, who continued to act as Minister of War after changes had been made in the ministry, wrote to Antonio Barata, the Minister of the Treasury, on April 3, 1821, and

[4] R. Gil de las Quadras to the Council of State, January 25, 1821, ibid., 88-3-13. Such a decree dated January 24, 1821—presumably obtained from O'Donojú—was quoted by Gutiérrez del Mazo (Aviso al público, September 17, 1821).

[5] "Acuerdo" of a committee of the Council of State, February 9, 1821, A.G.I., Audiencia de México, 88-3-13.

[6] "Actas del Concejo," February 10, 1821, in A.H.N., legajo 23 d; R. Feliú to the Council of State, March 28, 1821, ibid.

[7] Alamán, Historia de Mexico, V, 237-238, gives the date of the royal order which he quotes as January 25, 1821. In other particulars it closely resembles the royal decree of January 22, 1821, cited supra, n. 4. On April 15, 1821, Secretary of War Moreno informed Secretary of the Treasury Barata that the royal treasury was to bear the expense of transporting O'Donojú and his family to Mexico (in A.G.I., Audiencia de México, 95-6-4). His wife later followed him there.

[8] Minuta de las instrucciones reservadas dadas al jefe político de Nueva España, Don Juan O'Donojú, March 2, 1821, f. 8, in A.G.I., Audiencia de México, legajo 1676.

enclosed the names of sixteen individuals who had been selected by the King to sail with O'Donojú to New Spain. With the exception of a chaplain and a physician, all of them were military men.[9] Minister Moreno soon decided that O'Donojú and Marshal Juan de la Cruz Murgeon, who had been appointed the chief magistrate of the Viceroyalty of New Granada, should sail in the same frigate.[10]

There is no doubt that Mexican deputies to the Cortes played an influential part in the appointment of O'Donojú. Manuel Gómez Pedraza asserted that Miguel Ramos Arizpe, who was a deputy from the province of Coahuila, had urged the selection of the general upon Liberal ministers in the belief that the independence of Mexico would thus be facilitated.[11] Ramos Arizpe, an impetuous Creole who, after serving as a deputy to the Cortes, had been thrust into a Spanish prison in 1814 because of his liberal views, thus explained his part in promoting the transfer of O'Donojú to New Spain:

"This virtuous General, comprehending the extraordinary condition of Mexico and with rare discernment realizing the difficulties which would confront him in promoting the welfare of both Old Spain and New Spain, hesitated more than once about accepting the position and even wished to decline such an important office. As I realized, however, the importance of the arrival in Mexico of a general whose talent and virtues of every sort were well known to me, I used all the resources of an old and tried friendship and whatever else was in my power to secure his appointment. A correspondence carried on for five months and incredible exertions at court put O'Donojú in condition to embark by May 30."[12]

The new magistrate was aware of the delicate colonial problems which confronted the harassed constitutional government of Spain. It does not appear, however, that on the eve of his departure any suspicion had entered his mind that a formidable rebellion was spreading over the Viceroyalty of Mexico. Included in the party which sailed for America on the *Asia* were some of his relatives and Colonel Francisco de Paula Álvarez, who served as his secretary.

On June 12, 1821, Minister of the Colonies Ramón López Pelegrin undertook to explain anew to O'Donojú the government's attitude

[9] Moreno to Barata and enclosure, April 3, 1821, in *ibid.*, 95-6-4; Mier, *Memoria política-instructiva enviada desde Filadelfia en Agosto de 1821*, p. 126 n., stated that O'Donojú had thirty officials with him.

[10] Moreno to Barata, April 15, 1821, in A.G.I., Audiencia de México, 95-6-4.

[11] Gómez Pedraza, *El Chantre Ramos Arizpe*, p. 3.

[12] As quoted in Presas, *Juicio imparcial sobre las principales causas de la revolucion de la América Española*, pp. 94-95.

toward the Spanish Indies. Pelegrin declared that Ferdinand VII desired not only to terminate the devastating war but also to promote by every possible means the welfare of the colonists. The King accordingly wished positive reports concerning the condition of New Spain and other colonies so that he might be able to take the measures which seemed necessary. "His Majesty commands me to make known to your Excellency this tentative measure," wrote Pelegrin, "for your guidance in order that, in case need should arise, you may make that use of it which you believe most conducive to public tranquillity."[13]

Perhaps it was an interpretation given to these vague directions after they had been printed in Mexico which caused an English agent there to assert in March, 1823, that the "private instructions" to O'Donojú found among his papers showed that, in case the Mexicans declared their independence, he was authorized to make the best terms he could for Spain.[14] In a dispatch dated June 7, 1821, however, the French ambassador at Madrid, who, partly because of the Bourbon Family Compact, was sedulously watching the Spanish political situation, wrote to his government that O'Donojú had been entrusted with "very confidential instructions concerning the desires made known by the Mexican deputation."[15] With respect to the insignificant expeditionary force sent to restore Spanish rule in Mexico, the Minister of the Colonies subsequently explained to the Cortes that his government had done all that it was able to do under the circumstances. "What aid can the Peninsula furnish," he asked in despairing tones, "to carry on the war against the independence of the colonies?"[16]

Contemporaries did not agree concerning the political sentiments of the new Viceroy of Mexico, as he was sometimes mistakenly designated. Upon learning of the appointment of O'Donojú, Padre Mier stated that he had been a fellow-prisoner with him in Saragossa during the Spanish war against the French. The inveterate revolutionary alleged that the Spanish Liberal had no knowledge of Mexico nor of her controversy with Spain, that he had stigmatized the Mexicans as rebels, and that the consequences of such a foolish notion were apt

[13] As quoted in a copy of Iturbide's circular, September 21, 1821, to Chihuahua and Santa Fé, in A.N.M., no. 3035, Santa Fe. This was printed in Iturbide, *Comunicación oficial del primer gefe del ejército imperial de las Tres Garantías*, which began as follows: "El Excmo. Sr. D. Juan O'Donojú, con fecha de este día se ha servido comunicarle la real orden siguiente. . . ."

[14] Paxson, *The Independence of the South-American Republics*, pp. 168-169.

[15] Duke Laval-Montmorency to Baron Pasquier, June 7, 1821, in A.A.E., Espagne, vol. 713.

[16] *Gaceta de Madrid*, February 14, 1822.

to be horrible.[17] In contrast with that opinion and more indicative, it would seem, of his real sentiments were the views which O'Donojú was quoted as having expressed to Ramos Arizpe shortly before sailing from Spain:

"I wish to convince the Mexicans that I am their friend rather than their chief; that I am one of those persons who deserve their confidence; that I shall act with them to promote their welfare; that sacrifices will cost me nothing, if in that manner I can promote their happiness; that my government will not be stained with blood but shall be distinguished in history because of the great events which happened under it. . . ."[18]

Early in July the *Asia* cast anchor in a port of Venezuela.[19] Long before that time Mexicans had heard of the appointment of their new chief magistrate. As early as June 17 Antonio López de Santa Anna had written from Jalapa to Iturbide that certain citizens of Vera Cruz had planned that, upon the arrival of O'Donojú's party, they would march inland and take possession of Fort San Carlos at Perote.[20] When the *Asia* reached the castle of San Juan de Ulúa, its passengers were amazed to learn that insurgents had actually made an assault upon the city of Vera Cruz.[21] It appears that Governor Dávila promptly acknowledged O'Donojú as the Captain General of New Spain.

O'Donojú had already indicated that he intended to support the partisans of Spanish rule. He sent a dispatch to Madrid describing the deplorable condition in which he found Mexico, without money, without provisions, and without troops. He asserted that, if the government could not send him military aid, all would be lost, and that consequently he would return to Spain. Meanwhile he had written to the Captain General of Cuba in support of a request made by the cabildo of Vera Cruz for the aid of armed forces from that island. Besides, he asked that a detachment of royalist soldiers should be transferred from Venezuela to Mexico. In dire distress he even contemplated impressing the crew of the *Asia* into his service.[22]

From the besieged city, on August 3 O'Donojú issued a proclama-

[17] *Memoria política-instructiva enviada desde Filadelfia en Agosto de 1821*, pp. 95-96.
[18] Extract from a letter of May 28, 1821, printed in *El Sol*, April 24, 1824.
[19] *Le Moniteur universal*, September 16, 1821, p. 1319.
[20] Santa Anna to Iturbide, June 17, 1821, in MSS, C.
[21] J. Espinosa to J. Liño, August 1, 1821, in A.M.C., D/481.3/1841.
[22] To the Minister of the Colonies, July 31, 1821, in A.G.I., Audiencia de México, 1680; printed in part and inaccurately in Cuevas, *Historia de la iglesia en Mexico*, V, 104.

tion which breathed liberal sentiments. He said that he did not depend upon a tyrannical King or a despotic government; he did not come from an immoral people; nor did he land in Mexico to become a dey or to accumulate riches. He stated that the new regime in Spain had uprooted despotism, that his mind was full of philanthropic ideas, and that he was bound by friendship to the Mexican deputies who had encouraged him to make the long voyage to Vera Cruz. Declaring that he was without an armed force, he avowed that, if his government did not suit the Mexicans, at the slightest sign of dissatisfaction he would allow them freely to select their own ruler. Nevertheless, he suggested that they should suspend the projects which they were meditating until they received fresh news from Spain.[23] So impressed was the commander of the Army of the Three Guarantees with the conciliatory spirit of this proclamation that, upon reaching the city of Puebla, he had it reprinted so that his countrymen might learn the liberal views of the new Spanish agent. Iturbide informed the director of his military press that two officers whom he had sent to confer with O'Donojú were not to discuss whether Mexico could aspire to enter the ranks of free nations, but that they were instead to treat about the manner of sanctioning her independence.[24]

Another proclamation, which the Superior Political Chief issued on August 4, breathed a different spirit. He lauded the remarkable defense which the people of Vera Cruz had made of their city. He praised them for the valor, discipline, and love of order which they had preserved without staining the Spanish name. He expressed regret "at the blindness of those persons who without a legitimate object or a just motive separate from our society and declare themselves to be our enemies!"[25] From this it appears that on second thought O'Donojú was tempted to listen to the advice of those royalists who were holding the city of Vera Cruz and the adjacent castle, that he was in a distracted state of mind, or that he wished to fathom their sentiments.

Soon after he had set foot on Mexican soil, O'Donojú met Captain Manuel Santa Anna, a brother of Antonio Santa Anna. News soon reached the Army of the Three Guarantees that the Spanish expedition had anchored at Vera Cruz.[26] From Jalapa on August 5 Colonel

[23] Bustamante, *op. cit.*, V, 223-225.

[24] Iturbide to "Sr. Director de la imprenta del Ejército," August 3, 1821, *Gaceta del gobierno de Guadalajara*, August 25, 1821.

[25] O'Donojú, *Segunda proclama . . . á los dignos militares y heroicos habitantes de Vera Cruz.*

[26] Olagaray, *Coleccion de documentos historicos mexicanos*, II, 148. In the

JUAN O'DONOJÚ, CAPTAIN GENERAL AND SUPERIOR POLITICAL CHIEF
OF NEW SPAIN
From Manuel Rivera Cambas, *Los Gobernantes de México*

Joaquín Liño wrote to Iturbide to notify him that the Superior Political Chief had arrived without any military force. Liño asserted that he had received reports that O'Donojú was animated by the most philanthropic sentiments and that his appointment was the work of Mexican deputies.[27]

It is clear that, as O'Donojú became acquainted with conditions existing in the Viceroyalty and especially with the amazing spread of the Iturbidista revolution, his views concerning New Spain were modified. The fact that some of his companions, including two nephews, were stricken with yellow fever, which was endemic at Vera Cruz, may also have influenced his judgment.[28] In a justificatory letter which he later addressed to the Spanish government, he thus described the situation which confronted him:

"All the provinces of New Spain had proclaimed their independence. Either by force or by virtue of capitulations, all the strongholds had opened their gates to the champions of liberty. They had a force of 30,000 soldiers of all arms, organized and disciplined—an armed citizenry among whom liberal ideas had been effectively spread, soldiers who remembered the weaknesses (to which they gave another name) of their former governments. This army was directed by men of talent and character. At the head of these forces there was a commander who knew how to inspire them and how to secure their favor and their love. This commander had always led them to victory. He had on his side all the prestige that is usually bestowed upon heroes."[29]

The Captain General, as he was sometimes designated, addressed a letter to Iturbide on August 5 stating that he had appointed two agents to confer with him. On the next day O'Donojú presented his

---

draft of his memoirs Antonio Santa Anna wrote thus about O'Donojú: "Tres días después del desembarco, el Virrey me invitó á una entrevista, lo q. tuvimos en la Alameda.

"El Virrey pretendió: un tratado basado en las condiciones contenidas en el Plan de Iguala; pa. así facilitar entre los beligerantes la buena inteligencia." (Mis memorias. Escritas de mi puño y letra sin ayuda de nadie, en mi último destierro, f. 6, Genaro García Collection, in MSS, U.T. Library.)

[27] August 5, 1821, in A.M.C., D/481.3/1840.

[28] Alamán, *Historia*, V, 211. In an undated letter written to Count Toreno in 1822, Señora O'Donojú stated that one half of the officials in the party died at Vera Cruz (*El Sol*, May 22, 1822, p. 213).

[29] O'Donojú, *Modelo de virtud y filantropía, loor eterno al exmo. señor capitán general Don Juan O'Donojú, carta de remisión al gobierno español del tratado celebrado en la villa de Córdova por el exmo. Señor Don Juan O'Donojú*, pp. 1-2. The original dispatch, addressed to the Minister of the Colonies, is dated August 31, 1821 (in A.G.I., Audiencia de México, 1680).

views about the condition of Mexico in a letter to the insurgent commander whom he addressed as "amigo." Declaring that his government entertained liberal sentiments, the newly arrived magistrate expressed himself favorably with respect to Iturbide's views as set forth in the epistle of March 18 addressed to Venadito. He enclosed copies of his first proclamation. In particular O'Donojú expressed a desire to negotiate a treaty which would maintain tranquillity in Mexico, pending its approval by the King and the Cortes. Entrusting the letter to Colonel Manuel Gual and Captain Pedro Vélez, who were authorized to place before the revolutionary leader the matters mentioned therein, the Spaniard asked Iturbide for a safe-conduct so that he might proceed to a conference with him.[30] The Generalissimo replied that reports which had reached him about O'Donojú's liberal ideas and political talent had convinced him that the Spaniard would use this opportunity to gain certain advantages for the Mexicans which Marshal Novella could not secure. Iturbide reasoned that the latter did not have the authority to enter into legal and binding agreements.[31]

O'Donojú had meantime sent dispatches to the Spanish government describing the deplorable plight in which he found Mexico. By August 13 he had reached the conclusion that he could do no more than to secure as many advantages for the motherland as were consistent with the independence of New Spain, which he had decided was inevitable. Accordingly he suggested that he should be furnished with fresh instructions which suited the altered condition of the country or else that he should be recalled.[32] It appears that no response to this communication was ever written.

Iturbide wrote to Colonel Anastasio Bustamante on August 13 to inform him that O'Donojú had written to Novella recognizing him merely as a marshal.[33] On the next day in a letter from the town of Toquipa to Colonel Pedro Telmo Primero, Iturbide described the situation as follows:

"Here I am in correspondence with Señor Novella. I have received satisfactory communications from O'Donojú, who is in Vera Cruz without any armed force and without hope that any aid will reach him. His thoughts are much occupied with the liberal ideas of the

[30] *Noticia documentada de las últimas occurencias con el Sr. D. Francisco Novella, . . . mandadas publicar por el Sr. D. Agustín de Iturbide*, pp. 2-3.

[31] Bustamante, *Cuadro historico*, V, 230.

[32] The Council of State to Ferdinand VII, December 12, 1821, in A.G.I., Estado, México, 23. The council mentioned letters from O'Donojú dated July 31, August 5 and 13.

[33] In A.M.C., D/481.3/1846.

age. He has sent two commissioners to me with special, official letters. In order that he may proceed to the town of Córdoba, I have furnished him with an escort of honor composed of my grenadiers so that in this climate, which is more healthful than that of Vera Cruz, we may arrange treaties which will conclude our great work."[34]

A formal report of the arrival of General O'Donojú at Vera Cruz had meantime reached Mexico City. A letter from him addressed to Marshal Novella stated that he would proceed from Vera Cruz to the capital to take charge of the military and political administration of New Spain as Captain General and Superior Political Chief. An inspired article that followed an epitome of the letter which was printed in a special issue of the *Gaceta del gobierno de México* intimated that O'Donojú ought to bring with him the instructions concerning the policy which he was to follow in the Viceroyalty. This article asserted that, though the King and the Cortes had kept the Mexicans in ignorance of their policy, the government of Mexico would never be at odds with decisions of the supreme authority in Spain.[35] Novella soon appointed a commission to confer with the new chief magistrate.[36]

Novella's attempt to initiate negotiations with O'Donojú was fruitless. A report published in a special number of the official gazette on August 18 stated that three viceregal officials appointed to confer with the new magistrate had been turned back by Iturbide. In a letter written three days earlier that commander had informed the Acting Viceroy, whom he designated merely as the temporary commander of the soldiers in the capital of Mexico, that he could send to O'Donojú two commissioners who would be treated with consideration by the army of independence. Iturbide also stated that arrangements had been made for a brief interview between himself and the Captain General.[37]

Because of measures taken by Novella for the defense of the capital, so imminent did hostilities between the opposing parties appear that Iturbide's wife, who was lodged in a metropolitan convent, fled toward her native city. Her fellow-citizens welcomed her outside its gates and drew her homeward in a triumphal coach which, among other festive adornments, was decorated with a crown of laurel.[38]

[34] *Ibid.*, D/481.3/187.
[35] *Gaceta extraordinaria del gobierno de México*, August 14, 1821, p. 842.
[36] *Noticia documentada de las últimas occurencias con el Sr. D. Francisco Novella*, p. 3.
[37] *Alcance al suplemento de la gaceta extraordinaria del gobierno de México*, August 18, 1821, p. 863.
[38] *Entrada pública en Valladolid de la Señora Doña Ana Huarte de Iturbide*, pp. 1-4.

Meanwhile Iturbide had written from the city of Puebla to O'Donojú to express the opinion that they were in agreement concerning the political condition of both Old and New Spain. Further, the insurgent commander explained that two commissioners whom he had sent to confer with the Spaniard would make known his desire that the latter should proceed upland to Córdoba, where, free from the contagion infecting the Gulf coast, an interview could be held in which, if it were possible, the finishing touches could be given to the great work of ensuring the happiness of Mexico. The commander added that he would soon send coaches to the city of Vera Cruz so that his correspondent could make the proposed trip with every possible convenience. Besides, Iturbide directed Antonio Santa Anna to select a military escort to accompany O'Donojú to Córdoba.[39] On his part, the Captain General was not sanguine that he could secure from Iturbide any advantage for Spain. Realizing that he ran the risk of becoming a prisoner of the revolutionary partisans if they lacked good faith, he apparently undertook the trip with the firm intention of not agreeing to anything that seemed unjust or improper. To an extent the way for an agreement had been prepared by his interchange of views with Iturbide's commissioners.[40] Indeed it seems that the Generalissimo might have sketched a Mexican-Spanish convention.

Just before he left Vera Cruz for Córdoba, O'Donojú issued a proclamation explaining as follows his purpose in proceeding to a conference with Iturbide:

"We shall consider in that interview the reciprocal interests of both Spains. It appears to me that the love which I have for Old Spain, the fondness which I cherish for the Mexicans, the worthy desires which animate me, and the rectitude of my intentions are now well known. Informed of these conditions, the public will be persuaded that my journey is indispensable as the only means of assuring public tranquillity and of ensuring the happiness of these people. . . . I assure you that on my part no negotiations in which I may engage will prejudice the legitimate interests of Spain, that is to say, . . . that a reliable guarantee of the persons and the fortunes of the Europeans residing in New Spain is one of the most sacred objects which I have undertaken to secure. According to the correspondence that I have had with the revolutionary leader, he is disposed to agree with my views so far as they are rational and just. . . ."[41]

[39] Olagaray, Coleccion de documentos historicos mexicanos, II, 162-163.
[40] O'Donojú, Modelo de virtud y filantropía, pp. 3-4.
[41] Manifiesto, August 19, 1821.

On August 19, the very day on which O'Donojú issued this proclamation, an indecisive conflict took place at Atzcapotzalco between royalist forces and a contingent of independents who were marching upon Mexico City.[42] Four days later the commander of the Army of the Three Guarantees approached Córdoba. Despite the fact that it was raining, wrote an annalist, some citizens met him on the highway, unhitched the mules from his coach, and dragged it into the town. Bustamante further recorded that when Iturbide and O'Donojú met in the presence of a brilliant company, they embraced one another and displayed cordial feelings. On the forenoon of August 24 each of them heard Mass. When Iturbide reached the house where O'Donojú was lodged, he evidently said that in view of the good faith and harmony with which they entered into negotiations, he supposed that it would be a very easy matter to untie the knot which bound Mexico to Spain.[43] To quote the words which presumably were put into Iturbide's mouth by his secretary, José Domínguez, the commander declared:

"I found in O'Donojú a chief animated by good intentions. I even noticed that he was anxious to be generous with me, that, doing justice to the character of honesty which distinguished the Mexicans, he had entered among them with confidence and had entrusted the security of his person to their virtues. Scarcely had I expressed the views which I had set forth in the Plan of Iguala when I noticed with admiration as much deference to my ideas on his part as though he had himself aided me to compose that plan. This was scarcely to be expected from a general with respect to whom there had been circulated notions of a conservative nature which were very contrary to the liberality of his principles. Accordingly it appeared to me to be even more just than politic to link to the plan of our felicity an official who showed by the scars on his body the most convincing proofs of his philanthropy and who did not consider it supererogatory to record his vote among those of the most ardent patriots of Mexico."[44]

After some discussion the agreement between the two men was put into writing by Iturbide's secretary. The draft of a treaty was then submitted to O'Donojú, who altered only a few phrases, which were said to have been in praise of himself.[45] The preamble of the treaty

[42] Bustamante, Cuadro historico, V, 236-237.

[43] Ibid., pp. 230-231.

[44] Proclama hecha á Iturbide q. no quiso firmar el comandante general en Xefe del exército de las tres garantías, Puebla, August 30, 1821, in MSS, C. Iturbide's name is appended to this document, but not his rúbrica.

[45] Bustamante, op. cit., V, 231; Alamán, Historia, V, 211.

stated that the two signatories had discussed the steps which, under the existing circumstances, were necessary to reconcile the interests of Mexico and Spain. The celerity with which they had reached an agreement on August 24, 1821, was probably in large part due to the circumstance that, advised by his commissioners who had met O'Donojú, Iturbide had had the foresight to prepare for the conference.[46] The results of the important interview were soon made known to the Army of the Three Guarantees in the pages of Iturbide's new vehicle of propaganda, the *Diario Político Militar Mejicano.*

The convention provided that the Mexican nation, henceforth to be styled the Mexican Empire, should be recognized as independent. The government was to be a constitutional monarchy. In the first place King Ferdinand VII was to be invited to reign over the former Viceroyalty. Should he decline to accept the Mexican crown, it was to be offered in turn to Prince Carlos, to Prince Francisco de Paula, and to Prince Carlos Luis. If no one of those princes would accept the crown, it was next to be offered to a person designated by the Cortes of the Mexican Empire. The new monarch was to establish his court in Mexico City, which should be the imperial capital. Two commissioners selected by O'Donojú were to proceed to the Court of Madrid to place in the hands of Ferdinand VII a copy of the convention with an accompanying memorial. The King should be asked to allow a prince of his family to proceed to Mexico. According to the Plan of Iguala, a council was at once to be formed to which O'Donojú should belong. This Junta was to choose its President and to select from its members a Regency of three persons who were to serve as the executive power of the nation. Legislative authority was to be vested in a Cortes convoked by the Junta. Europeans domiciled in Mexico were to be at liberty to leave with their persons and property. Opponents of Mexican independence should be required to depart. O'Donojú agreed to use his influence to secure the evacuation of the capital by royalist troops without bloodshed.[47]

The Treaty of Córdoba accordingly approved the Plan of Iguala

[46] O'Donojú, *Modelo de virtud y filantropía,* pp. 3-4. Antonio Santa Anna claimed to have taken part in the conferences which preceded the signing of the treaty (*Mi historia militar y politica,* p. 8). In the draft of this account there was no mention of the presence of Santa Anna at the interview. Inserted in it in a different hand after a mention of the conference between Iturbide and O'Donojú, however, was the following phrase, "y tomé una parte muy activo en el feliz resultado que tubieron" (*Mis memorias* . . . , f. 7, Genaro García Collection, in MSS, U.T. Library).

[47] García, *Documentos historicos mexicanos,* IV, contains a facsimile of the *Diario Político Militar Mejicano,* which printed the text of the Treaty of Córdoba on September 3, 4, and 5, 1821.

with certain modifications. It excluded the deposed Viceroy from membership in the Junta but included O'Donojú. Only by implication did it endorse the abolition of caste distinctions and the preservation of clerical privileges as specified in the Iguala Plan. It contained no stipulation to the effect that the future monarch must be selected from a European dynasty. Indeed its most significant clause was one which provided that if none of the personages named in the treaty deigned to accept the crown, the Emperor should be selected by the Congress of Mexico. "O'Donojú, engrossed in securing the throne of Mexico to princes of the Spanish dynasty," said Alamán plausibly, "did not notice the very important alteration which Iturbide had introduced, an alteration which was enough to undermine the entire structure that had been erected."[48] Yet the Mexican leader could not have been unaware that the way was thus cleared for the choice by his compatriots of a native-born ruler. For the time being, however, the governmental authority was to be vested in a council which presumably was to be selected by the commander of the Army of the Three Guarantees.

One week later O'Donojú undertook to justify the Treaty of Córdoba to the Court of Madrid. He avowed that he would rather die than be responsible for the loss to the Spanish crown of a rich and beautiful country. Declaring that nothing could prevent Mexican independence, he maintained that a limited constitutional monarchy was the best form of government for a country whose population did not possess the virtues necessary for the success of a republic or of a federation. Though he admitted that a people had the right to select their own ruler, yet he asserted that the article of the treaty which provided that a Spanish prince was to be the Emperor of Mexico would become one of the glories of the motherland. He stated that he had appointed a commission to notify Ferdinand VII of this convention. He reasoned that it would please those Mexicans who desired to be ruled by a member of the Spanish dynasty.

He maintained that the article providing that Mexico City was to be the capital of the Mexican Empire was a suitable arrangement but of no importance to Spaniards. Articles VI to XIV were mainly intended to preserve order in Mexico while the new system was being put into operation. With regard to a stipulation in Article VII to the effect that he was to have a seat in the provisional Junta, he stated that this clause was inserted at his desire, for he hoped that he might thus be able to influence favorably the attitude of the Mexicans toward

[48] *Historia*, V, 213.

Spanish interests. Articles XV and XVI aimed to conserve the life, liberty, and property of Europeans in the new Empire. That provision alone, he explained, should not fail to gain for him the indulgence of the King and of the entire Spanish nation. He declared that he could not oppose Article XVI which stipulated that persons opposed to the new system should leave Mexico. With regard to his own functions, he declared that they would cease at the moment when the first Congress of Mexico assembled, but that he would remain there until the chosen monarch arrived or until the Spanish government decided otherwise.[49]

Aware that he had negotiated a treaty without the express authorization of his government, on August 26, when he sent a copy of it to the governor of Vera Cruz, O'Donojú explained that the agreement had as its object the happiness of both Old and New Spain and that it also aimed to put an end to the horrible disasters of an internecine war: "This measure is supported by the law of nations; it is guaranteed by the spirit of the century, by the general opinion of enlightened people, by the liberality of the Cortes, by the beneficent purpose of our government, and by the paternal wishes of the King." O'Donojú also voiced the thoughts which thronged his mind when he signed the convention that he hoped would cement the eternal alliance of two nations. "Humanity is horrified," he declared, "upon contemplating provinces which are inhabited by people of the same origin, with the same faith, living under the same laws, speaking the same language, and with the same customs being sacked and ravaged by persons who a few months earlier cultivated those lands and depended upon their fertility for their food and that of their families—persons who were happy when they enjoyed peace, but who were unfortunate, indigent, vagrant, and needy in time of war." Furthermore, he undertook to explain the attitude of the motherland toward Spanish-American independence at the time of his appointment:

"In truth, before my departure from the Peninsula, the national legislature considered preparing for Mexican independence. And in one of its committees, with the assistance of the ministers of state, the bases for such action were prepared and approved. There is no doubt that before closing its sessions, the ordinary Cortes should have settled this matter which is important to both Old Spain and New Spain—a

---

[49] O'Donojú, *Modelo de virtud y filantropía*, pp. 5-7. This document, printed in Mexico in 1821, is followed by the date "Septiembre de 1821." The original dispatch, addressed to the Minister of the Colonies, is dated August 31, 1821, in A.G.I., Audiencia de México, 1680.

matter in which the honor of both parties is compromised and upon which the eyes of all Europe are fixed."[50]

This explanation is of special significance. It makes clear that O'Donojú now brought up as a justification for the convention with Iturbide his impression that upon the eve of his departure from Spain, the Cortes was preparing to recognize the independence of Mexico. When officials in the Spanish ministry of the colonies learned of O'Donojú's interpretation of their government's policy, however, they declared that it was false.[51]

Unfortunately for the immediate and complete triumph of the revolution, neither Governor Dávila nor Marshal Novella approved the Córdoba Treaty. Indeed opinions concerning the policy approved in that treaty varied widely. Some Mexicans hailed the news of the agreement between Iturbide and O'Donojú with joy. Among others, a revolutionary named Francisco Narvaez wrote to the patriot commander as follows: "I congratulate you on the fresh glory which you have acquired in your dealings with Señor O'Donojú and hope that the Lord Almighty will allow your Excellency to enter triumphantly into the capital of Mexico as a reward for many important labors."[52] One of the most pointed criticisms was that made by a royalist named Casimiro Leal from a coign of vantage in Cuba. Leal denounced the convention as "a deceptive veil used to conceal a treasonable act, a most scandalous and unprecedented proceeding . . . that was the result of a lamentable and dangerous situation in which unfortunately the chief authority of New Spain was placed when O'Donojú arrived there. . . ."[53] On the other side of the Atlantic, the pact signed by O'Donojú was not altogether without support. Intimating that the extreme caution of the Cortes had prevented it from favoring the separation of the Indies from the motherland, an author who subscribed his name as "Luli" published a pamphlet in Madrid which audaciously declared that the Spanish general had "cut the knot of indecision and apathy which was prejudicial to both worlds."[54]

[50] *Oficio del exçmo. Señor Don Juan O'Donojú dirigido al Señor gobernador de la plaza de Vera Cruz*, pp. 1-2.

[51] Governación de Ultramar, expediente no. 43 (undated) in A.G.I., Indiferente General, 146-1-17. Alamán declared that O'Donojú's assertion about the attitude of the Cortes toward Mexican independence was baseless (*Historia*, V, 437). See further *infra*, pp. 157-158.

[52] August 29, 1821, in A.M.C., D/481.3/191.

[53] *Refutación con notas interesantes al parte que dirigió al superior gobierno el teniente general Don Juan O'Donojú sobre el tratado que firmó en Córdoba*, pp. 9-10.

[54] *Refutación contra la memoria presentada por Don Miguel Cabrera Nevares sobre las Américas*, p. 24.

Iturbide's views concerning the effects of the treaty were expressed in his correspondence. In an interpretative order addressed to José A. Andrade, the commandant of the city of Guadalajara, he declared that it had put an end to the colonial regime in Mexico: "Articles have just been signed with . . . Lieutenant General Don Juan O'Donojú which have decided the great question of our independence. It is agreed that the places still occupied by the Spanish government are to be delivered to the military forces of this Empire."[55] In a letter to Andrade, Iturbide subsequently interpreted the Córdoba Treaty to mean that discontented Peninsular Spaniards were free to emigrate wheresoever they wished, but that they would have to conform to the regulations of the provisional government in such matters as the payment of export duties.[56] When he wrote to the Bishop of Puebla the Commander in Chief expressed his views with a different emphasis.

"Participate in the joy which thrills me because we have just given the finishing touch to the great work which I took upon myself for the welfare and happiness of my country. His Excellency, Señor O'Donojú, a man of culture, with a frank disposition and suave manners, animated by ideas of liberty and of love for his fellow-men, has agreed with me that the war and its evils should end completely. In general, he has adopted the plan which I proclaimed and swore to support at Iguala. Orders are being issued to Señor Novella to the effect that he should arrange the capitulation of Mexico City in a manner very similar to that by which other cities have surrendered. This capitulation would, as in other cases, leave everyone in full liberty to move wherever he may like or to remain among a people who have liberated themselves in a manner which has no precedent in the history of nations. . . . Let us congratulate ourselves on such good fortune and let us confess, however wrong it may seem to philosophers and to the incredulous, that neither chance nor the regular order of events have conducted us to this point but rather the hand of Providence, whose designs may not be thwarted without malice nor confounded without error."[57]

The tone assumed by the writer implied that Bishop Pérez heartily approved the Treaty of Córdoba. The Archbishop of Mexico, however, was critical. Fonte expressed dissatisfaction in a letter to the Spanish signatory because a Spaniard residing in Mexico who refused to accept the pact would be left outside the pale of the provisional

[55] August 24, 1821, *Gaceta del gobierno de Guadalajara*, September 19, 1821.

[56] *Ibid.*, September 26, 1821.

[57] Copy, undated, Gates MSS, no. 223, in MSS, T.U.

regime. Yet he admitted that he was ready to adhere to the new order, pending action upon the convention by Ferdinand VII.[58] In reply O'Donojú admitted that he had negotiated it without special instructions from Madrid. He reasoned, however, that he could not have better carried out the wishes of his government than by agreeing to it.

"I have sent to the King an account of the events and of my conduct. There is no doubt in my mind that the treaty deserves his approval; for it was justified by necessity and by principles of justice and convenience. If by a mischance, however, I have not succeeded, and if what I have approved is not confirmed, I have besought him to consider the step as due to my good intentions, and in case of his disapproval, have asked him to notify me in order that I may return to the country of which I am a citizen with rights which I wish to retain. In view of this, it may be deduced that my sojourn and representation in this Kingdom, as well as my adherence to the new order of things, may last only until His Majesty deigns to make up his mind. . . ."[59]

Significant is the implication in this epistle that the Spaniard considered the treaty with Iturbide as a temporary expedient, one which he would continue to support only if Ferdinand VII made known that he approved it. Yet O'Donojú could scarcely have been ignorant of the fact that the independent cause was constantly gaining new adherents. On the very day when the Córdoba Treaty was signed, on behalf of the Interior Provinces of the West, a junta at Chihuahua had declared in favor of the Plan of Iguala.[60]

Iturbide's achievements were noticed with interest by partisans of independence in South America. Simón Bolívar, who by his victories over the royalists at Boyacá on August 7, 1819, and at Carabobo on June 24, 1821, had liberated Venezuela and New Granada from Spanish rule, addressed on October 10, 1821, a letter to the Liberator of Mexico to voice the pleasure with which he had learned about the winning of Mexican independence. Bolívar stated that the Republic of Colombia was about to send a minister to the new government of Mexico. He expressed the hope that Iturbide would act "in such a manner that

[58] Copy, September 15, 1821, in A.H.I.N.A.H., 50-0-7.
[59] Copy, O'Donojú to Fonte, September 20, 1821, *ibid.*
[60] *Gaceta del gobierno de Guadalajara*, September 19, 1821. The *Provincias Internas* of New Spain varied in extent from time to time. After the struggles for independence began, those provinces located on the northern frontier were organized in two divisions, the East and the West. In 1821 the Interior Provinces of the West included Nuevo México, Nueva Viscaya, Sinaloa, and Sonora.

Colombia and Mexico would be displayed to the world as linked together by their hands and even by their hearts."[61]

In a letter to José de San Martín, however, the Liberator of Colombia expressed apprehension about the Treaty of Córdoba. He feared that, if a European principality were set up in Mexico, the Spanish government would not only put forth pretensions to all the free states which had been formed in Spanish America but would also wish to end the war with them in the same fashion. Hence he reasoned that, because of the changes which he dreaded might take place in the Spanish Indies, it was imperative to complete the expulsion of the Spaniards from the entire South American continent.[62]

Other contemporaries considered the convention from various viewpoints. What would any other sensible man who did not wish to inundate Mexican soil with patriot blood have done about the relations between Spain and Mexico, asked Señora O'Donojú, except to conserve the lives and property of numerous compatriots who inhabited the country, thus securing the greatest possible advantages for both nations?[63]   After a searching analysis of the motives which might have animated the Spanish signatory of the Córdoba Convention, Lucas Alamán, the Mexican historian of this period who was best acquainted with conditions in Spain, justified O'Donojú's step by stating that he was denounced as a traitor even though he had performed for his country the only service which was possible under the circumstances.[64]   A contemporary Spanish journalist declared that his only regret was that O'Donojú had not secured more advantages for his country by the treaty.   On the other hand a Spanish biographer of Iturbide later reasoned that Spain gained no advantage which had not been conceded to her by the Plan of Iguala.[65]

The dilemma which faced the Spaniard when he landed in Mexico was aptly propounded by his opponent.   In his autobiography Iturbide declared that if O'Donojú had commanded an army superior to his and with sufficient resources, he might have refused to sign the Treaty of Córdoba on the ground that he lacked the authorization of his government.   In view of the widespread approval of the plan for independence, however, unable to procure exact information of the

[61] Bolívar, Cartas, II, 404.   [62] Ibid., p. 412.
[63] Josefa O'Donojú to Count Toreno, undated, El Sol, May 22, 1822, p. 214.
[64] Alamán, Historia, V, 215.   Cf. Banegas Galván, Historia de Mexico, I, 487 n. 1; Bustamante, Manifiesto histórico á las naciones y pueblos del Anáhuac, pp. 8-9.
[65] "Examen de la memoria del ministro de ultramar leido en las córtes el día 6 de Marzo de 1822," El Mercurio Ultramarino, May 15, 1822, p. 94; Navarro y Rodrigo, Iturbide, p. 109.

actual state of affairs, ignorant of the terrain, shut up in an infected city with a hostile army in front of him, and the remaining royalist troops commanded by an upstart officer, the Superior Political Chief was almost helpless. He must have signed the Treaty of Córdoba, declared Iturbide, "or have become my prisoner, or have returned to Spain. He had no other alternative. If he had chosen the last-mentioned course, all his countrymen would have been compromised and the Spanish government would have lost all hope of gaining the advantages which it then secured—advantages which it would certainly never have acquired if I had not been in command of the patriot forces, and if O'Donojú had not been an able politician as well as an excellent Spaniard."[66]

Though the Treaty of Córdoba had endorsed the main features of the Plan of Iguala, it was silent with respect to some important issues. In particular, it contained no stipulation concerning the relations which were to exist between Iturbide and O'Donojú pending the occupation of Mexico City by the insurgents. Neither did it contain any provision about the role which the Captain General was to play after the capital had surrendered. Evidently neither of its signatories considered it to be a species of capitulation on the part of the Spanish general.

Although Iturbide continued to act as the director of the campaign of liberation, yet, as he retraced his steps toward the city of Puebla, he kept O'Donojú informed about military affairs and also solicited his co-operation. From Orizaba on August 26 he asked the Captain General, who was still at Córdoba, to order the commander of the fort at Perote to surrender that stronghold at once to Antonio Santa Anna.[67] On the same day the patriot general wrote another letter to O'Donojú to inform him about troop movements, to urge him to proceed to Puebla, and to state that coaches would soon be available for him so that he could journey wherever he pleased. "I am anxious," said Iturbide, "for the day to arrive which Mexico will celebrate eternally."[68]

At Puebla the Commander in Chief published an agreement reached on August 29 between the commandant of the Interior Provinces of the East and Comanche Indians who were hovering around the northern frontiers of Mexico. In this pact the Comanches not only agreed to recognize the independence of the Mexican Empire but

[66] Iturbide, *Carrera militar y politica de Don Agustin de Iturbide, ó sea memoria que escribió en Liorna*, p. 16.
[67] Iturbide to O'Donojú, August 26, 1821, in A.M.C., D/481.3/1843.
[68] *Ibid.*

also to refrain from aiding its enemies.[69] On September 9 Iturbide notified O'Donojú that in discussing an armistice with commissioners of Novella he had not only refused to recognize that Marshal as the Viceroy and Captain General of Mexico but had also insisted that he could merely designate him as the commander of the soldiers of Mexico City, Guadalupe, and adjacent places. "Very soon," added Iturbide, "I expect to have the pleasure of embracing you at Tacubaya. I shall proceed there this afternoon because at that place we shall have better lodgings."[70]

News of the Iturbide-O'Donojú convention evoked varying comments from European observers of the American scene. The clever and prolific writer Abbé Dominique Dufour de Pradt reasoned that, in view of the convention, there remained only one thing for the motherland to do, which was to acknowledge promptly the independence of the Spanish-American states. He maintained that she should henceforth occupy herself merely in forming commercial relations with them based upon sound principles.[71] The Spanish Minister of the Navy later expressed his views in a message to the Cortes that evidently was thus epitomized by the French legation at Madrid: "O'Donojú . . . appeared to be devoted to the constitutional system which the nation had welcomed with enthusiasm, signed with the rebel Iturbide an armistice containing provisions diametrically opposed to the instructions that had been given to him as well as to the interests of those persons who were sincerely devoted to the motherland. These terms were injurious to the dignity and the decorum of the Spanish nation."[72]

Upon learning of the convention, which the Captain General sent him from Córdoba, the Acting Viceroy promptly convoked representatives of leading civil and ecclesiastical organizations of the capital to consider what action should be taken. He responded to the overtures of O'Donojú by declaring that this junta entertained doubts concerning his authority to sign a binding agreement and questioned the advantages proposed by the moot treaty; further, it was neither in harmony with the early measures of the Captain General nor had it been approved by the Cortes.[73] During a conference which took place at

[69] *Noticias plausibles comunicadas por las Provincias Internas del Oriente.* In 1821 the Interior Provinces of the East included Coahuila, Texas, Nuevo León, and Nuevo Santander.

[70] Iturbide to O'Donojú, September 9, 1821, A.M.C., D/481.3/1843.

[71] *Examen du plan présenté aux cortès,* p. 88.

[72] Translation, March 6, 1822, in A.A.E., Espagne, 718. Cf. *Diario de las discusiones y actas de las cortes, diputación general de los años 1822 y 1823,* pp. 3-4.

[73] Bustamante, *Cuadro historico,* V, 241-243.

Puebla between O'Donojú and agents of Novella, the former stigmatized as criminal the conduct of those persons who had deposed Viceroy Venadito. Moreover, he stated that he would proceed to enter the capital in order to set up a provisional government which would establish the bases of the new Empire so that, according to the Treaty of Córdoba, a prince of the Spanish ruling dynasty could occupy the Mexican throne.[74] On September 7 Iturbide and Novella agreed to an armistice which provided that a line of demarcation should be drawn between the viceregal forces and the Army of the Three Guarantees. The truce was to remain in force for six days, pending the capitulation of Mexico City.[75]

Declaring that he was the legitimate authority in Mexico, on September 11 O'Donojú proposed that he and Novella should hold an interview. In an epistle of the same date the Marshal, who had fought against the French in Madrid on May 2, 1808, again demurred at accepting the Córdoba Treaty. He intimated that his correspondent might have to use force to gain possession of the capital. To this letter O'Donojú replied bluntly that he did not recognize Novella's authority: he promised that the instructions which authorized his acts would eventually be published; he arraigned the Acting Viceroy for opposing his authority, and demanded that the viceregal soldiers should be placed at his disposal. Further, he stated that, if upon the termination of the truce he had not received a reply to his demand, he would consider all persons obeying Novella as liable to the same punishment as the Marshal himself.[76]

As the soldiers of Iturbide had advanced to a line extending from Guadalupe to Chapultepec, after a brief armistice Novella finally decided to discuss the issue with his antagonists. On September 13, accompanied by his escort and the *ayuntamiento* of the capital city, the Acting Viceroy proceeded to the hacienda of Patera, which was located near the shrine of Guadalupe. There Novella and O'Donojú discussed the situation at length. After Iturbide joined the conference, an agreement was reached. Upon being shown papers concerning O'Donojú's appointment, Novella either became convinced that the Spaniard was the titular Captain General of New Spain or he considered it wise to yield to circumstances. Waiving the vital question concerning that official's authority to negotiate the Treaty of Córdoba, the Marshal recognized him as a royal agent. An anonymous chron-

[74] Copy, J. de Vial to L. García Noriega, September 8, 1821, Documentos relativos á independencia, 1802-1821, Genaro García Collection, in MSS, U.T.

[75] *Armisticio celebrado entre los señores Don Agustín de Iturbide . . . y Don Francisco Nobella*; Torres Lanzas, *Independencia de América*, V, 347.

[76] Bustamante, *op. cit.*, V, 247-253.

icler stated that at this interview Novella not only recognized O'Donojú as the Captain General and Superior Political Chief of New Spain but also agreed to place himself and the garrison of Mexico City under O'Donojú's orders. Moreover, Novella apparently decided that the capital was to be evacuated by the Spanish soldiers.[77]

The pseudo-Viceroy soon took steps to relinquish his authority. At a meeting of public officials in the viceregal palace Novella made known the results of the Patera interview. He formally declared that he recognized O'Donojú as the Captain General and Superior Political Chief of Mexico who had been appointed by the King.[78] At the instance of the new chief magistrate, Ramón Gutiérrez del Mazo, the local intendant, notified colonial officials that, pending the arrival of O'Donojú in Mexico City, he was to serve as its political chief.[79]

An order which Novella soon addressed to royalist soldiers informed them that he had recognized O'Donojú as the Captain General. Gutiérrez del Mazo published an announcement dated September 17 stating that O'Donojú had directed him for the time being to assume the political authority in the capital city in accordance with the Spanish Constitution and the decrees of the Cortes. On the same day General Liñán issued a notice to the royalist soldiers in or near the capital that he had been directed by the Captain General to take charge of them.[80] On the other side, from his camp near Mexico City, Iturbide had meanwhile issued an appeal to its garrison which voiced his desire for peace, invited them to join the standard of liberty, and assured them that they would thus become worthy of participating in the enormous benefits which would follow the triumph of the independent cause.[81]

A critical stage had been reached in the Mexican struggle for independence. After the capital of the Viceroyalty had been yielded by Novella, what were to be the relations between Iturbide and O'Donojú? Was the Superior Political Chief of New Spain or the Commander in Chief of the insurgent army to assume control of the former Viceroyalty? Were they to act jointly? As no trace of an agreement between them on this significant issue has been found, the only

[77] *Ibid.*, pp. 319-320. "Descripción de la entrada del ejército trigarante en México," *Boletin del archivo general de la nacion*, vol. X, no. 3, p. 483.

[78] *Gaceta del gobierno de México*, September 18, 1821, pp. 978-979.

[79] Gutiérrez del Mazo to the superintendent of the mint, September 15, 1821, in A.G.N., Virreyes Recepción, 1782-1821, vol. 284.

[80] Gutiérrez del Mazo, *Aviso al público*, September 17, 1821; *Gaceta del gobierno de México*, September 18, 1821, pp. 978 *et seq.*

[81] *El Primer gefe del ejército imperial á la guarnición de Méjico*.

THE CONFERENCE OF O'DONOJÚ, NOVELLA, AND ITURBIDE AT LA PATERA HACIENDA ON SEPTEMBER 13, 1821

From a painting in the Museo Nacional de Historia

answer available at present is that which is implied in the course of events.

From Tacubaya on September 17 O'Donojú issued a proclamation to the Mexicans in which he declared that they owed the liberty which they enjoyed to one of their own compatriots. He added that, once the regime outlined in the Córdoba Treaty was established, he would be the first person to offer his respects to it. "My functions," he continued, "will be confined to representing the Spanish government, to occupying a place in your government in accordance with the terms of the Treaty of Córdoba, to aiding the Mexicans to the extent of my ability, and to sacrificing myself most willingly for the sake of Mexicans and Spaniards."[82] From the same place, two days later, Iturbide issued a proclamation congratulating the Mexicans on the fact that in seven months they had erected an Empire without shedding the blood of their countrymen.[83] At his military headquarters there, on September 20 he issued an address to the people of Mexico City inviting them to welcome cordially the soldiers who in order to liberate them had suffered hunger, misery, and nakedness.[84] As if to place the capstone upon the structure which he was seeking to erect, on the following day the patriot commander published the royal instructions that Pelegrin had sent to O'Donojú concerning the policy of pacification which was to be followed in Mexico. In explanation of that action Iturbide declared that this document, which had just been sent him by O'Donojú, was made public in order to encourage those Mexicans who wished to see Spain acknowledge the independence of their country, whatever might be the time, the occasion, and the motives of the recognition.[85] On September 25 O'Donojú sent a note to Iturbide to inform him that, as Mexico City had been evacuated by the royalist soldiers, he had fulfilled Article XVII of the Treaty of Córdoba, and that, as the capital had been occupied by insurgents, he could not hold any other command than that of Captain General until the new government was established. He reasoned that, according to the Spanish Constitution, his political authority had devolved upon the local intendant. On the same day he notified the provincial deputation that he would enter the capital city on September 26 in full possession of his authority.[86]

[82] *Noticioso General*, September 21, 1821, p. 4.

[83] *Gaceta del gobierno de Mexico*, September 22, 1821, p. 996. Another proclamation of Iturbide dated September 19, 1821, has been printed in Miquel i Vergés, *La Independencia mexicana y la prensa insurgente*, pp. 331-332.

[84] *El Primer gefe del ejército imperial a los habitantes de México*, p. 1.

[85] *Comunicación oficial del primer gefe del ejército imperial de las Tres Garantías*.

[86] Cuevas, *Historia de la nacion mexicana*, p. 476; Olagaray, *Coleccion de documentos historicos mexicanos*, II, 208.

Meanwhile Iturbide had taken up the reins of government. On September 25 he had informed Gutiérrez del Mazo that he was to continue to exercise political authority until a junta was installed. On the next day he ordered him to announce that the accustomed liberty of the press had been restored.[87] As royalist soldiers had withdrawn from the capital, Filisola's troops had occupied its barracks, and other insurgent soldiers had taken possession of the castle of Chapultepec. From Tacubaya the Commander in Chief addressed a letter to the Archbishop of Mexico to inform him that on September 27 his army would march into the capital city. Iturbide also stated that a provisional legislative junta and a regency would soon be installed. Such important events, he added, called for extraordinary manifestations of recognition addressed to the Supreme Arbiter of Nations. Accordingly he suggested to Archbishop Fonte that a *Te Deum* should be chanted in the cathedral at 12:30 P.M. on the day when the triumphal entry into the capital was to take place and further that a solemn Mass should be celebrated in the cathedral before the junta took an oath of obedience to the new government.[88]

Several months later a report was printed of the arrival at Habana of the deposed Viceroy of Mexico on a vessel from Vera Cruz laden with some three hundred passengers and three and one-half million dollars. *Niles' Weekly Register* also mentioned the arrival of Novella there on the next day en route to Spain on a sloop which also bore refugees and treasure.[89]

Before the middle of October, 1821, partly as the result of an unratified treaty negotiated by a royal official who had not been authorized to agree to the independence of the Viceroyalty, the revolutionary movements which had distracted Mexico since 1810 were stilled. Little more than the castle of San Juan de Ulúa and the City of Vera Cruz remained in royalist hands. What O'Donojú's reaction would have been had he become aware of the unfavorable attitude of the home government to the convention which he had felt constrained to negotiate with Iturbide may be imagined. It is possible that he might have become fully converted to the independent cause. On the other hand, if the Spanish government had agreed to accept the Treaty of Córdoba, New Spain would perhaps have remained for the time being attached to the motherland as a species of appanage.

It seems plain, however, that the acceptance of a Bourbon prince

[87] Gutiérrez del Mazo, *Aviso al público*, September 26, 1821.
[88] Valle, *Iturbide*, p. 71.
[89] December 15, 1821, p. 244.

as a ruler would not have pleased some Mexicans. Early in September, 1821, in an oration delivered in the church where the Hero of Independence had been baptized, Manuel de la Bárcena, the archdeacon of that cathedral, compared the liberated Mexicans to the Israelites after they had crossed the Red Sea. Divine Providence, he declared, had guided the Liberator of the Mexican nation. The finger of God had directed the revolutionary movement. "Religion, union, and independence," he exclaimed, "are the three celestial guarantees, the three indestructible columns which the artificer has laid so that upon them there may be built with solidity the national edifice which is to be maintained eternally!"[90]

Eloquent exhortations which praised the success of the long struggle for separation from Spain generally ignored the havoc which had been wrought. In an official report Secretary of Justice Domínguez sketched a gloomy picture of the social and economic effects of the ten years' war. Domínguez stated that every class in society had suffered losses. Business was paralyzed. Fountains of prosperity and riches had been drained completely. Many fields lay untilled. Livestock had vanished from the pastures. The country was threatened by a flood of lawsuits between debtors and creditors. Roads and bridges were in a dilapidated state.[91] Long before Iturbide met O'Donojú, the church establishment had fallen into decay. Some parishes were without priests; the holy sacraments were not everywhere regularly administered.[92] Three-fourths of the benefices, said Secretary Pablo de la Llave in 1823, had been ravished.[93] The treasury of the Viceroyalty, which the revolutionary leaders had inherited, was completely empty.[94] An English traveler, who visited Iturbide's native province three years after the triumph of the revolution, noticed that many haciendas still remained in a ruinous condition.[95] During the war a not inconsiderable part of the male population had been uprooted, crippled, or killed.

[90] *Oración gratulatoria a Dios que por la independencia mejicana dijó en la catedral de Valladolid de Michoacán . . . el día 6 de Septiembre del año de 1821,* p. 3.

[91] *Memoria presentada al soberano congreso mexicano por el secretario de estado y del despacho de justicia y negocios eclesiásticos,* 1822, pp. 4-5; Poinsett, *Notes on Mexico,* pp. 328-329.

[92] Hernández y Dávalos, *Coleccion de documentos para la historia de la guerra de independencia de Mexico de 1808 a 1821,* v. I, 1043.

[93] *Memoria que el secretario de estado y del despacho universal de justicia y negocios eclesiásticos presenta al soberano congreso constituyente sobre los ramos del ministerio de su cargo leido en la sesión de 8 de Noviembre de 1823,* pp. 17-18.

[94] Pérez Maldonado, *Memoria que el ministro de hacienda presenta al soberano congreso sobre el estado del erario,* 1822, p. 22.

[95] Hardy, *Travels in the Interior of Mexico in 1825, 1826, 1827, & 1828,* p. 44.

CHAPTER VII

New Issues

IT NOW BECAME the task of Iturbide to direct the new-born statesmen who undertook to establish an independent government. Though many persons viewed him as the Saviour of Mexico, few were qualified to advise him what steps to take. Among military leaders, General Pedro Negrete ventured his opinion. Even before the capital city fell into the hands of the revolutionists, he had written their leader a letter outlining a program. Denouncing the corruption which existed among public employees, he declared that the central government should be re-formed.

"According to the treaty which you have negotiated with Señor O'Donojú, we should expect that the national government of Mexico will soon be organized. I repeat to you in frankness and invariable friendship that in Mexico City or in some other place, we urgently need a government with national authority in order to establish a general congress and the liberty of the press. You, my friend, will be our Washington—greater than all the conquerors of the world. We need a government, I repeat, in order that it may aid us to arrange for taxes and to preserve order, for we run a great risk that misery and discontent may cause the formation of factions. We need a liberal government, . . . and with our invincible bayonets we shall secure the recognition of our independence from all the world."[1]

From Tacubaya on September 25 Melchor Álvarez, the head of the General Staff, issued orders for the entry into Mexico City of the victorious soldiers, who numbered some fifteen thousand.[2] The appointed day, September 27, was Iturbide's thirty-eighth birthday. Álvarez directed that the division of the army which was under the command of General Anastasio Bustamante should lead the van, while Filisola's troops were to leave their quarters in the capital in order to join the procession. The members of the military staff were to

[1] Negrete to Iturbide, September 17, 1821, in I. MSS, 11.
[2] Revilla, "Estudios históricos, 27 de Setiembre de 1821," El Museo Mexicano, II, 233. The Noticioso General, October 1, 1821, pp. 1-3, stated that the army numbered more than 14,000 private soldiers, 1,200 officers, and 80 commanders.

ride by the side of Iturbide, who had directed that, in spite of the lack of uniforms, the jubilant soldiers were to enter the city in the best possible order. They were to treat the inhabitants with due consideration, "thus furnishing proof of their discipline, subordination, and good conduct." A notice prepared by order of the Generalissimo expressed the hope that the people would maintain the same order as had been observed in all the other cities which had been occupied by the liberating army.[3]

The procession began to enter the capital about ten o'clock. At the head was the Commander in Chief, who was followed by his aides, his staff, and his retinue. Upon arriving at a triumphal arch which had been erected near the Franciscan monastery, he dismounted in order to receive the greetings of leading municipal magistrates. The senior alcalde, José Ormaechea, presented him with keys of gold upon a platter of silver, emblematic of the freedom of the city. With a few well-chosen words, Iturbide returned the keys and then remounted his horse. Rome, said the official gazette, had never beheld such a spectacle as the celebration which followed the entry of the victorious army into the former capital of the Aztec Empire.[4]

Iturbide found O'Donojú awaiting him. From the chief balcony of the palace of the viceroys, with the Spanish General by his side, the Hero of Independence then reviewed the largest army that had ever been seen in the City of Mexico. "Amidst the most lively and extraordinary demonstrations of joy," wrote an anonymous chronicler, "the First Chief was incessantly proclaimed by the people as their Liberator. Salvos of artillery, the general pealing of bells, and the immense number of rockets, as well as the flowers and the poems which were showered upon him from the balconies and the roofs of the houses, furnished a climax to the joy of that happy day."[5]

After the liberating army had marched past the palace, the soldiers went to their barracks. Accompanied by his retinue, Iturbide proceeded to the spacious cathedral. Clad in pontifical robes, Archbishop

[3] The quotation is from Alamán, *Historia de Mexico*, V, 753; copy, J. I. Negreyros to R. Gutiérrez del Mazo, September 26, 1821, Documentos históricos. Don Agustín Iturbide, 1821-1827, Genaro García Collection, in MSS, U.T. Library.

[4] *Gaceta imperial de México*, October 2, 1821, p. 3.

[5] "Descripción de la entrada del ejército trigarante en México," *Boletin del archivo general de la nacion*, vol. X, no. 3, pp. 483-486. See further Bustamante, *Cuadro historico de la revolucion mexicana*, V, 327-329. A Mexican writer asserted that on his way to the palace Iturbide tossed a plume from his sombrero to the balcony of his inamorata (Peza, "La bella 'Güera' Rodríguez," *Excelsior*, September 27, 1921). Bustamante asserted that O'Donojú entered the capital on September 26, where he was received joyfully as the Captain General.

Fonte escorted him to the altar. According to a journal designated the *Noticioso General*, which was published in Mexico City, he took the seat ordinarily reserved for the Viceroy. While musicians performed a *Te Deum*, he gave thanks to Almighty God for having favored the partisans of independence. The cabildo then served a banquet in the palace in honor of Iturbide, his chief officers, and other personages. One of the *regidores* recited an ode which contained these lines:

¡Vivan por don de celestial clemencia,
La *Religion*, la *Unión*, la *Independencia*![6]

Iturbide soon issued a manifesto to the people of Mexico. After stating that since he had proclaimed Mexican independence at Iguala, they had passed from slavery to liberty, he vaingloriously declared that he had reached the capital of an opulent empire without having left behind him "rivulets of blood, or desolated fields, or disconsolate widows, or unfortunate children. . . ." He added the following exhortation: "Now you have entered the world of freemen. . . . I urge you to forget the words of alarm, of foreboding, and of extermination and to mention only union and intimate friendship. If you feel that the service which I owed my country deserves a recompense, accord me only your submission to the laws, allow me to return to the bosom of my beloved country, and from time to time think of your friend Iturbide."[7] In sharp contrast with this obsequious profession of humility was the view expressed by one of his critics, namely, that only unforeseen circumstances had frustrated a plan to proclaim him the Emperor of Mexico at the time of his triumphal entry into the capital.[8]

Early on September 28 the personages who had been selected by Iturbide to serve on the Junta specified in the Plan of Iguala assembled in the palace. Those thirty-eight men, said Alamán, included the most notable persons in the capital city by virtue of their birth, the posts which they occupied, and the reputation which they enjoyed.[9] Among the members, who were all upper-class Mexicans, were the Liberator, the Captain General, and the bishop of Puebla.[10] They

[6] *Noticioso General*, October 1, 1821, pp. 1-3; Bustamante, *op. cit.*, V, 331.
[7] *El Primer jefe del exército imperial a los habitantes de México*, p. 1.
[8] Rocafuerte, *Bosquejo ligerísimo de la revolución de Mégico*, pp. 113-115. By September, 1821, Rocafuerte was in New York City. See his letter to Mier, July 21, 1821 (Correspondencia de Mier, 1819-1830, Genaro García Collection, in MSS, U.T.).
[9] Alamán, *Historia de Mexico*, V, 252; cf. Rocafuerte, *op. cit.*, pp. 111-112, who, mentioning the choice of the Junta by Iturbide said: "Esta Junta se componia de sus mas adictos aduladores, de los hombres mas ineptos, ó mas corrumpidos, mas ignorantes ó mas serviles; en fin, y de la gente mas odiada ó desconceptada de Mégico. . . ."
[10] Bustamante, *op. cit.*, V, 334-335.

soon asked Iturbide to become their President. Strange though it may appear, neither the partisans of the early movement for independence nor the advocates of a republican form of government were represented in that council.

The new chief magistrate soon displayed qualities of political leadership. Declaring that the day of liberty and glory for his native land had just dawned, in an address to the Junta, he undertook to outline its functions in the nebulous state:

"To name a regency which is to be entrusted with the executive authority, to determine the manner of convoking an assembly of deputies that is to enact the constituent laws of the Empire and to exercise the legislative power until a national Congress is installed. . . . Perhaps the time during which you remain in charge of affairs may not permit you to employ all the means necessary to secure the prosperity of the State, but you will omit nothing that will preserve order, stimulate public spirit, sweep away the abuses of arbitrary power, abolish the tortuous methods of despotism, and demonstrate in practice the undeniable advantages of a government which limits its activity to what is just."[11]

As in Chile and Peru, so also in Mexico, independence was formally declared by a group of personages. The "Act of Independence of the Mexican Empire," which was signed by both creole and Spanish members of the Junta on September 28, briefly declared that the Mexican nation was emerging from the oppression under which she had lived for three hundred years. After praising the achievements of the politico-military Hero, the Act stated that, having resumed the exercise of rights conceded to her by the Lord Almighty, New Spain solemnly declared through the Junta that she was "a sovereign nation, independent of Old Spain." Further, New Spain declared that in the future "she will maintain no other union than that of a close friendship" with Old Spain according to "the terms prescribed by the treaties which will establish friendly relations with other powers, exercising with respect to them whatever acts other sovereign nations are able to perform." Without sketching a frame of political organization, the Act announced that Mexico was about to organize her government according to the bases furnished by Iturbide in the Iguala Plan and the Treaty of Córdoba.[12] This Declaration of Independence of

---

[11] Bustamante, *Cuadro historico*, V, 332.

[12] The Act was published in the *Gaceta imperial de México*, October 16, 1821, pp. 53-55. A facsimile of the original Act is printed in Sierra, *México, su evolución social*, I, opposite p. 164; in the English edition of Sierra's work the facsimile is opposite p. 160. Banegas Galván, *Historia de Mexico*, II, 2, ascribes the authorship of the Act of Independence to Espinosa de los Monteros.

the Mexican Empire was not published until it had been approved by the Regency.

During the evening of the same day the Junta assembled again in order to choose those persons who were to act as regents. Instead of selecting three of its members as specified in the Treaty of Córdoba, it decided to appoint five. Besides the personages who had signed that convention, it named as regents the philosopher-priest Manuel de la Bárcena, Isidro Yáñez, who had served as a member of the audiencia of Mexico, and Manuel Velásquez de León, the one-time secretary of the Viceroyalty. As Iturbide was made the President of the Regency, the Junta selected the bishop of Puebla to succeed him as its presiding officer. It also made Iturbide the military and naval Commander in Chief of the new state.[13]

During its second session the Junta framed regulations which defined its functions. It declared that, until a congress was assembled, the Junta was to be the legislative authority as provided in the Spanish Constitution so far as that organic law was not repugnant to the Treaty of Córdoba. Legislative authority was to be exercised as provided in the treaty. Executive authority was to be the function of the Regency. A manuscript journal, which recorded its proceedings, shows that it generally approved the nominations to office submitted by its President as well as the appointments which he had made during the campaign of liberation.[14] Among the regulations which the Junta framed was a provision that the decrees and laws which it passed should begin in the following style: "The Regency of the Empire which is governing ad interim in the lack of an Emperor . . . has ordained and decreed the following. . . ."[15] When the President of the Regency attended the meetings of the Junta, he was to have the seat of honor. A sharp line was not drawn between the functions of the executive and the legislative departments.

At once Iturbide grasped the helm of the ship of state. Acting as a member of the Junta, on September 28 he addressed a letter to O'Donojú, "a member of the Supreme Governmental Junta of the Mexican Empire," not only to notify him that an independent government had been set up in accordance with the Plan of Iguala but also to state that the bonds which had united the Kingdom of New Spain with the Spanish nation had been untied. Further, the President of

[13] Bustamante, *op. cit.*, V, 334-335.

[14] Secretario de Guerra y Marina, libro 1º, f. 8, 9, 14v., 18, 27, 39, 52, in A.M.C., D/481.3/7807.

[15] *Reglamento para el gobierno interior de la soberana junta provisional gubernativa del Imperio Mexicano*, p. 23.

the Regency declared that by virtue of this action the functions of the Captain General and Superior Political Chief of New Spain had ceased. Iturbide added that, as O'Donojú had shown "moderation, justice, integrity, exactitude, and love for humanity," his memory would be revered throughout Mexico.[16] Sonnets printed in the city of Puebla lauded the achievements of the signatories of the Treaty of Córdoba.[17] The sovereignty which Spain had exercised over the Mexican Viceroyalty thus virtually came to an end on September 28, 1821.

Soon after reaching the capital city, the last Captain General of New Spain became ill. Although his name followed that of the bishop of Puebla among the signatories of the Act of Independence in a broadside issued by Gutiérrez del Mazo on October 13 and was likewise printed at the foot of that Act in the *Gaceta imperial de México* three days later, yet his signature did not actually appear beside the signatures of Iturbide and Pérez at the foot of the original Act.[18] Declaring that it was of the utmost importance to preserve the life of O'Donojú, with whom he had formed an intimate friendship, on October 1 Iturbide directed the official board of viceregal physicians to make a careful diagnosis of the case and to recommend curative measures.[19] Nevertheless, seven days later, the ailing Spaniard died. Though strange rumors were circulated concerning the cause of O'Donojú's death, yet it seems clear that he died of a pulmonary complaint.[20] Alamán stated that the disease was pleurisy. Judging that crucial political differences would soon have arisen between O'Donojú and the Liberator, the historian made this interpretative comment:

"Odious imputations have been vaguely cast upon Iturbide because of the death of O'Donojú; but they are absolutely without foundation. The illness from which he died was well known; and, besides having been attended in it by the physician who had accompanied him from Spain, by order of Iturbide the entire board of viceregal physicians was directed to visit the patient. There had not been time for dissensions to develop between Iturbide and O'Donojú—dissensions which in a short time would have broken out. The death of O'Donojú,

---

[16] Iturbide, *Correspondencia privada*, p. 204.

[17] *Elogio de los excmos. Señores D. Agustín de Iturbide y D. Juan O'Donojú, individuos de la regencia del nuevo Imperio Mejicano que en los siguientes sonetos hizó el editor de La Abeja Poblana. . . .*

[18] Sierra, *México: su evolución social*, I, 184.

[19] Iturbide to S. Presidte. de Tribunal del Proto Medicato, October 1, 1821, in A.M.C., D/481.3/1843.

[20] *Gaceta imperial de México*, October 11, 1821, p. 35; May 16, 1822, p. 288 and n.

happening when it did, doubtless freed him from grievous cares."[21] On October 10 his body was ceremoniously interred in a sepulcher in the chapel of the kings of the metropolitan cathedral. Among others, Vicente Guerrero expressed deep regret. He avowed that words were inadequate to voice his sorrow at the death of a man who had given such unequivocal proof of his love for Mexico.[22] Fernández de Lizardi mourned the passing of "a valiant general, a wise publicist, and, above all, an estimable man who was our friend. . . . In conjunction with the heroic Iturbide, he opposed the slavery of our country. To him, in large part, your fathers owe their liberty."[23] As a token of appreciation, the Junta granted a pension of twelve thousand pesos per annum to O'Donojú's widow so long as she might remain in Mexico.[24] An anonymous writer composed a poetic epitaph which lamented the death of a noble Spaniard who had helped to tranquilize "the Indian Empire."[25] As O'Donojú was proscribed by the government at Madrid, his widow remained in Mexico, where she died many years later, a victim of neglect and poverty.[26]

A fear that anarchy would soon afflict the country induced Fernández de Lizardi on September 29 to address a pamphlet to the President of the Regency in which he argued that that official should be acclaimed the supreme ruler. "The army and the people desire that you should become Emperor," said the pamphleteer. "I know well that Don Ferdinand VII cannot come to Mexico; for he would have to abdicate the throne of Spain in favor of one of the infantes, . . . I do not believe that the elevation of your Excellency to the Mexican throne would make the commanders of the imperial army jealous."[27]

[21] Historia, V, 277-278. Cf. the imputations of Mier made after Iturbide had abdicated as Emperor, Actas del congreso constituyente mexicano, II, 206. Bancroft (History of Mexico, IV, 737) agrees with Alamán. In an undated letter written to Iturbide months after O'Donojú's death asking for financial aid, Señora O'Donojú made no mention of dissension between him and her husband, "el mejor Europeo que pisó las costas de Nueva España" (I. MSS, 11).

[22] See Guerrero's letter of October 9, 1821, in the Noticioso General, October 12, 1821, p. 4.

[23] Pésame que el Pensador Mexicano da al excelentísimo Señor generalísimo de las armas de América, Don Agustín de Iturbide, pp. 6-7.

[24] Coleccion de ordenes y decretos de la soberano junta provisional gubernativa y soberanos congresos generales de la nacion mexicana, I, 16.

[25] J. M. V., Desahogo del sentimiento de un Americano en la sensible muerte del excmo. Sr. D. Juan de O'Donojú.

[26] The decree of proscription dated May 1, 1824, was printed in the Suplemento á la Gaceta de Madrid, May 20, 1824; Bustamante, Apuntes para la historia del gobierno del general D. Antonio López de Santa-Anna, p. 76.

[27] El Pensador Mexicano al excmo. Señor general del ejército imperial americano, D. Agustín de Iturbide, pp. 4-6.

Shortly after victorious soldiers were quartered in the capital, Iturbide directed that the official gazette should henceforth be published by Alejandro Valdés.[28] The first number of that journal under the new regime appeared on October 2, 1821. It bore the title *Gaceta imperial de México*. In the second issue the statement was made that it would be published regularly by the imperial press on Tuesdays, Thursdays, and Saturdays.[29] According to custom, it continued to serve as the organ of the Mexican government. Stating that all authority in Mexico now emanated from the Empire, on October 5 the Junta decreed that governmental officials who were exercising authority in accordance with the Iguala Plan and the Treaty of Córdoba were confirmed in their positions.[30]

The Junta soon ordered that all the inhabitants of the Empire should take an oath to support its independence.[31] Typical perhaps of a growing national sentiment was the minting at the capital city of a medal to commemorate the last Mexican Declaration of Independence. The medal bore upon one side an inscription which gave the date, October 27, 1821, when independence was to be solemnly proclaimed in Mexico City. On the other side, inspired perhaps by a legend of the Nahuas, was a representation of an eagle adorned with a crown, with a serpent in its beak, perched upon a nopal which was growing upon a rock in a lake.[32] In a broadside issued early in 1821 the Regency announced that this device, with the omission of the serpent, should replace the Spanish coat of arms throughout the Empire. Perhaps it was in anticipation of the adoption of a monarchical form of government that the legislative authority had stipulated that the eagle should be adorned with an "imperial crown." Further, the Junta had decided that both the national flag and the military standard should be perpetually a tricolor which was to bear in vertical stripes the colors green, white, and red, the very colors which, according to tradition, had been displayed on the banner of the patriot army. On the white stripe there was to be depicted a crowned eagle.[33]

Disquieting rumors which reached Iturbide incited him to publish

[28] C. de la Torre to the Regency, October 3, 1821, in A.G.N., Justicia, legajo 21.
[29] *Gaceta imperial de México*, October 4, 1821, p. 16.
[30] *Noticioso General*, October 12, 1821, pp. 1-2.
[31] *Gaceta imperial de México*, October 27, 1821, pp. 101-104.
[32] Betts, *Mexican Imperial Coinage*, p. 6.
[33] A broadside of Gutiérrez del Mazo dated January 21, 1822, quotes a decree of the Junta dated January 16, 1822, in part as follows: "Que las armas del Imperio para toda clase de sellos sea solamente el nopal nacida de una peña que sale de la laguna y sobre el parado en el pie izquierdo una aguila con corona imperial." See further Iguíniz, *El Escudo de armas nacionales*, pp. 24-27.

a justificatory manifesto which furnished an inkling of his political thought. Replying to certain critics who had argued that the Mexicans were not bound by the Plan of Iguala because the people had not sanctioned it, he reasoned that he had acted in accordance with the supposed desire of the people. He asserted that the nation had ratified "what was done in her name and by her representatives at Iguala and Córdoba." He disclaimed aiming at any other glory than that of securing the liberty of his country. Furnishing perhaps a clue to his inmost thoughts, he added that "Numa did not cease to respond to the ambassadors of Rome who offered him the crown by saying that 'if in my person there are found certain talents, they will be exactly those which should make me avoid the throne, namely the love of respose and of a retired life.' "[34]

Such statements concerning his retirement from public service, which Iturbide reiterated in different words during his public career, should not be entirely discredited. For there is no doubt that rural life and the management of his estates attracted him strongly. As time went on, however, he was drawn more and more to a public career. In fact, shortly after his ceremonious entry into Mexico City, he made a careful study of the civil, commercial, and ecclesiastical institutions existing in the Empire.[35] By November 8, 1821, he had formed a revealing plan for the convocation of Congress. His notion was that its members, whom he styled deputies, should be selected to represent certain more or less definite classes of society. Subject to modification by the Junta, the ratio which he proposed was that public officials should have twenty-four seats; ecclesiastics and littérateurs should have eighteen apiece; laborers, miners, artisans, and merchants should each have ten seats; the army, the navy, and the rest of the people should each have nine; and the class of persons bearing titles of nobility should be allotted three seats.[36] Iturbide evidently wished to ensure the influence of the clergy and the bureaucracy.

For a time, however, certain features of the administrative system were not radically changed. Intendants still acted as financial agents of the government. The audiencia located in the capital city continued to function as a high judicial tribunal. But shortly after Iturbide became the President of the Regency, he issued an order which provided

[34] *Breve manifiesto del excmo. Sr. D. Agustín de Iturbide*, pp. 2-4.

[35] Escrito de Iturbide sobre la "Audiencia," "Diputación Provincial," "Ayuntamiento," "Arzobispo," "Cabildo Ecco," "Consulado y Minería," in I. MSS, 13.

[36] Iturbide, *Pensamiento que en grande ha propuesto el que subscribe como un particular para la pronta convocatoría de las proximas córtes.*

that the existing territorial divisions should be grouped into five districts, each of which was to be in charge of a military officer who was to be designated Captain General. The largest of these districts included both the Interior Provinces of the East and of the West. In consequence the jurisdiction of the Captain General of those united districts not only comprised the northern section of present Mexico but also portions of the southwestern part of the present United States.[37] Evidently both Upper and Lower California were to continue to occupy a unique place in the administrative system.

The Regency decided on October 4 that four executive departments should be established: the Treasury, War and the Navy, Interior and Exterior Relations, Justice and Ecclesiastical Affairs. A former fiscal agent named Rafael Pérez Maldonado was soon appointed the Secretary of the Treasury; Antonio de Medina, who had some knowledge of naval affairs, was made the Secretary of War and the Navy; Iturbide's one-time secretary, José Domínguez, was placed at the head of the department of Justice and Ecclesiastical Affairs; and José Manuel de Herrera became the Secretary of Relations. To Herrera, who had served as a foreign agent for early Mexican insurgents, there fell the task of corresponding with officials in outlying sections of the Empire and also of establishing relations with foreign states.[38]

At the instance of its President, on October 12 the Regency decreed that certain officers who had played influential roles in the struggle for independence should be signally recognized. Among other promotions which were accordingly made, Pedro Negrete was appointed Lieutenant General; Anastasio Bustamante, Luis Quintanar, and Vicente Guerrero were each accorded the title of Marshal. In addition, Guerrero was made the Captain General of the district of the south.[39] On the same day the Junta provided that the Commander in Chief by land and sea should be granted a salary of 120,000 pesos per annum beginning February 24, 1821.[40] In a long letter to the Regency, however, Iturbide at once declared that his sacrifices for the liberty of Mexico had been amply compensated by the happy conclusion of the campaign for liberation. He refused the stipend allowed him for the period extending from February 24 to September 29, 1821, when he had not held an appointment from the Mexican government. He wished that this sum, which amounted to 71,000 pesos, should be used for the benefit of the army.[41]

---

[37] Gaceta imperial de México, October 23, 1821, pp. 89-90.
[38] Gaceta imperial extraordinaria de México, October 5, 1821, p. 17.
[39] Gaceta imperial de México, October 25, 1821, p. 96.
[40] Ibid., October 18, 1821, p. 74.
[41] October 12, 1821, quoted by Andrade in a circular, November 8, 1821, pp. 2-3.

Though many towns and cities had proclaimed their intention to support the new government, and though the Junta and the Regency had been installed in Mexico City, a delay took place before imperial dignitaries took an oath to maintain independence. In accordance with a decision of the Junta and the Regency, on October 13 Gutiérrez del Mazo, the political chief of the capital, ordered that preparation should be made for the solemn proclamation of independence there.[42] Iturbide appointed a commission to censor the theatrical pieces proposed for that occasion.[43] On October 27 public buildings and private residences were brightly decorated. Members of the cabildo and of certain corporations took oath to support the Plan of Iguala and the Córdoba Treaty. Bells were rung in the cathedral towers. A manifesto was published announcing that a general pardon had been granted. Around the massive, bronze, equestrian statue of Charles IV in the Plaza de Armas, allegorical statues were displayed. Among these was that of an eagle perched upon a nopal plant, a representation which symbolized the liberty of the nation. Another figure represented a throne near which there were displayed a scepter and an imperial crown. One of the rubrics near the pedestal of the throne was this:

> Al solio augusto asciende,
> Que ya de nadie tu corona pende.[44]

By the adaptation of a colonial practice, during the afternoon the *Paseo del pendón imperial*, a procession which bore aloft the imperial banner, passed through important streets of the capital. When the parade returned to the central plaza, the first alcalde announced in a loud voice that the city had sworn to support the independence of the Mexican Empire according to the bases proclaimed at Iguala and Córdoba.[45] The national spirit was stimulated when news reached the capital city that on October 27 the port of Vera Cruz had fallen into the hands of the patriots. On the same day an edict of the Regency was issued which announced that a writer who attacked any one of the Three Guarantees would be considered guilty of *lesa nación*.[46]

By the middle of November Iturbide was convinced that the Plan of Iguala was being accepted throughout Mexico. In a private letter

---

[42] *Gaceta imperial de México*, October 27, 1821, pp. 101-104.

[43] Iturbide to A. Quintana, October 20, 1821, Miscelanea de documentos relativos al E. S. D. Agustín de Iturbide, no. 10, in MSS, B.N.M.

[44] *Gaceta imperial de México*, October 30, 1821, p. 111.

[45] *Ibid.*, p. 116.

[46] *Ibid.*, November 3, 1821, pp. 133-134.

to a friend named José Trespalacios he expressed the following sentiments: "It is my duty to make certain that all those persons who are
working for the liberty of the country should learn that fortunately
our independence from Spain has been irrevocably declared and that
never again shall we agree to be treated as colonists."[47] On the very
day that its President wrote this letter, the Regency directed that a
decree of the Junta should be published which provided not only that
he should be considered the Commander in Chief of the armed forces
by land and sea, but also that he should have the title of *Alteza*, a
title which was strange to Mexican ears.[48] What wonder that Iturbide
was no longer willing to contemplate his native land merely as a
Spanish appanage! Whatever view he may have expressed in public
at this time concerning the nominal relation that should exist between
Spain and the Mexican Empire, it seems clear that in his heart he felt
that his compatriots should never again bow their necks to the Spanish
yoke.

To celebrate the anniversary of his departure from the capital to
begin the campaign for independence, on November 16, on the occasion of the feast of the Immaculate Conception of the Virgin Mary,
a magnificent festival was held in the church of the Franciscan monastery in that city. The opportunity was employed by the Generalissimo to give thanks to the Lord Almighty for the success which by
his hand had been accorded to the enterprise of liberating the Mexican
Empire. The beautiful temple was adorned with many wax candles
in silver chandeliers. The flag of the Three Guarantees decorated the
altar of Saint Francis. A stately procession composed of the Regency,
the chief corporations of the capital, and the leading local and provincial officials was received in the patio of the chapel by Franciscan
friars. An account of the ceremony printed in the *Gaceta imperial de
México* stated that at the entrance of the temple a friar offered holy
water to the Regents who received it under the pallium according to
the Roman ritual. After they were seated, the monastic choir and
the choir of the cathedral chanted a *Te Deum*.

"When the function was over," so ran the report in the official
journal, "the Regency returned to the imperial palace amidst the
acclamations of the people whose fervor was increased at the sight of
their Liberator." The report concluded with these words: "This is a
positive demonstration that the Mexican people, rightly appreciative

---

[47] Copy, November 14, 1821, Documentos relativos al Imperio de Iturbide, 1821-
1824, f. 31, Genaro García Collection, in MSS, U.T. Library.
[48] *Gaceta imperial de México*, November 27, 1821, pp. 210-213.

of the merit and the virtues of the Liberator of the country, know how to respect religious ceremonies and how to manifest their pleasure in moderation."[49] The *Gazette* declared that the elaborate function was at the expense of the President of the Regency. An item amounting to 1900 pesos for the outlay was preserved in his accounts.[50] This ceremony shows how the paraphernalia of the Roman Catholic Church were employed to cast luster upon the imperial regime.

Unwilling to remain in Mexico under the new system, an exodus of prominent Spanish officeholders soon took place.[51] Among them was Miguel Bataller, who refused to remain, said Alamán, although Iturbide declared that he would answer for the safety of that Spaniard with his own head.[52] Because of their inexperience in politics, few Mexican leaders realized that many other delicate problems confronted the imperial government. Perhaps the most discerning among those who foresaw threatening evils was General Negrete. On December 3, 1821, he again gave voice to his apprehensions in a letter to Iturbide which contained passages that showed an insight into Mexican society.

"It is essential that the people should become free, but it is necessary to begin by explaining to them what liberty means. Otherwise, they would inevitably abuse their freedom and would be disgraced. It is necessary to make them landed proprietors, because neither society nor the people who compose it will ordinarily be respected without this; and, because of necessity, when men do not own property, they become turbulent. . . . It is necessary to allot the public lands and the large haciendas as well as the rural properties which are in our hands. In this matter I am not of opinion that we should take property from the friars or from the religious foundations. . . . It is necessary to teach the people subordination, for then they will receive kindly the new institutions which are so important to them and because, where that spirit is lacking, there is no real society. . . . It is necessary to make the people religious, for unfortunately they are simply idolatrous or superstitious; but this change is impossible without the reform of the ecclesiastical establishment, especially while institutions of public instruction do not exist. . . ."[53]

[49] *Ibid.*, November 17, 1821, pp. 180-181.

[50] E. M. Aromír y Bustamante, Razón de los gastos erogados en la solemne fiesta que el 16 del presente mes mando celebrar S.A.S. el Señor Generalísimo de mar y tierra en este Imperio Mexicano, Dn. Agustín de Iturbide, November 22, 1821, in I. MSS, 23.

[51] A list of persons who had asked for passports to leave Mexico is found in the *Gaceta imperial de México*, November 27, 1821, pp. 213-215.

[52] Alamán, *Historia*, V, 282-283.

[53] Castillo Negrete, *Mexico en el siglo xix*, XV, 154-158.

As a check to opponents of the new regime, Iturbide undertook to reform the army. Near the end of 1821 he ordered that the infantry should be reorganized into eight regiments and that the cavalry should be grouped into ten regiments.[54] Many soldiers were rewarded by promotions. Former captains soon appeared attired in the uniform of colonels. The number of officers was greatly increased.[55] A Mexican historian has calculated that at a review of the soldiers stationed in the capital city in December, 1821, the ratio was about one officer or musician for every two privates.[56] The Commander in Chief's purse was available to impecunious officers. Among his papers there is found a memorandum which records that about this time he advanced to Marshal Guerrero, presumably at the latter's request, money and specie valued at some 27,000 pesos.[57] Iturbide's interest in agriculture was indicated by his recommendation to the Junta in February, 1822, that a society should be founded to promote the economic development of the country.[58]

Months passed before the aegis of the new Empire was extended over the northern part of the former Viceroyalty. The chief leader of the insurgent movement in that vast region was General Negrete, who was styled the commander of the Reserve Army of the Three Guarantees. At his instance, in the city of Chihuahua on August 26, 1821, Alejo García Conde, the commander of the Interior Provinces of the West, took an oath to support the independence of Mexico. Early in the following month Negrete captured Durango, the capital of those provinces.[59] In a letter addressed to Iturbide, the cabildo of that city declared that the independence of the northwestern provinces of Mexico was thus assured.[60] When news of independence came to settlements in Texas, acting as representatives of the Mexican Empire, agents of the cabildo of San Antonio de Béxar treated for peace with chiefs of the Comanche Indians. After reports of events at Durango reached Santa Fé, the capital of New Mexico, on January 6, 1822, the governor and the populace celebrated the establishment of independence. Among the congratulatory addresses which showered

[54] Ramírez y Sesma, *Coleccion de decretos, ordenes y circulares expedidas por los gobiernos nacionales,* pp. 1-4.
[55] *Gaceta imperial de México,* December 13, 1821, pp. 300-304; Alamán, *Historia,* V, 344, 767-771.
[56] Olavarría y Ferrari, *México independiente,* p. 43.
[57] Partidas qe. ha. recibido Guerrero, annexed to a letter of Guerrero to Iturbide dated November 2, 1821, which solicited aid, in I. MSS, 13.
[58] *Estatutos para la sociedad económica mexicana de amigos del pais,* p. 3.
[59] Alejo García Conde to Iturbide, September 18, 1821, in A.M.C., D/481.3/204.
[60] *Gaceta imperial de México,* November 29, 1821, pp. 249-251.

Iturbide was one from that capital which pledged its fidelity to union, independence, and Roman Catholicism.[61]

Some inhabitants of Upper and Lower California, however, were loath to relinquish their allegiance to Spain. Hence on February 8, 1822, the President of the Regency ordered that a detachment of the army should be sent to occupy that region, to administer the oath of independence, and to unfurl the flag of the Empire.[62] Before the imperial soldiers started on the expedition, a report reached the Regency that a courier bearing dispatches to the governors of the Californias had been ejected from a Franciscan mission in that region as though he lay under an interdict.[63]

Shortly afterward Iturbide wrote instructions for Agustín Fernández de San Vicente, who was to proceed to Upper California to gather information.[64] Before that commissioner arrived there, however, Governor Pablo Sola had convoked at Monterey on April 9 a meeting which included ecclesiastics, military officers, and the commanders of the presidios of Santa Barbara and San Francisco. The assembly decided to recognize the authority of the junta which had been installed in Mexico City. It declared that Upper California was dependent upon the Mexican Empire and that it was independent of any foreign state. Two days later the members of the convocation, the soldiers of the garrison, and the people of the vicinity took an oath of obedience to the new regime. The secretary of the presidio of Monterey reported that the ceremony was concluded by music, illuminations, and salvos of musketry and cannon.[65]

Iturbide's revolution had also affected regions lying south of the capital city. On September 8, 1821, a junta in the district of Chiapas, which belonged to the Captaincy General of Central America, took an oath to support the Plan of Iguala.[66] Upon being informed by the governor of Tabasco that his province had taken similar action, on September 15, under the direction of the governor of Yucatan, a meeting was held at Mérida attended by military officers, the intendant, and members of the cabildo. That junta announced that the province of Yucatan was independent of Spain and that this step was demanded by justice, by necessity, and by the desire of the inhabitants.

---

[61] *Ibid.*, December 4, 1821, pp. 268-270; March 23 and 26, 1822, pp. 85-93.
[62] Richman, *California under Spain and Mexico*, p. 231.
[63] Fermin de Tarbe to Iturbide, February 6, 1822, in A.G.N., Californias, vol. 45.
[64] Instructions to San Vicente, April 1, 1822, in A.G.N., Provincias Internas, vol. 23.
[65] *Gaceta del gobierno imperial de México*, August 3, 1822, pp. 585-587.
[66] *Gaceta imperial de México*, October 4, 1821, pp. 10-12.

It further declared that the announcement was made in the supposition that the system of independence was not inconsistent with civil liberty.[67]

Indeed partly because of the wide acceptance of the Iguala Plan, it seemed as though the leaders of the new Empire were being lured into a career of expansion beyond the boundaries of the former Viceroyalty.

[67] Ancona, *Historia de Yucatán*, III, 496-498; Banegas Galván, *Historia de Mexico*, II, 111-113.

CHAPTER VIII

Policies

WITH REGARD to the five provinces of Central America, Iturbide took the initiative. On October 19, 1821, he addressed a letter to Gabino Gainza, who was the Captain General of that region, to express the opinion that Central America was not able to govern itself, that it might become an object of foreign ambition, and that it should unite with his country to form an Empire in accordance with the Iguala Plan and the Treaty of Córdoba. Iturbide added that a large army would soon march to protect that Captaincy General.[1]

In fact the Mexican movement for independence had already influenced Central America. Writing to Iturbide from Guatemala in November, 1821, leading citizens declared:

"The proclamation of independence which your Excellency made at Iguala did not discourage discontented persons. The government tried to increase their confidence in itself by issuing a proclamation which treated the person of your Excellency with disdain and by spreading reports which were contrary to the accounts that reached us about your glorious achievements. This progress rejoiced the hearts of those who favored independence. Our papers spread the news in Central America with such happy results that by the thirtieth of the next month not a single drop of blood had been shed in support of our independence. On September 15 the patriots triumphed."[2]

A junta summoned by the Captain General assembled on that day in the governmental palace of Guatemala City. It declared in favor of independence from Spain and the convocation of a Central American congress, but allowed Gainza to remain at the head of the government.[3] In Comayagua, the capital of the province of Honduras, on September 28 a junta proclaimed that that province was independent

---

[1] Marure, *Bosquejo historico de las revoluciones de Centro-America*, I, 35.

[2] P. Molino and Others to Iturbide, November 3, 1821, Hernández y Dávalos Collection, 14-3-1450, in MSS, U.T.

[3] Valle, *Valle, prólogo y selección*, pp. 1-6.

of the motherland.[4] During the same month a similar step was taken in the capital of the province of Nicaragua. Early in 1822 the province of Salvador took action which not only favored independence from Spain but also union with the Mexican Empire.[5]

As Count Cadena, who had been directed to march to Chiapas, could not proceed on that mission, on December 27 Iturbide ordered General Vicente Filisola to take charge of a military expedition that was to protect those Central American provinces which had acted in favor of independence from Spain.[6] Iturbide wrote to Gainza on December 28:

"I have just learned that the Republican party, which is active in Guatemala City, has finally broken through the dykes of moderation and justice. It has thus started hostilities against those peoples who, having declared their adhesion to the Mexican Empire, do not wish to be independent except under the plan which I proclaimed in Iguala and in harmony with the treaty that I later negotiated in Córdoba. Never did I believe that democratic fervor would lead to such a scandalous outbreak in which, disregarding the rights of humanity and deaf to the voice of reason, attention would be paid merely to the tumultuous demands of passion so as to dissolve the bonds of society and to destroy order. With much regret I have seen renewed in two expeditions which have marched against Gracías and Tegucigalpa the tragic scenes that inundated Spanish America with blood. . . . I would betray my trust, if, viewing with indifference these events, I did not take the means in my power to protect the provinces which, detaching themselves from the system adopted in Tegucigalpa, have been admitted as integral parts of this Empire."[7]

Imperial soldiers who had been sent to the province of Guatemala, added Iturbide, would not appear anywhere in the odious role of conquistadors. Assuming that this province desired a republican form of government, he declared that it should not be of such a character as to disturb other Central American provinces which preferred a monarchical system. There is no doubt that he had other objects in mind than the liberation of Middle America from Spanish

[4] C. Bosque to Iturbide, February 19, 1822, in A.G.N., Historia, Guatemala, vol. 268.

[5] Marure, *op. cit.*, I, 36-39.

[6] Filisola, *La Cooperación de México en la independencia de Centro América*, II, 107-108.

[7] M. Terán, Copia de las instrucciones formadas por órden del serenísimo Señor Dn. Agustín Iturbide, Generalísimo y Almirante del Imperio Mejicano, para el Señor brigadier D. Vicente Filisola, Gefe de la expedición auxiliar del Reyno de Guatemala, in A.G.N., Historia, Guatemala, vol. 268.

domination. Even before he sent Filisola to Central America, he had addressed a significant letter to Fray Ramón Casus y Torres, the Archbishop of Guatemala. After a survey of the movement for Mexican independence, he mentioned "the impartiality, the justice, and the political talents" of O'Donojú. Expressing the opinion that the example of Mexico should have an influence upon the fate of other Spanish possessions in America, he directed attention to the West Indies.

"The island of Cuba, by virtue of its interesting position for European commerce and the character of its population," he reasoned, "is much in danger of becoming a prey to the maritime ambition of the English of the Eastern or of the Western Hemisphere, or of being disrupted by internecine struggles which nowhere in America could be more disastrous or more fatal. Mexico cannot be indifferent to either of those contingencies. . . . She believes that she is obliged to offer to the Cubans an intimate union and an alliance for the common defence."[8] In thus realizing the importance of Cuba to American states, Iturbide anticipated the views of leading publicists of both the New World and the Old.

After several cabildos of Central America had voted in favor of union with Mexico, Gainza notified Iturbide that on January 2 a provisional junta had decided that the Captaincy General should be included in the new Empire.[9] Three days later the Captain General issued a manifesto which stated that annexation to Mexico had just taken place.[10] On January 9 he circulated a proclamation which announced that anyone who might criticize or censure either orally or in writing the decision in favor of the union of Central America with Mexico should be punished for sedition. All good citizens were asked to report to the authorities any person who was suspected of conspiring against that union. This achievement was to be signalized by a celebration lasting three days.[11] Writing to Iturbide on January 11 the Marquis of Arcinena stated that Guatemala City had been illuminated and that salvos of artillery had been fired there in honor of annexation to Mexico.[12] A month later the Mexican Junta and the President of the Regency undertook to make provision for a representation of the Guatemalan provinces at the inauguration of the Mexican Congress.[13]

[8] October 10, 1821, Expedición de Filisola á Guatemala, in A.G.N., 1821-1822.
[9] Gaceta imperial de México, January 23, 1822, pp. 446-447.
[10] Valle, La Anexión de Centro América á México, II, 27-31.
[11] Gaceta imperial de México, February 26, 1822, pp. 557-559.
[12] In A.G.N., Historia, Guatemala, vol. 269.   [13] Valle, op. cit., II, 62-63, 78.

Reports of the transformation which had taken place in Mexico eventually reached her northern frontier. On August 6, 1821, General Gaspar López, who was the temporary commander of the Interior Provinces of the East, issued a circular to officers and cabildos within his jurisdiction urging them to make the neighboring warlike tribes acquainted with the peaceful changes which had taken place in Mexico.[14] Ten days later, at Monterrey, Nuevo León, a treaty was signed between that General and a Comanche chief by which the latter solemnly recognized the independence of the Mexican Empire. Furthermore, this chief promised that he would not furnish succor to any individual, corporation, or foreign power that might entertain designs upon it.[15] On behalf of the President of the Regency, on November 3, López issued a proclamation to Indians on the frontier informing them that Iturbide had given liberty to a vast Empire and exhorting them to cease their wars upon its inhabitants.[16]

Foreigners had meanwhile been developing schemes to plant settlements in Mexico. In January, 1821, General Joaquín de Arredondo had granted to an enterprising American named Moses Austin permission to introduce three hundred families of his countrymen into Texas.[17] After that empresario's death, his son Stephen took up the task. Because of the establishment of the independent regime in Mexico, the younger Austin had to apply to it for a confirmation of the land grant made to his father.[18] Before he reached Mexico City, in addition to European applicants for lands, Captain José M. Piedad y López had addressed a plea to Iturbide urging the new regime to establish a presidio in the region where the Colorado River emptied into the Gulf of California. The captain felt that this would check encroachments by both Americans and Russians.[19] Though certain Mexican commissions undertook to consider the problem of colonization, no decision was reached before Congress assembled.

Among the delicate problems which confronted the national government was the policy to be adopted toward the Roman Catholic Church. Clauses in the Plan of Iguala and the Córdoba Treaty which pledged that the Church would be assured the enjoyment of its time-honored privileges had been viewed with favor by devout

[14] *Gaceta imperial de México*, December 4, 1821, p. 266.
[15] *Diario Político Militar Mejicano*, September 13 and 14, 1821, in García, *Documentos historicos mexicanos*, vol. IV.
[16] *Gaceta imperial de México*, December 11, 1821, p. 295.
[17] Gammel, *The Laws of Texas*, I, 25-27.
[18] Barker, *The Austin Papers*, part I, pp. 518-519.
[19] October 26, 1821, in I. MSS, 13.

laymen and ecclesiastical dignitaries. In certain regions churchmen had not only allowed military officers to collect tithes but had also contributed to the support of the revolutionary army.[20] On October 19, 1821, Archbishop Fonte advised the clergy of his diocese to obey the civil authorities of the Empire.[21] A month later the Regency decided that religious houses would be allowed to continue the initiation of novices.[22] Among the constitutional principles soon announced by it as fundamental was one mentioned by Gutiérrez del Mazo in a broadside, namely, that only the Roman Catholic religion was to be tolerated.[23]

Vacancies which had from time to time occurred in the ecclesiastical hierarchy during the revolution had involved issues related to the exercise of the *Patronato Real*. As nominations customarily made by the Spanish King to ecclesiastical vacancies had been seriously interrupted at times or entirely prevented by the prolonged insurrection, and as cathedral and other ecclesiastical positions had meantime fallen vacant, the imperial government was disposed to fill such vacancies. In October, 1821, Iturbide had raised the question of the exercise by the imperial government of the right to nominate candidates to ecclesiastical positions. He asked the Archbishop of Mexico to express his opinion concerning the method by which provision might be made for appointments to cathedral offices until an agreement could be reached with the Holy See concerning this patronage.[24] During the following month, in view of the merits of a curate named José Guridi y Alcocer, who had supported the cause of independence, the Regency saw fit to approve his nomination by King Ferdinand VII to a position as canon in the metropolitan cathedral.[25]

On November 24, 1821, after conferring with representatives of Mexican bishops who had met in the capital, Archbishop Fonte expressed the opinion that, as the Mexican Empire had declared its independence, the right of Spain to nominate candidates for ecclesiastical positions in the former Viceroyalty had terminated. He stated that his advisers had maintained that this right had been conceded by the Papacy to the monarchs of Castile and León, and hence that, if

[20] Cuevas, *Historia de la iglesia en Mexico*, V, 121, discusses the complicated situation.

[21] Vera, *Colección de documentos ecclesiasticos de Mexico*, II, 106.

[22] J. Domínguez to A. Medina, November 19, 1821, in A.M.C., D/481.3/4338.

[23] December 20, 1821.

[24] *Coleccion ecclesiastica mejicana*, I, 15. By 1826 six of the nine bishoprics of Mexico were vacant (Leturia, *La Acción diplomática de Bolívar ante Pío VII*, p. 113 n.).

[25] *Gaceta imperial de México*, November 29, 1821, p. 249; Alamán, *Historia de Mexico*, V, 354 n. 15, mentions two other such appointments.

the new government of Mexico desired to exercise this privilege, it would have to secure an identical concession from the Papacy. The Archbishop's clerical advisers had reasoned that, in the meantime, according to canon law, the right of making ecclesiastical appointments in each diocese belonged, not to the imperial government, but to the respective bishop.[26]

The Regency thereupon invited the ecclesiastical hierarchy to select suitable persons to discuss the thorny question of the ecclesiastical patronage until such a time as "circumstances would permit the establishment of relations with the Holy See."[27] Archbishop Fonte then asked the diocesan administrators to select clerics to represent them in a conference.[28] On March 11, 1822, a council of ecclesiastics formally decided that, as the independence of the Mexican Empire had been sworn to, the exercise of the right of appointment to vacancies in Mexican churches which had been conceded by the Vatican to the monarchs of Spain had ceased.[29]

Meantime the President of the Regency had actually undertaken to appoint ecclesiastics to vacant military chaplaincies, a species of office distinct from appointments in civil life. At a meeting of civil and ecclesiastical officials which subsequently discussed the relations between Church and State, José Domínguez, the Secretary of Justice and Ecclesiastical Affairs, declined to accept the view that the right of ecclesiastical patronage in Mexico had lapsed. On April 17, 1822, he reasoned that the decision of the ecclesiastical council was not just.

"For it does not accord with the fundamental principle that governed the *Patronato Real* which the monarchs of Castile exercised in this territory in the precise, unique, and indispensable belief that they were its sovereigns. By virtue of this, it neither can nor should be doubted that, because of the complete independence of the Mexican nation, sovereignty now resides in her and in her representative government which has been legitimately installed. In consequence that government should be invested with all the rights and prerogatives essentially accessory to and inseparable from sovereignty such as is the patronage; that is, in the manner of exercising it on the same

[26] *Coleccion ecclesiastica mejicana*, I, 16-17.

[27] Domínguez, *Memoria presentada al soberano congreso mexicano por el secretario de estado y del despacho de justicia y negocios ecclesiásticos*, 1822, p. 12.

[28] *Dictamen de la comisión de patronato leido en sesión pública del soberano congreso mexicano*, p. 3.

[29] *Ibid.*, pp. 15-20. Cf. Cuevas, *op. cit.*, V, 119.

terms and by the same title as those employed by the monarchs of Castile."[30]

An influential official of the independent regime thus maintained that the right of exercising in Mexico the same authority with respect to ecclesiastical appointments as that which had been exercised by the monarchs of Spain had automatically passed to the new government. In 1823 and 1824 governmental commissions appointed to consider the *Patronato Real* in Mexico took the same view. As the years passed, without any necessary connection with the views thus early set forth by Mexico, other independent governments of Spanish America undertook to uphold a similar doctrine. The stage was thus set for struggles between Church and State.

Because of the depleted condition of the viceregal treasury, serious problems arose concerning the financiering of the Empire. Early in October the Junta approved the reduction of the *alcabala* which had been announced by Iturbide at Querétaro.[31] A special committee of the treasury recommended that the Manila merchants whose convoy of specie had been seized by his soldiers should be at once repaid by hypothecating certain funds due to the government from four cathedrals.[32] On November 22 the Junta decreed that, pending the choice of an Emperor or action by Congress, the coins minted in Mexico should bear the same image and superscription as in 1820.[33] About three weeks later it approved a schedule of the duties which were to be levied on imports and exports passing through seaports of Mexico.[34] Near the end of 1821 Iturbide circulated a proclamation soliciting voluntary subscriptions in order that the nakedness of the soldiers might be clothed.[35] To relieve the financial stringency, early the next year the Junta authorized him to float a loan of 1,500,000 pesos.[36]

On January 4 Iturbide submitted a report to that body complaining that his pleas in behalf of the pressing financial needs of the army, which at that time, including the militia, numbered some 68,000 men,[37]

[30] *Dictamen de la comisión de patronato leido en sesión pública del soberano congreso mexicano*, p. 5. In an unsigned and undated manuscript entitled "Informe á la regencia" is the following passage: "Debe por tanto mantenerse el ejercicio del Patronato en el gobierno actual esperando solo de la Silla Apostólica la declaración de el igual á que obtuvieron los Reyes de Castilla y quizas con mas ampliación como exigen las circunstancias del día y las luces del siglo" (I. MSS, 14).

[31] *Gaceta imperial de México*, October 13, 1821, p. 45.

[32] *Coleccion de ordenes y decretos*, I, 77-78.

[33] *Ibid.*, I, 37.   [34] *Ibid.*, pp. 48-56.

[35] F. Melgar to certain alcaldes, December 30, 1821, in A.N.M., 67.

[36] *Coleccion de ordenes y decretos*, I, 84-85.

[37] Medina, *Memoria presentada al soberano congreso mexicano por el secretario de estado y del despacho de la guerra*, 1822.

had been disregarded. It was impossible, he argued, to preserve discipline among soldiers who were not fed.[38] As the condition of the treasury did not improve, on February 1 the Regency presented a report to the Junta which stressed the urgent need of funds for the support of the army.[39] Indeed the income and the expenditures of the government were made to balance only because large sums were transferred to the treasury from the *consulado* of Mexico City, from the mint, and from the funds which had been donated for pious purposes.[40] In fine, the financial history of this period was largely made up of a series of attempts by the government to make ends meet by the adoption of one expedient after another.

Iturbide felt compelled to make a fresh appeal to the Church. On January 9, 1822, he requested the cathedral of Guadalajara to furnish 400,000 pesos within six months.[41] In a similar fashion a loan of 150,000 pesos was demanded of the bishopric of Durango.[42] The bishop of Oaxaca was asked to contribute 200,000 pesos.[43] It cannot be assumed, however, that this forced loan was forthcoming at once in every case. The Augustinian Order in the bishopric of Michoacán responded to Iturbide through the Provincial that, although the Order did not have the money with which to pay the contribution, it would give the government any one of its haciendas so that by the use of its products the required exaction could be met.[44] Because of a lack of funds with which to meet current expenses, the Academy of San Carlos had to close its doors.[45]

Expenditures incurred by the imperial household rendered the financial stringency more acute. According to a memorandum of Francisco de Paula Tamariz, the comptroller of the army, from October 8, 1821, to March 20, 1822, the Commander in Chief received from the public treasury the sum of 77,884 pesos on account of his salary.[46] Among the data concerning almsgiving, a receipt found among Iturbide's papers shows that the Generalissimo received from the imperial steward 200 pesos which were to be distributed during January, 1822,

---

[38] Iturbide to the Regency, January 4, 1822, Hernández y Dávalos Collection, 15-8-3005, in MSS, U. T. Medina, *op. cit.*, estimated the annual expense of maintaining the army at 8,958,025 pesos.

[39] *Coleccion de ordenes y decretos*, I, 104.

[40] See the report dated January 12, 1822, printed in the *Gaceta imperial de México*, January 26, 1822, pp. 456-457.

[41] J. Cruz to Iturbide, February 20, 1822, in A.H.H., Donaciones y Préstamos, 698.

[42] Iturbide to Pérez Maldonado, March 14, 1822, *ibid.*

[43] *Idem* to *idem*, April 14, 1822, *ibid.*   [44] *Idem* to *idem*, March 14, 1822, *ibid.*

[45] *Gaceta del gobierno supremo de México*, February 24, 1824, p. 116.

[46] March 28, 1822, in A.H.I.N.A.H., 48-25-2.

among the poor of his native city.[47] Though in addition to paying Iturbide a salary and meeting his incidental expenditures, the government paid the expenses of the *Casa Imperial*, and though some of the funds may have been used unwisely, yet no evidence has been found to prove that Iturbide lined his private purse with funds filched from the public treasury.

In fact the Junta took special steps to reward the Commander in Chief for his service to the nation. On February 21, 1822, acting on the recommendation of a committee appointed to consider his domestic household, the Junta voted that, in order to reward him for "giving liberty to the Mexican nation and founding the Empire," properties of the extinct Inquisition should be set apart for him to the value of 1,000,000 pesos. Further, it provided that a portion of land "twenty leagues square in the province of Texas" should be granted to him. Although in March, 1822, Congress passed a decree reducing the pay of civil and military officials, yet it provided that the stipends of Iturbide, of his father, and of O'Donojú's widow were not to be affected.[48]

Signs had meanwhile not been lacking of dissatisfaction with the new regime. Carlos Bustamante undertook to deflate the reputation of the Liberator by founding a weekly journal entitled *La Abispa de Chilpancingo* which he dedicated to Morelos. In its pages he exalted the achievements of leaders in the early Mexican revolution. A notable expression of dissatisfaction with Iturbide's rule was the publication in December, 1821, of a pamphlet by Francisco Lagranda entitled *Consejo prudente sobre una de las garantías*. This tract argued against the doctrine of union among Mexicans. Lagranda even urged the Spaniards to dispose of their property and to leave Mexico.[49] Hence on December 11, 1821, certain officers of the Army of the Three Guarantees sent to Iturbide a strong protest against the circulation of tracts which aimed "to destroy the union of Americans and Europeans, to disturb tranquillity, and to plunge the Empire into an abyss." These military leaders not only urged him to suppress Lagranda's pamphlet but also to punish those authors who abused the freedom of the press.

Iturbide accordingly directed the censor to prevent the circulation of the "execrable" leaflet. In a letter to the Regency he denounced other authors who had criticized the new order. "The views which the army expresses," he said, "are those of the nation, especially of that part of it which is the most intelligent, the most discerning, and

[47]Receipt signed by A. Camacho, January 24, 1822, in I. MSS, 23.
[48] *Gaceta imperial de México*, April 4, 1822, p. 125.
[49] Lagranda, *Consejo prudente sobre una de las garantías*, pp. 2-4.

the most jealous of the prosperity of Mexico."[50] The Junta thereupon issued a decree which denounced Lagranda's pamphlet, suspended the departure of mail from the capital, and commended the Plan of Iguala as well as the Córdoba Treaty.[51] Lagranda was condemned to six years' imprisonment.[52] Nevertheless, criticism of the new government did not cease.[53]

Early in 1822 opposition to governmental policies had become so pronounced that Secretary Domínguez authorized an inquiry. In a report to Iturbide he stated that a plot against the existing regime was being formed in the capital, and that, in case a complaint by the conspirators was not well received, the chief magistrate was to be seized by armed force. A manifesto was then to be issued to justify this arbitrary act. Emissaries were to be sent into outlying districts to gain adherents. Placards were to be distributed decrying the virtues of the Commander in Chief, censuring his conduct, and ridiculing the activities of the Junta. Important personages supposedly implicated in the conspiracy were Generals Miguel Barragán, Nicolás Bravo, and Guadalupe Victoria. Bravo had been among twenty-seven persons arrested in November, 1821, on suspicion of disloyalty.[54]

Various denunciations of the chief magistrate were lodged in the ministry of justice. An anonymous complainant accused "the perfidious Iturbide" of being not only the King but also the Pope of Mexico. Another critic alleged that this magistrate had undertaken to delay the convocation of Congress in order that his own despotic rule might be maintained.[55] In November, 1821, however, the Regency published detailed regulations framed by the Junta concerning the election of deputies to Congress. This procedure was based largely upon the electoral practices recently followed in Spain. In an announcement of the Regency explaining the electoral regulations, as well as in the proclamation of Iturbide concerning them, stress was laid upon the duty of Congress to frame a constitution.[56]

That Iturbide was anxious to keep in touch with intelligent Mexi-

[50] *Gaceta imperial extraordinaria de México*, December 13, 1821, pp. 309-313.

[51] *Coleccion de ordenes y decretos*, I, 44.

[52] *Gaceta imperial de México*, December 22, 1821, p. 341.

[53] *Ibid.*, March 21, 1822, p. 74.

[54] Domínguez to Iturbide, January 17, 1822, in A.G.N., Justicia, 32; *Gaceta imperial de México*, December 1, 1821, p. 258; Alamán, *Historia*, V, 314.

[55] Copias de los anónimos que se hallan agregados á la causa criminal formada al Sor. Brigadier Dn. Nicolás Brabo y complices acusados del crimen do conspiración, Año de 1822, in A.G.N., Justicia, 32.

[56] *Gaceta imperial extraordinaria de México*, November 27, 1821, pp. 217-230; *Proclama del generalísimo a sus conciudadanos para la convocatoría del congreso*, p. 1.

cans concerning important political issues was demonstrated by a questionnaire which he distributed early in 1822 to leaders in various districts about the form of government which was most desired. Unedited documents collected by the Mexican scholar Genaro García show that opinion in favor of inviting a foreign prince to occupy the Mexican throne was not strong, that some persons desired a republican system, and that there was considerable sentiment in favor of a limited monarchy. Antonio de Santa Anna wrote from the city of Vera Cruz on April 15, 1822, that the intelligent part of the population favored "a constitutional, monarchical form of government," that the republican faction had few partisans, and that its adherents were considered "weak, fickle, or superficial. There are not lacking judicious partisans," he continued, who favor a republic, "either because they do not wish to see a Spanish monarch or a stranger of whom they would be jealous upon the throne of the Empire, or because they do not desire to risk internal dissensions in case Congress should invite a Mexican to occupy the throne."[57]

In April, 1822, Fernández de Lizardi presented in the form of a dream his impressions concerning the consequences of the accession to the Mexican throne of a prince belonging to a European dynasty. The Mexican Thinker imagined that, translated to the port of Vera Cruz, he had found erected there a stone upon which there was sculptured in black letters an "Epitaph to the Liberty of Mexico." He depicted the European prince as announcing in the hall of Congress that the separation of Mexico from Spain was an act of usurpation. Not only did the pamphleteer imagine that the tricolored flag of the Three Guarantees was cast into the flames but also that the banner of Castile was again unfurled over the castle of Chapultepec. He urged that, instead of inviting a European prince to Mexico, the new government should solicit the recognition of its independence from all the world.[58]

International politics had an influence upon the policy of the Mexican government. Though Iturbide had written to Juan Gómez de Navarrete to inform him of the Treaty of Córdoba, it appears that he left the Mexican deputies to the Spanish Cortes free to act as they judged proper. As an historian later pointed out, it was peculiar that commissioners were not sent to Madrid to negotiate an adjustment with the motherland as had been stipulated in the Córdoba Conven-

---

[57] Copy, Documentos relativos al imperio de Iturbide, 1821-1824, f. 149, Genaro García Collection, in MSS, U.T. Library.

[58] Fernández de Lizardi, El Sueño del Pensador no vaya á salir verdad, pp. 5, 12-15.

tion.[59]   Upon learning of that treaty, the Spanish Council of State expressed the opinion that Spain would not consent to the dismemberment of her transatlantic dominions.[60]   As a retort to allegations that General O'Donojú had the authority to sign the moot treaty, a board in the ministry of the colonies decided that a circular should be addressed to all the military, civil, and ecclesiastical authorities in Spanish America to notify them that, instead of having authorized O'Donojú "to celebrate this treaty or to negotiate any transaction which provided for independence as a basis, His Majesty was engaged in taking the measures demanded by the condition of the colonies."[61]

On December 7, 1821, Minister of the Colonies Ramón Pelegrin accordingly addressed a circular to civil and ecclesiastical authorities in the Spanish Indies to notify them that as the King and the Cortes were actually engaged in the pacification of Spanish America, his government "had not granted to O'Donojú or to any other person the authority to negotiate conventions acknowledging the independence of any transatlantic province."[62]   The Council of State soon decided not only that the erring Captain General should be recalled at once but also that foreign nations should be notified that, in negotiating the Treaty of Córdoba, O'Donojú had acted without any authorization from his government.[63]   Moreover, apparently still ignorant of his death, on December 21, 1821, it appointed Marshal Juan Moscoso to replace him as the chief magistrate of Mexico.[64]   By way of a reply to criticism of his government's attitude toward the revolution in Mexico, in February, 1822, the Minister of the Colonies declared to the Cortes that the world did not realize that the deplorable conditions existing in Spain had seriously affected her colonial policy.[65]

At the instance of the Council of State, Pelegrin sent a dispatch to the Spanish ambassador at Paris to inform him that, as doubts might arise concerning the directions to O'Donojú, he wished to make known that that official did not have any instructions which were

[59] Alamán, *Historia*, V, 361.

[60] Minute of the Council of State, November 7, 1821, in A.G.I., Indiferente General, 146-1-17.

[61] Gobernación de Ultramar, sección de gobierno, negociado político, reservado, númo. 30, *ibid.*, 146-1-18. In June, 1821, Ferdinand VII had informed the French ambassador at Madrid that he would never consent to the dispatch of a Spanish prince to America (Villanueva, *La Monarquía en América: Fernando VII y los nuevos estados*, p. 84).

[62] Páez Brotchie, *La Nueva Galicia a través de su viejo archivo judicial*, p. 79.

[63] The Council of State to Ferdinand VII, December 12, 1821, in A.G.I., Estado, Audiencia de México, 23.

[64] S. Salvador to A. Barata, December 21, 1821, in A.G.I., Audiencia de México, 95-6-4.

[65] *Gaceta de Madrid*, February 14, 1822, p. 253.

inconsistent with Spanish constitutional principles.[66] After an animated debate, on February 13, 1822, the Cortes passed a decree which provided that the government should send commissioners to the revolted colonies who were to transmit to Spain the proposals of the insurgents. The decree announced that the Treaty of Córdoba was illegal and void. It further provided that the government should inform other nations that Spain would always consider the recognition by them of the independence of her American colonies as a violation of existing treaties.[67] Her ambassadors at important European capitals were instructed to bring the policy which she had thus formally announced to the attention of those courts. Accordingly on March 6, 1822, the Spanish chargé d'affaires at St. Petersburg sent a note to Count Nesselrode, the Russian Minister of Foreign Affairs, which summarized the decision of the Spanish Council of State disavowing the Iturbide-O'Donojú Treaty.[68] Similar disclaimers were sent by Spanish ministers to the governments of Austria, France, Prussia, and England.[69]

Pelegrin's circular repudiating the O'Donojú-Iturbide negotiations was printed in the *Gaceta imperial de México* on March 28, 1822. In a comment upon the disavowal of the Treaty of Córdoba that journal denounced Spain's colonial policy, justified the movement for the independence of Mexico, and declared that her people would never submit to Spanish rule. During the next month the Congress which had been convoked in Mexico passed a decree directing that the inhabitants of all her cities, towns, and villages should take a solemn oath to acknowledge the sovereignty of the nation. The Regency ordered that this decree should be observed by the civil, ecclesiastical, and military dignitaries of every class as well as by the armed forces.[70]

The unqualified disavowal by the liberal Spanish government of the convention signed by Iturbide and O'Donojú gave a fresh stimulus to those Mexicans who favored absolute independence. The prospect of an adjustment that would have allowed the motherland to hold Mexico as an appanage faded away. This outcome pleased those partisans who desired absolute and unqualified independence. On the other side, the repudiation of the Córdoba Treaty displeased a not

[66] Pelegrin to Casa Yrujo, February 11, 1822, in A.H.N., Estado, 6843.

[67] *Colección de los decretos y órdenes que han expedido las cortes generales y extraordinarias*, VIII, 272-274.

[68] P. A. Argaiz to Nesselrode, March 6/18, 1822, in A.G.I., Estado, Audiencia de México, 23.

[69] Dated respectively March 8, March 10, February 22, and February 26, 1822, *ibid.*

[70] *Gaceta del gobierno imperial de México*, April 23, 1822, pp. 203-204.

inconsiderable faction which had favored the Plan of Iguala because it held promise of preserving some of the bonds that linked Mexico to Spain. When the Colombian Secretary of Foreign Relations heard that the Cortes had disavowed the Treaty of Córdoba, he expressed the opinion that the deputies had been mad to reject publicly an agreement from which Spain could have secured "immense advantages."[71]

Mexico took the initiative early in 1822 in regard to her relations with independent nations of the New World. On January 3 the Junta decided that, as the independence of the Mexican Empire had been proclaimed, it should send envoys to London, Rome, and Washington.[72] Five days later Iturbide wrote a letter to President James Monroe notifying him that Captain Eugenio Cortés had been appointed as agent to the United States in order to buy ships with which a beginning would be made in the formation of a navy for the Mexican Empire.[73] On January 10 Iturbide wrote instructions directing Cortés to proceed to that country to purchase a frigate and some corvettes for the government.[74] In response to a letter introducing the commissioner in which Iturbide expressed gratitude because of the service of Henry Clay in favor of the mission of Cortés,[75] that statesman replied in a letter dated March 15, 1822, that he took the greatest interest in everything pertaining to the independence and prosperity of Spanish America and especially of Mexico. "I offer your Excellency my most cordial congratulations upon the great achievement which has freed that Kingdom from the yoke of Europe," wrote Clay, "and my sincere wishes that this revolution, so happily consummated with little bloodshed, will result in the firm establishment of liberty and of a liberal government."[76]

Cortés wrote to Iturbide from Baltimore to report that he had met Clay, who treated him with urbanity. The agent mentioned Monroe's recent message to Congress urging that Spanish America had a right to recognition which should not be denied.[77] In an undated letter to the American President, Cortés suggested that Mexican independence should be acknowledged by the United States.[78] Secretary of State John Quincy Adams wrote to Secretary of Relations José

[71] O'Leary, Memorias del general O'Leary, XIX, 267.
[72] Coleccion de ordenes y decretos, I, 115.
[73] Iturbide to Monroe, January 8, 1822, in D.S., Notes from Mexican Legation, vol. 1.
[74] Copy, Hernández y Dávalos Collection, 15-8-3010, in MSS, U.T.
[75] Clay, Private Correspondence, p. 64.
[76] Spanish translation in Castillo Negrete, Mexico en el siglo xix, XV, 137-138.
[77] Gaceta del gobierno imperial de México, April 30, 1822, pp. 231-232.
[78] Notes from Mexican Legation, 1, in D.S.

Manuel de Herrera on April 23, 1822, to state that President Monroe was willing to receive a diplomatic agent from Mexico and further that his government would reciprocate by sending an agent to the Mexican capital.[79] On May 4 Monroe signed a bill which appropriated funds for the establishment of legations in independent Spanish-American countries.[80]

At this time the international adventurer, James Wilkinson, who was cooling his heels in Mexico, felt called upon to portray the Mexican Liberator to the government at Washington. On May 11, in a letter to Monroe, Wilkinson wrote that Iturbide was formed very much after that President's mold, "and would pass anywhere for a Citizen of the United States. His manly muscular Figure is adorned by a sweet expression of Countenance, and [with] manners at once easy, unaffected, and captivating, you cannot conceive of a gentleman of a more popular address. . . . He told me last Evening, with great frankness, that it was his intention to finish his public Career, by following the example of our incomparable Washington."[81]

The uncertainty which for a time prevailed concerning the status of the Central American provinces complicated issues which were involved in the summons for a Mexican Congress. Despite the views expressed by Iturbide, who wished congressmen to represent classes or social groups, both the Junta and the Regency finally agreed upon a plan for congressional elections which was based mainly upon provisions in the Spanish Constitution. On November 17, 1821, the Junta adopted a decree which provided that electors chosen by the cabildos should on January 28 following assemble at the capital of each province in order to choose deputies to a bicameral legislature which was to frame a Constitution for the Empire. The decree further specified that the intendancies and other districts were to elect to that assembly one hundred and sixty-two deputies and twenty-nine substitutes. It mentioned twenty-one provinces as being territorial divisions of Mexico.[82]

Directions framed by the Junta for the election of the deputies stated that they were empowered to act upon matters affecting the general welfare. Further, they were to organize the government of Mexico

---

[79] La Diplomacia mexicana, I, 73-74.
[80] Robertson, "The United States and Spain in 1822," American Historical Review, XX, 783.
[81] Wilkinson to Monroe, May 11, 1822, in M. MSS, vol. 20.
[82] Gaceta imperial extraordinaria de México, November 27, 1821, pp. 222-230. As will be shown later, the proposal that there be two houses of the legislature was forgotten or ignored.

according to the bases laid down in the Iguala Plan and the Treaty of Córdoba. In particular they were to provide for the complete separation of executive, legislative, and judicial authority so that these functions could never be exercised by the same individual.[83] Obviously there was a prevailing desire among the members of the Junta to prevent the concentration of governmental power in the hands of one person. Whether or not this was the reason which impelled Iturbide to oppose the electoral arrangements is not certain, but it is plain that he was not satisfied with them. In his autobiographical sketch he wrote of the electoral arrangements with aftersight:

"The first duty of the Junta after being inaugurated was to form an electoral summons for a congress which was to frame a constitution for the monarchy. The Junta took more time to perform this task than was justified. Grave errors were committed in framing the summons. This was very defective; but with all its faults it was approved. I could do no more than to notice the evils and to regret them. It did not consider the population of the provinces; in such a manner that, for example, it conceded one deputy to a province that contained one hundred thousand inhabitants, and four deputies to another province that had only one half that number. Neither did the Junta consider that representation in Congress ought to be in proportion to the intelligence of the respective constituencies; that from one hundred educated citizens three or four persons might well be selected who possessed the qualifications required to make a good deputy; and that among a thousand citizens who lacked education and were ignorant of political principles scarcely one person could be found with sufficient native ability to know what was conducive to the public welfare. . . ."[84]

In a proclamation addressed to the people of Mexico, in November, 1821, Iturbide declared that he awaited with impatience the meeting of the deputies, that he would joyfully relinquish his position, and that, if Congress so desired, he would retire to the bosom of his family or would execute any commission with which he might be charged. He declared that, if the Empire was happy, he had been rewarded.[85]

Aside from the populace who were in part devoid of political opinions, during the early months of 1822 three factions which may be denominated parties were emerging in Mexico. Persons who might be styled "Republicans" more or less covertly favored the establishment

[83] *Ibid.*, pp. 222-237.
[84] Iturbide, *Carrera militar y política de Don Agustín de Iturbide, ó sea memoria que escribió en Liorna*, pp. 19-20.
[85] *Gaceta imperial extraordinaria de México*, November 27, 1821, pp. 239-240.

of a form of government resembling that of the United States. Another faction was composed of "Bourbonists" or "Royalists," who wished to see a political relationship of some sort preserved between Mexico and the motherland. Some persons desired to see that bond maintained in accordance with the Plan of Iguala; while others, especially after Spain had rejected the Treaty of Córdoba, even contemplated with favor the relapse of the country into its former colonial status. Sometimes these loyalists were called "Serviles." Affiliated at times with the "Bourbonists" but breaking away from them in April, 1822, were those clerical and military adherents of the chief executive who were sometimes designated "Iturbidistas," many of whom eventually became monarchists. Increasingly active after the arrival of O'Donojú were individuals who had become affiliated with Masons of the Scottish rite.[86]

Newly founded journals disseminated foreign political doctrines. Among the Masonic lodges founded at this time was one called El Sol, which eventually sponsored a journal bearing that name. Its founder was a physician who had arrived in Mexico with O'Donojú.[87] In the first number of this periodical, which was dated December 5, 1821, the editors declared that their purpose was explained by its title. They added the following exhortation: "Mexicans, you know well that this is the time when you are to decide between ignorance and knowledge, between darkness and light, and between tyranny and liberty!" Several days later the Semanario Político y Literario de México published Spanish translations of the Declaration of Independence of July 4, 1776, the Articles of Confederation, and the Constitution of the United States. On January 23, 1822, the Semanario justified the publication of this Constitution by explaining that many Mexicans wished to read the great charter which had ensured the happiness of their neighbor. There is no doubt that Mexican upper classes were being affected by the leaven of American political philosophy.

[86] On the Masons, see Mateos, Historia de la masonería en México desde 1806 hasta 1884, pp. 8-15.

[87] Alamán, Historia, V, 313; Taylor to Adams, June 6, 1822, in S.D., Consular Letters, Vera Cruz, vol. 1.

CHAPTER IX

The Liberator Becomes a Monarch

O N FEBRUARY 24, 1822, one hundred members of the "Sovereign Constituent Congress" of Mexico ceremoniously proceeded to the metropolitan cathedral accompanied by members of the Junta and the Regency. There, placing his right hand upon the Holy Scriptures, each deputy took a solemn oath to protect the Roman Catholic religion, to support the independence of the Mexican nation, to form her Constitution according to the bases laid down in the Plan of Iguala and the Córdoba Convention, and to keep distinct the three departments of government. Up to this time, said Stephen Austin, Iturbide had acted "as the liberator of a Nation, as the Hero of Iguala ought to have acted."[1] The installment of the legislature was indeed the prelude to differences between it and the executive department similar to those which had harassed earlier insurgent governments in Mexico.

The Junta and the Regency escorted the congressmen to the former Jesuit temple of San Pedro and San Pablo, where a hall had been selected to serve as a legislative chamber. Congress soon elected its President and two secretaries. According to José M. Bocanegra, who was a deputy from Zacatecas, when the President of the Regency entered the hall, he took the most prominent seat. This step provoked a protest to which Iturbide retorted that he had been accorded the highest place in the sessions of the Junta.[2] After shifting to a place at the left of the President of Congress, Iturbide, who seldom missed a chance to express his views, delivered an address in which he congratulated the Mexican people upon coming into the possession of their rights. He declared that this glory was one of the motives which had induced him to form the plan of independence. He expressed pleasure at beholding the congressmen installed where they could frame good laws, without enemies at home or abroad. He

---

[1] *Actas del congreso constituyente mexicano*, I, 1-2. The quotation is from Barker, *The Austin Papers*, part 1, p. 587.
[2] Bocanegra, *Memorias para la historia de México independiente*, I, 40.

warned them, however, that foreign powers were jealously watching their proceedings. He voiced the hope that Congress would set the limits which justice and reason prescribed to liberty so that it might neither be forced to succumb to despotism nor to degenerate into license.[3] Thus early did he foresee a situation that has often confronted Latin-American magistrates.

As inexperienced hands were hewing a new state out of the side of an old one, it was natural that delicate constitutional problems should have arisen. The first decree enacted by Congress declared that the sovereignty of the Mexican nation was vested in the deputies, that Roman Catholicism was the religion of the state to the exclusion of any other faith, that the government was to be a moderate constitutional monarchy entitled the Mexican Empire, and that it invited to the imperial throne the persons designated in the Treaty of Córdoba. Congress further declared that the executive, legislative, and judicial departments should not remain united and that it possessed the entire legislative authority. For the time being, it delegated the executive power of the nation to the Regency, while judicial authority was to be exercised by the existing tribunals and by other courts which might be created. Furthermore, the deputies formulated an oath of fidelity to the new regime which was to be taken by the members of the Regency. Among other stipulations the oath provided that the regents should acknowledge that the sovereignty of the Mexican nation was vested in the deputies. Thus as early as February 24, 1822, the Congress of Mexico threw down the gauntlet to the chief magistrate.[4]

On the same day Congress passed a decree that prescribed the manner in which it should receive the Regency. A day later Iturbide addressed a letter to José Odoardo, a member of the audiencia of Mexico who had been chosen as the President of Congress, to inquire about his seat in that assembly. He proposed that it should concede him by special favor a place superior to those seats occupied by congressmen. He expressed the opinion that such pre-eminence would furnish a just recognition of the perils and privations he had suffered during the transformation of Mexico from an enslaved colony into

[3] *Actas del congreso constituyente mexicano*, I, 2-5. In a letter written in June, 1823, Padre Mier, who was in Congress at this time, alleged that when it opened, Iturbide ordered that the garrison in Mexico City should be supplied with bullets and cartridges so that they might coerce the deputies (Cossio, *Historia de Nuevo León*, V, 39-40).

[4] *Coleccion de ordenes y decretos de la soberana junta provisional gubernativa y soberanos congresos generales de la nacion mexicana*, II, 1-2.

an empire.[5] The secretaries of Congress replied that this matter of court etiquette had been considered prior to the receipt of his letter. They explained that, although Iturbide had redeemed the Mexicans from Spanish domination and was the first citizen of the Empire, the legislature could not give him the highest seat.[6] At the same time its secretaries informed Iturbide that it had assigned to him, as the Liberator of the country, the seat most honored after that which belonged to Odoardo. They stipulated, however, that his personal escort was not to enter the hall of Congress and that, while attending its sessions, he should not unsheath his sword.[7]

The legislature announced on February 25 that the Junta had ceased to function. On the following day it passed a decree providing that all public officials should take the same oath of obedience to Congress which had been sworn by the Regents. Moreover, it stipulated that the executive power was to publish congressional decrees preceded by this preamble: "To all those persons to whom these present may come, the Regency of the Empire, authorized to govern temporarily in the absence of an Emperor, makes known that the Sovereign Constituent Congress of Mexico has decreed as follows. . . ."[8] On March 1 it declared that February 24, March 2, September 16, and September 27 were to be national feast days, which should be celebrated by Masses and by salvos of artillery. Ten days later it took tentative measures to reform the financial administration by requiring local fiscal officials to file reports regularly with the Secretary of the Treasury. It also prohibited them from making certain expenditures of public money without his authorization. On the same day the intendants were ordered to make reports concerning the receipts and the expenditures of their respective districts.[9] Iturbide was considering further reorganization, because in a letter which he wrote to the intendant of the province of Puebla, he mentioned the need of reaching decisions about the strength of the army, the creation of a navy, and the framing of a constitution.[10]

The Mexican legislature soon enacted certain remedial measures.

[5] Cuevas, El Libertador, p. 319; Bustamante, Continuacion del cuadro historico de la revolución mexicana, VI, 44-46.

[6] C. Bustamante and M. Argüelles to Iturbide, February 27, 1822, in A.M.C., D/111-1-107.

[7] Odoardo and the secretaries of Congress to Iturbide, February 27, 1822, ibid. Cf. Bancroft, History of Mexico, IV, 760.

[8] Gaceta imperial de México, March 16, 1822, p. 58.

[9] Coleccion de ordenes y decretos, II, 5-9.

[10] Iturbide to García Rebello, March 13, 1822, W. B. Stephens Collection, no. 949, in MSS, U.T.

On March 16, 1822, it passed a decree which undertook to stop the collection of the forced loan as well as to stipulate that the proceeds were to be used for the support of the army.[11] Soon afterward Iturbide informed the Secretary of the Treasury that though religious communities had subscribed 280,000 pesos to the loan, and ecclesiastical cabildos had subscribed an enormous sum, he feared that the entire amount of the loan would not be forthcoming. A report had indeed been received from the bishopric of Sonora to the effect that it could not subscribe a single real. This happened at a time when the transportation of officers of disbanded royalist troops from Vera Cruz to Habana caused an additional expense to the imperial treasury.[12]

Stephen F. Austin, who had proceeded to Mexico City to importune the government for a land grant, recorded that the capital was in an agitated condition, party spirit was raging, and public opinion was vacillating with regard to the form of government that should be adopted.[13] Yet despite the critical condition of the nation, in some sections the enthusiasm for independence ran high. Basil Hall, who visited the Pacific shores, saw ladies wearing in their hats tricolored cockades emblematic of the revolutionary guarantees. Everywhere the conversation dealt with political topics. "The borders of the ladies' shawls were wrought into patriotic mottoes; the tops of the newspapers and play-bills bore similar inscriptions; patriotic words were set to all the old national airs; and I saw a child one day munching a piece of gilt gingerbread, stamped with the word Independencia!"[14]

Relations between the imperial government and the Holy See were still unsettled. As indicated in a previous chapter, when once independence was attained in Mexico, members of the clergy insisted that the right to make ecclesiastical appointments there had lapsed to the Vatican. Leading officials of the new government did not feel inclined to agree with this contention. A Mexican writer, who had access to unpublished documents, quotes a significant decree of the government dated April 18, 1822, which declared that the sovereign people of Mexico, who had succeeded to the prerogatives of the Spanish monarchs and were consequently invested with the *Patronato Real*, should firmly maintain the right of the new government to make

---

[11] *Coleccion de ordenes y decretos*, II, 13.

[12] Iturbide to R. Pérez Maldonado, March 29, 1822, in A.H.H., Donaciones y Préstamos, legajo 699; *Gaceta imperial de México*, April 9, 1822, p. 139.

[13] Barker, *The Life of Stephen F. Austin*, p. 49.

[14] Hall, *Extracts from a Journal Written on the Coasts of Chili, Peru, and Mexico*, II, 279.

appointments to ecclesiastical positions.[15]   Furthermore, a decree of May 4, 1822, displayed the intention of the legislature to secure control of politico-ecclesiastical authority. This decree stipulated that the instructions which were to be framed for an agent to Rome should, unlike the directions to other diplomatic agents, be submitted to Congress.[16]   Soon afterward Secretary of Relations Manuel Herrera requested that the ecclesiastical junta should furnish information which would aid him to prepare instructions for an envoy to the Holy See.[17]

Meanwhile General Dávila in Vera Cruz had been nourishing the hope that Iturbide was not yet lost to the cause for which he had strenuously fought. On March 23 the Spaniard addressed a significant letter to him. After a survey of the struggle for independence, Dávila argued that it could not succeed in Mexico. He even ventured to propose that to avoid the misfortunes which awaited that country the turncoat should rejoin the royalists.[18]

Particular phrases in the letter caused Iturbide to entertain grave doubts concerning the loyalty to the new regime of certain members of the Regency and also of some congressmen. At a session of Congress, where he occupied a seat near its President, he brazenly took occasion to assert that, according to documents in his possession, there were traitors in its hall. According to Alamán, one of the deputies threw this accusation into his teeth. When Congress examined Dávila's letter, which appears to have been the evidence submitted in support of the accusation, it found nothing to confirm Iturbide's suspicions. Indeed certain congressmen felt that by corresponding with an enemy of the State, the head of the Regency had himself acted treasonably. To adapt a congressman's account of the resulting scene, Odoardo then exclaimed with respect to Iturbide's accusation: "Caesar has crossed the Rubicon!" That phrase, energetically pronounced, said Alamán, made a deep impression, "although the majority of the deputies did not know what the Rubicon was. Neither did they know why Caesar crossed it." This occurrence brought the excitement to a climax.[19]   Just after the dramatic scene, the Hero of Iguala

---

[15] Pérez Lugo, *La Cuestión religiosa en México*, pp. 18-19. See further for the clerical view Cuevas, *El Libertador*, pp. 75-76.

[16] Ramírez Cabañas, *Las Relaciones entre Mexico y el Vaticano*, p. 3.

[17] *Coleccion eclesiastica mejicana*, I, 36.

[18] *Cartas de los Sres. generalísimo D. Agustín de Iturbide y teniente general Don José Dávila*, pp. 3-5.

[19] Bustamante, *Continuacion del cuadro historico*, VI, 76; Alamán, *Historia de Mexico*, V, 408.

replied to Dávila's invitation to rejoin the royalists in eloquent words that left no doubt concerning his attitude:

"What interest, what recompense, could persuade me to commit so outrageous an infamy? . . . Let the Mexican Empire become happy and independent and I shall be rewarded! With this glory, and in another niche than the one which you crave, I shall not desire the distinguished place in society that you offer me in the name of the Spanish King. Nothing which that King and the entire Spanish nation could give me would, in my estimation, equal the price of the absolute independence of my country. Absolute independence is what I proclaimed and that is what I have to maintain. The conciliatory measures which you propose . . . could not in substance be anything else than the former onerous dependence of Mexico upon Spain which lasted three centuries. . . ."[20]

To make his views known to the public, Iturbide insisted that his correspondence with Dávila should be printed in the official gazette. Obviously the intransigent attitude which he thus publicly assumed toward reconciliation with Spain did not lessen the rift that had already become visible between the Bourbon monarchists and the Iturbidistas.[21] Another sign of dissidence was shown in Congress on the night of April 11, 1822, when changes were made in the personnel of the Regency.[22] Deputy Bocanegra asserted that this move was a victory for the Bourbon faction.[23]

The deputies were not unaware of the dangers involved in precarious relations with the chief executive. On April 6, 1822, Carlos M. Bustamante had addressed to him a letter which broached the issue. Enclosing, as a token of his esteem, a pamphlet recently published in Madrid which honored Iturbide publicly, he ventured to urge him to act in harmony with the legislature. "Be assured, my dear Sir," he wrote, "that union with Congress is the device with which you should be presented to the world in order to make yourself happy and to crown your glory. . . . Your Excellency will not find much wisdom among us, but you will find good intentions and the desire for an intimate union in order to save this country which has cost so much."[24]

[20] *Gaceta imperial extraordinaria de México*, April 10, 1822, pp. 150-151. Bustamante's account of this incident written in 1823 is found in his *Manifiesto histórico á las naciones y pueblos del Anáhuac*, pp. 14-15.
[21] Bocanegra, *Memorias*, I, 49.
[22] *Gaceta imperial de México*, April 13, 1822, pp. 166-167.
[23] *Op. cit.*, I, 50, 140-141.
[24] Castillo Negrete, *Mexico en el siglo xix*, XV, 34.

Iturbide was not much inclined to take this advice to heart. In reply to Bustamante's plea, he declared that he had much respect for the legislature and wished to see its laws obeyed. He asked, however, why he should be considered so stupid as not to understand the advantage of co-operating with it. He characterized Congress as the bulwark of liberty and the hope of the country which was his idol. Asserting that he was not an enemy of the congressmen and that he had given them proofs of his appreciation, he complained that some of them were waging war upon him. He intimated that they had been the first persons to oppose the harmonious co-operation of powers which should always act as body and soul. On the other side, a committee of Congress reached the conclusion that the command of the armed forces ought not to be a function of the President of the Regency.[25]

At this time, when Iturbide was pleading for funds to support the army[26] and when his relations with Congress were near the breaking point, an incident took place which showed that he was not averse to co-operating with it when the public welfare demanded. In March, 1822, Miguel Santa María, a Mexican by birth, who had been appointed the minister of the Republic of Colombia, which at that time included both Venezuela and New Granada, reached Mexico City. By a decree of April 29 Congress declared that it solemnly recognized Colombia as a free and independent nation.[27] Three days late Santa María was privately introduced to Iturbide. On May 13 he was formally received by the Regency. He delivered to its President letters entrusted to him by Simón Bolívar which expressed high esteem for the Liberator of Mexico. In response Iturbide declared that the Regency wished to improve Mexico's relations with Colombia.[28] During the same month the international adventurer, James Wilkinson, paid a visit to Iturbide, who received him with courtesy. Wilkinson informed an American friend that he chatted with that magistrate and his wife for more than an hour, during which the revolutionary did not utter a single sentiment; "he returned my visit with the parade of two Coaches & six," wrote Wilkinson, "and at that interview he assured me, he would make the Career of our great Washington the

[25] Ibid., 76-77; Proyecto de reglamento provisional de la regencia del imperio, pp. 1-2.
[26] El Generalísimo al público, pp. 2-3, 6-7.
[27] Gaceta del gobierno imperial de México, May 4, 1822, p. 251.
[28] Cadena, Anales diplomáticos de Colombia, pp. 237-239.

model of his Conduct, i.e., to give liberty to His Country & retire to private Life. . . ."[29]

In response to the recommendation of Iturbide, who praised Santa Anna's services to the cause of independence, the Regency promoted that colonel to the rank of a brigadier in the national army.[30] On the other hand, the relations between Iturbide and Congress had reached such an impasse that he undertook to relinquish his authority. For, in response to his request that it should provide for an army of 35,000 regular soldiers and 30,000 militia, the legislature voted to place a smaller armed force at his disposal. The thwarted chief magistrate thereupon resigned his dual post as President of the Regency and Generalissimo.[31] On May 15, before his resignation had been acted upon, he addressed a significant note to the Secretary of War concerning military needs, a note which presumably he intended should be transmitted to Congress. He made an urgent plea for a large standing army. Without such an army, he reasoned, all that had thus far been accomplished for the independence of Mexico would be lost. Moreover, he expressed apprehension that certain foreign powers were already jealous of the new nations that were rising in America:

"In London, in Paris, and in Lisbon, there are emissaries of our former masters. Vienna, Berlin, and St. Petersburg have already made an attack upon liberty in Naples. Unless compelled by force, the Europeans will never consent to the establishment on this continent of governments independent of them. All the European nations are aware that once the Americans are organized into well-constituted societies, those peoples will become the depositaries of light, of power, and of riches; and that within one hundred years the European nations will be with respect to us what the Greeks and the Romans were to the rest of Europe after the death of Alexander and the destruction of the Eastern and the Western Roman empires."[32]

Explaining that although he was only a soldier, yet he had some

[29] "James Wilkinson on the Mexican Revolution, 1823," *Bulletin of the New York Public Library*, vol. III, no. 9, p. 362.

[30] *Noticioso General*, May 17, 1822.

[31] Taylor to Adams, June 6, 1822, in D.S., Consular Letters, Vera Cruz, 1.

[32] *Papel de S. M. Imperial dirigido al supremo consejo de regencia en 15 del corriente mes de Mayo*, pp. 4-5; cf. the text in Castillo Negrete, *Mexico en el siglo xix*, XV, 162. In Poinsett (*Notes on Mexico*, pp. 289-292), this letter is called Iturbide's Message to Congress. Cuevas (*El Libertador*, pp. 340-342) prints a version of the document which differs from that of the *Papel* quoted in the text; but, as with respect to many other documents included in his collection, he neglects to state where he obtained it. A manuscript copy of it (in A.H.I.N.A.H., 50-1-7/10) bears the date May 17, 1822.

knowledge of political affairs, Iturbide inquired what means his compatriots had with which to oppose aggression. He reasoned that Oliver Cromwell, the Prince of Orange, William Tell, and George Washington had saved their countries from tyranny by their military leadership. He asked:

"What has been the condition of Mexico up to the present time? Without a constitution, without an army, without a treasury, without the separation of governmental powers, without being recognized as an independent state? Without a navy, with all her flanks exposed, with her inhabitants distracted, insubordinate, abusing the liberty of the press and the freedom of customs, with officials who are insulted, without judges, and without magistrates. What is Mexico? Is this country properly designated a nation? And in what a grievous condition is the army which laid the first stone of the edifice of liberty. Those persons who owe Mexico their fortunes, their political existence, and their very lives taunt and despise her. . . ."[33]

After sketching this dark picture of the Mexican scene, the dissatisfied chief magistrate stated explicitly that, if the deplorable military situation was not remedied and if provision was not promptly made for an army of 35,000 regular soldiers, he would consider that his resignation had been accepted and would relinquish all his authority.[34] In a letter from the Mexican capital to Secretary John Quincy Adams, William Taylor, who had been appointed a consul of the United States, declared that Iturbide's resignation "was rather whispered about than generally known" until Saturday, May 18, when the alarmed Congress yielded to his demand. But it had made too long a delay. The die was "already cast."[35]

Long before his incisive message was penned, suggestions had been made that the Liberator should be elevated to a throne. Rocafuerte asserted that, even before his triumphal entrance into the capital, Iturbide had intrigued to have himself proclaimed the monarch of his native land. After that entry, this critic added, "the efforts of his adulators increased, his ambition was awakened, and a second attempt was made to proclaim him as Emperor on the very day when the oath was taken to support independence."[36] Immediately after the Act of Independence was signed, the Mexican Thinker proposed that Iturbide should be made Emperor.[37]

[33] *Papel de S. M. Imperial*, p. 5.   [34] Castillo Negrete, *op. cit.*, XV, 164.
[35] Taylor to Adams, June 6, 1822, in D.S., Consular Letters, Vera Cruz, 1.
[36] Rocafuerte, *Bosquejo ligerísimo de la revolución de Mégico*, pp. 115-116; Alamán, *Historia*, V, 449 and n. 39.
[37] Fernández de Lizardi, *El Pensador Mejicano al excmo. Señor general del ejército imperial americano, D. Agustín de Iturbide.*

Bocanegra recorded in his memoirs that, shortly after Congress assembled, a committee was appointed to consider offering the crown of Mexico to a Bourbon prince.[38] In certain towns suggestions had been made that the selection of the victorious military commander as the monarch would not be unwelcome. Among the persons who sponsored the most dramatic act in his rise, according to a contemporary, was his intimate friend, Anastasio Bustamante. It seems that a scheme had been formed to proclaim Iturbide as the imperial ruler on the morning of May 19 but that for some reason the evening of May 18 was finally selected as a more auspicious time.[39]

As events turned out, the chief actor in that scene was Pío Marcha, a sergeant in Iturbide's regiment of Celaya, which was stationed in the capital. In a romantic story told more than a year later, Marcha implied that he was incited to promote the fortunes of his beloved commander by a lovely maiden.[40] In a sober account composed in June, 1822, however, he declared that, as early as the preceding January, he had confided his plan for the proclamation of Iturbide as Emperor to certain comrades. He stated that the motives which impelled him to urge that momentous step were a fear of the evils which might befall his country if a prince of the Bourbon dynasty should be placed upon the Mexican throne and a belief that a worthy son of Mexico deserved that distinction.[41] Members of Marcha's regiment justified the step by explaining that their first sergeant believed that a son of their country "would view us with the eyes of a loving father from whom with less timidity and more confidence we could ask the remedy which we need."[42]

On the evening of May 18 sergeants of the Celaya regiment led by Pío Marcha proclaimed Iturbide as Emperor Agustín I. The cry was taken up by a rabble which was lurking in the streets. Public buildings were suddenly illuminated. A motley crowd proceeded to the mansion occupied by the Liberator, where they acclaimed him as the Emperor. The congressional committee later chosen to pass upon his proposal to retire from public life wrote a jaundiced account of this spectacular event which alleged that some seditious persons joined

[38] *Memorias*, I, 56-57.
[39] Rocafuerte, *op. cit.*, pp. 205-206.
[40] Castillo Negrete, *Mexico en el siglo xix*, XIV, 234-236. Cf. Fuente, "El Sargento Pío Marcha," *Boletín de la sociedad de geografía y estadística de la república mexicana*, 5th series, I, 26-27.
[41] Memoria of Pío Marcha, June 26, 1822, Hernández y Dávalos Collection, 15-4-1815, in MSS, U.T.
[42] *Manifiesto á los Mexicanos del regimiento infantería de línea número 1*.

AGUSTÍN DE ITURBIDE ACCLAIMED AS EMPEROR OF MEXICO AT MONCADA
PALACE ON MAY 19, 1822
A painting in the Museo Nacional de Historia

by "the despicable populace of one of the districts" of the capital city
and led by "some officers who were not highly esteemed in their own
regiments" had given "a more serious aspect to the tumult."[43]

While living in exile, Iturbide composed a disingenuous story of
the manner in which he received the news of this acclamation:

"My first impulse was to go forth and make known to the people
my reluctance to accept a crown whose weight already oppressed me
excessively. If I restrained myself from appearing before them for
that purpose, it was in compliance with the advice of a friend who
happened at that moment to be at my side. 'They will consider it to
be an insult,' he scarcely had time to say, 'and, believing themselves
treated with contempt, an irritated people can become a monster.
You must make this fresh sacrifice for the public good. The country
is in danger; remain a moment longer undecided, and you will hear
the death shouts.' I felt it necessary to submit to this misfortune
which was the greatest I had yet suffered. I spent all that night,
which was fatal for me, allaying enthusiasm and persuading the people
and the soldiers to allow time for consideration and to obey the
decision of Congress, the only hope which remained to me. I went
out repeatedly to speak to the populace and used the intervening time
to prepare a brief manifesto which I circulated on the following
morning."[44]

It seems possible that the reluctance which Iturbide thus expressed
about accepting the imperial crown was not altogether simulated. A
resident of the capital city named Miguel Beruete, who had served as
a special revenue officer under Viceroy Venadito, recorded in his diary
that Miguel Cavaleri kissed the hand of Iturbide, that all night long the
people shouted "long live Agustín I!" and for the death of those who
opposed him, and that occasionally cries of death to the Spaniards,
to the Serviles, and even to the congressmen were heard.[45] At three
o'clock the next morning, cavalry and infantry regiments stationed in
the capital directed a letter to Iturbide to state that with complete
unanimity they had proclaimed him the Emperor of "Mexican
America."[46]

In his manifesto the newly proclaimed monarch said that he
addressed the Mexicans as a fellow-citizen who desired to preserve

[43] *Actas del congreso constituyente mexicano*, IV, 161.

[44] *Carrera militar y politica*, p. 27.

[45] Beruete, Diario, f. 3-4, in MSS, T.U. Another account of the event is found
in Rocafuerte, *op. cit.*, pp. 207-210.

[46] Copy, addressed to "Señor," May 19, 1822, was found by the writer in A.N.M.,
legajo 67, when those papers were in the Library of Congress.

order. He declared that the army and the people of the capital had just made an important decision which the rest of the nation would have to approve or disapprove. Expressing pleasure at the action of the populace, he exhorted his countrymen to refrain from violence, to repress all resentment, and to respect their rulers. "Let us leave for tranquil moments," he implored, "the decision concerning our political system and our fate. . . ." He importuned the people to listen to the deputies who represented the nation: "The law is the will of the people; there is nothing superior to it. Listen to me, give me the ultimate proof of your love, which is all that I desire. That is the height of my ambition. I utter these words with my heart on my lips!"[47]

The manifesto was read to an extraordinary session of the legislature on the morning of May 19. A memorial bearing that date which emanated from public officials, both civil and military, and was signed among others by Pedro Negrete, Anastasio Bustamante, and José Echávarri, was laid before the deputies. Citing a representation prepared by certain regiments which had proclaimed Iturbide as the Emperor of Mexican America, the signatories suggested that the legislature should consider the issue which had thus been raised.[48] Beruete wrote in his dairy that Congress assembled at 6 A.M.; eighty-seven deputies were present; after messages had been sent to him, Iturbide joined them at 12:00. "The people unhitched the horses from his coach and drew it to the hall of Congress. This assembly was insulted and threatened with death by the populace."[49]

When Iturbide entered the legislative hall, he was accompanied by certain generals. The keynote of the opposition to the immediate proclamation of imperial rule was struck by José Guiridi y Alcocer, a legislator well versed in the law, who argued that the powers of the deputies were limited and that the important issue should be referred to their constituencies. Other legislators proposed that action should be postponed until at least two-thirds of the provinces had increased the authority of their representatives. Deputy Valentín Gómez Farías of Zacatecas finally introduced a proposal signed by many congressmen which reasoned that, as the Plan of Iguala and the Córdoba Treaty had been undone, Congress now had the power to vote in favor of the coronation of Iturbide, thus rewarding the merit and the service of the Liberator of Anáhuac. Otherwise, they asserted

[47] *Gaceta del gobierno imperial de México*, May 21, 1822, p. 304.
[48] *Actas del congreso*, I, 279-281.
[49] Diario, f. 4*v*., in MSS, T.U.

that peace, union, and tranquillity would perhaps disappear from Mexico forever.[50]

Antonio Valdés, who was a deputy for Guadalajara, argued that, as the Spanish government had rejected the Plan of Iguala and the Córdoba Treaty, the Mexicans were not obliged to observe Article III of that treaty by selecting as their monarch a prince belonging to a European dynasty. In a flight of oratory a member named Lanuza then praised Iturbide, the virtuous, valiant, charitable, humble, and peerless man whom the Almighty had destined to break the iron chains with which the Mexican eagle had been bound for three centuries. Two other speakers expressed the opinion that they had enough authority to confirm the choice made by the army and the people. Another speaker argued that Congress should first frame a constitution for the nation. Declaring that the welfare of the people was the supreme law, a deputy from Iturbide's native province maintained that the people, the generals, and the army favored his election as Emperor; that more than one half of the deputies desired it; and that to block such action might provoke a bloody revolution. Applause followed this speech as well as another by Valdés, who stated that he favored a limited monarchical form of government, which he considered a happy political invention. A motion was then introduced that propounded an alternative: should the Commander in Chief be proclaimed the monarch at once or should the provinces be consulted on the issue? Among the members present who participated in the vote, according to the official record, sixty-seven were in favor of the immediate proclamation of Iturbide as Emperor, while fifteen voted to refer the question to the provinces for decision.[51]

The official record of the debate stated that the President of Congress promptly yielded his elevated seat under a canopy to the newly

[50] *Actas del congreso*, I, 283-285.

[51] *Actas del congreso*, I, 286-301; see also the *Noticioso General*, May 22, 1822. Cf. Iturbide, *Carrera militar y politica*, p. 30 and n. 14, where he stated that 94 deputies were present in Congress when his election as Emperor took place, that 2 left the hall without voting, and that he was elected by a vote of 77 to 15. The congressional committee which passed upon the abdication of Agustín I stated that the 82 deputies in Congress on May 19, 1822, were surprised at the proposal to make Iturbide Emperor (*Actas del congreso*, IV, 161). James Wilkinson stated that the vote was about 75 to 15 ("James Wilkinson on the Mexican Revolution, 1823," *Bulletin of the New York Public Library*, vol. III, no. 9, p. 363). Consul Taylor informed Secretary John Quincy Adams on June 6, 1822, that 72 congressmen voted to elect Iturbide Emperor, "those who were purposely absent and consequently opposed to him, 63. Total number of 150 votes" (S.D., Consular Letters, Vera Cruz, 1). Bustamante (*Manifiesto histórico á las naciones y pueblos del Anáhuac*, p. 17) agreed with the official record. Cf. Bancroft, *History of Mexico*, IV, 773 n. 28.

chosen monarch, that the populace shouted "Long live the Emperor, long live the Sovereign Congress," and that his Imperial Majesty then departed from the legislative hall "amidst the most enthusiastic demonstrations of joy."[52] Beruete recorded that, when Agustín I returned to his palace, his carriage was drawn by Franciscan friars and other ecclesiastics, and that acclamations of the new sovereign lasted all that night. The diarist added that subsequently the clerics of La Profesa kissed the hand of the Emperor-Elect, that banners were displayed which denounced the Masons and the Spaniards, and that chimes were heard from the cathedral towers.[53]

Years later Alamán expressed the opinion that the approval of Iturbide's election given by the legislature was "not legal, because in order to give it only eighty-two votes were cast, when, in order to make the action legal, according to the regulations of Congress, one hundred and one deputies should have voted." In June, 1822, the Mexican Congress held that 102 members should be in attendance to constitute a quorum. Obviously a quorum was not present in Congress when Iturbide was elected Emperor.[54]

On May 19 Congress adopted a formal declaration, which was soon published in a broadside by the Regency, that Iturbide had been elected "the Constitutional Emperor of the Mexican Empire . . . according to the bases proclaimed in the Plan of Iguala and generally accepted by the Mexican nation, bases which are to be described in the formula of the oath that he is to take before Congress on May 21."[55] After mentioning, as motives for the election, the events of the previous night, as well as the acclamation of the people, the resolution explained that the rejection of the Treaty of Córdoba by the Spanish Cortes, which released the Mexican nation from the obligation to carry out that treaty, had left Congress at liberty to elect an Emperor. The legislature decided on May 20 that the Regency was to cease its activities at the very time when Agustín I began to exercise his functions. Congress soon enacted a long, formal decree which declared that Article III of the Córdoba Treaty had conceded to it the right to select the sovereign.[56]

[52] Actas del congreso, I, 302. Cf. the view of the congressional committee which passed upon the Emperor's abdication with regard to the attitude of the populace (ibid., IV, 162). A recent account of the imperial election is in Cotner, The Military and Political Career of José Joaquín de Herrera, pp. 48-49.

[53] Diario, f. 4-5, in MSS, T.U.

[54] Alamán, Historia, V, 457; Actas del congreso, II, 93-94.

[55] By J. M. Herrera, May 21, 1922. An official account of the election was published in the Gaceta del gobierno imperial de México, May 23, 1822, pp. 316-318.

[56] Actas del congreso, I, 303, 309.

In a proclamation issued by Congress the election of Iturbide as Emperor was justified because of the obstinate opposition of General Dávila to the new regime, because of a conspiracy formed by the Spanish expeditionary force, and because of the silence of the Court of Madrid. "These are unequivocal proofs," so ran this document, "that that court does not wish to recognize the independence of the Empire nor to approve the Córdoba Treaty and consequently that it does not accept the invitation extended to the Bourbon princes to proceed to Mexico." After mentioning the Spanish decree which disavowed that treaty, the legislators alleged that the Bourbons had "declared General O'Donojú to be a traitor" and also that they had stigmatized the Hero of the Mexican Nation as "a dissenter," while the Cortes had urged that vigorous steps should be taken for the reconquest of Mexico.

"The Court of Madrid had not deigned to address a single word directly to the government of Mexico or to its representatives. . . . Article III of the Treaty of Córdoba is the best justification of the proceedings of the Mexican government. That treaty left Mexico at liberty to establish her government in the form that seemed the most suitable to her and to elect a monarch in case the royal dynasty of Spain did not undertake to occupy the throne."[57]

On May 21 a committee of Congress informed the Emperor-Elect that he should appear in its halls to take an oath which had been carefully formulated. This oath might be likened to that taken by King John to support Magna Carta. Because the Mexican monarch was required to swear "by the Lord Almighty and by the Holy Gospels" that if he did not observe the Constitution and the laws, if he dismembered the Empire, if he took property away from anyone, if he did not respect the liberty of every individual, he ought not to be obeyed, and that whatever he might have done contrary to his oath was to be null and void.[58]

Declaring that he was bound by a chain of gold, on May 21 the new sovereign took the prescribed oath.[59] On the next day he addressed a manifesto to the soldiers in which, after mentioning his election and his confidence in their fine, civic qualities, he reasoned that their task was not yet finished. The representatives of the nation

[57] *Gaceta del gobierno imperial de México*, May 23, 1822, pp. 312-314.

[58] *Ibid.*, pp. 316-317. A criticism of this oath under fifteen heads was made in *Mando nuestro Emperador que ninguno le obdezca.*

[59] *S. M. el Emperador, después de haber jurado en el congreso, pronunció el discurso siguiente*, p. 2.

had still to act. He even asserted that the title which he most valued was that of the first soldier of the Army of the Three Guarantees.[60] On May 29 he wrote a letter to the Liberator of northern South America containing a passage which breathed a spirit of humility that perhaps he did not possess:

"The political position which you hold requires that one should give you timely information concerning those events which will form an epoch in history—events which have an influence upon the actual condition of societies. Notice, therefore, most worthy President of Colombia, that the sovereign Congress of Mexico, seconding the desires of the army and the people, elevated me on May 19 to the throne of this Empire. I do not know what they saw in your fellow-citizen that should have made them confer upon me so great an honor. In the belief that I deserved it, they placed a crown upon my head; but I am far from considering as a benefit an act which lays upon my shoulders a burden that oppresses me! I lack the strength needed to sustain the scepter. I abhorred it, but in the end I agreed to accept it in order to prevent evils to the country which was about to succumb anew, if not to the former slavery, at least to the horrors of anarchy."[61]

Soon afterward, in reply to a proposal made by General José de San Martín that a European prince should be invited to rule over independent Peru, Bolívar went so far as to declare that instead he would prefer to invite Iturbide to occupy the Peruvian throne. Months later José G. Pérez, a secretary of Bolívar, wrote to the new sovereign to express the admiration of the Colombian Liberator at the sudden transformation of New Spain into a nation. That event was styled "the marvelous work of the tutelar genius of Mexico."[62] This expression of sentiment seems much less surprising than at first blush when notice is taken of the fact that in his later years Bolívar at times acted like the uncrowned king of northern South America. Moreover, it is scarcely to be supposed that the Venezuelan Hero was fully aware of the arbitrary acts which stained the public career of the Mexican genius.

On May 23 Congress approved the recommendation of a committee concerning the title to be used by the monarch. It decided that to head

[60] *El Emperador al ejército*, p. 1.
[61] O'Leary, *Memorias del general O'Leary*, XI, 339-340. Valle (*Iturbide*, pp. 97-98) gives the date of the letter as May 22. A copy of it in A.G.R.E., 1-2-506, is dated May 29, which is correct. See Bolívar, *Cartas*, III, 116. A translation of a response by Bolívar is printed in Lecuna and Bierck, *Selected Writings of Bolívar*, I, 286-287.
[62] Lecuna, "La Conferencia de Guayaquil," *Boletín de la academia nacional de la historia*, vol. XXVI, no. 101, p. 63.

diplomas and dispatches he should employ the following simple formula: "Agustín, by Divine Providence and by the Congress of the Nation, the First Constitutional Emperor of Mexico." His signature should be merely "Agustín."[63] Congress soon decided that the treasury should furnish the Emperor with the funds which he needed and that the former palace of the viceroys should be placed at his disposal for use as a residence and as the seat of administrative offices.[64] The first Emperor of Mexico became known as Agustín I.

Various criticisms were made of the choice of Iturbide as Emperor. In reply to the charge that he was ambitious to become the imperial magistrate, he pointed out that the day on which he entered the capital would have been the most favorable time to carry out such a design. With respect to the allegation that, because of his presence, the legislature did not have freedom in the election, he later declared that he was present only because it had invited him and that, although the remarks of its members had sometimes been interrupted, neither the officers in its hall nor the populace had prevented liberty of expression. In regard to the contention that a quorum was not in attendance when the election took place, he maintained that many decrees of Congress had been enacted when only seventy or eighty deputies were present. Further, he reasoned that subsequent congressional action which made the crown hereditary in his family belied the charge that the legislative procedure had been improper.[65] From a different viewpoint, Lorenzo de Zavala later argued that though the moot election was a work of violence, it could scarcely be said that, under the circumstances, his fellow-countrymen would not have elevated Iturbide to the imperial throne in preference to anyone else.[66] Shortly after Agustín I had been acclaimed, Congress published a manifesto which stated that his election was demanded by the gratitude of the nation, was solicited by the vote of many towns and provinces, and was favored by the army and the inhabitants of the capital city.[67]

The national coat of arms adopted early in 1822 was still sometimes used but there were many variations in practice. On June 8 by order of the Emperor his secretary transmitted to the secretaries of Congress an exposition of Manuel López y Granda which accompanied his project for an imperial coat of arms. That plan depicted

[63] Gaceta del gobierno imperial de México, May 28, 1822, p. 339.

[64] Actas del congreso, II, 15-16.

[65] Iturbide, Carrera militar y politica, pp. 31-36.

[66] Zavala, Ensayo histórico de las revoluciones de México desde 1808 hasta 1830, I, 121.

[67] Gaceta del gobierno imperial de México, June 6, 1822, pp. 376-380.

an eagle which was to bear a specially fashioned crown. In January, 1823, the Council of State resolved that a decision concerning the design of the crown and the escutcheon should be made by the Academy of San Carlos.[68]

Scarcely had the imperial election become known when the new monarch was showered with felicitations from cabildos, provincial deputations, private individuals, and prominent military officers. In a broadside dated May 19 deputies of Honduras proclaimed that Iturbide was the Emperor of Middle America.[69] Praise of his election promptly reached him from the city of Guanajuato. The provincial deputation of Valladolid sent congratulations to her son who had been placed upon the throne of Anáhuac.[70] In a spirit of eulogy, Bocanegra later declared that there was scarcely a single group numbering one thousand inhabitants in the country which did not voice its approval at the elevation of the Commander in Chief to the imperial throne.[71] Certain greetings which were marked by a lack of cordiality, however, were quietly filed in the archives.[72]

Bishop Pérez sent a letter to Secretary Herrera to express his gratification at the election as Emperor of "a Father who had released Mexico from slavery and who was winning the hearts of his countrymen. . . ."[73] Guerrero wrote to Iturbide on May 28 to voice his pleasure at the imperial election. He expressed the opinion that the inhabitants of the Empire were confident that the leader who had set them free would not become a tyrant.[74] A week later, he addressed the Hero of Iguala again to report that in Tixtla "the election was celebrated by reveilles, general applause, salvos of artillery, and the pealing of bells." He added: "I congratulate myself at deserving the esteem of your Imperial Majesty whom I shall recognize as my sole protector during my entire life."[75] In reply Agustín I mentioned the heavy burden imposed upon him by his high office. He told Guerrero, however, that he relied upon the aid of his friends, of wise men, and

---

[68] *Ibid.*, January 29, 1822, p. 464; the First Secretary of State to the secretaries of Congress, June, 1822, Hernández y Dávalos Collection, 16-1-3144, in MSS, U.T. Minutes of the Council of State, January 31, 1823, Hernández y Dávalos Collection, 16-1-3147, *ibid.* See also Cuevas, *El Libertador*, pp. 87, 313.

[69] Signed by J. Lindo and others, May 19, 1822.

[70] *Gaceta del gobierno imperial de México*, July 9, 1822, pp. 494-496.

[71] Bocanegra, *Memorias*, I, 66-67.

[72] Felicitaciones al Emperador por su exaltación al trono, in A.M.C., D/481.3/222.

[73] *Gaceta del gobierno imperial de México*, May 30, 1822, pp. 354-355.

[74] Guerrero, *Felicitación del exmo. Señor D. Vicente Guerrero á S.M.I.*

[75] *Gaceta del gobierno imperial de México*, June 18, 1822, p. 416.

of Heaven. "You are one of those friends," he trustfully said, "upon whom your most affectionate Agustín will always count."[76]

In an address to his soldiers at Jalapa, Antonio Santa Anna declared that it was not possible for him to restrain his joy at the imperial election; for that action was suited to promote the general prosperity.[77] To the Emperor this commander wrote in fulsome words: "In common with the regiment of infantry of the line number eight which I command, and which under my direction was ready to take such a politic and glorious step much sooner than the present time, I regret that we were not the instruments of such a worthy recognition."[78]

General Anastasio Bustamante issued an address to the people of the eastern and the western Interior Provinces to congratulate them upon having a ruler who was not an arbitrary despot but "a friend and a fellow-citizen, whose hands would maintain their happiness."[79] Messages of congratulation to the new sovereign by Vicente Filisola and Diego García Conde were sent to Mexico City from distant Guatemala and Yucatan.[80] The *Noticioso General* printed an editorial on May 22 which bore the headline: "News of the Empire. Long Live Religion, Liberty, Union, Independence. Long Live Agustín I, Emperor of Mexico." Five days later, upon praising the election of Iturbide as Emperor, this journal declared that all Mexicans would make haste to consolidate the new order under his leadership, "which will make us invincible, even though all the nations of Europe conspire against our independence. Religion and union will be our device." *El Farol*, a new periodical published in the city of Puebla, asserted that the Emperor would preserve ecclesiastical privileges. Maintaining that the Iguala Plan had promised the security of the Mexican Church, that periodical said: "This security now arises from beholding the fulfilment of that plan fully assured because its pious author has recently been placed at the head of our government and upon the imperial Mexican throne."[81]

Among those persons who held that the election of Iturbide was null, Vicente Rocafuerte had a prominent place. He argued that

[76] *Cartas que S.M.I. con motivo de su exaltación al trono dirigió al excmo. Sr. capitán general del sur*, p. 7.

[77] *Gaceta del gobierno imperial de México*, June 15, 1822, p. 410.

[78] *Ibid.*

[79] Bustamante, *Habitantes de las provincias internas de oriente y occidente*, May 19, 1822.

[80] Filisola to the Prince Imperial, August 3, 1822, in A.M.C., D/481.3/222; Diego García Conde to M. Sota Riva, August 28, 1822, *ibid.*

[81] July 7, 1822.

seventy-four members of Congress, who did not take part in the electoral proceedings, tacitly disapproved of the choice of Iturbide, who was proclaimed the sovereign in the midst of a tumult without the vote of a sufficient number of deputies.[82] In view of the extraordinary circumstances attending the choice of the new monarch, the Colombian minister deemed it prudent to suspend his negotiations for a treaty between Mexico and Colombia while awaiting fresh instructions from Bogotá. To his government Santa María wrote that, because of the large number of deputies who did not vote in favor of the election, and because of the conditions which induced Congress to make its decision, the validity of its choice might become questionable.[83] Upon hearing of the imperial election, Mier, who had just been released from prison, expressed amazement that a republic had not been set up and that the populace and the soldiers of the capital had committed the great folly of proclaiming the Generalissimo as the Emperor of Mexico.[84] After he had turned against Agustín I, Guadalupe Victoria complained that the Mexican Congress had yielded to the threats of "a ferocious people."[85] Although presumably Iturbide welcomed the acclamation, there is no evidence at hand to prove that he had urged the populace to proclaim him Emperor.

The question of the legality and the wisdom of the imperial election is indeed one upon which varying judgments may be pronounced. These would largely depend upon the historical background of their authors as well as upon the political sentiments which they entertained. Whether designed by Iturbide or not, the Treaty of Córdoba had left a loophole which rendered feasible the election of a sovereign by the Mexican legislature. The choice by that assembly, however, was neither free nor technically legal. Because of the intimidating shouts of the populace who lauded their Hero and the presence of his soldiers in the hall of Congress, those members who elevated him to the imperial throne acted under duress. Indeed Simón Bolívar described the Mexican monarch as "Emperor by the grace of God and of bayonets."[86]

[82] *Bosquejo ligerísimo*, pp. 233-234.
[83] Cadena, *Anales diplomáticos de Colombia*, pp. 242-246.
[84] *Diez cartas hasta hoy inéditas de Fray Servando Teresa de Mier*, p. 27.
[85] Marcha, *Carta . . . á Don Guadalupe Victoria*, p. 2.
[86] Bolívar, *Cartas*, III, 92. See Poinsett, *op. cit.*, p. 68; and Barker, *The Austin Papers*, part I, p. 587, for further comment on the election of Iturbide as Emperor. Comments by Mexicans may be found in the following works: Alamán, *Historia*, V, 457; Bustamante, *Continuacion del cuadro historico*, pp. 132-133; Bocanegra, *Memorias*, I, 61-64. Views of ecclesiastical historians are found in: Banegas Galván, *Historia de Mexico*, II, 128-129; Cuevas, *Historia de la nacion mexicana*, p. 496. See also Olavarría y Ferrari, *México independiente*, pp. 76 *et seq.*

Some months later the government was compelled to resort to the issue of fiat money. On December 20 Congress decreed that 4,000,000 pesos of paper currency should be printed in denominations of one peso, two pesos, and ten pesos. It stipulated that during 1823 in both public and private transactions one-third of the payments were to be made in paper money while the remainder should be in silver.[87]

Despite innovations, the imperial government sought to maintain certain ties with the past. Though there were some nobles in Mexico, yet the imperial family was almost isolated amidst a population largely composed of middle and lower class people. After the exodus of many Spaniards, there were no tiers of nobles that might serve as steps to the throne.[88] As early as February, 1822, however, the Junta had shown a desire to sanction titles of nobility by approving a recommendation of the Regency to confer the title of viscount upon a certain worthy Mexican. On the other hand, not many days after the imperial election, certain congressmen who favored simplicity at court, led by José Joaquín de Herrera, voiced their opposition to such monarchical practices as "the kissing of the hand."[89] Nevertheless, Congress soon began to consider plans for the inauguration, the anointing, and the coronation of the new sovereign.

On June 22, 1822, a congressional committee submitted a report to the legislature concerning the method to be followed in the selection of a successor to Agustín I. Asserting that terrible evils were inseparable from a system of elective monarchy, the committee reasoned that by inviting various personages to accept the throne both the Plan of Iguala and the Treaty of Córdoba had undertaken to relieve Mexico from the convulsions which would ensue upon the introduction of an elective monarchical system. Therefore it recommended that the succession to the imperial throne should be hereditary; that, upon the death of Agustín I, the crown should pass to his eldest son; and that honorable titles should be accorded to the Emperor's nearest relatives.[90] In general Congress approved these recommendations. It provided that the heir to the Mexican throne should be styled Prince Imperial, that legitimate children of Agustín I should be designated Mexican princes, that his sister María Nicolasa should be called Princess Iturbide, and that his father should be known as the Prince of the Union.[91]

[87] Hernández, El Archivo historico de hacienda, pp. 12-13.
[88] Zavala, Ensayo histórico, I, 122.
[89] Cotner, The Military and Political Career of José Joaquín de Herrera, pp. 49-50.
[90] Actas del congreso, II, 94.
[91] Ibid., pp. 99-106; Gaceta extraordinaria del gobierno imperial de México, June 26, 1822, p. 448.

The ceremony of coronation, which was originally set for June 27, was postponed because of a slight illness that caused the Emperor to visit the neighboring baths of San Agustín de Cuevas. This delay provoked rumors that the coronation was strongly opposed by aristocratic Spanish families as well as by the Archbishop of Mexico. Fonte later explained that, faced by the dilemma of scandalously recognizing the upstart Emperor or of leaving the country, he eventually chose the latter alternative.[92] Elaborate preparations were meantime being made for the occasion. Andrés Castaldo drew up in Latin an elaborate plan for the ceremony. Alamán stated that gems were borrowed to adorn the imperial insignia and that an unsuccessful attempt was made to use jewels from the national pawnshop. Costumes for the Empress were designed by a French modiste after the fashion employed in the coronation ceremony of Napoleon.[93]

In the main the ceremony followed a program drawn up by a committee of Congress.[94] Files of soldiers lined the streets to be traversed by the imperial party. Houses and public buildings were decorated with pennants, streamers, and tapestries.[95] The procession, which included many civil and ecclesiastical dignitaries, started from Moncada Palace at ten o'clock on the morning of Sunday, July 21. A coach bearing Emperor Agustín I, clad, said Beruete, in the uniform of a colonel in the regiment of Celaya,[96] was escorted by a number of generals, while Empress Ana María, attired magnificently, was accompanied by ladies of the court. At the chief portal of the cathedral the procession was met by the ecclesiastical cabildo and also by the bishops of Puebla, Durango, Oaxaca, and Guadalajara who were to take part in the ceremony. Alleging that he could not officiate without the authorization of the Pope, Archbishop Fonte had not only declined to anoint the ruler but had actually withdrawn from the capital. Fonte later asserted that in soliciting the attendance of these bishops at his anointment in the cathedral of Mexico City, the Emperor had promised that he would protect the church and its ministers.[97]

Upon their arrival at the cathedral, the monarchs, newly adorned

[92] Medina, *La Santa Sede y la emancipacion mexicana*, pp. 195-196.
[93] Castaldo, *Ceremonías de la iglesia en la unción y coronación del nuevo Rey ó Emperador escritas en Latin . . . y traducidas al Castellano*; Alamán, *Historia*, V, 475-476, and n. 33.
[94] *Proyecto del ceremonial que para la inauguración, consagración y coronación de su magestad el Emperador Agustín Primero se presentó por la comisión encargada de formarlo al soberano congreso en 17 de Junio de 1822, passim.*
[95] *Gaceta imperial de México*, July 30, 1822, pp. 565-569.
[96] Diario, f. 20v., in MSS, T.U.
[97] Bocanegra, *Memorias*, I, 69-74; Medina, *op. cit.*, p. 196.

in imperial vestments, were escorted to improvised thrones. After Bishop Cabañas had heard the monarch's profession of faith and had anointed him at the foot of the Churrigueresque high altar, Rafael Mangino, the President of Congress, placed an imperial crown, which had been fabricated in Mexico, upon the head of the kneeling Emperor. With his own hand the sovereign then placed a tiara upon the brow of his wife.[98] The bishop of Puebla delivered an eloquent sermon on the text *Et clamavit omnis populus, et ait. Vivat Rex.* He reasoned that the choice of Agustín de Iturbide as the monarch of Mexico had, like that of Saul as the King of Israel, been inspired by God.[99]

Before the ceremony was completed, Mangino made an address in which he declared that the Church with its august ceremonies had set the keystone in the new political edifice. He expressed hope that the Emperor's paternal government, his zeal for the observance of the Constitution and the laws, his anxiety for the conservation of the Roman Catholic faith, his enlightened desire for the advancement of art and science, and his heroic endeavors to maintain Mexican liberty and independence would secure for him the blessings of his subjects.[100] Agustín I did not hesitate to voice his reactions to this advice. According to the official gazette of August 3, he emphatically declared that all his vigilance would be used to secure the real happiness of the Mexican people. "I shall conserve the religion, the independence, and the union of the Mexicans," he said, "and, faithful to my oaths, I shall also preserve public liberty and shall march steadily along the path charted by the Constitution."

In phrases which lacked the bright color of descriptions by sympathetic Mexicans, Consul Taylor portrayed the inauguration in the huge, gloomy cathedral as "a most tiresome Pantomime," a ceremony which lasted five hours, during which General Wilkinson, who accompanied him, "had two good naps."[101] The latter described the ceremony as clumsy and tinseled.[102] Carlos María de Bustamante likened it to a theatrical farce performed in a magnificent temple.[103]

When it ended, the procession returned to Moncada Palace. On

[98] Taylor to Adams, August 4, 1822, in D.S., Consular Letters, Vera Cruz, 1.

[99] Pérez, *Sermon predicado en la santa iglesia metropolitana de Mégico el día 21 de Julio de 1822, passim.*

[100] *Gaceta del gobierno imperial de México,* August 3, 1822, p. 581. A warning which he alleged was given Iturbide by Mangino is mentioned by Alamán, *Historia,* V, 485, and also Iturbide's response.

[101] Taylor to Adams, August 4, 1822, in D.S., Consular Letters, Vera Cruz, 1.

[102] "James Wilkinson on the Mexican Revolution, 1823," *Bulletin of the New York Public Library,* vol. III, no. 9, p. 362.

[103] *Manifiesto histórico á las naciones y pueblos del Anáhuac,* p. 22.

July 22 the *Noticioso General* published an interpretative comment on the event. After lauding the achievements of the Liberator of Mexico, it reasoned that by accepting this high investiture from representatives of the people, the Emperor had confirmed the solemn oath which he had recently taken. Thus he sanctioned the political axiom that monarchs were born for the people, and not the people for the monarchs. "By a marvelous relationship due to the influence of philosophy," it continued, "a limited monarchy today unites all the liberties of a republic with the vigor of monarchical unity without the perils to which democratic governments of antiquity and absolute monarchies of recent centuries were always exposed."

A son of the church gave the eleborate ceremony his blessing. In an adapted translation of a Roman ritual which was opportunely published in Mexico City, the bishops who presented the candidate for the imperial crown were represented as having said to the chief prelate: "Holy Mother Church wishes, O Reverend Father, that you should deign to elevate this excellent military man to the imperial dignity." That prelate then asked: "Do you consider him worthy and fit for this dignity?" To which the bishops responded: "We know him and are convinced that he is useful to the Church of God and well fitted for the government of this Empire."[104]

Thirty-eight years of age, Agustín I was in the prime of life. Slightly above the middle height, he had an erect and well-proportioned figure. Of athletic build, with a military carriage, he had a nimble step. Brown hair crowned an oval face; his complexion was fresh and ruddy, more like that of a German than that of a Spaniard. Reddish whiskers bordered his cheeks. Although in society his manners were gracious and insinuating, he could be bitter and unrelenting. At times he became imperious. His hazel eyes were sometimes averted from his interlocutor or cast upon the ground.

His bearing, said an admiring Mexican, was "manly and gracious, easy and natural."[105] Of his mental traits an English visitor to Mexico recorded that he was "shrewd, cautious, and reserved."[106] It appears that his private morals did not improve after he was elevated to the imperial throne. In describing his interview with the Emperor, an American critic wrote, "I will not repeat the tales I hear daily of the

[104] *Benedición que nuestra madre la santa iglesia da al nuevo Rey ó Emperador en el día su coronación sacada del pontifical romano y traducida del Latin al Castellano,* p. 1.
[105] As quoted by Romero de Terreros, *La Corte de Agustín I,* p. 5.
[106] James Henderson, Memorandum Respecting Mexico, in F.O., 72/265.

character and conduct of this man."[107]   An observant Mexican, however, could not refrain from mentioning in his diary a bit of court gossip. In October, 1822, Beruete made an entry to the effect that some foreign journals had mentioned with effrontery the amorous relations of the Emperor with Antonia, the daughter of La Güera.[108]   It should not be forgotten, however, in passing judgment upon his conduct, that in addition to temptations which occasionally confronted princes, the Emperor lived in an age and in a society where, as a contemporary remarked, the standard of sexual morality was not high.

Among the tokens struck off in Mexico City to commemorate the coronation was a silver medal which bore at the top an eight-pointed star. On the field was a five-line inscription as follows: *Inauguración de Agustín. Primer Emperador de México. Julio 21 de 1822.* On the right the field was bordered by a palm wreath, and on the left by a wreath of olive. The reverse side bore an eagle perched upon a nopal. The eagle's head was adorned with a crown.[109]

The imperial household had meantime been planned. A list of the persons composing "the imperial family" which was printed in the official gazette on July 20 made known that the Marquis of San Miguel de Aguayo had been appointed the major-domo, while the Marquis de Salvatierra had been made the captain of the guard. Eight military officers, including General Gabino Gainza, and Brigadiers José Echávarri, Luis Cortazar, and José de Armijo, had been appointed the aides of the Emperor. The Bishop of Guadalajara had been made the chief almoner, and the Bishop of Puebla was appointed the chief chaplain. A friar named José Treviño, who had been born in Iturbide's native province, was made the confessor to his Majesty. The Empress and the Prince of the Union were also to have confessors. Their imperial majesties were to be provided with six chaplains, besides thirteen honorary chaplains, four preachers, and four honorary preachers. Isidro de Icaza was to serve as the master of ceremonies. Eleven persons were to act as gentlemen of the chamber. In addition, there were to be pages, physicians, surgeons, chamberlains, ladies of honor, and maids of honor.[110]

Alejandro Valdés, who published the *Gaceta*, was appointed the printer to the imperial house. Meticulous regulations were framed for the superintendent of the imperial palace, who was to have charge of

[107] Poinsett, *Notes on Mexico*, p. 68.
[108] Diario, f. 43v., in MSS, T.U.
[109] Betts, *Mexican Imperial Coinage*, pp. 6-7.
[110] *Gaceta imperial de México*, July 20, 1822, pp. 536-539.

the servants and minor officials of the domestic establishment.[111] Specifications concerning the conduct and the dress of the ladies belonging to the suite of the Empress emphasized honesty, neatness, and moderation. For the imperial household was expected to serve as an example to the rest of the nation.[112]

The former palace of the viceroys had naturally been selected as the proper place for the executive offices of the national government as well as the official residence of the imperial court. Yet, as that building was being renovated and repaired, the members of the Iturbide family had been lodged in a mansion (later known as "Hotel Iturbide") which had been erected by a Mexican nobleman in the Renaissance style. Refurnished by the Emperor, it became known as "Moncada Palace."[113] If we may trust the recollections of Gómez Pedraza, who upon his return from Spain had an interesting interview with his old friend, it was not without embarrassment that the monarch viewed in perspective the transformation which had taken place in his political fortunes.[114] It would seem that, like a stranger in a desert, he was lured on by an entrancing mirage.

From this time forth, viewing the bond which had linked Mexico to Spain as an ominous yoke, the Emperor gathered up more and more of the powers of the State. The story of his life almost becomes a history of Mexico during a critical period. Step by step the legislature undertook to lay broad foundations for a monarchical regime. On May 31, declaring that it wished to organize the government pending the formation of a constitution, Congress passed a decree providing for the establishment of a Council of State to be composed of thirteen persons selected by Agustín I from a list of thirty-nine congressional nominees. The decree further provided that the council was to confer with the chief executive about proposed laws.[115] Among the persons chosen to serve on this council in June, 1822, were Barcena, Bravo, and Negrete.[116]

The legislature soon formulated regulations concerning the coins which were to be struck off in imperial mints to replace tokens bearing the effigy of a Spanish King. A certain deputy proposed that the

[111] Indicaciones para el establecimiento de la Superintendencia del Palacio Imperial, in I. MSS, 14.
[112] Reglamento que han de observar la camarera mayor, damas y camaristas de s.m. la Emperatriz en los vestidos y adornos . . . qdo. se hallen en servicio.
[113] Romero de Terreros, op. cit., p. 23.
[114] Manifiesto que Manuel Gómez Pedraza . . . dedica á sus compatriotas, p. 12.
[115] Gaceta del gobierno imperial de México, June 8, 1822, pp. 389-390.
[116] Actas del congreso, II, 87; Señores consejeros de estado nombrados por S.M.I. a consequencia de la propuesta hecha por el soberano congreso constituyente.

legend on the media of exchange should be in the language of the Aztec Indians or of the Toltecs. Congress, however, decided that the silver coins were to bear upon one side the bust of the Emperor and the inscription *Augustinus Dei Providentia*; and upon the other side the Mexican coat of arms encircled by the legend, *Mexici Primus Imperator Constitutionalis*.[117] At this time the Spanish silver peso, which was perhaps worth one dollar and a half in United States currency, was the common unit of value.[118] Although the silver coins known as the peso, the peseta, the real, the medio-real, and the gold onza continued to be coined at Mexican mints after July, 1822, yet both the image and the superscription on those coins were changed. The gold onza of the First Mexican Empire bore on one side the effigy of the nude bust of Iturbide in profile. Encircling the image was the legend *Augustinus Dei Providentia*. The reverse side depicted an eagle bearing a crown and with extended wings perched upon a nopal plant with five leaves to which there were attached Aztec war clubs, a bow, and three quivers of arrows.[119]

Manifold changes and innovations naturally involved additional expenses which had to be paid by the already embarrassed exchequer. As early as June, 1822, the Emperor had authorized Secretary Herrera to initiate negotiations with James Barry of London for a loan of some ten million pesos.[120] According to an official certificate drawn up near the end of 1822, during the period from May 19 to December 31 of that year certain payments made on account of the imperial household aggregated 123,400 pesos.[121] Another financial report which covered the period from April 18, 1822, to March 20, 1823, summarized the amounts paid by the national treasury on account of that household at 254,889 pesos.[122] Among records of specific expenditures is an account aggregrating 1,679 pesos, which was the cost of the uniforms of the imperial equerries, chamberlains, and pages of honor.[123]

Shortly after the imperial election, Congress confirmed a decree of

[117] *Actas del congreso*, I, 336; *Gaceta del gobierno imperial de México*, June 27, 1822, p. 450.

[118] Haggard, *Handbook for Translators of Spanish Historical Documents*, p. 106.

[119] Betts, *Mexican Imperial Coinage*, p. 16.

[120] Iturbide to J. M. Herrera, June 26, 1822, in A.M.C., H/122.32/822.

[121] By A. Batres and R. Mangino, without date, in A.H.I.N.A.H., 48-25.

[122] Copy, Razon de las cantidades que se han ministrado por esta tesorería general á Don Pablo Rodríguez para los gastos de la casa imperial, Documentos relativos al Imperio de Iturbide, 1821-1824, f. 65-67, Genaro García Collection, in MSS, U.T Library.

[123] Cuenta del costo que han tenido los uniformes de los pages de honor, uxieres y ayudas de camera de su Magd. el Emperador, July 31, 1822, in I. MSS, 23.

the Junta which, in accordance with a plan long entertained by Iturbide, provided for the founding of an honorary society to be known as the Imperial Order of Guadalupe.[124] The Virgin of Guadalupe, the patron saint of Mexican revolutionists, was declared to be "the celestial protector" of the organization. As its Grand Master, Agustín I was to have the inalienable right to name the members of the society as well as to formulate its regulations. Its members were to be ranked in three classes: cavaliers of the first class, who were to be decorated with the Grand Cross of the Order; cavaliers of the second class; and those persons belonging to a third class, who were to be styled supernumerary cavaliers. Citizens admitted to the fraternity must be Roman Catholics who had performed distinguished services to the State. Though the insignia of these classes differed from each other with respect to decorative details, yet the cross of each class was to bear an image of the Virgin of Guadalupe.[125]

A list of the persons chosen to membership was printed on July 25, 1822, in the *Gaceta del gobierno imperial de México*. Each of the four princes of the imperial family was awarded the Grand Cross. Prelates honored by the same insignia were the bishops of Guadalajara, Puebla, Guatemala, Oaxaca, and Nicaragua. Among the military men awarded that honor were Generals Pedro Negrete, Anastasio Bustamante, Luis Quintanar, Domingo Luaces, and Vicente Guerrero. Other persons included in the distinguished list were Manuel de la Bárcena, Miguel Cavaleri, and Pedro del Paso y Troncoso. Most worthy was the deceased O'Donojú, who was thus honored as though he were still living. Included in the second class of the order, in company with such personages as Filisola, Bravo, and Santa Anna, were a number of the Grand Master's friends who had not distinguished themselves. Among members of the third class were José Malo, José Manuel Zozaya, and Gómez de Navarrete. Obviously Iturbide believed in honoring his friends, his associates, and his relatives.

Early on the morning of August 13, accompanied by municipal corporations, the personages elected to the fraternity assembled at Moncada Palace to accompany the coach which was to take the imperial family to the revered church at Guadalupe. His Imperial Majesty was there placed upon an improvised throne. Thence he was

---

[124] *Gaceta del gobierno imperial de México*, June 20, 1822, pp. 425-426.

[125] *Constituciones de la Imperial Orden de Guadalupe*, pp. 2-6. The insignia of this order are illustrated in *ibid.*, pp. 27 *et seq.* and also in Romero de Terreros, *La Corte de Agustín I*, p. 42.

escorted to a dais upon which the Bishop of Puebla was seated. There, after taking the oath required by the statute of the order, Iturbide was adorned with the Grand Cross and a colored mantle. Other cavaliers then took oath as a group to maintain the Roman Catholic religion, to defend the Constitution of the State, and to protect the person of the Emperor. Symbolic of the initiation, one member from each class was then adorned with the mantle and the cross of his respective grade. It appears that the Prince of the Union added to his coat of arms a representation of the Grand Cross and the mantle of the chivalric order surmounted by a crown.[126]

The inauguration of the fraternal order increased the prestige of imperial rule among certain classes of Mexican society. Many years later, however, an historian declared that the establishment of the fraternity merely completed "the farce of the coronation." He added that the mantles of the cavaliers, as well as their sombreros, which were adorned with tricolored plumes, became objects of ridicule.[127] Certain contemporaries, however, flattered the Grand Master. One adulator even styled him "the Man of God."[128]

On the other hand, at the end of his sketch of the Mexican revolution which was published in Philadelphia after he had left the valley of Mexico for the banks of the Potomac, Rocafuerte drew a dark picture of the Mexican sovereign, whom he evidently wished to discredit. "Sanguinary, ambitious, hypocritical, proud, false, the executioner of his brothers, a perjurer, a traitor to every party, accustomed to intrigue, prostitution, theft, and iniquity—never has he experienced a generous emotion. Ignorant and fanatical," the Ecuadorian added, "he does not even know what fatherland or religion is. . . . O Mexicans! is there not a secret curse in Heaven, a bolt of wrath which with implacable fury will blast the evil man who erects his own fortune upon the ruins of his country?"[129]

A characterization of Agustín I which much influenced North American opinion was that of Joel R. Poinsett, a South Carolinian who had consorted with revolutionists in South America. In July, 1822, he was directed by President Monroe to proceed to Mexico on a mission of inquiry.[130] Furnished with a letter of introduction from

[126] *Gaceta del gobierno imperial de México*, August 15, 1822, pp. 621-624; Ortega y Pérez Gallardo, *Historia genealógica de las familias mas antiguas de México*, vol. III, part II, p. 1, of the section pertaining to the Iturbide family.

[127] Alamán, *Historia*, V, 488.

[128] Valle, *Iturbide*, p. 114.

[129] Rocafuerte, *Bosquejo ligerísimo*, pp. 247, 252.

[130] On Poinsett, see Rippy, *Joel R. Poinsett*, p. 90. On his appointment, see further,

Henry Clay to Agustín I,[131] the American agent was presented to the Emperor on November 3, 1822. Salient traits of that sovereign Poinsett described in the following passage:

"His usurpation of the chief authority has been the most glaring, and unjustifiable; and his exercise of power arbitrary and tyrannical. With a pleasing address and prepossessing exterior, and by lavish profusion, he has attached the officers and soldiers to his person, and so long as he possesses the means of paying and rewarding them, so long will he maintain himself on the throne; when these fail he will be precipitated from it."[132]

Some Mexican leaders entertained serious doubts about the wisdom of the decision to create a new monarchical regime. Prominent among the skeptics was Padre Mier. On July 15, 1822, he took a seat in Congress as deputy for the city of Monterrey, Nuevo León. In a stirring speech he declared that he had made known to Agustín I his desire for a republican form of government such as had been erected in other countries of the New World. Though willing to put up with a monarchical system, if it was conducted with moderation, yet he declared that under other circumstances, he would become its irreconcilable enemy. Speaking of the monarch, he said in warning tones:

"We beseech God that he may inspire us to maintain not simply independence but also liberty. Turkey is independent; the Barbary States are independent; but their inhabitants are slaves. We do not desire independence merely for its own sake but for the sake of liberty. . . . We have not been engaged for eleven years in staining with our blood the fields of Anáhuac in order to secure an independence which is useless. What we want is liberty and, if this is not attained, the war for independence has not yet ended. All the heroes have not perished, and defenders of the country will not be lacking!"[133]

On the other side of the Atlantic, Abbé de Pradt commented in a similar fashion upon the elevation of Iturbide to the imperial throne. He declared that the military leader had achieved a most daring *coup de main* but that his reign could be supported only by the means which had created it. The abbé intimated that Mexican imperial rule would be destroyed by violence. Pertinently did he inquire: "How

---

Poinsett to Monroe, July 20, 1822, in M. MSS, 20. Cf. Cuevas, *Historia de la nacion mexicana*, p. 499, where it is erroneously asserted that Poinsett was given secret instructions to promote the annexation of northern Mexico to the United States.

[131] *La Diplomacia mexicana*, I, 67.

[132] Poinsett, *Notes on Mexico*, p. 68.

[133] *Actas del congreso*, II, 277. Cf. Mier, *Diez cartas*, p. 29.

can Iturbide flatter himself that he is firmly seated upon his throne in the midst of that nursery of republics which occupies the entire soil of America?"[134]

News of the political transformation which had taken place in the City of Mexico penetrated the Mexican hinterland slowly. The citizens of Santa Fé did not celebrate the proclamation of Iturbide as the Emperor until December 12, 1822.[135] In Central America coins were eventually minted bearing inscriptions that commemorated the elevation of Iturbide to the throne.[136]

The enthronement of the Mexican Generalissimo was a logical outcome of events. His elevation to the supreme civil command was not in sharp contrast with measures taken during the heroic period of Spanish-American history in some other rising states. In South America, upon more than one occasion, the hero of independence was urged to become the chief executive of the country which he had been largely instrumental in liberating from Spanish rule. Simón Bolívar was made the President of Colombia by a small number of revolutionists. José de San Martín was invited to become the chief executive of Chile by a small group of patriots, and later actually proclaimed himself the Protector of Peru, without waiting for the form of a popular election.

In certain particulars, however, events in Mexico during this period differed from happenings in other Spanish-American countries. Unlike the political measures taken in Colombia, Peru, Chile, and La Plata, a monarchical form of government was formally set up in Middle America. It was not unnatural that certain leaders who had lived under a paternalistic monarchy and who feared that their countrymen were not ready for a republic should have favored the establishment of a monarchical regime. In Mexico it was largely the leadership and the prestige of Iturbide which brought about the adoption of such a system. Her statesmen were less influenced by inherited traditions than the publicists of Brazil, where the Braganza dynasty had been transplanted from Portugal and where the transition to an independent status did not cause an abrupt break with the past. Mexicans of the Age of Iturbide were presumably more affected by such traditions, however, than were those Haitian patriots who in their Constitution

---

[134] L'Europe et l'Amérique en 1822 et 1823, II, 247.

[135] Relaciones de las demonstraciones de juvilo con qe. felicitó la ciudad de Sta. Fé capital de la Provincia del Nuevo México la jura y proclamación del Sr. Dn. Agustín primer emperador constitucional mexicano, verificado el doce de Dbre. de 1822, no. 141, in the series covering the period of Mexican rule, A.N.M., Santa Fe.

[136] Valle, Iturbide, pp. 112-113.

of 1805 proclaimed Jacques Dessalines as their chief magistrate with the title of Emperor Jacques I. When he heard of the coronation of Iturbide, Bolívar wrote to his compatriot, General Santander, and declared that few monarchs of Europe had a title more legitimate than Agustín I.[137] Pamphlets were soon printed in Mexico, however, which criticized him because he had accepted the imperial dignity. To many of his countrymen that step was unpardonable. Some of them ascribed his acceptance of the crown to personal ambition.

A youth who had been nurtured in a family where the King and the Church were adored, an estate manager who had figured in the society of aristocratic and prosperous landowners of Michoacán, Agustín de Iturbide naturally became a champion of monarchy. Despite the influence of doctrines emanating from France and from the United States, the ambitious Creole had become convinced that his countrymen were not ready for democratic institutions. Accordingly it was not strange that he should have undertaken to surround his household with the paraphernalia of an imperial court. He evidently believed that such an entourage would help to secure support for his throne by influential ecclesiastical, military, and political dignitaries.

There were, however, forces working toward a different end. During the same year in which Iturbide was crowned, Francisco Molinos planned a series of pamphlets concerning the rights of man.[138] His first tract, which contained Spanish translations of six constitutions adopted in the Thirteen Colonies during the American Revolution,[139] was prefaced by an apothegm which declared that this collection would become "the book of the principles of liberty, the depository of the elements of happiness."[140] Yet, even before the year 1822 expired, the Mexican Secretary of the Treasury had realized the enormous difficulties which faced the new sovereign. Pérez Maldonado likened Agustín I to an architect who, entrusted with the construction of a new edifice, found that to erect it he was confronted only with a mass of ruins and rubbish, the remains of a magnificent structure which had been overthrown by a violent earthquake.[141]

[137] Bolívar, *Cartas*, III, 158.
[138] *Declaraciones de los derechos del hombre en sociedad*, p. 4.
[139] *Ibid.*, pp. 1-31.
[140] *Ibid.*, p. iv.
[141] *Memoria que el ministro de hacienda presenta al soberano congreso sobre el estado del erario*, 1822, pp. 21-22.

CHAPTER X

Early Steps of Agustín I

THE NEW SOVEREIGN early showed a disposition to follow certain precedents which had been set concerning Spanish law and custom soon after the termination of the war for independence. Even before Iturbide was crowned Emperor, the *Patronato Real* was again under consideration by the Mexican hierarchy. In June, 1822, a junta of clerics considered the need of making appointments to vacancies in the churches of Chiapas, Comayagua, and Valladolid. It also discussed the creation of new ecclesiastical positions subject to appointment. Though it took the view that the right of appointment which had been exercised by the Spanish King had ceased, yet it desired that the Holy See would grant that right to the Emperor and his successors, for such action would promote the spread of the Roman Catholic religion. Nevertheless, the junta decided that, for the time being, there was no other solution than to allow the cabildo of a church where an episcopal seat was vacant to submit to Agustín I the names of worthy candidates so that he might select a number for consideration by that council. Once its choice had been made, he was to seek confirmation by the Holy See.[1] As time passed, the Emperor undertook to increase his power of appointment by the selection of judges whose choice had formerly been controlled by political chiefs under the direction of Spanish officials.[2]

In June, 1822, the ecclesiastical junta began to consider making alterations in the liturgy so that it would be in harmony with the political changes which were taking place. Among other alterations the junta proposed that the prayer *Pro imperatore* in the Roman missal should no longer be used in any Mass; for that prayer was suited to the ruler of the Romans but not to Agustín I. It decided that in place of the words *Rex, regni* in the prayer *Pro rege* there should be substituted the phrase *Imperator, Imperii.*[3]

[1] Vera, *Colección de documentos eclesiasticos de Mexico*, I, 37-39.
[2] L. Quintanar to J. Domínguez, November 18, 1822, in A.G.N., Justicia, 29.
[3] Vera, *op. cit.*, I, 48.

On July 11 the junta resolved to ask the Emperor to solicit the Pope to extend to all the inhabitants of Mexico, without the need of a papal dispensation, the privilege which had been conceded by Pope Paul III to the Indians, namely, that of contracting marriages when such unions were within a certain grade of consanguinity. It also solicited Agustín I to ask the Vatican to allow Mexican ecclesiastics to convoke a national council for the purpose of regulating many difficult matters that could not otherwise be adjusted. In case the request was granted, the Pope was to name the ecclesiastic who was to preside over the council. During a session of the junta a question was raised about the personage who would become the head of the imperial Mexican Church. A response was made that a French journal had suggested that, as the Mexicans now had an Emperor, they already had a Pope.[4] Thus, as early as 1822, the crucial issue of a national Roman Catholic Church was broached in Mexico.

At this time the *Gaceta* published a list of books on sale, which included *Paradise Lost, Orations of Cicero, Virgil's Works, Don Quixote*, and the *Representación de los diputados Persas*.[5] On September 27, 1822, Agustín I had issued a broadside forbidding the circulation of books which contained doctrines that were not orthodox. The decree prohibited the introduction into Mexico or the ownership of certain works that were at variance with Roman Catholic doctrine. Among these volumes were *The War on the Gods, Origine des cultes*, and *Meditaciones sobre las Ruinas de Palmyra*.[6] By issuing the prohibitory edict the Emperor assumed a function that had been exercised in colonial days by officials of the Inquisition. He soon submitted to Congress certain regulations which he had formulated concerning books on the prohibited list.[7] Moreover, he declared that he was much disturbed because of insults to "the holy religion of Jesus Christ by the large number and diverse character of irreligious and impious books which, despite the precautions of the government, had been introduced into the Empire clandestinely."[8]

Archbishop Fonte, however, did not readily yield to the secular power the practice of censorship. In November, 1822, he issued a broadsheet announcing that certain books and pamphlets should not be read by the faithful. Various publications which had already been

---

[4] *Ibid.*, pp. 51-54, 65.
[5] July 11, 1822, pp. 506-508; foreign works were evidently in translations.
[6] *The William Gates Collection*, no. 231.
[7] *Colección de órdenes y decretos de las soberana junta provisional gubernativa y soberanos congresos generales de la nación mexicana*, II, 84-85.
[8] *Gaceta del gobierno imperial de México*, October 5, 1822, p. 806.

formally condemned were now declared to be heretical, blasphemous, impious, irreligious, and obscene. A person who dared to peruse any of those works was to be placed under the ban of excommunication. The use of clothing or furniture bearing sacred images, immodest figures, or the insignia of Freemasonry was prohibited. This edict was to be read publicly in all the churches of the archbishopric.[9] A peculiar problem arose because of the intransigent attitude of the Archbishop. A minute written months after Iturbide became Emperor shows that an official in his confidence was of opinion that Fonte, who had refrained from taking the oath of allegiance to the independent regime, should not be allowed to abandon his archdiocese. In the memorandum Agustín I was declared to be "the protector of the discipline of the church."[10]

In September, 1822, the Emperor appointed José Manuel Bermúdez Zozaya, who was an honorary member of the Council of State, envoy extraordinary and minister plenipotentiary at Washington. Asserting that he had been called to the throne by the free vote of all the Mexicans, Agustín I directed the minister to propose the negotiation of treaties between Mexico and the United States and to solicit that government to recognize his country as independent of Spain and ruled by an imperial dynasty. Soon after Zozaya had sent to the American Secretary of State a copy of his credentials, on December 12, 1822, John Quincy Adams presented him to President Monroe as the minister from Mexico.[11] The United States thus recognized the independence of the Mexican Empire. Accordingly the report of Joel Poinsett to his government in January, 1823, concerning the political condition of Mexico, in which he predicted that Agustín I could not long maintain himself upon the throne and also expressed himself unfavorably concerning the recognition by the United States of an American monarchical government, arrived too late to affect the recognition policy of the Monroe administration.[12] On February 6, 1823, the *Gaceta del gobierno imperial de México* joyfully announced that Zozaya had been received by Monroe with the same etiquette and ceremony employed in the reception of ministers of other nations.

Though the Mexican Congress had recognized Colombia as an in-

[9] November 13, 1822.

[10] The quotation is from Salido del Arzobispo, undated and unsigned, in I. MSS, 12. Fonte left his archdiocese for Spain in February, 1823.

[11] *La Diplomacia mexicana*, I, 76-77; Robertson, "The Recognition of the Hispanic American Nations by the United States," *Hispanic American Historical Review*, I, 260-261.

[12] Rippy, *Joel R. Poinsett*, p. 102.

dependent state soon after Iturbide became Emperor, Minister Santa María notified Secretary of Relations Herrera that he would merely transmit the news of that political change to Bogotá. In a letter to Secretary Pedro Gual of Colombia, however, the minister stated that he had decided to suspend negotiations with the imperial government.[13] This decision, as well as his failure to attend the coronation ceremony, evidently displeased the monarch. On August 14 Herrera informed Santa María that, pending the receipt of new credentials from the Colombian government, his public functions would cease.[14]

In contrast to the policy of Colombia, which was evidently loath to recognize a regime which might be ephemeral, was the attitude of Peru. On November 20, 1822, José de Morales, who had been made her minister to Mexico, addressed a note to Herrera to announce his arrival at Acapulco. Appointed before news of the coronation of Iturbide had reached Lima, Morales was vested with authority to negotiate a treaty of alliance, commerce, and friendship with Mexico.[15] In the following January, after the imperial government had issued a decree recognizing the independence of Peru, Morales was formally received by Agustín I.[16] Measures announced by the imperial government to establish legations in England and France,[17] however, were not carried out.

Steps had meanwhile been taken by Spanish diplomats which foreshadowed the policy their country would adopt toward the revolted colonies. In accordance with the decree of the Cortes which disavowed the Treaty of Córdoba, in May, 1822, Secretary of State Martínez de la Rosa addressed to Spain's ambassadors at leading European courts a manifesto concerning Spanish America. In brief he stated that Ferdinand VII was willing to negotiate with its revolutionary authorities; but that the maintenance of an independent existence did not invest a colony with the right to be acknowledged by foreign states as an independent nation.[18] When this manifesto was published in the *Gaceta del gobierno imperial de México*, its editor denounced the colonial policy of Spain. He declared that with Agustín I at the head of his victorious army, no pronouncement would convince Mexico that

[13] Cadena, *Anales diplomáticos de Colombia*, p. 243.

[14] *La Diplomacia mexicana*, I, 28.

[15] *Ibid.*, pp. 131-132.

[16] Bocanegra, *Memorias para la historia de México independiente*, I, 192.

[17] *La Diplomacia mexicana*, I, 121-124; Valadés, *Alamán*, pp. 139-140. On French policy toward Mexico at this time, see Robertson, *France and Latin-American Independence*, pp. 214, 232-233.

[18] Robertson, "The United States and Spain in 1822," *American Historical Review*, XX, 789-792.

she had been guilty of evil-doing, no promise would deceive her, no argument would seduce her—she would part with her dearly earned liberty only after her last citizen had perished.[19]

In the meantime the establishment of a new regime had caused some changes in the administration of frontier regions. Upon being appointed by Agustín I as the commandant general of the Interior Provinces of the West, Brigadier Antonio Cordero issued a proclamation which lauded the achievements of the "singular genius" who had laid the foundation of the Empire.[20] One of the administrative reforms instituted by the Emperor was concerned with those provinces. As a question had been raised about the authority rightly charged with the circulation of laws, decrees, and orders throughout that region, in September, 1822, Secretary Herrera issued a definitive circular. He announced that Agustín I had decided that the Superior Political Chief of the Interior Provinces of the East was to be considered the Captain General of both divisions of those provinces and that the provisional commandant general of the Western Interior Provinces was a subordinate of that Captain General in both civil and military affairs.[21] Shortly afterward, in a proclamation addressed to the inhabitants of Nuevo Santander, Anastasio Bustamante, who was in charge of the eastern district, accordingly styled himself the "Captain General and Superior Political Chief of the Interior Provinces."[22] General Wilkinson, who undertook to advise the Emperor on matters of policy, in vain urged in November, 1822, that Texas should be divided into two provinces, one of which should be designated "Iturbide."[23]

Iturbide became the ruler over a domain which at its largest extent stretched from northern California to the Isthmus of Panama. It possessed great natural resources. An American visitor calculated near the end of 1822 that the population was about 6,500,000, and that the inhabitants of the capital city numbered some 150,000. Throughout the Empire there existed classes which here and there had hardened into castes. Negroes had been so thoroughly absorbed into the rest of the population that their descendants could scarcely be distinguished from the hybrid class who were known as mestizos. In Mexico City some mestizos who were designated *léperos* were beggars and idlers, readily inclined to participate in uprisings or armed revolts. In large

[19] August 27, 1822, pp. 662-666.
[20] Copy, August 5, 1822, in A.N.M., legajo 67.
[21] Cordero to J. Viscarra, November 3, 1822, A.N.M., no. 125, Santa Fe.
[22] Copy, undated, *ibid.*, no. 118.
[23] Bolton, "General James Wilkinson as Advisor to Emperor Iturbide," *Hispanic American Historical Review*, I, 179.

part the *léperos* belonged to the laboring class, which included all blends and colors. The Indians generally lived upon inferior farm lands or because of their debts were bound to large landed estates. They were not infrequently treated like slaves. In the magnificent cathedral of Puebla, Poinsett noticed that miserable, scantily clad natives were wandering about.[24] In frontier districts aborigines were not infrequently seen bearing arms such as their ancestors had used in the time of the Spanish conquest.[25] Higher in the social pyramid were the creoles, who sometimes held landed estates, or local offices, or titles of nobility. At the apex of the social pyramid were the aristocratic nobles, the large landowners, and the holders of important public offices. Some officials were Peninsular Spaniards.

The clergy occupied an important and influential place, especially in the capital. Poinsett estimated in 1822 that there were in that city 550 secular clergy and 1646 members of regular orders. The income of ecclesiastics varied from the slender yearly stipend of a curate of an Indian village, which was about $100, to that of the Archbishop of Mexico, which amounted to $130,000 annually.[26] The same author estimated that the estates belonging to the clergy were worth perhaps $3,000,000. He expressed the opinion that there was "no country in Europe or America, where the superstitious forms of worship" were more strictly observed than in Mexico.[27] An Englishman who visited her Pacific coast, however, beheld a Spaniard, "to the infinite delight of the company," mimicking the ceremony of a priest reciting Mass.[28]

An influential group was the military class. In his *Notes on Mexico* Poinsett recorded that an official report estimated the total armed force at some 68,000, of which less than one half were militiamen. Near the end of 1822, the regular army had apparently decreased in number to about 11,000, while the militia remained at 30,000. The same observer estimated that there was in the capital city a force of infantry and cavalry of about 3,500.[29] "I have found the peasantry of this country, both Indians and castes," said Poinsett, "an amiable and a kind people, possessing the utmost good nature, and great natural politeness. . . . When drunk, they are ungovernable, and are savage and brutal in the extreme. . . ."[30]

[24] Poinsett, *Notes on Mexico*, p. 39.

[25] Hall, *Extracts from a Journal Written on the Coasts of Chili, Peru, and Mexico*, II, 221-223.

[26] *Op. cit.*, pp. 84-85.

[27] *Ibid.*, p. 87. Stephen Austin expressed similar views (Barker, *The Life of Stephen F. Austin*, p. 47).

[28] Hall, *op. cit.*, II, 205-206.

[29] Poinsett, *op. cit.*, pp. 113-114.　　　　[30] *Ibid.*, p. 200.

EMPEROR AGUSTÍN ATTIRED FOR THE CORONATION CEREMONY

A portrait in the Museo Nacional de Historia

EMPRESS ANA MARÍA IN HER CORONATION ROBES
A portrait in the Museo Nacional de Historia

Farming was the chief occupation. The most important crop was corn. On the highlands, barley, rye, wheat, tobacco, and sugar cane were raised. Bananas, manioc, cotton, and rice were produced in the lowlands. Rich mines were located in the region around the city of Guanajuato, where deposits of gold and silver were found. After the close of the struggle for independence, attention was turned from the mining of iron and mercury to the extraction of gold and silver.[31] In various places there were factories of cigars, boots, shoes, hats, cotton goods, pottery, silverware, and gold thread. Poinsett estimated that the articles manufactured in Mexico had decreased in value from 8,000,000 pesos, which they aggregated at the time of Humboldt's visit, to about 4,000,000 pesos.[32]

This decline had naturally affected the exchequer of the Empire. In a letter to Secretary John Quincy Adams in June, 1822, Consul Taylor explained that, besides excise taxes such as those on pulque, the main sources of income were the government monopolies of tobacco, salt, gunpowder, and playing cards, certain revenues collected from the clergy, and the duties levied on exports and imports.[33] An American visitor mentioned that in October, 1822, upon entering the harbor of Vera Cruz, imports paid a duty of 8 per cent. At the customhouse in that city duties were also collected on certain exports. Goods conveyed to the capital were charged the *alcabala* tax which amounted to 12.5 per cent ad valorem. The Spanish tax on stamped paper was retained for a time after independence was proclaimed.[34]

To offset the steadily mounting debt, the government resorted to forced loans from churches, monasteries, and mercantile tribunals. Soon after Iturbide was proclaimed Emperor, a friar informed the Secretary of the Treasury that, in order to meet the demands of the government for a loan of 20,000 pesos, the head of the ecclesiastical province of Santiago de Predicadores had placed some of its landed estates on sale and had also ordered that the silver plate in its temples should be melted. This ecclesiastic declared that no receipt was necessary for money contributed to the national treasury because the proved honor of Agustín I was more highly valued than empires.[35]   A few

[31] *Ibid.*, pp. 145-151, 170-173.
[32] *Ibid.*, pp. 100-102; cf. Bullock, *Six Months' Residence and Travels in Mexico*, pp. 105-109, 210-212, 225-228.
[33] June 6, 1822, in S.D., Consular Letters, Vera Cruz, 1.
[34] Poinsett, *op. cit.*, p. 14. A decree had specified what imposts were to be imposed upon liquors (*Gaceta del gobierno imperial de México*, August 17, 1822, pp. 629-631).
[35] L. Carrasco to R. Pérez Maldonado, May 30, 1822, *Noticioso General*, June 19, 1822.

months later in response to a protest that the silver utensils of a certain monastic establishment would have to be melted to meet his demands, the Emperor discredited the notion that the government wished churches to transform their silver plate into coin of the realm.[36]

On June 11, 1822, Congress directed the government to solicit a loan from the *consulado* of the capital city to the amount of 400,000 pesos which was to be levied proportionately among the merchants. If that sum could not be raised from them, it was to be demanded of the mercantile tribunal of Puebla. Moreover, 5,000 pesos were to be requested from the *consulado* of Vera Cruz.[37] Fourteen days later, a decree was issued authorizing the government to float in foreign countries a loan of some thirty million pesos. As security for the payment of that loan, it was empowered to hypothecate the national revenues.[38]

It was not merely in a figurative sense that Beruete wrote in his diary in July, 1822, that as the soldiers had not been paid, the Secretary of the Treasury was going from door to door asking for money. The government was soon compelled to resort to direct taxation.[39] On August 2 an order was issued that a tax of 2 per cent was to be levied on all the gold, silver, and copper money that might pass through certain customhouses.[40]

The imperial household was dislocated. Although in November, 1822, the Emperor was residing in Moncada Palace, yet the former palace of the viceroys was ordinarily used for public functions. Though elaborate arrangements had been made for an imperial court,[41] yet when an American visitor called upon Agustín I, it had not been completely set up. Joel Poinsett was received at the palace of government by a numerous guard and escorted up a large stone stairway lined with sentinels to a spacious room where a general presented him to the sovereign, whose entourage was composed simply of two favorites.[42] Poinsett recorded that the pictures he saw of Iturbide, which presumably were painted by the best artists in Mexico, were "very bad specimens" of the condition of the fine arts.[43] It appears that by this time the remarkable statue of King Charles IV by the Mexican sculptor

[36] Agustín I to M. Puebla, October 2, 1822, in A.H.H., Donativos y Préstamos, legajo 699.
[37] *Gaceta del gobierno imperial de México*, June 20, 1822, pp. 423-424.
[38] Dublán y Lozano, *Legislacion mexicana*, I, 617.
[39] Diario, July 19, 1822, f. 19v., in MSS, T.U.
[40] *Gaceta del gobierno imperial de México*, August 17, 1822, p. 633.
[41] Romero de Terreros, *La Corte de Agustín Primero*.
[42] *Notes on Mexico*, p. 67.
[43] *Ibid.*, p. 118.

Manuel Tolsa had been removed from the center of the Plaza de Armas, which was being used as a bull ring.[44]

Some not inconsiderable demands were made upon the treasury by the imperial household. Here a few illustrations must suffice. The Iturbide Papers contain a bill for chocolate for Empress Ana María which amounted to 448 pesos.[45] An expense ascribed to Miguel Cavaleri was 300 pesos for a saddle of bearskin with a seat of green velvet bearing leather trappings and adorned with gold.[46] Another bill, which aggregrated 1074 pesos, was on account of clothes made for the Emperor and certain princes of the imperial house.[47] Statistics published by Banegas Galván indicate that from January 1 to November 30, 1822, the government of Mexico had contracted a debt of almost two and a half million pesos.[48]

Moreover, soldiers who had fought for independence under Hidalgo or Morelos asked Agustín I to reward their services.[49] All those persons who had held the title of general, of colonel, of intendant, or of deputy, wrote Lorenzo de Zavala in exaggerated terms, "all those persons who had lost their property by promoting the cause of independence, either by destruction, or by confiscation on the part of the Spanish government; those persons who had been incapacitated for labor because of wounds which they had received—in fine, one half of the nation asked for this or that recompense."[50] Such was the later view of one who in 1823 had served as a deputy for Yucatan.

A Mexican historian of this period took the view, however, that the Emperor had actually been economical in the management of his household establishment. Alamán stated that the chief magistrate had set aside 500,000 pesos, one third of the sum that had been assigned to him for the expenses of the imperial house, for the promotion of the mining industry. Further, that writer mentioned the "noble disinterestedness," in which Iturbide had had few imitators, as typical of the fiscal policy of that ruler after he came to power.[51] In his apologetic memoirs the former Emperor mentioned other problems which he had anticipated would confront him after he accepted the crown: "I was fully convinced that my fortunes were infinitely injured;

[44] Alamán, Historia de Mexico, V, 533.
[45] Mes de Enero de 1823, in I. MSS, 26.
[46] El Exmo. Sor. D. Miguel Cavaleri á Ignacio Mendoza, debe, undated, ibid.
[47] Cuenta of M. P. Gómez, January 15, 1823, ibid.
[48] Historia de Mexico, II, apéndice, 16-18.
[49] El Clamor de la justicia de las antiguas patriotas tituladas insurgentes, pp. 11-12.
[50] Ensayo histórico de las revoluciones de México, I, 126.
[51] Historia, V, 519.

that I would be persecuted; that envy would cause many persons to be displeased with the measures which would have to be adopted; that it was impossible to satisfy everyone; that I was about to contend with an assembly full of pride and ambition, an assembly which, although denouncing despotism was nevertheless endeavoring to monopolize political authority, reducing the monarch to a mere phantom, and securing for itself not only the power to make the laws but also the authority to administer them and to judge of their infractions. . . . If Congress had been able to carry all its projects into effect, the Mexicans would have had less liberty than the people of Algiers. . . ."[52]

Thus did Iturbide subsequently formulate the main issue between himself and Congress, an issue which even before he was acclaimed Emperor had appeared as a menacing cloud upon the horizon. Indeed a Mexican historian has taken the view that the entire reign of Agustín I hinged upon the relations between him and the legislature.[53] The situation was complicated in July, 1822, when rumors were rife of republican conspiracies against the imperial regime. During the next month, when the Emperor expressed his approval of a law directed against conspirators, he elucidated his political faith. He expressed the opinion that persons who intrigued against the nation's independence were as much "enemies of the country, as guilty of *lesa nación*, and as abominable to reason and justice as those individuals who conspired against the established government." Such persons were as guilty as those who plotted against Congress or the Emperor or any of the guarantees accepted by the people. He asked:

"Which one of such sacred objects could be destroyed without undermining the entire social structure, without burying beneath its ruins the entire social edifice, and without burying the liberty for which our forefathers fought, the holy liberty to which man naturally aspires, that liberty which we acquired by facing perils, and which we purchased at the cost of incalculable sacrifices? By a miracle of politics the powers of government were divided, and limited monarchies were established. These are undoubtedly the best type of government. States were thus formed in such a manner that they could be stable, and so that their citizens could enjoy peace and tranquillity, without being constantly exposed to the convulsions of democ-

---

[52] Iturbide, *Carrera militar y política de Don Agustin de Iturbide, ó sea memoria que escribió en Liorna*, p. 37. In 1822 Álvarez asserted that Congress was undertaking to establish a worse despotism than that which existed in Morocco (*Santa Anna hasta 1822*, pp. 12-13).

[53] Banegas Galván, *Historia*, II, 141, 146.

racy or the insults of despotism. Any person who may conspire against the harmony that should exist among the powers of government, the harmony which is essential to general happiness and which is the first support of public prosperity, should be considered as a criminal, a monster who should without delay be excluded from society. . . ."[54]

Congress had on July 24 decreed the conditional pardon of all persons who had been accused of disaffection toward the government since May 18, 1822. Furthermore, early in August the Council of State recommended to the Emperor not only that special military tribunals should be set up in the capitals of all the provinces to deal with cases of disaffected citizens or of conspiracy against the State but also that all persons who might act contrary to Mexican liberty or independence were to be considered as being guilty of sedition.[55]

Discontent was encouraged by Padre Mier. A critic of monarchy and an ardent republican, he became one of the most bitter opponents of Agustín I. A contemporary asserted that that deputy likened the inaugural ceremony of the Imperial Order of Guadalupe to a barbaric dance of Indians called Huehuenches (little old men). Republican opposition to imperial rule was re-enforced by Masons belonging to the Scottish rite. Their activity was stimulated by José Mariano de Michelena, who had recently returned from Spain.[56]

Rumors of conspiracies against the imperial regime eventually involved deputies who had opposed the Emperor's policies. He accordingly issued an order that such persons should be arrested.[57] On the night of August 26 several members of the opposition were accordingly seized by soldiers and incarcerated in the monastery of San Domingo. Among congressmen thus imprisoned were Carlos María de Bustamante, José Fagoaga, José Joaquín de Herrera, Padre Mier, and José del Valle. A citizen of the United States, who was in Fagoaga's house when the arrest was made, stated that the deputy was seized by a lieutenant at the head of a file of soldiers who avowed that this was done by order of the Emperor, that they were not aware what crime was charged against the prisoner, and that the only authorization for the arbitrary act was the imperial bayonets.[58] At the same time some

[54] *Actas del congreso*, II, 406-407.
[55] Council of State to Agustín I, August 3, 1822, in A.G.N., Justicia, 32.
[56] Alamán, *Historia*, V, 490-492.
[57] Iturbide, *Carrera militar y política*, p. 40.
[58] W. Taylor to Adams, September 25, 1822, in D.S., Consular Letters, Vera Cruz, 1.

forty other persons were thrust into prison.[59] Congressmen demanded that their imprisoned colleagues should be set free and placed at their disposal. To refute their arguments Agustín I maintained that by arresting deputies he had not infringed Article CLXXII of the Spanish Constitution which was provisionally in force. Further, he made a new profession of political faith which veiled a threat.

"I have sworn to the nation to rule according to a constitutional system. I shall be faithful to my word, and shall respect what actually exists so far as the welfare of the Empire allows. Yet, if because of the faults of its organization or the passions of its agents, a desire is displayed to convert that system into an instrument of anarchy, the nation herself by the use of her sovereign rights, will provide a new legislative representation. I shall be the first to invoke such a legislature, so that, furnished with laws that will safeguard the general welfare of the citizens, I shall lessen the enormous burden of administration, which I neither ought nor wish to exercise despotically. In accordance with my principles and the most fervent desires of my heart, I shall be a constitutional monarch, subject to all the laws which emanate from the legitimate organs established by the nation."[60]

The official gazette declared that the object of the conspiracy was either the establishment of a republican government or the bestowal of the imperial crown upon a foreign prince. Its comment on the political situation presumably explained the attitude of the government. The gazette declared that certain deputies involved in the conspiracy had from the outbreak of the revolution been afflicted with "the fatal vertigo for a republic," a political system which would never suit Mexico, "where distances are so enormous, where classes are so unequal, so heterogeneous, and so much inclined to an inveterate aristocracy marked by inequalities of fortune, of culture, and of the essentials of civilization."[61]

A tract published by order of the government presented the view that the plot was far-reaching, and that among its members were Padre Mier and General Negrete.[62] Some of the plotters apparently wished to overthrow the imperial government and to found a federal republic. Oddly enough, the head of a commission appointed by the

[59] In an Indice de los individuous q. estan en arresto, sixty-eight names are listed, in I. MSS, 17.

[60] Sesiones extraordinarias del congreso constituyente con motivo del arresto de algunos señores diputados, p. L.

[61] Gaceta del gobierno imperial de México, August 31, 1822, p. 686.

[62] Idea de la conspiración descubierta en la capital del Imperio Mexicano en 26 de Agosto de este año, pp. 5-31.

government to investigate the conspiracy was Francisco de Paula Álvarez, who had become the secretary of Agustín I. Although Álvarez collected a mass of testimony which made clear that the object of certain Republicans was to depose the Emperor, yet evidently the inquest was never completed.[63] In a report to the Secretary of Relations on September 30, 1822, however, Álvarez stated that though some of the conspirators held that the Emperor should be put to death, the majority felt that he should be placed at the disposal of Congress. Álvarez reported further that the conspiracy was not skilfully formed, but that, as it was led by men of talent, its execution would have caused many evils.[64] In an account of his public life composed about a year later, Iturbide stated that among those contemporaries who approved of the arrests which he had made at this time were Bravo, Cortazar, Negrete, and Antonio Santa Anna.[65] However that may be, there is no doubt that the wholesale arrests increased the number and the bitterness of the Emperor's enemies. In satirical stanzas composed behind prison walls, Mier denounced him as a wicked traitor.[66]

When objections were raised in Congress to the imprisonment of its members, Secretary Herrera took the same view as the Emperor. He insisted that this step was not inconsistent with Article CLXXII of the Spanish Constitution which dealt with the arrest of legislators. At the instance of Fernández and Zavala, a motion was adopted on August 30 to the effect that, if certain deputies were accused of having conspired against the government, it was the duty of the legislature to investigate the charges. In the justificatory reply of Agustín I he argued that the Constitution had not been violated by the arrest of congressmen. He maintained that he had observed his oath to rule the nation under a constitutional system. He avowed again that he would be a constitutional monarch who was subject to all the laws enacted by the legislature. He directed the attention of congressmen to a Spanish law of April 11, 1821, aimed against conspirators which provided that they should be tried in a military fashion.[67] In this manner, said a leading deputy, the Emperor proceeded toward his ruin;

[63] *Publicaciones del archivo general de la nacion*, XXIII, 237-384.

[64] Iturbide, Manifiesto, September 27, 1823, f. 69-70, in F.O., 79/39b. Bancroft (*History of Mexico*, IV, 782 n. 8) quotes a French translation of an English version of this report.

[65] Iturbide, *Carrera militar y politica*, p. 40 nn. 23 and 24; and p. 44 n. 27.

[66] Bustamante, *Continuacion del cuadro historico*, pp. 24-25.

[67] *El Oficio que la comisión del soberano congreso presentó a S. M. I. y su contestación*, pp. 1-7.

with his own hands he dug the sepulcher in which he was to be immolated.[68]

So indignant were the colleagues of the imprisoned congressmen at the acts of the chief magistrate that they held secret meetings from August 27 to September 11 in order to consider what steps should be taken. A committee of four members was selected to investigate the charges against the accused legislators. The committee decided that, as Congress had done all that it could without precipitating a conflict with the Emperor, it ought to remain silent for the time being in the expectation that time would clarify occurrences which could not remain buried in oblivion and that it could then decide what course to adopt.[69] Deputy Gómez Farías, however, said that the minister should be held responsible for the arbitrary incarceration of his colleagues.[70]

In a record of the secret proceedings of the Council of State concerning the imprisoned congressmen the view was expressed that nineteen of them should be set free, that the cases of thirteen should be considered dubious, and that twenty-seven, whom it viewed as criminals, should remain in prison at the disposition of the judicial tribunal.[71] The object of the conspiracy appears to have been to seize the imperial family by the aid of the army, to declare the election of Agustín I null and void, and to allow Congress to form a republican system of government.[72]

Upon returning to Mexico after months of absence, Consul Wilcocks wrote to Secretary Adams from the capital city that the conspiracy would have become formidable but for "the bold and vigorous measures adopted by the Emperor for its suppression." Wilcocks expressed the opinion that presumably the people of the United States would not approve of the wholesale arrests ordered by Agustín I, but he justified them on the ground that it was the only way to prevent an uprising, which "would not perhaps have ceased but with the death

[68] Bustamante, *Continuacion del cuadro historico*, p. 18.

[69] *Sesiones extraordinarias del congreso constituyente con motivo del arresto de algunos señores diputados*, pp. cxxvii-cxxviii. The fly-leaf of the copy of this rare book in the library of the University of Texas bears a note by Carlos Bustamante dated July 31, 1832, which contains the following sentence: "La energía del Congo. contra la tyranía de Iturbide esta consignada en esta sesión, y spre. lo hará honor."

[70] *El Ministro es responsable á la prison de los ss. diputados*, p. 16.

[71] Borradores de las actas secretas, October 15-December 11, 1823, in I. MSS, 17.

[72] Under the rubric "Noticias del Imperio," on August 31, 1822, p. 686, the *Gaceta del gobierno imperial de México* began an account of the conspiracy thus: "En el noche del 26 se ha descubierto en esta Capital una meditada conspiración contra el actual Gobierno con la mira de establecer el Republicanismo, ó entregar el Trono á una dinastía extrangera."

of thousands and probably have ended in the greatest anarchy and confusion. . . ."[73]

Another serious difference between the Emperor and Congress arose because of the veto power which he undertook to use. Hence his secretary invited ministers, generals, congressmen, and the councilors of state to attend a meeting. The avowed object of the conference, over which Agustín I presided, was to quiet the dispute which had arisen between the executive and the legislature. Bocanegra, who was present, felt that its real purpose was to reduce the power of Congress.[74] Beruete mentioned that this group even considered dissolving it.[75] After some discussion, a committee was selected to study the relations of Congress with the Emperor. Lorenzo de Zavala, who was a member of the committee, presented a plan for political reform which involved the exclusion from the legislature of some members from those provinces that had a larger representation than they deserved according to their population. He also proposed that steps should be taken to frame a constitution which would provide for a bicameral legislature.[76] When Zavala's plan was laid before Congress, it appointed a committee which recommended that the Spanish Constitution should be adopted, that the sovereign should have the right of veto, and that, with respect to certain crimes, the provisions of a Spanish law of April 15, 1821, should be followed. The upshot was that the legislature refused to approve the proposed purge.[77]

Meanwhile, on September 26 a colonel of obscure origin named Felipe de la Garza, the commander of the Interior Provinces of the East, who had left the royalists after the Plan of Iguala was proclaimed and had sent to Congress a plea for the establishment of a republic,[78] addressed to Agustín I a memorial on behalf of the people of Nuevo Santander in which he denounced despotic tendencies in the national government. In addition Garza made five requests: (1) that the imprisoned deputies should be at once set free, (2) that all other persons who had been incarcerated on suspicion should be accorded similar treatment, (3) that Congress should be installed where it could deliberate freely, (4) that the Emperor's ministers should be removed from office and tried according to law, and (5) that military tribunals should be abolished.[79]

[73] September 28, 1822, in S.D., Consular Letters, Vera Cruz, 1.
[74] Memorias, I, 85-86.　　　　　　　　　[75] Diario, f. 44v., in MSS, T.U.
[76] Zavala, Proyecto de reforma del congreso, p. 8.
[77] Idem, Ensayo histórico de las revoluciones de México, I, 134-137.
[78] Iturbide, Breve diseño crítico de la emancipacion y libertad de la nacion mexicana, pp. 106-107.
[79] Bocanegra, Memorias, I, 152-154.

Two days later that colonel addressed a manifesto to the Mexican people. After praising the achievements of Iturbide and commending his elevation to the imperial throne, Garza denounced the imprisonment of the deputies as a violation of law, as an atrocious attempt to dissolve the national legislature, and as an outrage to the Mexican nation. He implored the Mexicans, in case a civil war should break out, "to enlist under the banners of liberty, not in order to serve against the worthy Emperor" but against a perverse clique which surrounded him.[80]

Agustín I took prompt measures to quell the incipient rebellion. On October 5, 1822, he sent an urgent, secret order to General Anastasio Bustamante. Stating that Garza was implicated in the conspiracy which had been unearthed in the capital city, the Emperor directed that Bustamante should circulate throughout the provinces under his command a notice that the rebellious officer had been proclaimed a traitor and that all persons who did not resist him or who aided him in any manner would be treated as traitors.[81] As the Minister of Colombia was suspected of being an abettor of the conspiracy, on October 16, by order of the Emperor, Secretary Herrera sent him his passports. General Cordero, the commander of the Interior Provinces of the West, accordingly issued a proclamation to announce that, if Garza acted openly against the imperial government, the inhabitants of those provinces would be expected to exterminate his followers who aimed to re-enact the horrors of the early Mexican revolution.[82] In the epigrammatic title of a broadside which was hawked in the streets of the capital city, the pursuit of the rebel colonel was thus described: Iturbide hunts the partisans of Garza without firing a gun.[83]

Prompt and vigorous action by loyal military officers soon caused the collapse of the movement. On October 26 the government issued a notice that the rebellion had been quelled and that the Emperor had pardoned all persons who were involved in it.[84] The Noticioso General contrasted this lenient treatment with the odious policies of European monarchs.[85] The discomfited colonel proceeded to the capital where,

[80] Copy, El Brigadier Garza á la Nación Mejicana, April 28, 1822, Hernández y Dávalos Collection, 15-5-1859, in MSS, U.T.

[81] Castillo Negrete, Mexico en el siglo xix, XIV, 318-321.

[82] October 25, 1822, in A.N.M., legajo 67. For a defense of Santa María, see Zubieta, Apuntaciones sobre las primeras misiones diplomáticas de Colombia, pp. 216-217.

[83] Iturbide caza Garzas sin disparar el fusil; Poinsett, Notes on Mexico, p. 195.

[84] Gaceta extraordinaria del gobierno imperial de México, October 27, 1822, pp. 385-388.

[85] Bocanegra, op. cit., I, 159-160.

by an act of rare magnanimity, he was pardoned by Agustín I, who even allowed him to return to his command. At the instance of the Emperor, the ministers soon took a decisive step. General Luis Cortazar was directed to see that the legislature was dissolved within ten minutes after an order to that effect had been placed in the hands of its President. Cortazar was further instructed that, if the deputies did not obey, they were to be dispersed by military force.[86] Agustín I explained that he had religiously performed his duty with respect to Congress in the confidence that it would enact useful laws which would properly organize the government and promote the welfare of the Empire; but that instead of doing so the congressmen had disappointed the nation by neglecting their duties and by assuming authority which they did not rightfully possess.[87] "Examine the acts of Congress," he wrote in his memoirs; "its principal task was to form the Constitution for the Empire. Not a single line of that document was written. . . . There were no funds with which to pay the soldiers or public officials. Neither a treasury department nor a fiscal system existed, for the establishment which had functioned under the Spanish regime had been swept away and nothing had been done to replace it."[88]

Agustín I announced in a decree dated October 31 that Congress was dissolved, and that to take its place until a new legislature could be assembled, a junta was to be set up, composed, besides substitutes, of two deputies for every province with a large population and of one deputy for each province with a small population. All of those members were to be selected by himself. He justified this arbitrary act by explaining that the legislators had not initiated the needed military and political reforms.[89] When Iturbide mentioned in his autobiography the dissolution of Congress, he explained that "in order that a body so respectable because of the manner in which it was established should not be swept away entirely, and lest it should be believed that I had arrogated the power of making laws, on the same day I replaced it by a junta which I called instituent. . . . Exclusive of eight substitutes, the members of the junta numbered forty-five."[90]

Bocanegra asserted that the imperial cabinet had a long and animated debate about the personnel of the Instituent Junta. He further

[86] Bustamante, *Continuacion del cuadro historico*, p. 20; Poinsett, *Notes on Mexico*, p. 63.
[87] *Gaceta del gobierno imperial de México*, November 5, 1822, p. 922.
[88] Iturbide, *Carrera militar y politica*, p. 24.
[89] *Gaceta del gobierno imperial de México*, November 5, 1822, pp. 922-923.
[90] Iturbide, *op. cit.*, p. 45.

recorded that, despite his opposition to the imperial government, Agustín I had invited him to serve as a member. That deputy held that this act showed that the Emperor wished to avoid extreme measures.[91] There appears to be no doubt, however, that a majority of the members of the new junta were deliberately selected from the congressional faction which had supported his policy.[92] A few days after the dissolution of the legislature, the Emperor notified the members of the rump Congress that they were to meet at once.[93] Despite the resentment of legislators at these proceedings, many Mexicans of the lower classes approved of the arbitrary measures of the chief magistrate. Carlos María de Bustamante later asserted in Congress that these acts were lauded by pamphleteers. Moreover, he stated that on November 1 a crowd of men preceded by musicians marched through the streets of the capital "shouting long live the absolute Emperor, insulting the guards who were posted around the monasteries where deputies were incarcerated, and loudly demanding that the prisoners should be turned over to them so that they might be put to death."[94] This deputy declared that the Instituent Junta was installed "with Asiatic pomp."[95]

Its first session took place on the afternoon of November 2 in the same hall which Congress had occupied. "About six o'clock," said Poinsett, who attended the meeting, "his majesty entered, preceded by a crowd of attendants bearing lights, and accompanied by the counsellors and ministers of state."[96] After being escorted to the throne, he read a speech in which he discussed the state of the nation. He ascribed the deplorable condition of the army to congressional neglect. He reasoned that, by following precedents set by the Spanish Cortes, the legislature had copied some of its mistakes. He maintained that when a government had directed an assembly to form a constitution, that body should not be entrusted with any other function. He ascribed the disasters which France and Spain had suffered to the manner in which the constituted authorities had "overstepped the bounds set to their power."[97]

Agustín I soon formed organic bases which outlined the functions of the Instituent Junta in fifteen articles. Among its duties was to

[91] *Memorias*, I, 98.
[92] Alamán, *Historia*, V, 506-507.
[93] Bocanegra, *op. cit.*, I, 162-163.
[94] Bustamante, *Manifiesto histórico a las naciones y pueblos del Anáhuac*, p. 28.
[95] *Ibid.*
[96] Poinsett, *Notes on Mexico*, p. 66.
[97] *Diario de la junta nacional instituyente del Imperio Mexicano*, I, 5-6.

be the framing of a constitution which would consolidate "the form of government that had been proclaimed and established in accordance with the bases adopted, ratified, and sworn to by the entire nation." Besides, it was to formulate regulations to govern the next congressional election; and, in co-operation with the executive authority, it was to organize the treasury so as to prevent deficits. Whenever important legislative matters were being discussed, "the orators of the government" were to be allowed to participate in the debate. The Junta was to make regulations for its meetings as well as to determine the extent to which the persons of its members should be considered inviolable. Its officers were to be a president, two vice-presidents, and four secretaries.[98] Soon afterward committees were selected to consider such matters as the *Patronato Real*, the condition of the national treasury, the plan for the election of a new Congress, and the drafting of a constitution for the Empire.[99] Rules which the Junta later approved contained elaborate provisions concerning the reception of the Emperor and other members of the imperial family when they attended its meetings.[100]

On November 13, 1822, the National Instituent Junta, as it styled itself, addressed a manifesto to the Mexican people. Declaring that the same hand which had laid the foundations of their independence was now directing them to the path of happiness, it outlined a plan of action. The program included the levying of such fiscal contributions as would enable the nation to make up the existing deficit, the summons for the election of a Congress, and the framing of a constitution which was to be submitted to the consideration of the legislature. Further, the Junta announced that it intended to enact a law of colonization which would allow foreign industry and labor to enter the country.[101]

The proceedings of the imperial government had meantime become a theme of public discussion. On November 18, 1822, Fernández de Lizardi published a lampoon entitled *Fifty Questions*. Among his pointed inquiries were the following: Should Congress not be installed soon? Should not all classes in the country be represented therein? Would the election of the new congressmen be carried on freely according to the Spanish system? Could the Mexicans sleep in

[98] *Ibid.*, pp. 3-9; *Gaceta del gobierno imperial de México*, December 5, 1822, pp. 1286 *et seq.*
[99] *Gaceta del gobierno imperial de México*, November 7, 1822, pp. 927-928.
[100] *Diario de la junta nacional instituyente*, I, 7-10.
[101] Bocanegra, *op. cit.*, I, 163-166.

security when thieves possessed the keys to their houses?[102] A writer who assumed the pseudonym of "Washington Napoleon" denounced the imprisonment of the deputies. He asserted that by such a usurpation of authority the Emperor had become a second Dionysius. With the cunning of a fox, he had concealed the designs of a lion.[103]

So far as his public life was concerned, the Emperor was not without defenders. Soon after he had dissolved Congress, there was published a pamphlet entitled *An Indication of the Origin of the Misconduct of the Mexican Congress that Caused Its Dissolution*, a tract which was probably inspired by the administration. The anonymous author reasoned that the attempt of Congress to exercise absolute sovereignty was due to factional opposition to the imperial form of government. He not only maintained that the nation had acquired the right to form a suitable constitution but also asserted that a national constituent representation would be formed in accordance with the Iguala Plan and the Treaty of Córdoba, both of which had been misrepresented by the Junta. He even accused a clique in Congress of scheming to reunite Mexico with Spain. He exhorted his countrymen, whether Mexicans or Spaniards, to rely upon the love and the vigilance of the Emperor.[104] Another side to the many-faceted political situation was revealed by the salvos of artillery and the ringing of bells which made known the safe delivery of a robust scion of "the invincible Hero who had secured Mexican liberty."[105]

The Instituent Junta had selected a committee to frame a provisional constitutional regulation for the Mexican Empire. The initiative in this matter was attributed by Zavala to the Emperor and his ministers.[106] Despite that deputy's opposition to the proceeding, there is no doubt that the committee prepared a draft of a constitution.[107] Among Iturbide's papers there is found what appears to be a fragmentary analysis of the plan. After stating that the Empire had thus far been governed by the Spanish Constitution, he reasoned that every people should have a constitution analogous to its religion, to its posi-

[102] Fernández de Lizardi, *Cincuenta preguntas del pensador á quien quiera responderlas*, pp. 1-3.

[103] *Retrato vivo del hombre que se llamó Emperador*, pp. 2-3.

[104] *Indicación del origen de los extravios del congreso mexicano*, pp. 4, 15-16. Cf. *Origen y destrucción del trono de Agustín Primero ó declamaciones de un buen patriota*.

[105] *Gaceta extraordinaria del gobierno imperial de México*, December 1, 1822, pp. 1013-1014.

[106] Zavala, *Ensayo histórico*, I, 144.

[107] Bustamante, *Diario historico de Mexico*, I, 83; cf. Alamán, *Historia*, V, 517.

tion, to its customs, to its international relations, and even to its prejudices.

This analysis contained interesting suggestions concerning the Emperor's political philosophy. He held that the Spanish decrees and orders which were still in force in Mexico should be enumerated or perhaps even edited. He maintained that an article in the committee's project which declared that Roman Catholicism should be the religion of state was redundant. He criticized a suggestion that friars should be accorded an exceptional position in society, as well as a proposal that other religions than Roman Catholicism should be recognized. In commenting upon the name proposed for the new political system, he said, "I would suppress the word representative. It would be enough to say a constitutional monarchy. That would indicate what is desired and what the system has been up to the present time." He reasoned that the term *citizen* should be defined so as to include not merely those persons who had already acknowledged the independence of the country but also such other persons as might in the future recognize that status. He held that the circumstances under which the national government might contract loans should be specified and that the executive authority should not have the right to exact contributions. He pointed out that, if every class in Mexican society was allowed to enjoy its existing privileges and exemptions, civil equality would be destroyed. He maintained that the press should be absolutely free but that publications might be censured if their authors had not respected the limits set by law to the liberty of the press. He thought that not even ecclesiastics should be excused from serving the country in case of military necessity. He urged that the exercise of sovereign authority by individuals or by corporations should be prohibited.[108]

Iturbide's disquisition on the project contained little criticism of the committee's proposals concerning the chief magistrate. No comment whatever was made on Article XXIX, which concerned the person of the Emperor. With regard to an article that defined his authority, he suggested a change of phraseology in the clause which described his role in the promulgation and the execution of laws. He believed that the chief executive should not have the power freely to dismiss his ministers, unless the cause for such action could be demonstrated legally. Agustín I objected to a provision which dealt with

[108] Without date or signature, it begins thus, La constitución Española . . . , f. 1-12, I. MSS, 13.

his authority to restrict individual liberty. Instead of it, he suggested that the following clause should be substituted:

"The Emperor may issue orders for the arrest of individuals, whenever this is required by the welfare and security of the State. He should place the person, who may be detained for a period of no more than fifteen days, in the custody of a competent official." He added that "the arbitrariness of the monarch would thus be restrained and an immediate conflict would be avoided."[109] Noteworthy was his view that it was never advisable for military men to exercise political authority. "Civil liberty," said he, "generally resents the dispositions made by soldiers."[110]

Some of the Emperor's emendations were taken to heart by the committee. Among these were his suggestions concerning the status of citizens and foreigners. Certain of his proposed modifications, however, such as that which waived the consent required of Congress to treaties negotiated by the chief executive, were rejected. On December 18, 1822, a "Project of Political Regulation for the Government of the Mexican Empire" was signed by the committee. It was read to the Instituent Junta on December 31.[111] The project provided that the Spanish Constitution was no longer to be in force; but that Spanish laws passed before February 24, 1821, which were not repugnant to the enactments of the Instituent Junta, should be valid. The Provisional Constitution provided that the government of the Mexican Empire was to be "monarchical, constitutional, representative, and hereditary."[112] Roman Catholicism was to be the exclusive religion of the Mexican people. Without prejudice to the rightful prerogatives of the civil power, the discipline, the authority, and the conciliar regulations of the Roman Catholic Church were recognized. The clergy were to retain their privileges according to Article XIV of the Plan of Iguala. All the inhabitants of Mexico, who in consequence of that plan had acknowledged her independence, were declared to be citizens of the Empire.

The proposed provisional constitution provided for executive, legislative, and judicial departments of government. Legislative authority was for the time being to be vested in the Junta. Judicial authority was to be exercised by a Supreme Court in the capital and by other courts to be established by law. At the head of each province there

[109] Ibid.
[110] Ibid.
[111] Proyecto de reglamento político de gobierno del Imperio Mejicano presentado a la junta nacional instituyente y leído en sesión ordinaria de 31 de Diciembre de 1822.
[112] Ibid., p. 8.

was to be a supreme political chief. Article XXIX provided that the executive authority, including the exercise of the *Patronato Real* in legal and canonical form, was vested exclusively in the Emperor as the supreme head of the State: "His person is sacred and inviolable," the project declared; "only his ministers are responsible for the acts of his government. Their respective authorization shall be necessary to put those measures into effect."[113]

In this project the powers of the monarch, who was to be the forefront of the system, were specified in detail. He was to defend the independence and the union of the Empire. He was to protect the Roman Catholic religion and ecclesiastical discipline according to the Plan of Iguala. He was to exercise the right of the *Patronato Real* in legal and canonical form. With the advice of Congress or of the Council of State, he might admit or exclude conciliar decrees and papal bulls which contained general provisions. He was made the Commander in Chief of the military and naval forces. He could declare war and negotiate treaties. He was to make appointments to all civil and military offices of the national government, including the ministers of state. He was to sanction, promulgate, and execute the laws. He could frame the ordinances necessary for their execution. In accordance with law, he could establish judicial tribunals. He could appoint judges upon the recommendation of the Council of State. He was accorded the power of pardon under the law. He was to allocate the funds to be distributed in each branch of the administration. He was expressly given the power to remove the ministers of state. Nothing was said about the right to veto laws enacted by Congress.

There were some express limitations upon the chief executive. He was prohibited from interfering with the legislative body, from transferring his authority to any other person, from departing from the soil of the Empire, from disposing of the territory or other property of the nation, from negotiating alliances with foreign powers without the consent of Congress, and from depriving any person of his liberty. Nevertheless, there was a clause providing that in case of internal convulsions, the chief magistrate should be clothed "with all the power of the law."[114]

These provisions of the constitutional project show that, though the subservient Junta was ready to vest extensive authority in the Emperor, such as the right to control the *Patronato Real*, and even to

[113] *Ibid.*, p. 14.
[114] *Ibid.*, pp. 14-19.

concede him dictatorial power during a crisis, yet it wished to prevent him under ordinary circumstances from interfering with the legislature. The proposed Constitution for the Mexican Empire demonstrates that certain leaders who had given careful thought to the political organization of their nation had decided to retain the existing frame of government with some modifications.

In the Junta on January 10, 1823, Zavala started the opposition to the proposal by questioning the authority of that body to abrogate the Spanish Constitution. Expressing the opinion that the Emperor had more authority to make such a change than the rump legislature, he urged that the committee on constitutional reform should instead frame a law providing for the convocation of a new Congress which should consider the plan.[115] A champion of the project was Toribio González, a deputy for the province of Guadalajara, who argued that it was a necessary, transitional arrangement pending the framing of a constitution which should be submitted to the consideration of the next legislature. On January 14, by a vote of twenty-one to sixteen, the Junta decided in favor of the Provisional Constitution.[116] The political discussion still continued, however, and the project was never put into force.

Pressing problems had arisen concerning unsettled lands in Mexico. At San Antonio de Béxar, on November 8, 1822, Colonel José F. Trespalacios, who had advanced in his checkered career by becoming the governor of the province of Texas, signed a significant agreement with Chief Richard Fields and other Cherokee Indians who had asserted a claim to lands in northeastern Mexico. The pact provided that a delegation of Cherokees was to proceed to Mexico City to treat with the Emperor concerning the settlements which they wished to make in Texas. The parties further agreed that, pending action by the imperial government, the Cherokees already in that province might till their lands "in free and peaceful possession," that such aborigines would become "immediately subject to the laws of the Empire," and that they should even be ready to take up arms in its defense.[117] It appears that in April, 1823, Agustín I approved an arrangement that Governor Trespalacios had reached with them by which they were to be allowed for the time being to continue to occupy the lands upon which they had squatted.[118] Steps were thus taken to safeguard the northeastern frontier of the Empire.

[115] *Diario de la junta nacional instituyente*, pp. 221-225.
[116] *Ibid.*, pp. 373, 394-395.
[117] Winkler, "The Cherokee Indians in Texas," *Quarterly of the Texas State Historical Association*, VII, 101-102.
[118] Yoakum, *History of Texas*, I, 216.

In the meantime the Junta had passed a decree concerning colonization which was approved by Agustín I on January 4, 1823. This law
declared that the government would protect the property, liberty, and
civil rights of all foreigners entering Mexico who professed the Roman
Catholic religion. The chief magistrate was to distribute land to persons who would undertake to plant settlements. An individual who
might wish to introduce at least two hundred families was to enter into
a contract with the executive authority specifying the industry which
was to be carried on by the settlers. For every two hundred families
thus brought into the Empire the impresario was to be allotted a
strip of land. In its distribution preference was to be given to native-
born Mexicans, especially to those persons who had served in the Army
of the Three Guarantees. Provisions were made for the political
organization of the colonists. Each of the new towns and cities was
to be provided with a sufficient number of priests. During the first
six years of a settlement no taxes whatever were to be levied upon
foreigners who might enter the country. Goods, machinery, and
merchandise introduced by such colonists for their own use were to
be partially exempt from taxation. The children of slaves who were
brought into the Empire were to be free at the age of fourteen.[119]

Stephen F. Austin accordingly petitioned the Mexican government
for the right to plant a colony of his countrymen in Mexico. In particular he asked for permission to found one or two towns in the land
assigned to him with the authority to dispose of lots to settlers.[120] On
March 11, 1823, Agustín I issued a decree which approved the action
of the Council of State that had conceded to Austin the right to
introduce foreigners into Texas and to found a settlement according
to the provisions of the colonization law. The concession was later
confirmed by the Constituent Congress of Mexico. A basis was thus
laid for settlements in Texas by citizens of the United States.[121]

Attempts had been made to improve the administrative system,
some social reforms had been initiated, and a provisional, organic law
had been framed to displace the Spanish Constitution which had been
tentatively in force. Yet discontent with the national government had
been gradually increasing. Despite the honors, rewards, and emolu-
ments by means of which Iturbide evidently hoped to gain support

[119] This decree was quoted by José Morán, Captain General of the province of
Puebla, in a broadside issued on January 10, 1823. An English version of the decree
is printed in Gammel, *The Laws of Texas*, I, 27-30. See further, Barker, *The Life of
Stephen F. Austin*, pp. 72-73.
[120] Gammel, *op. cit.*, I, 32.
[121] Filisola, *Memorias para la historia de la guerra de Téjas*, I, 116-119.

for his rule, the opposition that existed largely because of his acceptance of the imperial crown did not decrease. His quarrel with Congress strengthened the hands of the opposition. Sentiment in favor of the establishment of a republican form of government grew steadily among Mexican political and military leaders. Members of a large and fluctuating group that had found it difficult to decide upon the proper form of government for their native land now forsook the Iturbidistas for the Republicans. In the United States, as well as in Mexico, the belief spread that Iturbide was a despot. Upon declining to accept an appointment as the first American minister to Mexico, General Andrew Jackson declared that the unhappy condition of her oppressed people, who were "struggling for their liberties against an Emperor," had convinced him that no envoy from Washington could at that time secure "any beneficial treaty for his country."[122]

[122] Jackson to J. Q. Adams, March 15, 1823, in D.S., Dispatches from Mexico, 1.

CHAPTER XI

Mexican and Spanish Intrigues

DURING THE LAST months of 1822 the province of Vera Cruz became a storm center. The port was held by the Mexicans. General Dávila and a group of royalist refugees were in possession of the castle of San Juan de Ulúa. This fortification, built by the Spaniards at an enormous expense on the isle of Gallegos, a short distance northeast of Vera Cruz harbor, was equipped with heavy artillery and was defended by some six hundred men who were well supplied with food and munitions. The royalist governor of the fortress, however, allowed merchant vessels to enter the harbor subject to the payment of duties on their cargoes. Because Captain General Moscoso had not proceeded to Mexico as the successor of O'Donojú, in May, 1822, the Spanish government appointed the subinspector of engineers in Mexico, Brigadier Francisco Lemaur, the governor of Vera Cruz as well as the Captain General and Superior Political Chief of New Spain. On October 24 Lemaur arrived at Gallegos to take over the command from Dávila, who was rewarded by an important appointment in Spain. As an American visitor remarked, a strange state of affairs existed on the shores of the Mexican gulf: the most important port was in the possession of revolutionists, while the castle which dominated the best gateway to Mexico was held by royalists.

On October 23 General Lemaur issued a proclamation to the people explaining his intentions. He declared that he did not intend to renew hostilities with them and announced that Ferdinand VII wished to establish peace with Mexico. He added that the Cortes had disapproved the Treaty of Córdoba because General O'Donojú had lacked the authority to negotiate it.[1] A few days later Lemaur sent a letter to General Echávarri, who, as Captain General of the provinces of Puebla and Vera Cruz, had been making preparations to assault San Juan de Ulúa. The royalist commander expressed hope that a treaty might be negotiated to regulate the relations between the Spaniards and the city of Vera Cruz.[2]

[1] *Habitantes del Reino de Méjico.*
[2] *Gaceta del gobierno imperial de México*, November 9, 1822, pp. 933-935.

Hoping perhaps that the differences between the Empire and Spain might be peacefully adjusted or that he could facilitate the capture of San Juan de Ulúa, in November, 1822, at the head of a small force, Agustín I marched from the capital to Puebla, Perote, and Jalapa. It was evidently to question General Antonio Santa Anna about his failure to capture Ulúa Castle that the Emperor summoned the commander to report to him at Jalapa.

Just before leaving Jalapa, the Emperor not only summarily removed Santa Anna from his command but also directed him to report in the capital city.[3]   In an autobiographical sketch the deposed commander denounced this humiliating order. "So rude a blow wounded my military pride and tore the bandage from my eyes. I beheld absolutism in all its power; and I felt encouraged to enter into a struggle against Agustín I . . . . I proceeded rapidly to the city of Vera Cruz, where I addressed the people. At four o'clock in the afternoon of December 2, at the head of my soldiers, I proclaimed the republic."[4]

On that day he explained his political views in a proclamation addressed to his compatriots. After deploring the absolutism of the Emperor, he declared that their general desire was the establishment of a republican government based upon certain conditions, namely, the observance of the three guarantees proclaimed in the Plan of Iguala, the arrangement of an armistice with General Lemaur, and the removal of certain restrictions on Mexico's commerce with Spain. He assured the Mexicans that his men would vigilantly guard their persons and property.[5]   On December 3 he issued an address to his soldiers. He argued that Iturbide had become an unjust despot who had riveted anew the fetters fastened upon Mexico by Spanish despotism. In a spirit of self-glorification, he avowed that he was resolved to sacrifice his life and his fortune to promote the happiness of his country. In order to restore to the Mexican nation the liberty which a single individual had usurped, he asked of his followers valor, fidelity, and constancy.[6]

A fuller explanation of his defection was furnished in a letter which he soon addressed to Agustín I. After reminding that monarch

[3] Bustamante, *Diario historico de Mexico*, I, 9. In his *autobiografía* Iturbide justified this removal by declaring that Santa Anna had plotted to assassinate Echávarri and that there had been many complaints against him (*Carrera militar y politica de Don Agustin de Iturbide, ó sea memoria que escribió en Liorna*, p. 46). It has been alleged that Santa Anna had courted María Nicolasa de Iturbide and had thus antagonized the Emperor.
[4] *Mi Historia militar y politica*, p. 11.
[5] *Diario de Vera Cruz*, December 3, 1822.
[6] *Ibid.*, December 4, 1822.

that he had favored his elevation to the throne, and reasoning that he had sacrificed his own interests in order that the imperial dignity should be made hereditary in the Iturbide family, Santa Anna asserted that by such acts he had become odious to his countrymen. He declared that he had loyally undertaken to strengthen the Emperor's power, but that love for his native land was the paramount consideration which led him to renounce his obedience. He accused Agustín I of various offenses:

"I behold the entire nation agitated because of the terrible events which have afflicted Congress. The people of the towns all clamor for liberty. With an imperious voice they tell you that you have broken your oaths; that you have infringed the laws, the Iguala Plan, the Treaty of Córdoba, and all that is most sacred in society. Further, you have brought manifold evils upon the nation by obstructing commerce, paralyzing agriculture, and neglecting the mines. You have persecuted the deputies unjustly, exiling some, oppressing others, and imprisoning many of them until you have reduced Congress to what is designated the Instituent Junta, an assembly which is composed of your favorites. This has been done in order that they might yield to your designs and establish a formal constitution which would ensure the slavery of this people. . . . Lastly, they realize that there is not enough income or property in Mexico to sustain a throne with all the dignity and ostentation which an Emperor exacts."[7]

Santa Anna further maintained that a Congress should be assembled in order to form a constitution for the state upon "the worthy bases of religion, independence, and union." He reasoned that the legislature would reward the service of the Emperor by according him "a distinguished place in the nation." He implored that magistrate not to expose his life to the terrible catastrophe which his adulators had prepared for him.[8] Though this arraignment contained pertinent criticisms of the imperial regime, its anti-imperialistic spirit was doubtless due in part to personal resentment. Santa Anna had meantime engaged in correspondence with the commander of Ulúa Castle which led to an armistice between them. On December 5 he informed Lemaur of his intention to overthrow the imperial government.[9] Guadalupe Victoria, who had escaped from a prison into which the government had cast him and who had shown a desire to become

[7] Bustamante, Continuacion del cuadro historico, p. 52. Rivera Cambas (Historia antigua y moderna de Jalapa, I, 254) ascribes the framing of a proclamation and of the Plan of Vera Cruz to Miguel Santa María.
[8] Ibid.
[9] Castillo Negrete, Mexico en el siglo xix, XIV, 435; XV, 318.

reconciled with Iturbide, soon decided to join Santa Anna, the arch-enemy of the Empire.

At Vera Cruz on December 6, 1822, Santa Anna subscribed a verbose project to which he had secured the adhesion of the inveterate revolutionary Guadalupe Victoria. Like the Plan of Iguala, it eventually took its name from the place where it had been proclaimed. A preamble to the Plan of Vera Cruz explained that it was intended to restore to the Mexican nation "the imprescriptible rights and the true liberty" of which she had been deprived by the Emperor. The project declared that Mexico was vested with full power to establish her own government by means of the legislature. As Agustín I had acted in an arbitrary manner, he should not be recognized as Emperor but a reconstituted Congress should frame an organic law for the state. Meanwhile, the Spanish Constitution and the three guarantees of the Iguala Plan should be observed. An Army of Liberation was to be formed from supporters of the proposed system.[10] Electric fire, said Santa Anna later, did not spread more rapidly than a national spirit was formed.[11] On his part, Victoria explained that, as he detested oppression, he had again taken up arms, had proclaimed a republic and had resolved to perish, if necessary, in the attempt to establish it.[12] One of the first persons to acclaim the election of Agustín Primero, Santa Anna now announced his defection. This was an opportunistic metamorphosis which forecast his kaleidoscopic politico-military career.

Reactions to the Vera Cruz project were various. General José Echávarri, who had become a trusted champion of imperial rule, promptly denounced its author as a hypocrite who was unworthy of the uniform which he wore.[13] On December 10, 1822, the Emperor directed Echávarri to march against Santa Anna, and, in case of the defeat of the rebellious general, to prevent him from taking refuge in Ulúa Castle.[14] Echávarri promptly issued a proclamation to his soldiers in which he denounced the republican gesture of Santa Anna, who had gained the favor of Lemaur by promising to deliver to him

---

[10] Plan ó indicaciones para reintegrar á la nación en sus naturales é imprescriptibles derechos y verdadera libertad, de todo lo que se halla con escándalo de los pueblos cultos violentamente despotada por D. Agustín de Iturbide, pp. 1-22. The above title is that of the Plan of Vera Cruz found in the Sutro Branch, California State Library. The document printed by Bustamante (op. cit., pp. 64-71) differs from that cited above because Bustamante omits and inserts words, alters sentences, and makes additions to the text. The most striking differences are in the "Aclaraciones" or "Declaraciones," as Bustamante (ibid., pp. 67-71) styles them, at the end of the plan.

[11] Manifiesto . . . á sus conciudadanos, pp. 9-10.

[12] Proclama . . . las provincias de oriente y occidente, p. 2.

[13] Bocanegra, Memorias para la historia de México independiente, I, 168.

[14] Castillo Negrete, op. cit., XV, 102-103.

the port of Vera Cruz.[15] Meantime an article in the official gazette had stigmatized the conduct of the new leader of the Republican party as inconsistent, odious, and traitorous.[16] Soon afterward a decree was enacted by the Instituent Junta providing for the issue of 4,000,000 pesos of paper currency. The decree stipulated that one-third of the payments in commercial transactions should be made in this fiat money.[17]

On December 20 the Council of State undertook to consider the uprising. Its members felt that, if the rebellion spread, the safety of the nation would be imperiled; for without order, without union, and without respect for the public authorities, "there would be neither a Mexican nation, nor public liberty, nor independence, nor anything else than anarchy, confusion, and disaster." The council accordingly decided that, in addition to the officials residing in provincial capitals, subaltern agents should be appointed to serve under the political chiefs. Further, instead of being designated national or provincial, the militia should be styled imperial. Its officers should be appointed by the general government. Moreover, the council suggested that other precautions lay within the authority of the Emperor.[18] On the next day, the Instituent Junta published a broadside which provided that conspirators against independence, or the existing form of government, or the person of the Emperor should be subject to summary arrest and to trial by extralegal tribunals.[19] By order of Agustín I, Secretary of War Sota Riva directed Captain General Guerrero to execute the decree.[20] At that very time Santa Anna was defeated in an assault on Jalapa. Had it not been for the admonitions of Victoria, the author of the revolutionary plan might have taken ship for the United States.[21]

In this crisis Agustín I decided to call upon the church for support. He instructed Secretary Domínguez to send a circular directly to the clergy, both regular and secular, in all districts. In distributing that appeal, which was dated December 22, 1822, Domínguez exhorted the priests to give instruction from their pulpits concerning the justice, the necessity, and the convenience of Mexican emancipation under the existing regime, which was based upon the natural and imprescriptible right of all people. Further, that regime had been the anchor

[15] *Gaceta del gobierno imperial de México*, December 17, 1822, p. 1077.
[16] *Ibid.*, December 12, 1822, pp. 1058-1060.
[17] Hernández, *El Archivo historico de hacienda*, pp. 12-13.
[18] The Council of State to A. Quintana Roo and enclosure, December 20, 1822, Hernández y Dávalos Collection, 15-7-2062 and 2063, in MSS, U.T.
[19] December 21, 1822.
[20] *Ministerio de guerra y marina*, December 21, 1822.
[21] Alamán, *Historia de Mexico*, V, 529.

by which the Roman Catholic Apostolic religion had been maintained against "a false and dominant liberalism." Moreover, he urged that the clergy should convince their parishioners that they lay under an obligation "to protect and sustain at all cost the guarantee of union among the inhabitants of the Empire." Lastly, communicants were exhorted to observe "fidelity, respect, and gratitude" toward his Imperial Majesty because of his fine character, his great virtues, and his numerous sacrifices for the cause of liberty and independence.[22]

At Chilapa on January 13 Vicente Guerrero and Nicolás Bravo, both of whom had quietly departed from the capital city and renounced imperial rule, issued a manifesto which began by citing the preamble of the Vera Cruz Plan. They declared that they wished to vindicate the rights of the nation which the Emperor had usurped. Arguing that his election as the sovereign was null and void, they announced that they desired the re-establishment of Congress, which was the only legitimate representation of Mexico.[23] Moreover, Bravo published a proclamation to the Mexicans in which he denounced imperial rule. He stigmatized the Instituent Junta as a coterie of the Emperor's friends. He predicted that horrible scenes would soon be enacted in Mexico. "My object," he explained, "is not my personal interest; but I desire that, in accordance with the Plan of Vera Cruz, the use of her indisputable rights should be restored to the nation. . . ."[24] The denunciation of Iturbide's rule by these influential leaders gave an added impetus to the anti-imperialistic movement. Yet, in spite of disconcerting reports about the uprising, the bustle of bullfights and the pealing of bells continued in the capital city.[25]

In a later explanation of his conduct, after mentioning the usurpation of legislative authority by Agustín I, Guerrero thus explained the rejection of imperial rule by Bravo and himself:

"Up to this time we had been impartial spectators of events who silently lamented our misfortunes because our political existence was threatened. I was convinced that I understood the general opinion which never lost sight of the peculiar actions of the person who was called Emperor. Aware that those evils were approaching a climax, I no longer delayed declaring myself in favor of the cause which had just been proclaimed in Vera Cruz. Accompanied by Don Nicolás Bravo, I abandoned the gayety of the court, and amid threatening

[22] Domínguez, *Justicia y negocios ecclesiásticos, sección ecclesiástica*, pp. 2-3.
[23] *Plan ó indicaciones para reintegrar á la nación en sus naturales é imprescriptibles derechos y verdadera libertad*, p. 4.
[24] Bustamante, *El Honor y patriotismo del general D. Nicolas Bravo demostrado en los ultimos dias del fugaz imperio de Iturbide*, p. 19.
[25] Beruete, Diario, f. 68-68v., in MSS, T.U.

perils, I proceeded to Chilapa, where we unfurled the banner of liberty."[26]

When their defection became known to Guonique, a chief of the Comanche Indians who had just signed in the capital city a curious treaty which not only pledged him to maintain peace with the Mexican Empire but also to defend its northern frontiers, that chief avowed that he would help to keep the crown upon the brow of Agustín I. When he bade farewell to the monarch, Guonique apparently promised to place at his disposal several thousand redskins.[27]

Partly because of the peculiar relations existing between Santa Anna and Lemaur, on December 21, 1822, the imperial government had announced that the war for the independence of Mexico from Spain had been renewed.[28] Shortly afterward, in a letter to Echávarri, Agustín I discussed the international situation. With respect to the commissioners of Spain who were expected daily, he rightly imagined that their object was the pacification of Mexico rather than an acknowledgment of her independence. He maintained that the proceedings of the Spanish government showed no sign of an intention to recognize Mexico as an independent state. With regard to the fulfilment of the Treaty of Córdoba, he explained that the failure of his government to send agents to Madrid was due to a fear that they might be expelled from Spain. He maintained that Lemaur should not only refuse to protect Santa Anna but should also harry him. Lastly, he stated that, if need arose, he would himself lead General Echávarri's soldiers against the city of Vera Cruz.[29] In a letter to his secretary written from San Cosme shortly after the landing of the Spanish commissioners, however, the Emperor reasoned that their mission almost implied the recognition of the independence of Mexico. Meantime, according to Aláman, Echávarri had been initiated into a Masonic lodge and had succumbed to the influence of its members who wished to depose Agustín I. A diarist called the mansion at San Cosme where the Emperor was then sojourning the "Palacio de Escape."[30]

Unedited documents in the General Archives of the Indies reveal that Lemaur had meanwhile undertaken to play a role in the complicated situation. On December 15 he sent an intriguing letter to Echávarri, who had failed to capture Vera Cruz. The royalist commander argued that, under the imperial regime the lives and properties of his countrymen who had enriched Mexico by their toil were im-

---

[26] *Manifiesto . . . á sus compatriotas*, May 16, 1823, p. 2.

[27] *Gaceta del gobierno imperial de México*, January 30, 1823, pp. 51-52.

[28] Bocanegra, *Memorias*, I, 176-177.   [29] Cuevas, *El Libertador*, pp. 363-366.

[30] *Ibid.*, p. 372; Alamán, *Historia*, V, 539; Bustamante, *Diario historico*, I, 65.

periled. He asked if it would be strange that a Mexican leader should rise against such a system. Not only did he denounce the exactions which the Emperor had levied upon Spaniards residing in his dominions but he cricitized that magistrate because, unlike Santa Anna, he had been unwilling to negotiate a peace with Spain. Asserting that imperial rule had brought Mexico to the edge of a precipice, Lemaur concluded with a special appeal:

"In view of this fatal prospect, will you desire to debase yourself by becoming a blind instrument in the hands of a desperate party? I accordingly wish that you would fix your thoughts upon higher objects; and that, forecasting the welfare of this country, or better to say, undertaking to prevent its total ruin, you would aspire to the glory which you could achieve in such an enterprise. The path to such glory cannot be unknown to you."[31]

In that subtle manner the Spanish commander undertook to undermine the loyalty of a fellow-countryman who had been a faithful supporter of Agustín I. General Echávarri had meantime issued a proclamation at Jalapa in which he denounced the Plan of Vera Cruz, praised the Liberator of Mexico, and stigmatized Santa Anna as a hypocrite and a traitor.[32] Several days later the Emperor wrote to Echávarri that the Mexican troops who were investing Vera Cruz had been ordered to obey him. That general was directed to act with vigor so as to inspirit good citizens and to undeceive those persons who were misguided.[33] On January 17 the Commander in Chief wrote to him to reiterate his opinion that the speedy reduction of the besieged city was very important.[34] It was evidently an attempt to bolster the morale of the citizenry which led the Council of State to present to the Emperor a medal bearing an inscription which lauded the achievements of "the Liberator of the country, the founder of the Empire, the invincible Agustín I." On January 27, the very day when an account of the presentation was printed in the official gazette, the monarch unbosomed himself to his secretary in this paragraph:

"The evils which we suffer are the necessary result of the system followed by those persons who dominate the governmental junta and Congress. There is no disguising the fact that their object is to destroy the army and the treasury because they are the necessary means of preserving internal order and hence independence. They foment

[31] Copy, Lemaur to Echávarri, December 15, 1822, in A.G.I., Audiencia de México, 90-2-16.
[32] Bocanegra, op. cit., pp. 167-169.
[33] Cuevas, op. cit., pp. 359-360.
[34] Agustín I to Echávarri, January 17, 1823, Hernández y Dávalos Collection, 16-1-3114, in MSS, U.T.

envy in some people and resentment in other people; they flatter certain persons with complimentary suggestions; and they take advantage of the ignorance of many persons in order to make them the instruments of their machinations."[35]

Strange though it may seem, Santa Anna had also turned his face expectantly toward San Juan de Ulúa. On December 31, he assured Lemaur that Iturbide would be undone by the union which the Spaniard wished to arrange between Mexico and Spain and that, should Echávarri dare to attack the city of Vera Cruz, a single blow would be sufficient to punish him.[36] Echávarri was evidently torn by various emotions: a twinge of loyalty to the Emperor who had signally rewarded him by promotions in rank, a desire to circumvent the wily Santa Anna, a wish to play fair with his own soldiers, and a deep sympathy for his distressed countrymen in Mexico. This vacillating commander even addressed a communication to the Spanish Minister of War which contained an exposé of the precarious condition of Mexico.[37] Several days later, upon their arrival at Ulúa Castle, three Spanish commissioners who had been sent on a mission of pacification addressed a letter to Echávarri to inform him that their purpose was to promote a reconciliation between Mexico and Spain.[38] Soon afterward the commander of that castle wrote to Echávarri again, ostensibly to mention his desire to mediate between him and Santa Anna in order to prevent bloodshed. In reality his intention was to estrange Echávarri from the Emperor. A dispatch to the Court of Madrid from Lemaur contained a passage which revealed his motives. He stated that his object was to persuade Echávarri that "he should rise against Iturbide by proclaiming the re-establishment of Congress. . . . Instead of defending Iturbide against my charges, he endorsed them, but differed with me concerning the means of remedying the situation. However, the guarantees which he has offered me up to the present consist in the relinquishment of his command, if Iturbide should refuse to approve the armistice that Echávarri may adjust with me."[39] On the other side, during the last days of January, 1823, the Emperor

<hr />

[35] *Gaceta del gobierno imperial de México*, January 28, 1823, p. 46, describes the medal; the letter to Álvarez is printed in Cuevas, *op. cit.*, p. 370.

[36] In A.G.I., Audiencia de México, 90-2-16.

[37] Copy, January 9, 1823, enclosed in Lemaur's dispatch no. 3, *ibid.* Iturbide's opinion of Echávarri's conduct is expressed in his *Carrera militar y política*, pp. 49-50 n. 29.

[38] J. R. Oses, S. de Irisarri, and S. Oses to Echávarri, January 21, 1823, Hernández y Dávalos Collection, 16-1-3166, in MSS, U.T.

[39] Copy, Lemaur to M. López Baños, January 29, 1823, in A.G.I., Audiencia de México, 90-2-16.

took steps to rally imperial forces so as to check the rising tide of opposition to his authority.

It appears that Echávarri was ready to take a fateful step. His changing attitude was indicated by a letter which he addressed to Lemaur from his camp before Vera Cruz. He entrusted it to agents who were instructed to make oral explanations regarding the situation which confronted their commander. Stating that he had many influential friends throughout the Mexican provinces, Echávarri reasoned that before the cry of liberty could be given, certain obstacles to that step would have to be removed. Pointedly did he ask whether the Spaniard was interested in consolidating the fraternal relations between Mexico and Spain. Declaring that the moment when the public welfare demanded action from him had arrived, he stated that, if Lemaur did not oppose his project, the political situation would soon be altered.[40]

Evidently the hesitant imperial general received an assurance, which was desired by some of his officers, that, in case his treasonable project miscarried, they would be granted an asylum in the impregnable castle. The commander of that fortress soon explained to the Spanish Secretary of War that, as he had expected, Echávarri had turned against Agustín I. "His army was moved no less by the inconveniences of its situation," wrote Lemaur, "than by the agency of persons who on account of those disadvantages gave to the military commanders the impulse which I desired."[41] Accordingly it was not simply the machinations of Iturbide's enemies and the defection of Santa Anna that presaged the downfall of the First Mexican Empire but also the covert intrigues of Lemaur with Echávarri.

The tempest which had been gathering against imperial rule burst on February 1, 1823. In his headquarters at the "Casa de Mata," a magazine outside the southern walls of Vera Cruz, Echávarri and his officers, including Anastasio Bustamante, Luis Cortazar, and José M. Lobato, signed an act or rather a plan composed of eleven articles. Asserting that danger threatened the country because of the lack of a national legislature, they declared that sovereignty resided in the people and that a new Congress should be installed as soon as possible under the protection of their army. They proposed that the mode of electing congressmen should be the same as that employed in the choice of the former legislators, but that certain members of that body need not be re-elected. Soldiers who might favor the reform were to take an oath to support the new assembly at any cost. A committee

[40] Copy, January 28, 1823, *ibid.*
[41] Lemaur to M. López Baños, February 8, 1823, *ibid.*

was to be appointed to present the plan to the governor of the city of Vera Cruz, while another committee was to lay it before military officers stationed in Jalapa. Pending the receipt of an answer from the imperial government, the provincial deputation of Vera Cruz was to consider the mode of administering the proposed system. Article VII provided that a commission of the army was to place a copy of this program in the hands of Agustín I. The last article declared that, in the belief that the monarch was in favor of convoking a national Congress, the revolutionary soldiers would never harm his person.[42]

Despite the disclaimer, which presumably pleased some lukewarm monarchists, in view of the attendant circumstances, it is clear that in certain essentials Echávarri had accepted the views set forth by Santa Anna on December 2. Asserting that the deposition of Agustín I was the sole object of the Plan of Casa Mata, Alamán declared that "to this there agreed, even without understanding it, the numerous enemies whom the Emperor had made. . . ."[43] In fact Santa Anna had started a movement which foreshadowed the formation of a republic, seemingly in ignorance of the real nature of that political system. A Spanish writer not inappropriately remarked that just as Ferdinand VII was despoiled of his colony by the Plan of Iguala, so Agustín I was shorn of his power by the Plan of Casa Mata.

Not only was the Casa Mata Plan, like Santa Anna's scheme, a program which resembled the Iguala Plan, but its author also imitated Iturbide in the propaganda which he undertook. On the very day when he proclaimed his scheme, Echávarri sent copies of it to the cabildo of Vera Cruz and to the provincial deputation of Mexico.[44] If indeed it was his intention to overthrow Agustín I, he temporarily concealed that purpose. In a letter addressed to Ignacio Rayón on February 1, Echávarri said that, by agreeing to the plan, the officers of his division had undertaken to support the national representation and also to keep Agustín I on the throne. "Upon casting our votes for the installation of Congress, we regarded the conservation of the Emperor as a sacred duty," he asserted, "and in consequence these arms will attempt nothing against his august person which they re-

[42] The Spanish text of the Plan of Casa Mata is published in Navarro y Rodrigo, *Agustín de Iturbide*, pp. 424-426. The texts published by Bustamante in his *Diario historico de Mexico*, I, 170-173, and in *Continuacion del cuadro historico*, pp. 86-88, omit Article VII of the plan. An English translation from a text furnished by Iturbide is found in *A Statement of Some of the Principal Events in the Public Life of Agustin de Iturbide*, pp. 146-148.

[43] *Historia*, V, 541. Alamán stressed the Masonic influence in the formation of the plan, *ibid.*, p. 539.

[44] *Convenio del Sr. Chávarri con el ayuntamiento de Vera Cruz*, p. 2.

spect as inviolable." He reasoned that once Congress was installed and party struggles had terminated, harmony would be restored "between the legislature and the executive; and his Majesty will reign in the hearts of all his subjects. Otherwise, the nation will move with gigantic steps toward her own ruin."[45]

Three days later, in a letter to another correspondent, Echávarri declared that the revolutionary project was demanded by the unhappy condition to which the Mexicans had been reduced.[46] From his camp at Casa Mata on February 2 he had written to Lemaur to inform him concerning the new revolutionary plan. Further, the disaffected general sent an agent to Ulúa Castle who was to explain the delay which had taken place in reaching a decision which had not been the work of a moment. He added:

"In official replies and in private letters you have offered me your aid and friendship from the moment when I should resolve to take this step. I flatter myself that, as it is my intention to cement the relations of this country with Spain, you will co-operate on your part to gain so important an object—an object in which your attentive and reliable servant, José Antonio Echávarri, is as much interested as you."[47] To this letter, which showed that the recreant imperial commander was anxious to have an anchor to windward, the commander of Ulúa Castle promptly replied that the explanation had caused the anomalies of his correspondent's conduct to vanish. Lemaur also declared that Echávarri would not find him lacking in decision and efficiency but anxious to demonstrate by his acts "the sincere and ardent wish that this country should secure happiness in order that, as you have said, its friendly relations with Spain may be improved."[48]

On February 2 Santa Anna issued a manifesto to his countrymen. After mentioning the Plan of Vera Cruz, he declared that the army besieging that city was not only a valiant defender of the rights of Mexico but was also disposed to co-operate with him, while the proceedings of Lemaur conformed to honor and good faith. "I would prove false to my sentiments," he continued, "if I did not declare both by word and deed that the philanthropic general has manifested generous sentiments of conciliation."[49] Four days later, at the Puente del Rey, which spanned the river Antigua on the road between the Gulf coast and Jalapa, with the approval of Santa Anna, Victoria and

[45] In I. MSS, 13.
[46] Echávarri to J. M. González Arrana, February 4, 1823, *ibid.*
[47] Copy, *idem* to Lemaur, February 2, 1823, in A.G.I., Audiencia de México, 90-2-16.
[48] Lemaur to Echávarri, February 2, 1823, *ibid.*
[49] *Manifiesto . . . á sus compatriotas*, p. 6.

Echávarri reached an agreement by which the imperial garrison stationed at that strategic military position undertook to act in conjunction with Santa Anna's soldiers who had adopted the Plan of Vera Cruz.[50] Thus, with the support of Lemaur, the besieged in Vera Cruz and its besiegers undertook to proceed jointly against Agustín I. Lemaur promptly wrote to the Spanish Secretary of War that Echávarri, who had been besieging the city of Vera Cruz, had turned against the Emperor and joined Santa Anna. Moreover, he reported that neighboring towns were supporting this dissident movement.[51] Acclaiming the new plan, civilians and soldiers changed color like chameleons.

The Emperor had become aware early in February of the seriousness of the politico-military situation. In a letter to Miguel Cavaleri he expressed the belief that Lemaur was in touch was Santa Anna and that the royalist commander schemed to deceive that recreant general as well as Echávarri.[52] On February 7 Agustín I addressed a letter to the Marquis of Vivanco who had been made the Captain General of the province of Puebla. After expressing approval of the military steps taken by that commander, he wrote: "On the day after tomorrow I shall leave here in order to check the evil as far as possible and to prove to the rebels how much my soul is superior to theirs. I shall demonstrate to them that love of country and not my selfish interests served as the motive for all my operations."[53] Four days later, in a letter to an intimate friend, he declared that the ungrateful Echávarri had taken a step which covered him with opprobrium—a step which would give the Spaniards an opportunity to reconquer Mexico. Iturbide went on to say:

"After Santa Anna had proclaimed a republic and I had directed Echávarri to pursue him, the latter had a thousand chances to destroy that traitor and to occupy the city of Vera Cruz. ... I have no doubt that love for the land of his birth prevailed over Echávarri's duty to Mexico and that in accord with Lemaur he is negotiating concerning co-operation in the re-conquest of the Empire. ...

"I have never seen a worse combination of follies and contradictions than the anti-imperialistic proceedings. And I am astonished that our commanders and officials have been so grossly deceived. Since the tenth of last month there has been before the Instituent

<hr>

[50] Copy, Convenio que en lo reservado y que con previo conocimiento del Gral. Sta. Anna hicieron en el puente los grales. D. José Antonio Echávarri y D. Guadalupe Victoria, February 6, 1823, Hernández y Dávalos Collection, 16-2-3138, in MSS, U.T.

[51] Lemaur to M. López Baños, February 8, 1823, in A.G.I., Audiencia de México, 90-2-16.

[52] Cuevas, El Libertador, p. 376.   [53] Ibid., p. 377.

Junta a project prepared by a committee for the convocation of the new Congress. This plan was soon printed. Many copies of it were distributed. Some of them must now be in the hands of Echávarri's soldiers. Consequently they cannot protest that the government did not consider a matter so interesting. Echávarri and all the others know with certainty that the object of my previous measures with respect to the dissolved Congress has been no other than to free the Empire from the civil war into which it was being led by an assembly formed in contradiction to all the principles of public law and composed of representatives whose majority think only of the disruption or the complete destruction of the existing system in order to reorganize it after their own fashion, which is the worst that one can imagine."[54]

Iturbide later interpreted the Plan of Casa Mata as the upshot of congressional opposition to his rule.[55] News of Echávarri's defection stirred the capital city. Under date of February 8, Miguel Beruete, who was not a friendly critic of the imperial regime, recorded that a heated discussion had taken place among political leaders about the policy of adhering to that article of the Plan of Iguala which was aimed against the caste system. He alleged that a certain deputy had denounced that guarantee as the apple of discord. Six days later, the excited populace of the capital city shouted, "Long live the absolute Emperor and death to the Spaniards!" When the Emperor appeared in the street on horseback, he was greeted with the cry "Death to the Republicans and death to Echávarri!"[56] Meantime Agustín I was evidently pondering about the demarcation of a line which would protect those regions that had remained loyal from encroachments by the rebellious soldiers.

A Mexican who subscribed himself as "A Friend of the Truth" criticized supporters of the Casa Mata Plan. He said that Guadalupe Victoria, who was likened to Diogenes, had taken refuge in a cavern until he heard Iturbide's paean of liberty. Antonio Santa Anna, a cruel and violent warrior, had joined Victoria so as to ensure in a sanguinary fashion the triumph which he desired. Lemaur had protected both Victoria and Santa Anna in order to provoke the volcano which he thought might destroy the Emperor's partisans. The only article of the new project which was worthy of serious consideration was one which proposed that an armistice should be arranged with the

[54] Cuevas, op. cit., pp. 377-378.

[55] Iturbide, Carrera militar y politica, pp. 55-56. The report of Álvarez on the "sumaria" which Iturbide mentioned is found in Spanish among documents appended to his manuscript Manifiesto, September 27, 1823, f. 59-74, in F.O., 79/39b.

[56] Diario, f. 71-72, in MSS, T.U.

commander of Ulúa Castle.[57] On the other hand, in a diary which he kept at this time, Carlos María de Bustamante raised the question whether it would be wise to allow the discredited magistrate to remain in Mexico. This diarist asserted, however, that, if the Liberator should proceed to a foreign land, he would seduce many unwary persons and would prolong the evils of Mexico by waging cruel war upon her. Bustamante described Iturbide thus:

"He possesses the art of persuasion. His personality is interesting. He pleases everyone; and his arguments seldom fail to convince. . . . Although mild in time of peace, Iturbide is relentless during a campaign. He marches twenty leagues in one night. . . . He lassos a bull like a vaquero. He eats ravenously. He is patient, valiant, and constant in his endeavors, even though they may be rash. If Cataline had known him, he would have placed Iturbide second in command of the army. Cataline would have been pleased to meet a man formed after his own image not only in political matters but also in warfare and immorality."[58]

On February 10, 1823, basing his views upon the decision of the Council of State, the Emperor undertook to prepare instructions for commissioners who were to confer with the conspirators of Vera Cruz. On the next day he issued an address to the Army of the Three Guarantees. He appealed to the soldiers to save the country from anarchy. He denounced those persons who had tried to sweep away that army. He maintained that he had championed it upon every occasion in order to preserve Mexican independence, to prevent internal convulsions, and to consolidate the government. He warned the soldiers against being deceived by false representations.

"You should support the Christian religion, maintain the independence of our country, and preserve union among its inhabitants. You should also swear to maintain the limited constitutional monarchy; for it conforms to the unanimous wish of the people of Mexico. . . . Neither an aged father, nor eight tender children, nor a lovely wife, nor anything else will prevent me from acting in accordance with my principles. On the contrary, from all these dear pledges of nature my honor receives fresh stimuli."[59]

The Plan of Casa Mata was brought to the attention of the Instituent Junta. When two deputies asked to be informed of the views of the Council of State, the Emperor appeared before the Junta to

[57] El Plan republicano del triunvirato de Veracruz, Santana, Victoria y Lemaur refutado por un amigo de la verdad, pp. 23-27.

[58] Diario historico, I, 166-167.

[59] Gaceta del gobierno imperial de México, February 15, 1823, pp. 80-81.

furnish an explanation. He stated that though the council had not
formulated an opinion in writing, it held that the leaders of the revolt
should be convinced of the vices of the defunct Congress. Further,
he maintained that the Instituent Junta should promptly issue a summons for the election of a new legislature. He declared that, if the
Junta did not issue the call at once, he would certainly be compromised.
Not to do so would be a very strange step, he reasoned, "for it would
give my subjects an impression of weakness which should be far
from the thoughts of one who is in command. Indeed I would rather
abdicate the throne."[60]

On February 11 a committee of the Junta criticized the Casa Mata
Plan. They declared that the plan was not only an attack upon the
established government but also that it disseminated subversive doctrines. Above all, they expressed their astonishment that Echávarri
had in the strangest manner proposed that the besiegers of Vera Cruz
should support the cause of the besieged and that jointly they should
solemnly constitute themselves the legislators and the supreme rulers of
the Mexican nation.[61] It seems curious that the committee did not
make any comment with regard to the Emperor's threat of abdication.

Secretary Herrera had meanwhile signed instructions for imperial
commissioners who were to confer with the officers who had subscribed to the Plan of Casa Mata. The directions began by stating
that the chief purpose of the proposed conference was to convince the
signatories of the plan that the Emperor still favored a limited constitutional monarchy. Those signatories were to be persuaded that the
soldiers of the so-called Army of Liberation should not be allowed to
advance beyond the towns of Jalapa, Córdoba, and Orizaba. The
commissioners were also to confer with local authorities in the city
of Vera Cruz. Though they were informed that Agustín I favored
the convocation of a Congress as proposed in Article I of the Casa
Mata Plan, yet they were instructed that he was opposed to elections
being arranged in the same manner as that which had been followed
in the selection of the previous legislature, because that procedure had
caused great inequalities in the representation of the provinces. The
agents were also told that other articles of the plan were inacceptable.
Nevertheless, they were instructed that under existing circumstances,
they should manage the negotiations prudently in order that their
mission would not be frustrated. Above all, they were to convince the

[60] *Diario de la junta nacional instituyente del Imperio Mexicano,* p. 380.
[61] *Ibid.,* p. 381.

insurgents that they owed obedience to the imperial government.[62]

Near the end of February the Emperor's thoughts were turning more and more toward the future. In a letter from Ixtapaluca addressed to the Captain General of the province of Mexico, he expressed his appreciation of an exposition sent to him by certain generals and other military officers. He declared that it was a document which would prove to posterity that all virtue had not vanished. He explained that, at the head of troops supporting a good cause, he would not be the first aggressor; that he would never be concerned with anything other than keeping order, reconciling differences, and preventing bloodshed. He avowed that, if eventually his life became the sacrifice necessary to appease the anger of Heaven, he would submit to that fate without the least sign of remorse. In conclusion he stated that, desirous to avoid bloodshed, he had appointed a commission to present his views to the dissatisfied soldiers. He declared that his diagnosis of the political situation had convinced him that, when they were assured that the government had decided to convoke a new Congress, discontented persons would either be pacified or their actual intentions would be revealed.[63]

During a session of the Instituent Junta on February 26, its vice-president described the main features of the revolutionary scheme. He explained that Agustín I wished to learn the views of the Junta about it in order that the summons for congressional elections should have the proper bases and so that a suitable declaration might be made concerning whatever touched his own person.[64] A committee appointed to give immediate attention to those problems submitted four recommendations which the Junta approved: 1. That elections to Congress should be arranged on more liberal principles than those set forth in the Spanish Constitution. 2. That the junta of the revolutionary soldiers should appoint commissioners to present its views to the Instituent Junta. 3. That, with respect to a demarcation line beyond which the "Army of Liberation" was not to pass until the new Congress was installed, the location of that line should be left to the Emperor. 4. That regulations concerning commerce and finance should be considered at the time when the electoral summons was issued.[65]

[62] Instrucciones para los comisionados á las tropas que subscrivieron las actas de 1º. del corriente constante en el alcance al Diario de Vera Cruz del 2, February 10, 1823, Hernández y Dávalos Collection, 16-1-3152, in MSS, U.T.

[63] Copy, Agustín I to J. A. Andrade, February 24, 1823, in A.H.I.N.A.H., 50-1-7.

[64] Diario de la junta nacional instituyente, p. 432.

[65] Ibid., pp. 432-433.

Meanwhile Álvarez, the imperial secretary, who was in touch with the commissioners of Spain, had warned the Emperor that both the besieged and the besiegers of Vera Cruz had agreed to the Plan of Casa Mata. Further, he stated that the province of Vera Cruz would not obey the imperial government and that the agents of Spain no longer cared to negotiate with him.[66]

Guerrero made public his views concerning the political situation in a justificatory manifesto dated February 18, 1823. He began by stating that the task of separating Mexico from Spain was not solely Iturbide's achievement. He denounced the seizure by force of congressmen in the legislative hall by a deceitful man who had not followed the immortal example set by Washington, Bolívar, and San Martín. He continued in this manner:

"There pertains exclusively to the august Congress . . . the choice of the form of government which the wisdom of worthy representatives, prudence, and harmony recommend. It is necessary, beloved compatriots, that the Congress should be protected, sustained, and aided by the entire, heroic nation which it represents. This is the one and only object which has impelled me and all of my companions to grasp the sword. It is nothing else than to restore to the country by virtue of the Plan of Vera Cruz that which Don Agustín de Iturbide has usurped. To promote such a sacred purpose I am resolved to lose a thousand lives rather than to desist."[67]

The perturbed state of mind of some Mexicans at this time is illustrated by a letter which Guadalupe Victoria wrote from Vera Cruz to the commander of Ulúa Castle. Victoria praised the military and political conduct adopted by Lemaur (of which he had been informed by Santa Anna) after Vera Cruz had proclaimed "the liberty of the Mexican nation." Moreover, he announced the dispatch to that castle of a military commission which was to present his respects to the Spanish General. He was quoted as having said that union with their Spanish compatriots was so dear to the Mexicans that they would support it with their lives.[68]

Signs of a lack of confidence in imperial rule had become increasingly apparent. On February 18, 1823, José Manuel de Herrera re-

[66] F. Álvarez to Agustín I, February 5, 1823, in I. MSS, 13.

[67] El Ciudadano Guerrero á la nación mexicana, p. 2. In this manifesto Guerrero had perhaps confused the Casa Mata Plan drawn up outside the walls of Vera Cruz with the Plan of Vera Cruz which was signed in that city.

[68] Copy, Victoria to Lemaur, February 19, 1823, enclosure no. 2 in Lemaur to J. M. Vadillo, March 8, 1823. Enclosure no. 2 is a copy of Lemaur's conciliatory reply dated February 20, in A.G.I., Audiencia de México, 90-2-16.

signed his post as Secretary of Relations.[69] Three days later Ramón Huarte sent word from Valladolid to his imperial relative that detachments of soldiers in that city were prepared to support Echávarri's plan, but that they were not aware of the scheme of Santa Anna and Victoria to establish a republic.[70] The commander of a battalion of the national army wrote from Chalco to declare that the dykes of order had been broken, that military discipline was not enough to inspire confidence in his soldiers, and that they were in an extremely agitated condition which would soon bring them to the edge of a precipice.[71] Further, many soldiers were deserting the imperial ranks. Moreover, from Vera Cruz to Guadalajara important cities had declared in favor of the Plan of Casa Mata.

Even before the end of February the Emperor held little more than the City of Mexico. He set up an armed camp at Ixtapaluca, a short distance from the capital. From various points such disaffected commanders as Bravo, Echávarri, and the Marquis of Vivanco converged on the city of Puebla, which now became the focus of discontent.[72] Meantime imperial commissioners and officers of the insurgent army had agreed that Congress should be convoked and that a demarcation line should be drawn between the opposing forces.[73] At Puebla on February 25 an agreement was reached between the Captain General of that region and imperial commissioners which sketched a line that should separate the soldiers defending Mexico City from the Army of Liberation.[74]

By order of Agustín I a notice was published in an extraordinary number of the official gazette to the effect that the negotiations of his commissioners with the signatories of the Plan of Casa Mata concerning the mode of convoking a new Congress would soon terminate. Yet whatever hope the monarch may have entertained for the cooperation of certain military commanders in measures against the rebellious faction was soon shattered. On February 26 the Marquis of Vivanco issued a proclamation to his soldiers which showed that he had also been won over to the new revolutionary project. Asserting that the cry of liberty had resounded from Casa Mata to Cali-

[69] *La Diplomacia mexicana*, I, 201.

[70] Huarte to Agustín I, February 21, 1823, in I. MSS, 17.

[71] A. Bustamante to *idem*, February 17, 1823, *ibid.*, p. 12.

[72] Alamán, *Historia*, V, 543-548; Bustamante, *Continuacion del cuadro historico*, pp. 81-86.

[73] Banegas Galván, *Historia*, II, 288-293, who cites documents secured from Mexican archives.

[74] *Gaceta del gobierno imperial de México*, March 6, 1823, pp. 118-119.

fornia, he cautioned them not to be seduced by false allegations. He declared that he wished to see the temple of the law occupied by representatives of the nation.[75]

In conjunction with local officials, the marquis undertook to hold a conference with commanders of recalcitrant soldiers at the city of Puebla. Meantime, acting in a manner that later provoked Iturbide to accuse him of being an insincere friend,[76] General Pedro Negrete, who was the dean of the Council of State, had joined the partisans of reform. Upon announcing at Puebla that Negrete had accepted the Plan of Casa Mata, Echávarri proposed that because of that general's rank, skill, and experience, he should be made the Commander in Chief of the anti-imperialistic forces. Negrete responded, however, that, being a Spaniard by birth, he would under no circumstances assume the command; for the imperial government had been spreading the report that the object of the Casa Mata Plan was to subject the Mexicans once more to the Spanish yoke. Hence he argued that it would be better to place Vivanco at the head of the liberating army, because the marquis was well acquainted with the important provinces of Mexico and Puebla; above all, he was a native Mexican, who could check the rumors circulated by enemies of the insurrection.[77]

Though Vivanco demurred at the nomination, and urged that the choice of Negrete as the Generalissimo would convince the world that both the Spaniards and the Mexicans in the Empire were united in favor of liberty, and though the provincial deputation of Puebla also urged Negrete to accept the post, the Spaniard persisted in his refusal. He argued that the cause of independence would be jeopardized by placing a native of Spain at the head of the army, for such an appointment would furnish ammunition to the enemies of Mexican liberty. Moreover, he added that he lacked topographical knowledge of the provinces of Puebla and Mexico in which it might be necessary to wage war, knowledge which his candidate for the supreme command possessed. After some discussion, the decision was reached that the Marquis of Vivanco should be the temporary commander of the disaffected troops.[78] The conference also decided that this commander, a commissioner of the province of Puebla, and a representative of revolutionary soldiers in other regions who adhered to the agreement, should constitute a junta to direct the operations of the Army of Liberation.

[75] *El Marqués de Vivanco á los militares.*
[76] Iturbide, *Carrera militar y politica,* pp. 28-29 n. 14.
[77] *Tercer trueno de la libertad en México,* pp. 1-2.
[78] *El General Negrete á sus compatriotas.*

Desirous to justify his sudden change of heart, in turn Negrete soon issued a proclamation. He asserted that when as an imperial commissioner he left the capital on February 10, he had contemplated arranging a reconciliation between the supporters of the Plan of Casa Mata and the imperial government. He explained, however, that after fulfilling his obligation as a public man, he had yielded to his duty as a citizen:

"I adhere to the plan because I am convinced that, when convulsions of this nature agitate the state, a citizen cannot remain neutral without becoming a traitor to the society to which he belongs, and also because the movement which these valiant soldiers sustain is the most just in the world. Lastly, I support that plan because I am persuaded that there can be neither prosperity nor even independence without civil liberty. Neither can such liberty exist without a national Congress which establishes and guarantees that freedom. Always a champion of the rights of this nation, I prefer death to beholding her in chains and to leaving my children here as slaves."[79]

This view stresses unduly the opinions of disaffected Mexicans who were leading the uneducated masses. Under the conditions existing in Mexico during this critical transitional period, the mistakes of Agustín I were not necessarily fatal to the existence of the new State, provided that he kept a tight hold of the reins of power. An intimate friend recorded the Emperor's remark that in certain matters he had acted upon the advice of Negrete or with his approval. Influenced by those persons who were called his friends, wrote Gómez Pedraza, the monarch committed errors.[80] Discussing the Plan of Casa Mata at a later time, Iturbide admitted that his mistake early in 1823 was that of not taking command of the national army as soon as he became aware of Echávarri's defection.[81] Neither does this allegation, however, fully explain the critical political situation. It appears that, justifying their proceedings by a plea of patriotism, affected by the infiltration of foreign political philosophy, encouraged by the increasing discontent with imperial rule, and at times instigated by the royalist commander of Ulúa Castle, influential Mexican politicians had deeply undermined the power and the prestige of Agustín I.

[79] *Ibid.*

[80] *Manifiesto que Manuel Gómez Pedraza, ciudadano de la república de Méjico, dedica á sus compatriotas,* p. 17.

[81] Iturbide, *Carrera militar y política,* p. 49.

CHAPTER XII

End of the First Mexican Empire

A DILEMMA confronted Agustín I. He had to decide upon a definite course of action. Among the decisions which still seemed open to him were the following: to place the fate of Mexico in the lap of the reassembled Congress, to issue a summons for the election of a new legislature, to reorganize the army of the Mexican nation, to assume boldly the leadership of the Army of Liberation.[1] Although he must have realized that his support had been gradually ebbing away, he decided to submit to the arbitrament of the existing Congress.

On February 25 the *Gaceta imperial de México* published a notice that the Instituent Junta had undertaken to arrange congressional elections on the most liberal bases. This Junta had resolved that the primary duty of Congress was to consider the formation of a constitution for the Mexican Empire. Moreover, it took the view that the bases of the political system should be independence, union, the Roman Catholic religion, the separation of powers, and a hereditary monarchy under the Iturbide dynasty.[2] On the same day an agreement was signed by leaders of the Puebla junta and commissioners of the Emperor which sketched a line that was to separate the regions occupied by their respective soldiers. The demarcation line was to be observed, so ran the compact, "until his Majesty had accepted the Plan of Casa Mata and the general adjustment had been decided."[3]

Meantime, José Andrade, a Creole who had been appointed Captain General of the province of Mexico, had issued a notice in which he declared, on behalf of the Emperor, that he hoped for an agreement with the dissident military leaders without any bloodshed.[4] That

---

[1] Iturbide later alleged that champions of the Plan of Casa Mata invited him to become head of the revolution (*Carrera militar y política de Don Agustín de Iturbide, ó sea memoria que escribió en Liorna*, p. 61 n. 36). See further Zamacois, *Historia de Méjico*, XI, 477-478.

[2] *Diario de la junta nacional instituyente del Imperio Mexicano*, I, 444.

[3] *Gaceta del gobierno imperial de México*, March 6, 1823, p. 119.

[4] *Aviso al público*, March 1, 1823.

step was apparently taken in the hope that agitated public sentiment might be soothed. If such was the intention of Agustín I, he was soon disillusioned, for he was informed by his commissioners, who had conferred with agents of the discontented army, that it did not favor the electoral plan which had been proposed by the junta in Mexico City. Furthermore, his commissioners recommended that the Congress which he had dissolved should be reinstated.[5] Agustín I had meanwhile shown a willingness to compromise, for he had suggested to Negrete that the right of hereditary succession which Congress had vested in his family might be relinquished.[6]

The upshot was that, yielding to the recommendation of the Council of State, at nine o'clock in the evening of March 4, Agustín I issued a decree directing that, in view of the existing circumstances, all the congressmen should reassemble at Mexico City in order to resume their sessions. He instructed the Secretary of the Treasury that the deputies who were in outlying provinces should be provided with the funds which might be necessary to ensure their attendance. Meantime the Secretary of War was to circulate this decree among the chief army officials. The monarch instructed his secretary to see that it was made known to the generals and other leaders who had signed the Plan of Casa Mata as well as to those persons who had later adhered to that pronunciamento. He even declared that, if upon assembling in the capital the deputies wished to shift the seat of the legislature to some other place, this might be done. José del Valle, the reputed author of the Guatemalan Act of Independence, who had represented the province of Tegucigalpa in the Congress of Mexico and had been informed while in prison of his appointment as the Mexican Secretary of Relations, printed the momentous summons in a special number of the official gazette. Evidently voicing the sentiments of his master, Valle added the sanguine comment that there was no longer any reason for differences among the Mexicans: "All the people should unite behind a government which has no other wish than their own. The Mexican nation should be one, ruled by wise and liberal principles—a distinct line ought to separate the present regime from that which recently existed."[7]

In a bitter comment dated March 5, which he wrote behind prison walls, Deputy Carlos María de Bustamante declared that the decision

---

[5] *Gaceta del gobierno imperial de México*, March 18, 1823, pp. 135-136.
[6] Cuevas, *El Libertador*, p. 382.
[7] *Gaceta extraordinaria del gobierno imperial de México*, March 5, 1823, p. 115. On José Valle, see Rosa, *Biografía de Don José Cecilio del Valle*, pp. 36-58; Valle, *Valle, prólogo y selección*, pp. xi-xiv.

to summon Congress was reached as soon as certain cities had adhered to the Plan of Vera Cruz. He asked "the braggart Iturbide" where his power was. "From every quarter one hears indignant voices raised against you," he continued; "everyone mentions your excesses; everyone denounces them. Soldiers arise from the land in order to vindicate their rights which have been humbled by your pride. The edifice constructed by your pride and ambition is falling and you are about to be buried in its ruins."[8] That the Emperor was changing his attitude toward the supporters of the Plan of Casa Mata was indicated by the fact that in response to a plea from imprisoned deputies praying for release and for permission to proceed to regions occupied by the Army of Liberation, Captain General Andrade promptly replied that they were to be set at liberty without delay and that Agustín I had decided to reassemble Congress.[9] Moreover, on the day after Bustamante had predicted the downfall of the Empire, a junta in Monterrey, Nuevo León, announced its adhesion to the Plan of Casa Mata with two modifications.[10] On February 26, 1822, the garrison of Guadalajara had declared in favor of Echávarri's scheme.[11]

At the summons of the Vice-President of Congress, on March 7 some fifty deputies assembled in its hall. To them Agustín I made a species of apology for his conduct in which he mentioned "the happy day of reconciliation." Asserting that the legislature now had all the liberty specified in the Plan of Casa Mata, he avowed that he was ready to sacrifice his life in order to promote the liberty and happiness of his native land. One of the secretaries of Congress then made known the agreement which had been reached between imperial commissioners and anti-imperialistic leaders concerning the line of demarcation to be drawn between the region dominated by the liberating army and the terrain occupied by the Emperor's soldiers.[12] It was not without significance perhaps that on the same day Deputy Bustamante, who complained of having been treated with contumely, was set free. On March 7 Fernández de Lizardi prematurely published a pamphlet commending Iturbide's renunciation of the crown as an example to European sovereigns.[13] The Emperor soon issued a procla-

[8] Bustamante, *Diario historico de Mexico*, I, 286.

[9] Anaya, *Representación de los diputados y otros presos por opinion que se hallan en el carcel público dirigido al exmo. Sr. capitán general de esta Provincia*, pp. 3-4.

[10] *Proclamación de la libertad en las Provincias Internas del Oriente*, p. 4.

[11] Copy, Acta de la guarnición de Guadalajara secundando el plan de Echávarri, 26 Febrero de 1823, Hernández y Dávalos Collection, 16-1-3177, in MSS, U.T.

[12] Bustamante, *Continuacion del cuadro historico*, pp. 105-106.

[13] *Exposición que el lic. D. Carlos María de Bustamante . . . hizó al Emperador*, pp. 1-3; *Por la salud de la patria se desprecia una corona*, p. 7.

mation to the Mexicans which indicated that he was actually contemplating such a step. He reasoned that one of his important obligations was to remain a soldier and to promote the welfare of his country. "Never will I relinquish my intention," he declared, "and once convinced that your happiness in this crisis depends upon my absence from the court, I could not delay my departure."[14] Meantime the insurgent junta at Puebla had made known its opposition to the rump Congress because, among other reasons, it did not consider that that body was free to act. On March 12 the junta appealed to the legislature to urge that Agustín I should depart from the capital or that the congressmen should migrate to the city of Puebla at once.[15] Far to the south, upon the receipt of news about the proceedings of the Puebla junta and of the reinstallation of the Mexican Congress, Filisola issued a manifesto announcing that a congress of the Central American provinces would assemble in Guatemala City.[16]

On March 13, at the instance of the Council of State, the Emperor proposed that Congress should act as a provisional government in the capital, that both the opposing parties should withdraw their forces to a distance of forty or fifty leagues from that city, that he should retire to a place selected by Congress, and that he would delegate his functions to an executive designated by it. This compromise proposal was promptly transmitted to Congress with the explanation that Agustín I did not wish to prolong existing evils.[17] The Puebla junta, however, demurred at recognizing the authority of the legislature until it was acting freely and legally. At the city of Vera Cruz both Guadalupe Victoria and Santa Anna approved anti-imperialistic measures adopted by that junta.[18] On March 17 General Lemaur addressed to the Spanish Minister of War a letter which included these revealing words:

"I enclose for your Excellency a copy of a dispatch and of documents that describe the condition of this country and also the approaching ruin which threatens the so-called Emperor of Mexico as a result of the conspiracy formed and supported in the city of Vera Cruz under

[14] *El Emperador*, March 11, 1823.
[15] *Acta de la junta de Puebla sobre la reinstalacion del congreso mexicano*, p. 4; *Oficio de la junta de Puebla a los diputados de México*.
[16] Vallejo, *Compendio de la historia social y política de Honduras*, pp. 357-361.
[17] Minute of Ignacio Alas, March 13, 1823, Hernández y Dávalos Collection, 16-2-3221, in MSS, U.T.; Valle to Congress, March 14, 1823, *Gaceta del gobierno imperial de México*, March 18, 1823, p. 139.
[18] Bustamante, *Continuacion del cuadro historico*, pp. 112-113. The proceedings of the junta were printed in the *Diario de Vera Cruz*, March 22, 23, and 24, 1823. See further, *Noticia extraordinaria sobre la rendición de la capital*, pp. 1-4.

my immedaite influence—a conspiracy which has now extended over almost the entire country. . . ."[19]

Agustín I soon took a decisive step. On March 19 he placed in the hands of Gómez de Navarrete, who was now the secretary of the Council of State, a document which that official promptly forwarded to Congress. This state paper was a formal Act of Abdication. The monarch stated that as the supporters of the Plan of Casa Mata had recognized Congress, there was no longer any reason why he should keep a part of the national army in the vicinity of the capital. Iturbide asserted that he had accepted the emperorship with reluctance only in order to serve his countrymen and, as it had become a pretext for internal disturbance, he was convinced that, even though there was no authority to which he might properly present his abdication, he ought to relinquish the crown. Declaring that his presence in Mexico would always be a pretext for discord and that schemes he had never entertained would be attributed to him, he stated that, in order to avoid the slightest suspicion concerning his actions, he would voluntarily leave his native country for a foreign land. He declared that in ten or fifteen days he could arrange his domestic affairs and make preparations for the departure of his family from Mexico. The only request which he made was that the legislature should pay certain debts which he had contracted on behalf of the government. For, though it had left him free to use the money which he needed, and though the Instituent Junta had granted him an allowance for expenditures, yet he had not been able to use these funds on certain occasions when he had learned of the crying needs of public officials or imperial soldiers.[20] On March 20 Gómez de Navarrete forwarded to Congress an elaborated version of the Act of Abdication in which Agustín I expressly declared that he relinquished his executive authority to the legislature.[21]

Widely different views have been expressed about his motives for abdication. A Mexican contemporary voiced the opinion that the Emperor had imagined that Congress would beseech him to keep the crown.[22] If that was his purpose, he must have been grievously disappointed. A more plausible view is one presented by a Mexican biographer of our own time, which is that the abdication of the throne

[19] In A.G.I., Audiencia de México, 90-2-16.

[20] Bustamante, *Continuacion del cuadro historico*, pp. 114-116.

[21] *Ibid.*, pp. 115-116. Drafts of this act addressed to Congress on March 20 are found in the Hernández y Dávalos Collection, 16-2-3238 and 16-2-3239, in MSS, U.T.

[22] Bustamante, *El Honor y patriotismo del general D. Nicolas Bravo*, p. 39.

was a sign of weakness and that, if the chief magistrate had displayed the energy and the valor which he had shown as a royalist commander, he might have been able to retain the imperial dignity.[23] The present writer's view of the enigmatical commander's character is that, in sharp contrast with the cruel and sanguinary conduct which he pursued as a royalist officer, after becoming the great champion of independence, his public conduct became considerate and humane. It seems that in the early months of 1823 he wished above all to prevent the shedding of Mexican blood. The blackamoor had been washed white.

Several months later Iturbide thus explained the motives which impelled him to relinquish the imperial throne:

"I gave up my authority because I was already free from the obligations which had forced me reluctantly to accept the crown. Mexico did not need my service against foreign enemies, for at that time she had none. With regard to domestic enemies, my presence instead of being helpful might have injured the country, because it might have been employed as a pretext for the charge that war was being waged on account of my ambition. . . . I did not relinquish my power because of fear of my enemies: I knew them all and what they could do. I did not act thus because I had declined in the esteem of the people or because I had lost the affection of the soldiers. Well did I know that at my call the majority of the troops would rejoin the valiant men who were already with me; and that the small number who remained would either follow their example in the first engagement or would be put to rout."[24]

The former Emperor's optimistic view of the potential strength of his position was not the same as that held by his enemies. Alamán recorded a remark by Lemaur to the effect that the imperial army had a greater number of officers and musicians than it had private soldiers.[25] Strange rumors were being circulated in the agitated capital city. Miguel Beruete, who had been thrust into a dungeon, wrote that the Emperor became inebriated every day. This diarist added that fears were entertained that Agustín I might end his reign by a murderous, bacchanalian orgy. Beruete even recorded an idle tale that, from a pulpit in the sanctuary of Guadalupe, the monarch had de-

[23] Cuevas, El Libertador, p. 100.

[24] Iturbide, Carrera militar y politica, pp. 56-57. Bullock mentioned Iturbide's "strength and prowess" (Six Months' Residence and Travels in Mexico, p. 248).

[25] Historia, V, 561 n.

clared he entrusted the welfare of his country to the Holy Virgin![26]

Iturbide delivered to the deputies on March 22 what has been styled a farewell address. On the eve of his departure from the capital city, he alleged that some of his advisers had convinced him that the happiness of his country depended upon certain measures which he had accordingly taken. He asserted that, after altercations broke out between himself and Congress, he was obliged to appear "either as a weak man or as a despot." He maintained that he had built a dyke which prevented the shedding of torrents of blood. He stated that he was aware that in various sections of Mexico he was still looked upon with favor but explained that he viewed with horror the prospect of discord and anarchy. He vowed that if there was any other step, in addition to his abdication, by which he could promote the welfare of his native land, he would willingly take it. Announcing that he was about to depart from Mexico with his entire family to take up his residence in a foreign land, he declared that, if Congress should succeed in ending discord, in promoting the public welfare, and in making the Mexicans happy, he would rejoice at this outcome and pass cheerfully to his grave. He suggested that General Bravo should be placed in charge of the party which was to escort him out of the country.[27] Thus did he profess to be ready for the sacrifice.

Because of his protestations of humility, certain Mexicans suspected Iturbide's sincerity.[28] An anonymous pamphleteer stigmatized him as "this wicked American Pygmalion!"[29] Other persons denounced him as pusillanimous. It is possible that in his heart the discredited monarch may have considered the odds against him too great to be overcome.

On March 24 Iturbide was notified of the conditions formulated in a conference between leading generals of the liberating army and congressional commissioners. These terms were that, while Congress was discussing certain problems involved in the abdication, the discredited magistrate should reside at Tulancingo or at some other specified place; that he should select five hundred men to serve as his escort; and that the commissioners should promptly make known the

[26] Maggs Bros., *Bibliotheca Americana et Philippina: Catalogue No. 465*, part IV, p. 445; cf. Beruete, Diario, f. 79, in MSS, T.U.

[27] Iturbide, *Breve diseño crítico de la emancipacion y libertad de la nacion mexicana*, pp. 125-132. An allegation has been made that after the Emperor abdicated he sold some family jewels and even his imperial mantle (Valle, *Iturbide*, p. 150 n.).

[28] Beruete, Diario, f. 80v., in MSS, T.U.; *Ya se va Agustín Primero desterrado y sin corona*, p. 1.

[29] *Segunda parte de la conducta de Iturbide*.

outcome of these proposals. Iturbide demurred at accepting them, however, because the cautious, recalcitrant generals had refused to grant him an interview.[30] The Council of State now showed a leaning toward the revolutionists, for it decided to favor Negrete's request that the soldiers of his army should be paid by the imperial treasury.[31]

On behalf of Iturbide, Secretary Valle authorized the Captain General of the district including the capital city to confer with the rebellious generals. At this time that office was taken over by Gómez Pedraza, who found Iturbide averse to bloodshed, willing to depart from the capital quickly, and ready to leave it in charge of the Army of Liberation.[32] Through that official on March 25 Iturbide proposed to General Negrete, who was acting as the agent of the approaching army, that he should withdraw from Mexico City with an escort of five hundred men, that the imperial soldiers remaining in its vicinity should pass under the control of the Captain General of the province of Mexico, and that he should depart from the New World by way of Acapulco, Panama, and Jamaica.[33] Though aware of the mortal fear haunting some of his compatriots that these proposals veiled a scheme to regain power, Negrete agreed to them, with the exception of the peculiar route which the former Emperor designed to follow.[34] On March 25 Secretary Valle notified the Council of State that, pending a decision concerning his abdication, Iturbide would not exercise any authority whatever.[35] During six days the distintegrating Empire was thus without a chief magistrate. Deputies of Central America soon took steps which anticipated its separation from Mexico.

Leading insurgent officers who had assembled at Santa Marta signed on March 26 an agreement that they would accord the former Emperor the treatment proposed by Congress, that he was to leave Tacubaya escorted by General Bravo, and that imperial troops near the capital were to be treated as though they belonged to the victorious army. The military junta also decided that its soldiers should enter Mexico City led by Bravo.[36] Apparently in response to a rejoinder by Iturbide, two days later with some minor modifications the leaders of

---

[30] Bustamante, *El Honor y patriotismo del general D. Nicolas Bravo*, pp. 41-43.

[31] Minute of the Council of State, March 24, 1823, Hernández y Dávalos Collection, 16-2-3252, in MSS, U.T.

[32] *Manifiesto que Manuel Gómez Pedraza . . . dedica á sus compatriotas*, p. 15.

[33] *Ibid.*

[34] Bustamante, *op. cit.*, p. 45; Iturbide to Gómez Pedraza, March 25, 1823, Hernández y Dávalos Collection, 16-2-3259, in MSS, U.T.

[35] Valle to the subdeacon of the Council of State, March 25, 1823, Hernández y Dávalos Collection, 16-2-3253, in MSS, U.T.

[36] Bustamante, *El Honor y patriotismo*, pp. 46-47.

the advancing army reaffirmed the agreement of Santa Marta.[37] Soldiers of the Army of Liberation marched into the capital on March 27, 1823.

Some Mexicans approved Iturbide's conduct. A friend, who subscribed the initials "J.I.V.," praised his renunciation of the imperial crown. This apologist argued that it was more glorious for the former sovereign to become a private citizen than to remain a monarch. The name of the Liberator of Mexico was far better than that of Emperor.[38]

On the other hand, enemies of Iturbide were not loath to erect barriers to prevent his return to the throne. When General Lemaur sent a report to Madrid about the downfall of the monarch, he stated that all the paths by which that recreant royalist officer might escape from the toils of his jailers had been closed by detachments of anti-imperialistic soldiers. Though the commander of Ulúa Castle felt that, under the circumstances, the expatriation of the former Emperor was the most prudent step which could be taken by the Mexicans, he doubted Iturbide's good faith. Apprehensive that the exile might intrigue to ensure his return to Mexico, he intimated that he was aware of the means by which his government could prevent the restoration of such an avowed enemy of Spain and the Spaniards. Lemaur urged that under no circumstances should the traitor be allowed to make himself again "the master of this unfortunate country."[39] El Sol declared on April 2 that ambition had blinded the man whom it had viewed as another Washington.

On March 29 Congress adopted a decree declaring that it now had full liberty to deliberate. It announced that the executive power which had exercised authority since May 19, 1822, had ceased to exist.[40] On March 31 the legislature passed an act which provided that, for the time being, the executive authority should be vested in a commission composed of three persons, who should not be congressmen, entitled the Supreme Executive Power. Each of its members was to serve in turn for one month as president of the commission.[41] Nicolás Bravo, Guadalupe Victoria, and Pedro Negrete were selected to serve provisionally as the plural executive. As both Bravo and Victoria

[37] Act signed by Vivanco and Others, March 28, 1823, Hernández y Dávalos Collection, 16-2-3265, in MSS, U.T.

[38] Agustín y Ana María triunfaron en algun día de todos sus enemigos, pp. 1-2.

[39] Lemaur to J. M. Vadillo, April 5, 1823, in A.G.I., Audiencia de México, 90-2-16.

[40] Colección de órdenes y decretos de la soberana junta provisional gubernativa y soberanos congresos generales de la nación mexicana, II, 88.

[41] Ibid., pp. 89-90.

were absent from the capital, José Mariano de Michelena and Miguel Domínguez, the one-time *corregidor* of Querétaro, were chosen to serve as their substitutes. In an address which the ruling Triumvirate made to their countrymen they exultantly declared that the representatives of the nation had been restored to the seats from which despotism had ejected them.[42]

An alleged illness of the former Emperor slightly delayed his departure from Tacubaya. On March 30, in a coach escorted by General Bravo at the head of fifty soldiers, Iturbide made the first move on his *via dolorosa*. Basing his opinion upon the unedited papers of Bravo to which he had access, Carlos María de Bustamante asserted that the prisoner of state—for such he really was—expressed regret at his downfall only because of his children.[43] During a sojourn at Tulancingo, Bravo checked a tumult which evidently aimed to prevent Iturbide's journey. A contemporary declared that the reserved, modest, and able General Bravo had been destined by Providence to tear the tyrant from the breast of Mexico.[44]

Scarcely had the party of some thirty persons reached Tulancingo, when Secretary José García Illueca, who had been placed in charge of the existing ministries by the Triumvirate, instructed Bravo to prevent Iturbide from performing any act of sovereignty, and, if necessary, to prohibit all communication with him. García Illueca further directed Bravo to exclude from Iturbide's party all persons who were neither servants nor relatives of the former ruler. Suspicious characters such as Francisco Álvarez, Miguel Cavaleri, and Pío Marcha, who might incite intrigue against the new government, were forthwith to be incarcerated at Perote.[45] When a list of those persons was submitted to the one-time monarch, however, he protested so strongly against the proposed exclusion of Álvarez and his family from the party scheduled for deportation that they were finally allowed to proceed with him.[46]

[42] *Gaceta del gobierno supremo de México*, April 8, 1823, pp. 175-177; Mier, *Diez cartas hasta hoy inéditas*, pp. 4-5; Bustamante, *Diario historico*, I, 343.

[43] Bustamante, *El Honor y patriotismo*, pp. 50-51.

[44] Manuscrito, manifiesto de Iturbide, comentado por Carlos M. de Bustamante con letra de el mismo, f. 51-51*v.*, Hernández y Dávalos Collection, 17-8-4255, in MSS, U.T.

[45] *Lista de los presos que fueron remitidos desde Tulancingo a Perote el día 10 de Abril por órden del ciudadano Nicolás Bravo*; Bustamante, *El Honor y patriotismo*, pp. 60-61. A detailed account by a Mexican scholar of Iturbide's trip from Tulancingo to Antigua is given by Iguíniz, "Iturbide en el destierro y en el cadalso," *El Universal*, September, 1921.

[46] Aláman, *Historia*, V, 570.

The report of a committee appointed to consider the Act of Abdication was meanwhile being considered by the legislature. The committee not only maintained that the action of Congress in the imperial election which took place on May 19, 1822, was unduly influenced by the populace but also that the dissolution of that assembly by the sovereign was a "monstrous act of despotism" which had provoked an insurrection. Furthermore, the committee held that Congress did not have the authority to elect an Emperor. Hence it would be "contrary to recognized principles to accept his abdication." Neither Iturbide nor anyone else had the right to rule a nation which had won the right to govern herself.

"The committee agrees with Iturbide that his presence in the country is unpleasant to him and inconvenient to the nation. . . . Everybody knows that he has friends and adherents who, incited by his presence, could some day resort to certain measures which, though they have at present lost their potential power, might, when the patriotism of our valiant men had cooled, occasion surprising events. Though indeed these could never be of serious consequence, yet they might nevertheless cause some injury to this afflicted country."[47]

The committee accordingly recommended to the Supreme Executive Power that Iturbide's pledge to leave Mexico at once should be promptly carried out. It also urged that the debts which he had contracted with various persons on behalf of the State should be assumed by the new government and furthermore that decent provision should be made for the support of himself and family. It took the view that the nation had a right to designate the country in which the exile was to reside. It submitted recommendations under eight heads: 1. Iturbide's coronation had been a work of violence. 2. All governmental measures resulting from that proceeding were accordingly illegal. 3. There was no need for Congress to discuss the Emperor's abdication. 4. The Supreme Executive Power should reach an agreement with him to the effect that he would depart from the soil of Mexico promptly. 5. At the expense of the nation, he was to leave with his family on a neutral vessel from a port on the Gulf of Mexico. 6. A pension of 25,000 pesos per annum during his life should be assigned to him on condition that he was to establish his residence at some place in the Italian Peninsula. 7. He should be accorded the title of "Excellency." 8. The Iguala Plan and the Treaty of Córdoba were no

[47] *Actas del congreso constituyente mexicano*, IV, 164.

longer to be in force; Mexico was to be at liberty to adopt whatever form of government suited her best.[48]

Certain features of this proposal provoked criticism both inside and outside of Congress. Fernández de Lizardi protested against the plan to exile Iturbide to Italy and to assign him a large pension. "Resentful, rich, and clever," said that thinker, he could with 25,000 pesos recruit tens of thousands of foreigners with whom he could invade Mexico and involve her in civil war.[49] Padre Mier was a bitter critic of the proposal. He intimated that O'Donojú had vanished from the Mexican scene because he was an obstacle to Iturbide's ambition. Mier even expressed the opinion that the former Emperor ought to be sent to the gallows. Mentioning a rumor that Iturbide had deposited money in foreign banks, he argued against conceding him a pension. Carlos María de Bustamante also opposed that grant. He feared that while sojourning in Italy, the vindictive exile might organize an expedition against his native land. Moreover, certain European princes might use him to make good their pretensions to Mexico. Again, he might return there as Napoleon had returned to France from Elba. The other side had no such eloquent champions. Becerra argued that it was improper for the government to deport a family whose head had raised the victorious cry for independence. He also maintained that 25,000 pesos per annum were not sufficient to equip a military expedition against Mexico. During the debate Bustamante delineated the Iturbide Period of Mexican history thus: "Agustín! Agustín! You gave us independence but deprived us of liberty!"[50]

On April 7, 1823, after a decision had been reached to omit the recommendations of the committee proposing that all governmental measures resulting from Iturbide's coronation were illegal and that the Iguala Plan and the Treaty of Córdoba were null and void, Congress approved the first seven resolutions.[51] Furthermore, influential congressmen expressed the opinion that both the Iguala Plan and the Treaty of Córdoba were null and void. They asserted that the nation was at liberty to adopt whatever form of government she might desire.[52]

The Mexican historian Alamán ironically asserted that the identical deputies who had advocated the choice of Iturbide as Emperor

[48] *Ibid.*, pp. 165-166.
[49] *Sentencia contra el Emperador propuesta en el soberano congreso.*
[50] *Actas del congreso*, IV, 201.
[51] *Ibid.*, IV, 165-166, 201-213.
[52] *Ibid.*, pp. 213-217.

had voted that his election should be adjudged to have no binding
force. Carlos María de Bustamante wrote in his diary that the first
day of real Mexican independence was April 8, 1823.[53] Seven days
later, a new journal entitled the *Aguila Mexicana,* which had announced its purpose of paying special attention to politics, declared
in its first number that the era of Mexican emancipation had just
begun. Its editors reasoned that the reconstructed regime demanded
consideration and wisdom on the part of the rulers in order to prevent discord, anarchy, and a return to slavery. They argued that
neither Europe nor the entire world would be able to reduce Mexico
to the abject condition of a colony or to transform her into an integral
part of a foreign political system.

The new government soon transmitted news of the overthrow of
imperial rule to outlying districts of the Empire. Shortly after the
abdication of Iturbide had been acted upon, the commandant of the
Interior Provinces of the West sent to the governor of New Mexico
a warning that anyone who might dare to acclaim Iturbide as Emperor
should be considered a traitor.[54] Meantime, Congress undertook to
supplement its measures concerning the abdication. One of its decrees
announced that the Mexican nation was beyond the jurisdiction of
any law or treaty which had not been drawn up by her own legally
chosen representatives, yet the guarantees of religion, independence,
and union were to remain in force. Another decree denounced the
coronation ceremony as a work of violence. The Supreme Executive
Power was directed to promote the departure of the former monarch
from a port on the Gulf of Mexico by a neutral vessel to a place to
be selected by him. Further, this decree assigned to Iturbide during
his life a pension of 25,000 pesos per annum on condition that he
should establish his residence in Italy. He was to have the title "Excellency," and upon his death his family was to be paid a pension of
8,000 pesos annually.[55] A few days later Congress decreed that the
eagle depicted upon the national ensign should no longer be adorned
with a crown.[56]

When the Secretary of War informed General Bravo of the decree
of April 8, he stated that an English frigate of four hundred tons

[53] *Historia,* V, 567; Bustamante, *Diario,* I, 371. For Mier's summary of the action
of Congress, see *Diez cartas,* p. 10.
[54] G. Ochoa to J. A. Viscarra, May 14, 1823, in A.N.M., no. 227, Santa Fe.
[55] Dublán y Lozano, *Legislacion mexicana,* I, 634-635.
[56] Bustamante, *Diario historico,* I, 373. Bullock, who visited Mexico City shortly
after the Emperor resigned, makes no mention of any reaction against the acts of
Congress (*Six Months' Residence and Travels in Mexico,* pp. 123 *et seq.*).

would soon be ready to receive forty persons belonging to Iturbide's company. Bravo was told that the most convenient route for the exiles to follow to the Gulf of Mexico was by way of Apam, Fort Perote, the hacienda of Lucas Martín, and the Puente del Rey. In particular, he was enjoined from passing through the city of Puebla, where Iturbide was supposed to have many devoted partisans.[57]

When the former sovereign was notified of these measures, after making a plea for the humane treatment of his faithful soldiers, he informed Bravo on April 11 that he wanted an assurance that his party would be comfortable and safe from attack on the voyage to Europe. He expressed a desire to sail in an English or an American ship with sufficient funds to enable him to establish a comfortable residence for his family.[58] Bravo peremptorily replied that he was acting in accordance with the orders of his government. He asked to be informed promptly at what place in Europe the exile intended to reside.[59] In response Iturbide mentioned the weak or infirm condition of certain members of his party whose ages ranged from a few months to eighty-five years. He added:

"I cannot risk finding the means of support in a strange land where I have no connections. I cannot undertake the voyage except in a good English or American frigate that has on board enough money to enable me to reside in Rome, Naples, or some other place in Italy which suits me best. I understand that the honor of the Mexican nation is involved in both of these matters as well as in relieving my honorable family of all annoyance until they embark."[60]

Iturbide addressed a letter to Negrete on April 13 in which he explained his reasons for desiring to proceed by the route which he had proposed. Appealing to that member of the Supreme Executive Power in the name of their old friendship, he said: "I should like to embark in Acapulco for Panama, and then to proceed to Jamaica. Thence I would continue my voyage to Italy by the most convenient route." Discrediting a rumor that he entertained designs upon Central America, the anxious father declared that the only motive which animated him was a desire to promote the welfare of his delicate family. "Negrete, my friend," he added, "if I were single and were free of everything, I would take fresh steps leading to new, heroic deeds. But how can I expose my beloved family to the scorn of a hostile

[57] Bustamante, *El Honor y patriotismo*, p. 65.
[58] *Ibid.*, pp. 67-68.
[59] *Ibid.*
[60] *Ibid.*, p. 68.

government or to the insults of unscrupulous pirates? . . . With a full knowledge of conditions, Iturbide has known how to confront with serenity the menace of a treacherous death as well as that of a gallows demanded by strong passions and by fear. . . ."[61]

Upon being apprised of Iturbide's views, José García Illueca, who had succeeded Valle as the Secretary of Relations, notified Bravo that the fallen Emperor was to sail for Italy on an English frigate mounting twelve cannon. García Illueca asserted that in view of the action of Congress it was not within the authority of the Supreme Executive Power to make arrangements about funds for the exile and that the payment of a pension to him was dependent upon the establishment of his residence in Italy. García Illueca added that, if the party embarking on the frigate exceeded thirty persons, individuals in excess of that number would be required to pay their own expenses. On April 4 he wrote to inform Bravo that Iturbide was to leave Tulancingo in a few days with an escort of eight hundred soldiers via Encero for a port on the Gulf of Mexico. General Victoria, who had been placed in charge of arrangements for the embarkation of the passengers, was directed to co-operate with Bravo.[62]

Although not satisfied with the assurances which had been given him concerning the comfort and security of his family on the voyage, Iturbide finally consented to leave Tulancingo. Escorted by a military officer, his party proceeded to the village of Apam, while Bravo marched to the neighboring hacienda of Buena Vista. At Apam the former Emperor decided that neither his aged father nor his frail sister María Nicolasa was able to continue the journey.[63] Ignorant of the fact that the Supreme Executive Power had taken steps to protect his party on their trip to Europe, on April 27 he asked Bravo that the schooner *Iguala* of the Mexican navy should convoy the vessel which was destined to transport him to the shores of Italy.[64] Bitterly dissatisfied with what he had learned about the arrangements made for his protection on the high seas against attacks by Spaniards or by pirates, on May 24 at an hacienda near Jalapa, he addressed to Bravo a species of ultimatum from which a salient extract is taken:

[61] Copy, April 13, 1823, Documentos relativos al Imperio de Iturbide, 1821-1824, f. 247-251, Genaro García Collection, in MSS, U.T. Library.

[62] Bustamante, *El Honor y patriotismo*, pp. 69-71; Rivera Cambas, *Historia antigua y moderna de Jalapa*, II, 291.

[63] Bustamante, *El Honor y patriotismo*, pp. 72-74.

[64] On April 22, 1823, the Supreme Executive Power had written to Bravo that steps had been taken to protect Iturbide's party and to provide for its comfort during the voyage, Hernández y Dávalos Collection, 16-3 bis-3732, in MSS, U.T.

"I assure your Excellency that there is no power capable of inducing me to act in a vile manner. Whatever sacrifices I have made were in favor of my country. I am disposed to make as many more sacrifices as I can; but I know that there is no advantage to Mexico in sacrificing my family, and therefore I shall not do so. In conclusion, I shall proceed with every assurance of security in order that my honorable family may not suffer the least insult or else I shall not proceed at all. In the latter case, your Excellency can inform the national government so that it may consign me to a prison or dispose of me in any other manner that it may wish. . . ."[65]

Bravo was evidently on his guard lest an attempt should be made to set his prisoner at liberty. Iturbide's representations, however, were not fruitless. Congress eventually decided that both his father and his ailing sister could reside in Mexico at a place to be approved by the government.[66] It appears that the Supreme Executive Power allowed Iturbide to choose the port in Italy where he wished to disembark.[67] In any case, before his party caught sight of the Mexican Gulf, Leghorn had been selected as the terminus of his voyage.

When his party reached Antigua—the site of old Vera Cruz—Bravo placed Iturbide in the custody of Guadalupe Victoria. Disturbed financial conditions had prevented the latter from securing by letters of credit more than one-half of the amount of the promised annual pension. Victoria soon sent to Iturbide letters of credit for 12,500 pesos and promised that the balance of the amount due him would eventually be placed at the disposal of properly authorized agents.[68] Upon acknowledging the receipt of this moiety, the deposed monarch stated that he would like to have the remainder of the allowance so that he could provide for the establishment of his home in Italy.[69] When an issue was raised about the examination of his outgoing luggage by Mexican customs officials on the banks of the river Antigua, Iturbide seemed not only willing but anxious that this should be done. He explained that he wished to convince people that, contrary to vile rumors to the effect that he had carried off all the gold from the mint,

---

[65] Bustamante, *El Honor y patriotismo*, pp. 81-82.

[66] The secretaries of Congress to J. García Illueca, April 28, 1823, Hernández y Dávalos Collection, 16-3-3294, in MSS, U.T.

[67] *El Sol*, April 19, 1823, p. 24.

[68] Victoria to García Illueca, April 22, 1823, Hernández y Dávalos Collection, 16-2 bis-3733, in MSS, U.T.

[69] Iturbide to Victoria, May 10, 1823, "Una correspondencia desconocida de Don Agustín de Iturbide," *El Universal*, September, 1921.

he had not cared to accumulate riches.[70] Influenced by his plea, the officials refrained from examining his baggage. The Supreme Executive Power had meanwhile sent directions to Victoria concerning the vessel which was to transport him.[71] With respect to his property in Mexico, Iturbide prepared instructions for its management by Nicolás Carrillo and Gómez de Navarrete.[72]

A contract for the transportation of the exiles signed by General Victoria with Captain Quelch of the armed merchantman *Rawlins* on April 26 stipulated that the vessel was to transport Iturbide's party, composed of from twenty-five to thirty members of his family and servants, from Vera Cruz to Leghorn. Unless compelled by wind or waves, the vessel was not to touch at any place during the voyage. In particular the ports of Spain were to be avoided. Quelch promised to submit to any quarantine that might be imposed by Italian authorities prior to the disembarkation of his passengers. On behalf of the Mexican government, Victoria agreed to pay the captain or his representative 15,550 pesos in Mexican silver for the transportation of the company. One half of this sum was to be paid on May 1; and the remainder three days before the *Rawlins* weighed anchor.[73]

It was presumably by the aid of Pedro del Paso y Troncoso, whom Iturbide had chosen to represent him, that supplies were embarked on board the *Rawlins*. Among the items mentioned in the manifest were 2 milch cows, 10 calves, 52 sheep, 16 lambs, 600 chickens, 6,000 eggs, 100 melons, 2 cases of Málaga wine, 30 cases of claret, and 12 barrels of Catalonian wine.[74] Many years later José Malo asserted that a bottle of bitters containing poison was surreptitiously placed among the provisions intended for the former Emperor.[75] Among the belongings

[70] Bustamante, *El Honor y patriotismo*, p. 84; Iturbide to N. Carrillo, August 2, 1823, in I. MSS, 17; cf. Bustamante, *Diario historico*, I, 318-319.

[71] The Supreme Executive Power to Bravo, April 22, 1823, Hernández y Dávalos Collection, 16-2 bis-3732, in MSS, U.T. In a letter to García Illueca, April 26, 1823, Victoria wrote, "devo advertir que la contrata se ha celebrado con arreglo á las indicaciones del Govierno para el transporte . . . ," Hernández y Dávalos Collection, 16-3-3285, *ibid.*

[72] Copy, Instrucciones para gobierno de los apoderados Don Juan Gómez Navarrete y Don Nicolás Carrillo, en el. giro y manejo de mi casa en México, Documentos relativos al Imperio de Iturbide, 1821-1824, f. 252-254, Genaro García Collection, in MSS, U.T. Library.

[73] M. M., *Verdadera noticia del embarque del Sr. Iturbide y cargamento que lleva*, p. 1.

[74] *Ibid.*

[75] *Apuntes historicos sobre el destierro, vuelta al territorio mexicano y muerte del libertador D. Agustin de Iturbide*, pp. 18-19.

of the exiled family embarked on the vessel were silverware, precious jewels, and paintings by old masters.[76]

The downfall of the First Mexican Empire was due to a variety of circumstances. As the founder of a state set up after ten years of revolutionary disturbance, the sovereign was compelled to surmount obstacles and to disentangle complications, without experience or precedents to guide him. What was even more of a handicap, he had to act without the aid of men trained in statecraft. Though many of his countrymen joyfully hailed the Liberator when he was suddenly elevated to the throne, yet it appears that, in the case of some influential politico-military leaders, those acclamations were little more than lip service. Some of the Emperor's most difficult problems stemmed from the fact that, ignoring the fundamental principle of the Plan of Iguala, he had accepted the imperial dignity without acknowledging subordination to the motherland.[77] Above all, though he declared himself to be the champion of a limited monarchy, yet in practice he became an almost absolute ruler. Expressing the views of some Mexicans, *El Sol* not inappropriately exclaimed: "What was our surprise when we saw that the same arms which had co-operated in order to liberate our native land had turned against it and fettered us with heavier chains than those which had oppressed us during previous centuries, so that we had merely replaced a foreign despot by a domestic tyrant!"[78]

Moreover, the large additional expense involved in the establishment of a monarchical regime added to the prevailing discontent. The cry for the establishment of a republic voiced by discontented leaders appealed to many Mexicans who were dissatisfied with the recognition which they had been accorded or who had become disgusted with imperial rule. Some of the malcontents evidently dreamed that they could at once attain individual prosperity and also promote the general welfare under a republican system of government—a system for which the Emperor had publicly declared his countrymen were not ready. As he pointed out on more than one occasion, prominent among those leaders who undertook to overthrow his political

[76] Inventory of various articles belonging to His Excellency Don Agustín de Iturbide and put under charge of the undersigned Fletcher, Macbean & Co., Leghorn, November 22, 1823, Hernández y Dávalos Collection, 16-6-3556, in MSS, U.T.

[77] Lemaur to M. López Baños, March 17, 1823, enclosed extracts from letters of correspondents who opposed imperial rule, in A.G.I., Audiencia de México, 90-2-16.

[78] November 23, 1823.

system were Echávarri, Santa Anna, and the Marquis of Vivanco.[79] Iturbide later avowed that his greatest sacrifice in 1823 was the abandonment of his beloved country, of an invalid sister and an idolized father, and of friends who had been the companions of his infancy and youth.[80] Indeed in 1823 the Mexican Thinker depicted Iturbide as an actor stripped of his imperial crown, mantle, and scepter who was lamenting the sudden disappearance of his friends.[81]

[79] The view of a Mexican biographer about the role of Santa Anna in the overthrow of Agustín I is found in Suárez y Navarro, *Historia de México y del general Antonio Lopez de Santa Anna*, pp. 32-33.

[80] Iturbide, *Carrera militar y politica*, p. 61.

[81] Fernández de Lizardi, *El Unipersonal de Don Agustín de Iturbide*, p. 1.

CHAPTER XIII

Iturbide in Europe

YELLOW FEVER was raging at Vera Cruz. Hence on May 11
Iturbide's party sailed from the mouth of the river Antigua, a
few miles north of the city. As some former members of his following had been allowed to rejoin him at Perote, besides the banished
Emperor, his wife, and their eight children, the passengers included
his old friend, José López; José Treviño, his confessor; José Malo, his
nephew; and Secretary Álvarez with his family. In addition, there
were ten dependents and servants.[1] A story was soon told with gusto
in the capital city that the former Admiral had scarcely embarked
before he became seasick.[2] On May 15, 1823, the Supreme Executive
Power announced, in a special number of the gazette, the departure
of the Hero of Independence. They unctuously declared that at the
moment when his moral and political virtues vanished, "and when
ambition and other mean passions" were substituted for them, the
country removed him "from its bosom by moderate measures" which
were almost unprecedented in history.

After his return from a sojourn in Europe, on April 10, 1823, Lucas
Alamán, who was described by a contemporary as wearing green spec-
tacles and having a Parisian accent,[3] had been appointed provisionally
the Secretary for Foreign Affairs as well as for Domestic Affairs.
Presumably by the direction of Secretary Alamán, long before Iturbide
had finished the voyage, the Mexican government had made arrangements for espionage. Instructions were framed for a Dominican friar
named José María Marchena who was directed to serve as an agent
to the Holy See as well as to watch secretly the activities of the proscribed Mexican. In addition to a passport in his own name, the spy
was furnished with another certificate which bore the alias Juan Villa-
franca. He was instructed that by means of the Austrian police he

[1] *Gaceta extraordinaria del gobierno supremo de México,* May 14, 1823, p. 242.
[2] Bustamante, *Diario historico de Mexico,* I, 400.
[3] Beruete, Diario, f. 85, in MSS, T.U.

was to prevent any attempt by Iturbide to return to his native land.[4]

Much to the chagrin of the exile, shortly after the *Rawlins* reached the high seas, an English frigate which had served as an escort turned her prow toward Mexico.[5] In a letter to a friend Iturbide complained that during the voyage he was treated like a prisoner. He expressed regret that he had not been able to catch more than a passing glimpse of the frowning fortress of Gibraltar.[6] Scarcely had he reached the shores of Italy when, in a letter to Nicolás Carrillo, he denounced the attitude which had been assumed by the Mexican government with regard to the payment of his pension.

"Despite the fact than on my part there has been nothing else than generosity, disinterestedness, and very obvious proofs of a true love for my country, the treatment accorded me has been almost incredible. It has been niggardly and marked by bad faith. In fine, I shall suffer with my family but shall always rest content with the testimony of my conscience concerning my conduct as a public man, a conduct which is free from ignominy. Imagine how I shall be able to maintain such a numerous family for six months in a strange country, without any money and with very little property that I can sell. . . . If the government has not honored my just claims, I shall feel myself forced to dispose of the greater part of the small collection of silverware and jewels which I owned before sailing from Mexico in order to pay part of my debts, so as to relieve as many of my friends as possible from actual loss."[7]

The *Rawlins* cast anchor in the harbor of Leghorn on August 2. In a letter written on that day to Juan Gómez de Navarrete, Iturbide stated that he desired to live in or near Rome or else in a country house near another city where he could give his children a good edu-

[4] Olavarría y Ferrari, *México independiente*, 104-105 n. As printed, the instructions to José María Marchena were without signature or exact date. In 1942 a copy of the original "Instrucción reservada" was, however, found by the writer in A.G.R.E., 40-11-2. Alamán, *Historia*, V, 599, alleged that Marchena had been sent to Europe by Masons. Yet a copy of a certificate dated March 29, 1825, which was ascribed to Alamán, begins thus: "Certifico: que Don José Marchena fue comisionado por el Gobierno Supremo de la Nacion para desempeñar encargos de la mayor importancia que debía evacuar en ultramar. De hecho se puso en marcha y lo desempeñó sin perdonar riesgos y toda clase de fatigas muy á satisfacción del mismo Gobierno" (Comisión reservada conferida al Padre Don José María Marchena, f. 54, Genaro García Collection, in MSS, U.T. Library).

[5] Bustamante, *Diario historico*, I, 413; Malo, *Apuntes historicos sobre el destierro, vuelta al territorio mexicano y muerte del libertador D. Agustin de Iturbide*, p. 16.

[6] To Gómez de Navarrete, Castillo Negrete, *Mexico en el siglo xix*, XV, 179-180.

[7] "Una correspondencia desconocida de Don Agustín de Iturbide," *El Universal*, September, 1921.

cation. He urged his correspondent to see that his father and his sister María Nicolasa were being adequately financed, if not by the Mexican government, then by funds derived from his property.[8] In a letter to a mysterious European correspondent whom he addressed as Mr. Bourdeaux, on August 2, 1823, the Mexican mentioned his plans for the future in more detail:

"I am not concerned about my own fate. But I regret the misfortune of an estimable wife and eight innocent children who are expatriated. The children may become orphans in strange countries which are far from home. Most of all I am harassed about the fate of my compatriots. May God grant that I am mistaken, and that they are happy! In that case I shall live placidly the rest of my days in the place where I settle, which, although I favor a country house near Rome, I have not yet selected. I should like to be able to reside in France, where I would select Bordeaux as my domicile and would have the satisfaction of enjoying your friendship. I cannot leave Italy, however, because in that case I would lose the pension upon which I depend for living expenses. . . ."[9]

Arriving from a region where yellow fever was endemic, the passengers on the *Rawlins* were required to remain in quarantine for one month. During a part of that period Iturbide lived on shipboard, the remaining time he spent in a lazaretto on the neighboring shore. Soon after reaching Leghorn, he received a courteous letter from Mariano Torrente, who was the consul in that port of the liberal government of Spain. The Spaniard congratulated Iturbide on his safe arrival in Italy, praised his love of liberty, displayed much interest in his plans, and expressed an ardent desire to meet him.[10] Ignorant of Italian customs, the former Emperor highly appreciated the friendly attitude of the consul, and soon placed much reliance upon his advice. After Torrente had been deprived of the consulate at Leghorn because of the restoration of Ferdinand VII to his throne by French intervention, Iturbide's intimacy with him did not decrease.

As the Congress of Vienna had restored the old dynasties to the Italian principalities, Ferdinand III, who had been made the Grand Duke of Tuscany by his father, the Emperor of Austria, was formally reinstated in Florence, the capital of the duchy. The exile soon became aware that he could not establish a residence in the country without the permission of the Grand Duke. So sympathetic did Tor-

[8] Castillo Negrete, *op. cit.*, XV, 180-194.

[9] *Ibid.*, p. 211.

[10] August 2, 1823, Hernández y Dávalos Collection, 16-6-3372, in MSS, U.T.

rente become that he consulted Marquis Garzoni Venturi, the governor of Leghorn, about the action required of a visitor. On his part, Iturbide conferred with Torrente about a petition which he undertook to prepare for the government soliciting permission to remain in Tuscany.[11] On August 11 the Mexican sent a letter to the Spaniard in which he declared that it would not be easy for him to explain properly in writing the motives which had impelled him to promote the independence of his native land. He asked Torrente to examine the draft of a plea addressed to Ferdinand III and to return it promptly with his comment so that it could be translated into Italian and forwarded to Florence.[12] Torrente replied on the same day that he had found this representation to be clear, precise, and suitable. He suggested, however, that, before the document was translated into Italian, the author might well burn a little incense before the throne of King Ferdinand VII.[13]

A few days later Iturbide addressed a letter directly to Governor Venturi. The petitioner stated that, having decided to reside in Leghorn for the time being, he considered it to be his duty to solicit the hospitality of the government.[14] For that purpose he enclosed an account of his public career addressed to the Tuscan Secretary of State which he wished forwarded to Florence. In that sketch, when discussing his part in the establishment of Mexican independence, the author not only justified his conduct as a public man but also tempered his statements in order to avoid antagonizing a legitimist ruler. He declared that his object in the revolutionary movement was simply a peaceful reform which would benefit a country that had been harassed for years by notorious evils of all kinds."[15]

Agents of legitimist governments in Italy soon became aware of the arrival of the one-time chief of the rebellious Mexicans. One week after the *Rawlins* reached Leghorn, Guillermo Curtoys, the Spanish minister at Lucca, which was the capital of the neighboring duchy of that name, sent word to his government that the former Emperor of Mexico had arrived in Italy with his family and would reside in Tuscany.[16] In order to carry out his plan concerning a resi-

---

[11] Torrente to Iturbide, without date, Hernández y Dávalos Collection, 16-6-3394, in MSS, U.T.

[12] Hernández y Dávalos Collection, 16-6-3395, *ibid*.

[13] August 11, 1823, Hernández y Dávalos Collection, 16-6-3397, *ibid*.

[14] Al Gobernador de Liorna, undated, Hernández y Dávalos Collection, 16-6-3400, *ibid*.

[15] Cuevas, *El Libertador*, p. 395.

[16] Curtoys to V. Saez, August 9, 1823, in A.H.N., Estado, 5741.

dence, Iturbide soon applied to the Vatican for permission to proceed to the Eternal City. On September 17, 1823, Monsignor Mazio, the secretary of the Conclave of Cardinals which had assembled there in order to choose a successor to the deceased Pope Pius VII, wrote to Signor Bernetti, the governor of Rome, to inquire whether there would be any objection to the sojourn in that city of Agustín de Iturbide,[17] "a person well known throughout Europe and celebrated in the history of these times."

Iturbide's purpose, as expressed in a letter sent directly to the Papal Secretary of State, was to offer his respects to the Pope as well as to examine the educational institutions located at "the capital of the world" with a view to placing his children in schools where they might become reverent communicants of the Roman Catholic Church. In consequence, an inquiry was made of Antonio de Vargas, the Spanish minister to the Holy See, concerning the proposed visit. "My reply to this question," wrote Vargas to Victor Saez, who had become the chief minister of King Ferdinand VII, was "that it is by no means likely that the King our master or the Regency or any loyal Spaniard would view with indifference the admission of Iturbide into the Papal States and the establishment of his residence there; for he has been one of the principal promoters of the revolution in Mexico against her legitimate sovereign and has even carried his audacity and ambition to the point of usurping the title of Emperor." The result was that, acting in accordance with the wishes of Vargas, the College of Cardinals notified Governor Bernetti that persons interested in Iturbide should be informed that his request for permission to visit Rome had been denied.[18]

Meanwhile the petitioner had become seriously concerned about his finances. Pedro del Paso y Troncoso had addressed a letter to him to state that, as soon as the *Rawlins* sailed, he had forwarded to him the duplicates of three letters of exchange amounting to 10,875 pesos drawn by the Mexican government on parties in Europe.[19] Directions sent to a Cadiz banker concerning one of these letters were that Iturbide was not to be paid the designated sum unless he took up his residence in Italy.[20] Early in August, a part of his allowance was paid to him at Leghorn.[21] On August 2 he addressed a letter to Gómez

[17] R. Mazio to J. Bernetti, September 17, 1823, in A.E.E.S.S., legajo 751.
[18] *Ibid.* The quotations are from Vargas to Saez, September 19, 1823, in A.H.N., Estado, 5757.
[19] May 14, 1823, Hernández y Dávalos Collection, 16-4-3319, in MSS, U.T.
[20] P. Echevarría to J. M. Irigoyen, May 5, 1823, in I. MSS, 17.
[21] Webb & Co. to Iturbide, August 6, 1823, Hernández y Dávalos Collection, 16-4-3387, in MSS, U.T.

de Navarrete in which he complained that the agreement which he had with the Mexican government about the payment of his pension had not been fulfilled.[22] Two months later he repeated this complaint in a letter to Pedro del Paso y Troncoso.[23] Lucas Alamán, who because of his secretaryship should have known the facts, calculated many years later that, after the necessary deductions had been made, the part of Iturbide's pension which was actually paid netted him only 9,700 pesos.[24] In the end of September, 1823, while living temporarily in Villa Guebhardt at Imbroggiana,[25] in an *Apologia pro vita sua*,[26] Iturbide undertook to refute accusations that he had filled his private purse while in office. He maintained that the best proof that he had not enriched himself was that he was not rich. He asserted that he did not possess as much property as he had when he undertook to establish the independence of Mexico. "Not only did I not misapply the public funds," he added, "but I did not even take from the treasury the appropriations which were granted to me. . . . I did not enrich my relatives by giving them lucrative employments."[27]

Iturbide's plea soliciting permission from the Grand Duke to reside in his dominions was favorably received. According to his own account, the petitioner was notified that he could reside anywhere in Tuscany that might please his fancy. With the assistance of Torrente, he found a residence to his liking in a former palace owned by Signor Fournier which was located in an attractive suburb of Leghorn. Alamán later stated that the expatriated Mexican leased this spacious villa for the modest sum of four hundred pesos per annum. Iturbide calculated that the rent which was paid in advance, the expense of furnishing Villa Fournier in suitable style, and his living expenses amounted to some 10,000 pesos.[28] In October, 1823, his

[22] Castillo Negrete, *Mexico en el siglo xix*, XV, 180.

[23] October 1, 1823, Hernández y Dávalos Collection, 16-6-3454, in MSS, U.T.

[24] *Historia*, V, 597.

[25] Webb & Co. to Iturbide, September 20, 1823, Hernández y Dávalos Collection, 16-6-3451, in MSS, U.T.

[26] Robertson, "The Memorabilia of Agustín de Iturbide," *Hispanic American Historical Review*, XXVII, 441-442.

[27] Iturbide, *Carrera militar y politica*, pp. 52-53, and n. 31. Cf. the translation into English made by Michael J. Quin entitled *A Statement of Some of the Principal Events in the Public Life of Agustin de Iturbide Written by Himself*, pp. 78-80. That translation, which incorporates some of the footnotes of the *memoria* into the *Statement*, was made by Quin while the former Emperor was in England (Robertson, "The Memorabilia of Agustín de Iturbide," *loc. cit.*, XXVII, 454).

[28] Alamán, *Historia*, V, 597 n. 38; Persecución de Y. venida Londres, f. 5v., Hernández y Dávalos Collection, 17-2-3843, in MSS, U.T.

family took up their residence there. The walls of the villa were soon adorned with paintings by old masters.

Early in November, Iturbide made a trip to Florence, where, according to his own story, Ferdinand III received him with consideration and honor.[29] Not only did the visitor become acquainted with some European dignitaries but he also called upon Lord Burghersh, the English minister to Tuscany, with whom he had become acquainted while that diplomat was enjoying sea baths at Leghorn. To Burghersh the man without a country expressed apprehensions concerning the future of Mexico. In particular he voiced a dread of the expansionist ambitions of the Americans, the French, and the Spaniards. To George Canning, the English Secretary of State for Foreign Affairs, Burghersh sent a "secret and confidential" dispatch which contained these statements concerning Iturbide:

"With England he was most anxious to contract engagements because he felt satisfied it was for the true interest of his country; for the true interest of that Empire to which he had given independence; and for whose prosperity and happiness his life had been and should continue to be devoted. In contracting these engagements he would not hesitate in offering every possible commercial advantage to the British nation. . . ." In reply to an inquiry concerning his attitude in case Ferdinand VII should ask him to enter the Spanish military service and reconquer Mexico for Spain, he replied that this "was so entirely contrary to his principles that if every prospect of wealth and power were offered to him on one hand, and certain destruction on the other, he would not accede to such a proposition. . . ." When sounded about a hypothetical proposal to send a Spanish prince to occupy the throne of Mexico, he replied that this was very unlikely but that "supposing the independence of his Country to be assured, he might be induced to listen to some proposal of that sort."[30]

Iturbide eventually became profoundly dissatisfied with the conditions under which he was residing in Italy. Not only was he much displeased with the indifference or neglect of the Mexican government concerning the payment of his pension, but he also became apprehensive of designs upon his liberty.[31] Near the end of 1823 the

[29] Persecución de Y. venida Londres, f. 1, Hernández y Dávalos Collection, 17-2-3843, ibid.

[30] Burghersh to Canning, November 11, 1823, f. 4-5v., in F.O., 79/38a. In his reply dated December 2, 1823, Canning advised the minister to avoid any appearance of encouraging the projects which Iturbide seemed to be contemplating (ibid., 79/39a).

[31] Persecución de Y. venida Londres, f. 2, Hernández y Dávalos Collection, 17-1&2-3843, in MSS, U.T.

Mexican agent to the Holy See sent to his government a message written in invisible ink in which he explained that he had been unable to do anything with regard to Iturbide in Tuscany because the Grand Duke had promised to protect him. "This Duke," continued José Marchena, "caused him to flee because King Ferdinand VII demanded his person in order to hang him."[32]

Iturbide's dream of abiding quietly with his family in Italy was shattered. "I remained there in tranquillity," he recorded, "until the beginning of November, when I was told that the ministers of Austria and France had become concerned about me. As this happened at the very time when the issue of the reconquest of Spanish America was being discussed in European journals, it seemed very significant to me. Soon I was given to understand that I needed a letter of identification."[33] Near the end of November he was given such a certificate promising himself and his companions protection by the government of Leghorn. The assurance was to be valid, however, for only one month.[34] "This policy of the government," said Iturbide, "so different from the frankness with which I had been received in August, convinced me of the accuracy of reports that had been given me by some friends. It also convinced me that, if I wished to be situated so that I might be able to return to serve my country, I ought to leave Leghorn without loss of time."[35]

Indeed in November Torrente had warned Iturbide that he did not consider him safe in Tuscany because of the unfavorable opinion entertained of him by European diplomats stationed in Florence who had stigmatized him as a "rebel." The Spaniard, who was still a Liberal, added that such proceedings were not strange in view of the intolerance openly professed "by the Holy Alliance which has not pardoned and will not pardon those persons who have undertaken either directly or indirectly to oppose its pretended legitimacy."[36] Although originally the so-called Treaty of the Holy Alliance was little more than a declaration of principles by the monarchs of Austria, Prussia, and Russia, yet the Holy Allies were eventually viewed as the instruments of legitimacy. In April, 1823, after the King of

---

[32] Castillo Negrete, *Mexico en el siglo xix*, XIV, 254.

[33] Persecución de Y. venida Londres, f. 2, Hernández y Dávalos Collection, 17-2-3843, in MSS, U.T.

[34] Cuevas, *El Libertador*, p. 402.

[35] Persecución de Y. venida Londres, f. 2, Hernández y Dávalos Collection, 17-2-3843, in MSS, U.T.

[36] Torrente to Iturbide, November 12, 1823, Hernández y Dávalos Collection, 16-6-3516, *ibid*.

France had joined the Holy Alliance, French soldiers marched into Spain, overthrew the constitutional government, and restored Ferdinand VII to absolute power. It is clear that the King of Spain wished the Allies to restore his rule over Spanish America.[37]

On November 22, 1823, Iturbide had deposited in the custody of Fletcher, Macbean, and Company, an English firm in Leghorn which was to serve as his agent, some furniture as well as gold and silver jewelry. He drew up instructions to the effect that, if he did not return from a projected journey, his horses were to be sold at the best possible price.[38] On November 28, he secured passage on the *George & Mary*, a small English vessel which had cast anchor at Leghorn.[39] Shortly afterward, furnished with letters of introduction by Lord Burghersh,[40] accompanied by his two eldest boys named Agustín and Angel, his nephew, his secretary, two priests, and Torrente, Iturbide embarked on that vessel bound for London.[41] His departure on a ship flying the British flag startled some diplomats of the Holy Allies.

Early in December the Spanish minister at Lucca sent a dispatch warning his government of Iturbide's "very secret and mysterious flight. He has wished to have it understood by the public," wrote Curtoys, "that the object of his voyage was simply to take his two eldest sons to an educational institution in England. After his departure his wife instituted the most rigid economy and at once dismissed five of her servants." As further shown by a tailor's bill sent to her husband, the family had been living in an extravagant style.[42]

Spanish journalists soon became aware of the former Emperor's movements. A notice of his departure from Italy published in the *Gaceta de Madrid* stated that certain letters from Paris had declared that he was accompanied by some Spanish revolutionaries who would go with him to Mexico; but that other letters implied that he would direct his steps toward London, for England had become the asylum

[37] V. Saez to the Duke of San Carlos, November 27, 1823, A.G.I., Estado, América en General, 5.

[38] "Inventory of various articles belonging to His Excellency Don Agustín de Iturbide and put under charge of the undersigned, Fletcher, Macbean & Co.," Leghorn, November 22, 1823, Hernández y Dávalos Collection, 16-6-3556, in MSS, U.T.

[39] Memorandum of G. Traill, November 28, 1823, Hernández y Dávalos Collection, 17-1-3770, *ibid*.

[40] Burghersh to Canning, November 27, 1823, in F.O., 79/39a.

[41] Burghersh to Canning, November 27, 1823, *ibid*. A copy of a memorandum by J. R. Malo (Documentos históricos, Don Agustín Iturbide, 1821-1827, f. 239, Genaro García Collection, in MSS, U.T. Library) states that the party sailed on November 29.

[42] The quotation is from Curtoys to V. Saez, December 2, 1823, in A.H.N., Estado, 5741; Conto al S. E. el Signor Agostino Iturbide ad Alessandro Vigo . . . . , September 28, 1823, Hernández y Dávalos Collection, 16-6-3566, in MSS, U.T.

for all the enemies of legitimist monarchies.[43] Marchena sent to Mexico from Rome on December 27 an instructive letter about the exile. He declared that during his entire sojourn in Italy the Mexican had lived a retired life without spending much money. "In fact, he behaved so much like a poor man that those persons who served him in certain matters received in return only medals commemorating his proclamation as Emperor."[44] A little later the spy reported that the protective attitude of the Grand Duke had prevented him from impeding Iturbide's journey.[45]

Early in December, 1823, Count Bombelles, the minister of Austria at Florence, notified Prince Metternich, the Austrian Chancellor often supposed to have been the *deus ex machina* of the Holy Alliance, of the flight of the former Emperor from Leghorn.[46] Seven days later the count wrote to Metternich that the revolutionary had returned to that port because of contrary winds. In the belief that the Mexican intended soon to re-embark, Bombelles sent a letter to Prince Neri Corsini, the Tuscan Minister of Foreign Affairs, in which he expressed a wish that the government at Florence would use all the means in its power to prevent Iturbide from leaving Leghorn a second time. Among important reasons for such a policy the writer stated that the arrival of the exile in England or in America would be viewed by continental powers as a major event fraught with ominous results. Bombelles argued that Grand Duke Ferdinand III could not allow Iturbide to depart from the soil of Tuscany without incurring the displeasure of the Allies, who were "united in heart and in interest to maintain the repose and the tranquillity of the world."[47]

Upon learning of these representations, Prince Metternich expressed the opinion that the departure of Iturbide for England had been provoked by the fear that his person would be demanded by the government of Spain. The reputed champion of legitimacy expressed regret that Bombelles had undertaken to act in conjunction with Prince Corsini to prevent the departure of the adventurer from Tuscany. "If the French minister [Maisonfort] had well-founded motives to oppose that departure," said Metternich, "he did well to act upon them. But with respect to us, not having had any motive to keep Iturbide in Tuscany, and not having given purely and simply our consent that

---

[43] January 3, 1824.

[44] *El Sol*, May 28, 1824, p. 1394.

[45] Castillo Negrete, *Mexico en el siglo xix*, XIV, 259.

[46] December 2, 1823, in H. H. u. S., Berichte aus Toscane, 10.

[47] December 9, 1823, and enclosure, a copy of Bombelles' letter to Corsini, December 9, 1823, *ibid.*

he should be admitted into that country, I should have preferred under these circumstance that you had allowed M. de la Maisonfort to act alone."[48] Meantime at more than one European court disturbing stories were rife of English relations with the stormy petrel of Mexico.

Reports of his departure from Italy were soon printed in Madrid and Vienna. Rumors concerning his movements caused excitement in French diplomatic circles. Viscount Chateaubriand, the Minister of Foreign Affairs, at once instructed Prince Polignac, the French ambassador in London, to find out what role the English government had played in Iturbide's departure from Italy. On December 18 the viscount wrote to Polignac and protested that an expedition against Mexico, supported directly or indirectly by England, would destroy all hope that Spain might gain some advantage from the loss of her revolted colonies.[49] In a letter to Count Talaru, the French ambassador at Madrid, Chateaubriand used the hasty voyage of Iturbide as an argument to reinforce his plea for mediation between Spain and her colonies by European powers.[50]

As his plan to proceed to England by sea was thwarted by a storm, Iturbide returned to Leghorn on December 7, 1823. A few days later, accompanied only by Torrente and by his two eldest sons, he started for London by an overland route. In a dispatch to his government the alert Curtoys reported that the chief reason for this departure was the refusal of the Grand Duke of Tuscany to declare formally in writing that Iturbide's person, property, and family would be protected at all times and under all circumstances.[51]

Six years later, upon being restored to favor in Spain, Torrente undertook to explain Iturbide's departure from Italy. In one of his volumes on the history of the revolution in Spanish America, the former liberal asserted that his Mexican protegé had become weary of an obscure life and that he was threatened by the Tuscan government, which could not allow to remain in its dominions "a revolutionist who was hated by Spain and persecuted by his own countrymen." Torrente also alleged that the refugee dreamed of finding in London the means of equipping an expedition resembling that of the ill-fated

---

[48] Metternich to Bombelles, January 4, 1824, in H. H. u. S., Weisungen aus Toscane, 11. On the policy of Metternich toward revolutions, see W. S. Robertson, "Metternich's Attitude toward Revolutions in Latin America," *Hispanic American Historical Review*, XXI, 538-558.

[49] Chateaubriand, *Correspondance générale*, V, 104.

[50] December 16, 1823, in A.A.E., Espagne, 724.

[51] To V. Saez, December 11, 1823, in A.H.N., Estado, 5741.

Mina or of initiating negotiations with the Spanish government for the founding of a Bourbon appanage in Mexico in conformity with the Plan of Iguala and the Córdoba Treaty.[52] The second of these allegations is at odds with the known intentions of Iturbide at this time. Indeed it was apparently the later notion of a Spaniard who had changed his politics in order to ingratiate himself with the absolute King of Spain. This interpretation seems more likely than to suppose that during his relations with the former Emperor the Spaniard had been acting as a spy.

European diplomats became excited upon learning of the alteration in the plans of the exile. Ministers of the Holy Allies in Tuscany had evidently agreed to oppose jointly the grant of a permit allowing the adventurous voyager to re-embark.[53] The envoys of both Austria and France at Florence expressed their regret to the Grand Duke that, "without giving them timely notice of its intention," his government had allowed "a person, whose motives must excite uneasiness on the part of their Allies, to make preparations to quit the country."[54] On December 22, 1823, Chateaubriand wrote to the French ambassador at Madrid that Iturbide had just passed through Turin.[55] When his movements came up for discussion between the viscount and Sir Charles Stuart, the capable English minister at Paris, the former admitted that the traveler had obtained a passport by the oversight of a French consul. Apparently the person of Iturbide had actually been demanded of the French government; because Chateaubriand added that, if the quarry should take a road leading through France, "he would immediately receive orders to return to the frontiers by the road he came, accompanied by a gendarme, for the French law does not permit any individual to be given up to a foreign Government. . . ."[56]

Iturbide gave a different explanation, however, of his escape from the toils of legitimists. "My departure was the more urgent," said he, "because my intentions had become known. Had I embarked again, there would have been sufficient time so that I could have been seized during the voyage. I went by way of Switzerland and the Low Countries to Ostend. If I had not travelled day and night, or if I had taken the road through France, I would have been seized on the way with-

[52] Historia, III, 365-366 n. 1, where Torrente alleged that he had always been a faithful subject of the King of Spain.
[53] Chateaubriand, op. cit., V, 104-105.
[54] Stuart to Canning, December 25, 1823, in F.O., 27/29.
[55] In A.A.E., Espagne, 724.
[56] Stuart to Canning, December 25, 1823, in F.O., 27/29.

out being able to avoid the consequences. . . ."[57] According to diarial
jottings found among unedited papers of Iturbide, after passing
through various Italian cities, he traversed the German principalities
of Baden, Wurtemberg, Hesse, and Prussia.[58] The draft of a letter
addressed by him at Ostend to Henry Pomier, the consul for Mexico
at Bordeaux, through whom he evidently kept in touch with friends,
shows that he was anxiously awaiting news of events in Mexico.[59]

His party reached London on January 1, 1824. He first secured
accommodations in St. Paul's Hotel. Voicing fear of the menace of
the Holy Allies to American independence, a menace which had become his bête noir, on February 13, 1824, Iturbide addressed to the
Mexican Congress an exposition in which he not only offered his
service on behalf of Mexico but also stated that he could bring with
him money, uniforms, munitions, and arms.[60] After advising his
traveling companion about the sale of paintings by Espagnoletto,
Rubens, and Velásquez, Torrente left London for Leghorn, via Paris.[61]
There the former consul had an interview with the Duke of San
Carlos, the Spanish minister to France. When he wrote to Iturbide
about that meeting, Torrente stated that San Carlos had said that the
Holy Alliance had more interest than Spain in destroying liberal ideas
in the New World. He added that when that diplomat astutely inquired whether it would be possible to induce the Mexican revolutionary to act in favor of Spain, in which case his fortune and that of his
family would be assured, he had replied vehemently that the former
Emperor would never act contrary to the principles which he had
recently championed. In conclusion Torrente, who laid himself open
to the suspicion of having transmitted a Spanish proposal that the
Hero of Iguala should renounce the cause of Mexican independence,
advised his correspondent to sail for the United States and to await
there the outcome of events.[62]

Instead of taking this advice, the exile soon addressed a letter to

[57] Persecución de Y. venida Londres, f. 3, Hernández y Dávalos Collection, 17-
1 & 2-3843, in MSS, U.T.

[58] Explicación del viaje desde Liorna á Ostend, Hernández y Dávalos Collection,
16-8-3671, ibid.; Iturbide, Correspondencia de . . . después de la proclamación del
Plan de Iguala, II, 250. The Journal de Paris, January 7, 1824, mentioned Iturbide's
stop at Brussels.

[59] December 29, 1823, Hernández y Dávalos Collection, 16-8-3670, in MSS, U.T.

[60] Breve diseño crítico de la emancipacion y libertad de la nacion mexicana, p. 134.

[61] Torrente to Iturbide, March 6, 1824, Hernández y Dávalos Collection, 17-1 & 2-
3913, in MSS, U.T.

[62] Castillo Negrete, Mexico en el siglo xix, XV, 247-250.

Secretary Canning to make known his arrival in London.[63] Iturbide was not very favorably impressed by the English metropolis, which he called "a Babylon. One can hardly walk in the streets," he wrote, "because of the amazing traffic of carriages, carts of every kind, and people on foot. . . . I have seen few buildings of great importance. The palaces of the King and of the House of Lords are old and do not appear either grand or beautiful."[64]

His arrival in England was soon bruited in the capital city. Among those persons who visited him was a native of Vera Cruz named Francisco de Borja Migoni who had been corresponding with the government of Mexico about the floating of a loan in London.[65] Early in January, 1824, Migoni wrote to Secretary Alamán to report the arrival of the former Emperor's party. When this Mexican agent met Iturbide in a coffeehouse, the conversation naturally turned to their native land. Upon being informed that Spaniards had been expelled from Mexico and their property sequestrated, the exile expressed much regret. Migoni summarized Iturbide's political views in a sentence:

"He was convinced that a republican government would not suit Mexico, for men could not suddenly pass from a state of slavery to a condition of unrestricted liberty. . . . I deduced that the journey of Don Agustín de Iturbide to England with so much celerity in the depth of winter had as its motive some ideas concerning Mexico similar to those which Napoleon had entertained in Elba concerning France."[66] Six days later the agent supplemented these views by another letter to Alamán in which he alleged that, if the revolutionist had proceeded to London with the idea of launching an expedition to protect Mexico against the Holy Alliance, he would be unable to do so; for the monarchs belonging to that alliance would not dare to attack the Spanish-American countries in the face of a decision which he alleged the Anglo-Saxon nations had reached to support the independence of those countries at all cost. "If Iturbide has proposed a plan to act with the refugees here," added Migoni, "that scheme would also be illusory because of the poverty and the very depressed spirits which afflict them. He would not be able to finance a regular expedition on his own account and the English would not aid him."[67]

[63] Canning to Polignac, May 18, 1824, in A.A.E., Angleterre, 618.

[64] Castillo Negrete, op. cit., XV, 228.

[65] Copy, J. M. Herrera to Alamán, August 14, 1822, in A.G.R.E., 6-18-3.

[66] January 4, 1824, in ibid., 40-11-2.

[67] Ibid. Cf. this letter as printed in the Gaceta del gobierno supremo de la Federación Mexicana, March 18, 1824.

After Padre Marchena had traveled from Rome to London, he undertook to supplement Migoni's reports. In February, 1824, he wrote to Alamán that Iturbide was leading a quiet life in a house with five servants, that he appeared infrequently in the streets but occasionally went to the theater, and that he sometimes rode in a green coach resembling one that he had used in Mexico City.[68] During the following month the friar reported that the refugee had become intimate with an Englishman named Powles who had formed a company for the exploitation of Mexican mines.[69] Iturbide informed Álvarez that he would stay in England only a short time. Yet, upon writing to Gómez de Navarrete in regard to his financial relations with the Mexican government, chafing at the barbed bit which had been thrust into his mouth, the exile instructed this agent to solicit from Congress permission for him to reside with his family wherever he liked, whether in Italy, in France, in the Low Countries, or in England.[70] About this time he was also attempting to secure the admission of his daughters into a convent at Amiens or Paris.[71]

On May 6 Marchena sent word to his government that Iturbide had selected a merchant named Matthew Fletcher, a member of the firm of Fletcher, Macbean, and Company, to serve him as a business representative. Further, the spy reported that, under cover of a mining enterprise, the proscribed Mexican was secretly preparing an expedition against his native land.[72]

Indeed shortly after the exile disembarked at Leghorn, placards had been posted in Mexico City announcing his prospective return.[73] During the autumn of 1823 monarchical plots were discovered there. In September, Beruete recorded that in the capital city the Iturbidistas had incited two conspiracies in three nights.[74] During the next month conspirators undertook to correspond with Captain Manuel Reyes who had been in the royalist army during the viceregal regime and had later served under Iturbide. A document found with the captain's instructions, which arranged for the seizure of the Supreme Executive Power, declared that the only slogan of the plotters should be Religion,

[68] Olavarría y Ferrari, *México independiente*, p. 105 n. The original in A.G.R.E., 40-11-2, bears no date.
[69] Copy, Marchena to Alamán, March 17, 1824, Comisión reservada conferida al padre Don José María Marchena, f. 34, Genaro García Collection, in MSS, U.T. Library.
[70] Castillo Negrete, *Mexico en el siglo xix*, XV, 242.
[71] *Ibid.*, pp. 234-235.
[72] *Ibid.*, XIV, 267-270.
[73] Bustamante, *Diario historico*, I, 538-540.
[74] Diario, f. 97 bis-98, in MSS, T.U.

Independence, the Sovereign Congress, and the Hero of Iguala.[75] In a letter to Reyes dated November 11, 1823, Manuel Caro declared himself in favor of the restoration of Iturbide to power.[76] An attempt by the conspirators to induce Gómez Pedraza to lead a revolution, however, failed.[77] José Joaquín de Herrera, who had become the Secretary of War and the Navy, issued a broadside in January, 1824, warning them to lay down their arms under penalty of being declared traitors.[78]

Nevertheless, agitation in favor of the restoration of imperial rule did not cease. Near the end of March, Beruete mentioned that placards had been posted on street corners in the capital city which portrayed Iturbide again adorned with the imperial insignia, while Echávarri, Antonio Santa Anna, and the Marquis of Vivanco were depicted in hasty flight.[79] On May 14 the same diarist wrote as follows: "Yesterday more than twenty persons were arrested who had formed a conspiracy. Their object was to assassinate the members of the Executive Power as well as some of the deputies, to establish a regency, and to proclaim Iturbide as the President of the republic."[80] A few days later Nicolás Bravo warned the Secretary of War that General Anastasio Bustamante was carrying out his pledge "to re-establish the tyranny of Iturbide."[81] Beruete recorded early in June that during a secret session of Congress an intercepted epistle of General Quintanar had been read which proposed the overthrow of the existing government, the despoliation of all the Spaniards, and the proclamation of Iturbide as the ruler.[82]

There is a possibility that at least one of the monarchical plans had been submitted to the former Emperor. For, among manuscripts pertaining to conspiracies in the Hernández y Dávalos Collection the writer found a "Plan to Restore the Liberty of the Mexican Nation and to Preserve her Independence" which bears an annotation in what appears to be the handwriting of Iturbide.[83] Further, an undated and

[75] Instrucciones á q. presisamte. debe seguir sus operaciones el q. ha de asegurar á las personas de los q. componen el Poder Executivo, Hernández y Dávalos Collection, 16-6-3508, in MSS, U.T.

[76] Hernández y Dávalos Collection, 16-6-3502, *ibid.*

[77] José M. Lobato and Others to Gómez Pedraza, January 21, 1824, Hernández y Dávalos Collection, 17-1 & 2-3789, *ibid.*; Gómez Pedraza to the Minister of Relations, January 24, 1824, Hernández y Dávalos Collection, 17-1 & 2-3788, *ibid.*

[78] January 24, 1824.

[79] Diario, f. 124-124*v.*, in MSS, T.U.

[80] Diario, f. 135*v.*, *ibid.*

[81] To M. Mier y Terán, May 19, 1824, in A.M.C., D/481.3/305.

[82] Diario, f. 141, in MSS, T.U.

[83] Plano para restaurar la libertad de la Nación Mexicana y conservar su Independencia . . . , Hernández y Dávalos Collection, 16-6-3442, in MSS, U.T.

unsigned memorandum concerning imperialistic plans, which was perhaps composed by him, suggested that Echávarri, Negrete, and Vivanco should be excluded from positions of trust under the projected regime.[84] Mexicans who were in touch with the exile evidently conveyed to him a hint of existing conditions. Upon acknowledging the receipt of three letters from him, Pedro del Paso y Troncoso replied that there was a prevailing fear in Mexico that the Holy Alliance would intervene there.[85] Declaring that he was suspected of being a notorious agent of the former Emperor, on January 31 Miguel Cavaleri wrote to Iturbide to state that he was en route to England, that frequent reports about conspiracies had provoked the persecution of Iturbidistas, and that nothing was known in Mexico about the naval designs of the Holy Allies.[86] On March 17 a Spanish official warned his government that a vessel which had just touched at Habana had on board Cavaleri, who had undertaken to bring the former Emperor back to his native land.[87]

Aside from underground plots, Mexican leaders were kept from forgetting Iturbide through casual notices of him which filtered into Mexican journals. On February 27, 1824, *El Sol* printed a letter from Paris which mentioned his departure from Leghorn. When it discussed his flight to escape the toils of King Ferdinand VII, the *Aguila Mexicana* added that no Mexican desired the ruin of a compatriot who had performed such noble service in favor of emancipation.[88] The editors of this periodical soon published an item which stated that they had seen a letter from Iturbide demanding the payment of his pension.[89] Upon printing a notice to the effect that the exile had proceeded to England in order to secure the aid of that government in his imperialistic designs, *El Sol* asserted that some of his partisans believed that he would be welcomed in the city of Guadalajara with open arms.[90] In Mexico City handbills were circulated which stated

[84] Hernández y Dávalos Collection, 16-6-3444, *ibid.*; *Lista de documentos inéditos para la historia de México*, p. 323.

[85] Paso y Troncoso to Iturbide, January 5, 1824, Hernández y Dávalos Collection, 17-1-3746, in MSS, U.T.

[86] *Ibid.* On the movement in favor of Iturbide, see Pérez Verdia, *Historia particular del estado de Jalisco*, II, 222-226; and Banegas Galván, *Historia de Mexico*, II, 475-484.

[87] Casa Yrujo to Ofalia and enclosure July 7, 1824, in A.G.I., Audiencia de México, 16. Conspiracies in favor of Iturbide are mentioned in Alamán, *Historia*, V, 586. Bustamante takes the view that Iturbide was aware of the conspiracies to restore him to power (*El General D. Felipe de la Garza vindicado de las notas del traidor é ingrato . . .*, p. 32).

[88] *Aguila Mexicana*, February 28, 1824.

[89] *Ibid.*, March 4, 1824.　　　　　[90] *El Sol*, March 13, 1824.

that Guerrero would be frightened by news of the impending return of the former monarch.[91]

Meantime it appeared to Migoni that, because of the firm opposition of the Court of London to intervention in Spanish America by the Holy Allies, Iturbide's intention to return to Mexico had become less apparent.[92] Evidently he was much in need of funds. In fact he solicited Migoni to advance him 12,000 pesos of a loan which he had succeeded in floating for the Mexican government. "He has assured me," wrote Migoni to Alamán, "that in order to subsist he has already sold some gems, that when he passed through Frankfort he left there pearl earrings and a string of pearls belonging to his wife which cost 14,000 pesos, and that for these jewels he was advanced only 3,500 pesos."[93] Taking pity upon the exile, a few days later Migoni offered to advance him money from his private purse.[94] To Gómez de Navarrete, Iturbide wrote on February 14, 1824, that he had received no funds whatever from the sale of his household furniture in Mexico and that inquiries about his haciendas had remained unanswered. He complained that he had not received a single real from his property in Mexico, that in place of 25,000 pesos which the government had promised would be placed on board the *Rawlins* to be transferred to him at Leghorn, it had given him only a little more than 11,000 pesos in letters of credit payable in London and Lisbon. He explained that he had originally planned to sojourn in Italy for several years. Moreover, he had counted upon "the exact fulfillment of what had been arranged by Congress" and promised by the government, besides some aid from this correspondent. Further, he declared that he was ignorant of what had been done with regard to the execution of the decree of the Junta dated February 21, 1822, which had granted him 1,000,000 pesos as well as extensive lands in California.[95]

Iturbide now met persons whom he had known merely by correspondence or by reputation. He became friends with Matthew Fletcher. Captain Basil Hall conversed with him about Mexican politics.[96] On May 6 he wrote to Lord Cochrane, who had played an

[91] Bustamante, *Manifiesto histórico á las naciones y pueblos del Anáhuac*, p. 30.

[92] Copy, Migoni to Alamán, February 9, 1824, in A.G.R.E., 40-11-2.

[93] *Ibid.* A different text of this letter from that found in A.G.R.E. was printed in the *Aguila Mexicana*, May 8, 1824.

[94] Migoni to Iturbide, February 12, 1824, Hernández y Dávalos Collection, 17-1 & 2-3866, in MSS, U.T.

[95] Cuevas, *El Libertador*, pp. 429-430.

[96] Hall, *Extracts from a Journal Written on the Coasts of Chili, Peru, and Mexico in the Years 1820, 1821, 1822*, part II, p. 52.

influential naval role in the liberation of Chile and Peru from Spanish rule, to solicit his aid in the capture of San Juan de Ulúa from the Spaniards, an achievement which he reasoned would not only enhance that mariner's fame but would also ensure the independence of Mexico.[97] The exiled Mexican also met Juan García del Río, a South American who had been sent by the independent government of Peru on a mission to England. As a token of esteem, this patriot sent him a number of Lima gazettes, papers concerning the negotiations of General San Martín with Spanish agents at Punchauca, and a biography of that Liberator, as well as some medals of gold and silver which had been struck off to commemorate the independence of Peru.[98]

Shortly after reaching England, Iturbide made a call upon an expatriated Spaniard known as Blanco White, who had edited *El Español*, a liberal Spanish periodical published in London. The journalist was not at home in Paradise Row when the Mexican made his visit, but he wrote to express his regret and to state that he would be pleased to meet him. Iturbide sent him for scrutiny a document which he wished to publish. Blanco soon wrote the author that he had perused it with much interest and that he would be ready to express his views about its publication in England. This paper could not have been any other than a copy of a memoir accompanied by illustrative documents that Iturbide had earlier sent to Lord Burghersh, a memoir which its author styled a *manifiesto* or a *memoria*.

It was reserved for an English friend, Michael J. Quin of Gray's Inn, who had written a book about his recent visit to Spain, to undertake the publication of the *memoria* in an English edition. Just before leaving London, Iturbide called on him in order to say farewell and to leave two bank notes as a small compensation for the pains which he had taken in translating this manuscript. Soon after the Mexican had sailed from Southampton, the Englishman wrote him to state that he had decided to publish the memoir immediately.[99] The preface to the first English version of it, prepared by Quin and dated June 3, 1824, was evidently in press before news of the author's untimely death reached London.[100] This translation was entitled *A Statement*

[97] Iturbide, *Breve diseño crítico*, pp. 141-142.

[98] García del Río to Iturbide, February 9, 1824, Hernández y Dávalos Collection, 17-1 & 2-3863, in MSS, U.T.

[99] Robertson, "The Memorabilia of Agustín de Iturbide," *Hispanic American Historical Review*, XXVII, 443. Bancroft's references to this *autobiografía* do not raise the question of its provenance (*History of Mexico*, IV, 782 n. 8 and 805 n. 64).

[100] *A Statement of Some of the Principal Events in the Public Life of Agustín de*

of Some of the Principal Events in the Public Life of Agustín de Iturbide Written by Himself.

On March 9, 1824, Iturbide left London for Bath. Padre Marchena wrote to Alamán that the banished Mexican seemingly planned to settle there with his wife and small children, who were expected soon to arrive from Italy. The spy stated that, in order to ascertain the schemes of Iturbide exactly, he was in need of funds with which to pay for espionage.[101] Meanwhile in distant Leghorn the firm of Fletcher and Macbean had disposed of silver plate and gold plate belonging to the Iturbide family, which brought some 5,000 pesos.[102] Matthew Fletcher wrote to Iturbide on March 18 to inform him that his diamonds had been sold at Frankfort.[103] Even more indicative of his intention was the fact that his wife was striving to induce certain European envoys at Florence to endorse a passport which had been granted to her by officials at Leghorn.[104] On March 19 Iturbide directed Fletcher that the furniture in Villa Fournier should be placed on sale.[105] His enemies at home were not idle. An anonymous tract was published in Mexico that contained a spurious letter from Iturbide to King Ferdinand VII in which words were put into the Liberator's mouth to the effect that he accepted the Mexican crown merely in order to hold the throne for a prince of the Spanish dynasty.[106]

Well pleased with Bath as a place of residence, he expressed regret at not having spent more time there instead of in the murky English metropolis.[107] In April the remaining members of his family arrived in London.[108] They were accompanied by José Malo as well as by Fathers López and Treviño. In addition, Charles Beneski, a Polish

---

Iturbide Written by Himself, p. xxiii. Michelena declared that a reply to this would not be generous and that it did not injure any member of his government (*La Diplomacia mexicana*, III, 119).

[101] Marchena to Alamán, March 17, 1824, Comisión reservada conferida al padre Don José María Marchena, f. 34-35, Genaro García Collection, in MSS, U.T. Library.

[102] Fletcher, Macbean & Co. to J. López, March 5, 1824, Hernández y Dávalos Collection, 17-1 & 2-3902, *ibid.*

[103] Hernández y Dávalos Collection, 17-1 & 2-3940.

[104] Copy, Fletcher, Macbean & Co. to M. Fletcher, March 16, 1824, Hernández y Dávalos Collection, 17-1 & 2-3954, *ibid.*

[105] Iturbide to Fletcher, March 19, 1824, Hernández y Dávalos Collection, 17-1 & 2-3954, *ibid.*

[106] *Ni Borbones ni Iturbide sino el congreso de la ley, exposición de D. Agustín Iturbide á Fernando VII*, pp. 1-2.

[107] Iturbide to H. Pomier, March 21, 1824, Hernández y Dávalos Collection, 17-1 & 2-3959, in MSS, U.T.

[108] The *Journal de Paris*, April 15, 1824, mentioned the departure of Señora Iturbide from Calais for Dover.

Colonel who had served Iturbide faithfully in Mexico and who had recently returned to Europe, presumably to convey messages to him from his adherents, had joined the party.[109] On May 6 Marchena wrote a letter to Alamán which contained this omnibus passage: "On the frivolous pretext of the arrival of his family, the traitor Iturbide, who will never be anything else than what he has always been, secured a passport for France, and in fact was actually in Paris, from which court he was demanded a short time ago in order that he might be delivered to Ferdinand VII of Spain."[110] During Iturbide's residence at Bath, said Quin, he received most urgent invitations to return to Mexico.[111]

Not aware as yet that he had been proscribed by King Ferdinand VII,[112] the former Emperor had made up his mind to depart from England soon. Early in May he addressed a letter to Quin in which he undertook to explain his state of mind. He said that the chief provinces of Mexico were in such a disturbed condition that her independence was imperiled. "Should she lose it," he maintained, "she must live for ages to come in frightful slavery.

"My return has been solicited by different parts of the country, which considers me necessary to the establishment of unanimity there and to the consolidation of the Government. I do not presume to form such an opinion of myself; but as I am assured that it is in my power to contribute in a great degree to the amalgamation of the separate interests of the provinces, and to tranquillize in part those angry passions which are sure to lead to the most disastrous anarchy, I go with such an object before me, uninfluenced by any other ambition than the glory of effecting the happiness of my countrymen, and of discharging those obligations which I owe to the land of my birth— obligations which have received additional force from the event of her independence. When I abdicated the Crown of Mexico, I did so with pleasure, and my sentiments remain unchanged. . . .

"I conclude by again recommending to your attention my children, in my separation from whom will be seen an additional proof of the real sentiments which animate the heart of your very sincere friend."[113]

---

[109] Copy, Migoni to Alamán, May 5, 1824, in A.G.R.E., 40-11-2; Malo, *Apuntes historicos*, p. 35.

[110] Castillo Negrete, *Mexico en el siglo xix*, XIV, 267-268.

[111] Iturbide, *A Statement of Some of the Principal Events in the Public Life*, p. xiii.

[112] A royal decree of May 1, 1824, announced a general pardon but excluded from it Iturbide as well as O'Donojú "of odious memory" (*Suplemento á la Gaceta de Madrid*, May 20, 1824).

[113] Iturbide, *op. cit.*, p. xv. *Niles' Weekly Register*, July 3, 1824, gives the date

At leisure moments the refugee had composed a farewell letter to be delivered to his eldest son, who was in school at Ampleforth. That epistle, which was dated April 27, began thus: "My son Agustín: We are about to separate. . . . Perhaps we shall not see each other again." He advised the youth that virtue and knowledge were possessions of inestimable value, that he should respect his teachers and those people with whom he might associate, and that he should make friends of persons who were both educated and virtuous. Repeating certain sentiments so that the youth should never forget them, he said that "the holy fear of God, a good education, and courteous manners," were the qualities which would ensure him happiness and good fortune. "To secure these benefits," continued Iturbide, "good books and good companions, much application, and the greatest care are necessary." Concluding in the same high moral tone, the father, who seemed to have a premonition of his fate, expressed hope that his eldest son would be adorned with the qualities needed to make him a good patriot so that he might fulfil in a worthy fashion the duties for which Divine Providence had destined him.[114]

On May 10 at the Royal Coffee House on Regent Street, Iturbide wrote a letter to a general who had arrived in London on April 25 en route from La Plata to the European Continent.[115] The Mexican expressed regret that he had not met that person when he called at his hotel. He asked the South American to visit him at the coffeehouse without letting anyone know that he had received such an invitation. "I believe that our good friend, Don García del Río," continued Iturbide, "will have said something to you about our interview. Because of this, and because I hope soon to have the pleasure of meeting you, for the present I shall only assure you that I am a true admirer of your merits and virtues."[116]

On the same day José María Marchena wrote to Secretary Alamán that the former Emperor had left London for a seaport on the preceding Saturday. Marchena added that, as Iturbide suddenly learned that "a certain general" who had been a champion of South American independence had arrived in London, he had decided to delay his

of this letter as May 5. That date was mentioned by Malo (*Apuntes historicos*, p. 34) as the day on which Iturbide departed from London for Southampton. On which see Castillo Negrete, *op. cit.*, XVI, 435.

[114] *Carta y despedida del Señor Iturbide á su hijo el mayor*, pp. 1-3.

[115] The passport issued to José de San Martín in London on September 8, 1824, was given a visa in Ostend on September 12; and on September 23 in Amsterdam, in A.S.M., caja 70, carpeta ostracismo, 1824-1849.

[116] San Martín, *San Martín, su correspondencia*, p. 332.

departure in order to meet him. After an interview with that person during which Iturbide stated that he was about to return to Mexico, the general evidently remonstrated with him regarding his decision. "He tried," so continued the spy, "to make Iturbide realize the disturbances, the civil war, and the other incalculable evils which would result from his return to Mexico. Iturbide responded, however, that the people had repeatedly urged him to return and that he would know how to check disorder and civil war. To this the gentleman replied that the people had made known their opinion when they banished him from the Empire. Iturbide retorted that his exile was a work of violence and the wish of only four persons. . . ."[117]

If we may trust Marchena's report—which was printed by a Mexican historian and corroborated by a Mexican scholar—this general, who was no less a personage than General José de San Martín, the Argentine Liberator and one-time Protector of Peru[118] who had renounced office in the hope of preventing discord, urged the Liberator of Mexico to follow his example and, for the sake of his beloved country, to remain in exile. But San Martín's efforts were in vain. Migoni soon wrote to Alamán that Iturbide had sailed from England. He expressed the opinion that the secrecy with which the former Emperor had arranged his departure indicated that his destination was the coast of Mexico. "It has not been possible for me to prevent this," added the agent, "for your Excellency well knows that in this country each person lives as he wishes. . . . Not even the government of England could have prevented that flight."[119]

Soon afterward Migoni warned Alamán that the returning exile had taken with him guns, munitions, and a printing press.[120] Unknown to Migoni, on the eve of his departure, Iturbide had addressed a letter to Canning describing his intentions:

"My object is to promote the consolidation of a government which will make Mexico as happy as she deserves to be, so that she may occupy the position to which she is entitled among other nations.

[117] Castillo Negrete, *op. cit.*, XIV, 272. A copy of this dispatch is found in Comisión reservada conferida al padre Don José María Marchena, f. 40-41, Genaro García Collection, in MSS, U.T. Library.

[118] Malo, *Apuntes historicos*, p. 34; a dispatch concerning Iturbide's departure from England was sent by F. Tacón and J. de Hereida to Count Ofalia, May 14, 1824 (A.H.N., Estado, 5475). Casa Yrujo to Ofalia, May 26, 1824, wrote of Iturbide, "Antes de su partida de Londres, donde tuvo una conferencia con San Martín, que acabó de llegar á la misma capital . . ." (*ibid.*).

[119] Copy, May 17, 1824, in A.G.R.E., 40-11-2. Quin said that Iturbide sailed from Cowes on May 11 (Iturbide, *A Statement*, p. xiv).

[120] Castillo Negrete, *Mexico en el siglo xix*, XIV, 273.

Having been repeatedly invited to return to Mexico by various parties, I am no longer able to turn a deaf ear to such entreaties. I do not return in order to seek an Empire which I do not desire; nor do I proceed like a soldier to foment discord or war, but to mediate between opposing parties and to secure peace. One of my first aims will be to determine the bases for firm relations of reciprocal interest with Great Britain."[121]

Quin wrote to Canning on May 15 to declare that he had been entrusted with "a private and confidential letter" to him and to ask for an interview.[122] In response the Minister suggested that, if his correspondent wished to add anything to his communication, it had better "be done in writing." Hence Quin soon forwarded Iturbide's letter to the Foreign Office accompanied by a note which declared that he had been commissioned to add verbally that, if Iturbide secured a dominant influence in Mexico, it was his intention to promote the establishment of a constitution there similar to the English Constitution, and that it was his desire to cultivate "the closest political and commercial relations with Great Britain." Further, Iturbide hoped that, as soon as he could make it appear that the government was consolidated and the country redeemed from discord, Canning would "not be slow to recognize the independence" of Mexico.[123]

Canning replied that he would have been happy to make the personal acquaintance of Iturbide during his sojourn in England, if it had been possible to do so "as a private individual, or without leading to inferences" which it was his duty to avoid, "inferences not only relating to important public questions, but likely to affect the pecuniary welfare of large classes of British subjects."[124] The minister was undoubtedly aware of the keen interest of some English investors in Mexico's political fortunes. Further, he was cognizant of the international significance which might be attributed to an interview with the former Emperor, especially as he had himself made known to certain European diplomats that he favored the founding of monarchies in Latin America.

Indeed Canning deemed it necessary to instruct Sir William À Court, the English minister to Spain, that his government had held no communication with Iturbide after his arrival in London.[125] Upon being

---

[121] Spanish text in Iturbide, *Breve diseño*, pp. 140-141, where the date is given as May 6; a translation is in F.O., 50/7, where the date is mentioned as May 12.

[122] Copy, in A.G.R.E., 40-11-2.

[123] Copy, May 17, 1824, *ibid.*

[124] Copy, May 17, 1824, *ibid.*

[125] Copy, May 17, 1824, in A.G.I., Estado, América en General, 5.

assured by a British agent that his government had not connived at the exile's journey to England, the Mexican government was pleased.[126] When the sudden departure of Iturbide from England, which caused a sensation in Parisian journals, became known to the French ambassador in London, he wrote to Chateaubriand to suggest that it might be wise to dispatch a French corvette with news of this event to Cuba and to the castle of San Juan de Ulúa.[127] On the same day Polignac sent a note to Canning in the hope of securing explanations about the trip because he feared that it would complicate the international problem of the status of the Spanish colonies.[128] The English Minister replied that during recent months he had had no communication with the exile, that he knew nothing about his movements except that he had left London for Mexico and that there was "no law in England which would authorize the government to interfere with General Iturbide's return to his native country.

"With what view he may be gone there, Your Excellency is just as well able to judge as I am. If I were to believe anonymous information (of which I receive abundance), I should suppose him to be gone, in concert with the Government of France, to intrigue for the restoration in Mexico of the ancient authority of the mother country. But I make no doubt, Your Excellency will be able to affirm, as confidently as I make the like affirmation on the part of my Government, that General Iturbide's proceedings are entirely without the participation or privity either of yourself or of your Government."[129]

Soon afterward, in a conversation with Sir Charles Stuart, the English ambassador at Paris, Chateaubriand took occasion to contradict statements in English newspapers that Iturbide was "proceeding to Mexico under the auspices of the French Government." Further, he declared that his government was ignorant of the motives which had impelled the revolutionist to return to his native land.[130]

It appears that the former Emperor of Mexico was transported to Italy by his government without a precise agreement about the place which was to be his future residence. After landing at Leghorn, he evidently meditated about establishing his residence at some other place in Italy, but was prevented from visiting Rome because of a prohibition laid by the government of the Papal States at the instance

[126] Webster, *Britain and the Independence of Latin America*, I, 452.
[127] Polignac to Chateaubriand, May 18, 1824, in A.A.E., Angleterre, 618.
[128] Copy, Polignac to Canning, May 18, 1824, *ibid.*
[129] Copy, Canning to Polignac, May 18, 1824, *ibid.*
[130] Stuart to Canning, May 22, 1824, in F.O., 27/309.

of the Spanish court. The regrettable delay by the Mexican government in the payment of his pension was possibly in part due to the difficulty encountered in making the proper financial arrangements because of the disturbed condition of international exchange and the embarrassed state of Mexico's finances. After Iturbide forsook Leghorn, the Mexican government felt justified in withholding his pension because he had violated the stipulation that he was not to leave Italy.

There is no reason to doubt that his hurried flight to England was partly due to fear of intrigues against his person by diplomats of the allied monarchs. Moreover, he was seriously contemplating a return to his native land for the purpose of defending it against what he considered the menace of the Holy Alliance. Historical research has shown that, like James Monroe and George Canning, the former Emperor overemphasized the danger of intervention by the Holy Alliance in Spanish America. Nevertheless, the belief that such action was impending was a potent incentive which stimulated Iturbide as well as Monroe.[131]

[131] In an anonymous pamphlet, which was published in Mexico in 1923, entitled *Proyecto de la república federal de México*, p. 1, the Holy Alliance was mentioned thus: "Los tiranos de la llamada Santa Alianza han jurado el exterminio de los gobiernos liberales, y no hay remedio ó los pueblos son esclavos para siempre ó es necesario que los reyes quedan eternamente sepultados bajo las ruinas de sus sacrilegios tronos."

CHAPTER XIV

The Return of the Exile

ON MAY 11, 1824, Iturbide sailed from Southampton on the
English vessel *Spring*.[1] Besides his wife and two small children,
Felipe and Salvador, José Malo accompanied him. There also belonged
to the party José Lopez and José Treviño; an Italian named Macario
Morandini; John Armstrong, an English printer, and Colonel Beneski.[2]
Iturbide's six eldest children were left behind in educational institutions.[3] Not only did the returning exile embark a printing press and
many papers concerning his career, but also thousands of pesos of
Mexican currency which had been struck off on red, white, and green
paper. He brought on board the remainder of the family jewels, some
books which were chiefly concerned with England, Latin America, and
military affairs, as well as many Mexican medals of copper, silver, and
gold. He also took with him a pendant bearing an image of the
Virgin of Guadalupe. Although a Mexican official who examined his
luggage apparently believed that Iturbide's imperial vestments were
not brought with him,[4] yet an anonymous chronicler asserted that they
were eventually found in his belongings, thus proving beyond doubt
that "he intended to regain his ill-fated throne which would have
caused many tears and much bloodshed."[5]

So stealthily had the preparations for the expedition been made
that six days elapsed before its departure was noticed in London newspapers. According to Quin, on May 14 mention was made on the
London stock exchange that Iturbide had sailed for Mexico and Peru,
"laden with money, jewels, and decorations" which he had received

[1] In an exposition drawn up at Padilla on July 19, 1824, Iturbide said: "mi salida
de Londres se verificó al 4 de mayo, y de la isla de Wight el 11, y no he tocado en
puerto alguno hasta mi legada á la barra de Soto la Marina . . ." (*Breve diseño
crítico de la emancipacion y libertad de la nacion mexicana*, p. 169).
[2] Garza, Nota de la familia que acompañaba al finado Sr. Iturbide, July 21, 1824,
in A.M.C., D/481.3/304.
[3] Iturbide, *A Statement of Some of the Principal Events in the Public Life of
Agustin de Iturbide*, p. xiv n.
[4] Garza to M. Mier y Terán, August 13, 1824, in A.M.C., D/481.3/304.
[5] *Noticias circunstanciadas de la muerto de Iturbide para los que no la creen*, p. 2.

from the Spanish ambassador "for the purpose of distributing them among the leading persons in those countries" and of exercising his influence in order "to persuade both Peru and Mexico to submit again to the rule of Spain." A more absurd report was soon circulated in the English metropolis to the effect that the author of the Plan of Iguala had reached a full understanding with the ministers of France and Spain and had even been appointed the Viceroy of Mexico.[6]

The *Courier* published on May 17 a more accurate story of the exile's departure for his native land, a story which, however, erroneously stated that the *Spring* had on board arms and other military stores. "We understand," added that newspaper, "he is assured of being joined by a numerous party in Mexico, when he arrives, who will assist him in recovering his abdicated throne." In consequence of such reports, Quin soon sent to the *Times*, the *Herald*, and the *Morning Chronicle* an English translation of a letter dated May 9 in which Iturbide stated that his only ambition was the glory of promoting the happiness of his countrymen and of fulfilling his obligations to his native land.[7]

Officials of the Spanish legation in London addressed a letter to Secretary of State Ofalia about Iturbide's sudden departure. They expressed the opinion that his secret plan was to disembark on the coast of Mexico in order to restore his authority by the aid of numerous partisans who had persuaded him to return. They thought that the expedition would probably touch at a port in the United States where its leader could secure the aid of adventurers and from which he could penetrate the Interior Provinces.[8] Shortly afterward, Canning directed Minister À Court to assure Ofalia that his government had not communicated with Iturbide since his arrival in England. The Secretary for Foreign Affairs insisted that the Court of St. James had taken no part in the exile's return to his native land.[9]

Spanish-American diplomats in London soon undertook to thwart the voyager's purpose. José Revenga, who had been sent on a mission to Europe by the government of Colombia, sent a letter to an American correspondent stating that Iturbide had left England with the intention of regaining his power in Mexico. Revenga believed that Iturbide would probably touch in the West Indies or at New Orleans

[6] M. J. Quin to Iturbide, May 22, 1824, in A.G.R.E., 40-11-2.

[7] *Ibid*. Comment on Iturbide's departure was printed in the *Times* August 5, 1824.

[8] J. de Hereida and F. Jacón to Count Ofalia, May 15, 1824, in A.H.N., Estado, 5475.

[9] Webster, *Britain and the Independence of Latin America*, II, 427.

in order to promote his design.[10] José Mariano de Michelena, whom the Mexican government had appointed as the head of a trio of confidential agents charged to promote friendly relations with England, addressed a letter to José Salazar, the Colombian minister in the United States, declaring that Iturbide would probably land at a North American port in order to perfect his plans. In the name of Spanish-American independence, Michelena urged Salazar to use all his influence to frustrate the ambitious projects of that inveterate enemy of Mexico.[11]

The financing of Iturbide's return voyage is a subject for conjecture. Despite his frequent complaints of the lack of resources, it is possible that he had on hand monies resulting from the sale of family silverware and jewels. Possibly some funds had been made available to him by Mexican correspondents. More than one contemporary hinted that he might have secured aid from financiers in London and Paris.[12] If indeed the former Emperor had deposits in foreign banks, presumably he drew upon them. Reports of his partisans about revolutionary discontent in Mexico had evidently convinced him that upon landing there he would get substantial support.

The motives which impelled Iturbide to return to his native land have been variously explained. José Malo stated that, before leaving England, the former Emperor had induced his eldest son to renounce whatever right he possessed to the Mexican throne by virtue of the act of Congress which in May, 1822, had established the new dynasty. "For Iturbide's intention in returning to his native land was not to reclaim the throne," Malo asserted later, "but to fight as a general and to maintain the independence which three years earlier he had achieved with so much glory."[13] Malo's contemporary explanation was that the purpose of his uncle was to escape the machinations directed against him by the Holy Allies. José López stated that Iturbide was not safe in Italy because representations were being made against him to the Tuscan government by diplomats of continental monarchies. Macario Morandini declared that the departure of the expatriate from Leghorn was due to his persecution by the allied monarchs of Europe. In response to inquiries made on August 17,

[10] Revenga to "Governor" Hyslop, May 17, 1824, in A.M.C., D/481.3/304.

[11] Michelena to Salazar, July 3, 1824, in A.G.R.E., 14-3-65.

[12] Beruete, Diario, f. 159-159v., in MSS, T.U.; Castillo Negrete, Mexico en el siglo xix, XV, 424.

[13] Malo, Apuntes historicos sobre el destierro, vuelta al territorio mexicano y muerte del libertador D. Agustin de Iturbide, p. 34.

1824, Father Treviño, who had served as the exile's confessor, expressed his views concerning Iturbide's motives as follows:

"That during the months which elapsed between his embarkation at Antigua and the time when Ferdinand VII was restored to absolute power, Iturbide did not contemplate anything else than to settle in one of the sections of Italy which suited him best. After that restoration, however, when he began to learn of measures which the cabinets of France and Spain were taking for the reconquest of Spanish America, he came to believe that because of his love of country and the welfare of his family, this conquest should not be allowed to take place, not even by virtue of apathy, and that, sacrificing his interests and his life, he ought to oppose the designs of these powers and of the entire Holy Alliance. Thus he believed that it was his duty to return to Mexico."[14]

Letters addressed to Iturbide by English friends with whom he had conversed convey other impressions. In a letter which Matthew Fletcher wrote to him in Spanish on May 21, after stating that the news of his departure had probably leaked out through Peruvian sympathizers in England, that merchant declared: "The public show a friendly disposition toward you. Persons interested in the public funds are satisfied that the existing obligations of the Mexican government will be respected under whatever aspect or change of circumstances. . . ."[15] Another English sympathizer addressed a letter to Iturbide which contained the following passages: "From your valor and influence the English people hope that the independence of Mexico (which has been confided by Providence to your hands) shall not be suffered to perish before the bayonets or the intrigues of the Holy Alliance. . . .

"Your great object is to put down without delay any obstacle from whatever quarter it comes which might impede the consolidation of the government. For I have every occasion to hope that as soon as you can make it evident to Mr. Canning that Mexico has organized and settled a government that is likely to endure, her independence will be acknowledged without delay by the Cabinet of Great Britain."[16]

From these letters it would appear that English confidants of the exile had gained the impression that there was not absent from his thoughts the notion of regaining supreme power. Mexicans who opposed the re-establishment of monarchical rule were certainly appre-

[14] Garza to S. Ruíz, August 3, 1824, in A.M.C., D/481.3/304.
[15] In A.G.R.E., 40-11-2.
[16] M. J. Quin to Iturbide, May 22, 1824, *ibid.*

hensive that such was his design. An anonymous pamphlet was published in Mexico City entitled *Plans of Señor Iturbide for the New Re-conquest of Mexico*. This tract quoted from a curious letter which was said to have been received from a Mexican residing in London. That person alleged that the Liberator had formed a fantastic plan of proceeding to St. Petersburg to secure the support of the Tsar, who was to be solicited to furnish military or financial aid for an invasion of the former Viceroyalty.[17] After the tragic denouement of Iturbide's expedition, Lucas Alamán who, after a brief interlude, was again serving as the Secretary for Foreign Affairs, expressed his opinion that the expatriated Mexican had cherished the design of regaining the imperial throne. Further, this Minister held that the arrival of Beneski in Europe with news of extensive ramifications of a conspiracy to restore imperial rule had precipitated the advent of Iturbide.[18]

While Iturbide was sojourning in England, another kaleidoscopic change had taken place in Mexican politics. A Constituent Congress had adopted an Act of Federation which designated the existing districts as states and territories. Executive authority was formally vested in a triumvirate designated the Supreme Executive Power.

Few reliable details are at hand concerning the route taken by Iturbide's party on the return trip. Many years later, in reply to a request from Lucas Alamán, who was then engaged in writing a history of Mexico, Iturbide's nephew wrote a brief narrative of the journey. In that sketch José Malo asserted that the *Spring* sailed to America by way of Guadeloupe, Jamaica, and New Orleans.[19] If he meant that the vessel stopped at those places, his assertion is not supported by the account of Iturbide. For he stated that the *Spring* did not touch at any port during the journey to the Gulf of Mexico.[20]

During the long voyage Iturbide prepared documents intended for distribution after he had landed in Mexico. Among them were representations intended for officials of Mexican provinces urging them to make known the critical political situation to the inhabitants of their respective districts, to explain the object of his return, and to prevent anarchy. Twenty-four expositions were prepared for military com-

---

[17] *Planos del Sr. Iturbide para la nueva reconquista de América*, pp. 1-2.

[18] "Reservada," addressed to M. Mier y Terán, August 21, 1824, Hernández y Dávalos Collection, 17-4-4053, in MSS, U.T. Alamán resigned his position on February 7, 1824, but was reappointed on May 15, 1824.

[19] August 17, 1852, Alamán MSS, Archivo relativo a su historia de México, 1808-1849, Genaro García Collection, in MSS, U.T.

[20] *Supra*, p. 287 n. 1.

manders which mentioned the imminent peril of subjugation threatening Mexico, declared that it was the duty of those persons who were armed to defend their native land, and explained that the former Emperor did not seek vengeance but would consider as his foes only such persons as were the enemies of his country. Notices were drafted for state legislatures declaring that, "if the national Congress would not accept his services, they could be promptly accepted by whatever Mexican state might consider them useful and might wish to oppose the views of the Holy Alliance." Explanatory circulars were addressed to various bishops. Several letters were composed which solicited cooperation from the author's friends. Four proclamations to the Mexican people were printed.[21]

In an undated exposition intended for the Central American provinces Iturbide declared that he was returning to America to maintain the liberty and independence of Mexico, to oppose the spirit of partisanship, to put an end to anarchy, and to restore peace. He argued that Central America was his country as well as Mexico, that the same enemies threatened both countries, and that his attitude toward them was identical.[22] In a broadside to the Mexicans dated June 8, 1824, which bore his coat of arms, the former Emperor described his motives in more detail. He stated that his sojourn in Europe had convinced him that his countrymen were threatened with immediate ruin. He explained that this menace had impelled him to return to his native land in spite of the snares laid for him by the Holy Allies:

"I come not as the Emperor but only as a soldier and a Mexican. . . . I come as the person most interested in the preservation of your independence and liberty. I come impelled by the regard which I owe to the nation in general, without any recollection of the atrocious calumnies with which my enemies or the enemies of my country wished to blacken my name. My sole object is to contribute with my voice and my sword to the support of Mexican liberty and independence."[23]

Shortly before reaching his destination, Iturbide directed Armstrong to strike off from the printing press an exposition addressed to Congress which included his representation dated February 13, 1824.[24] Reading carefully between the lines of such justificatory papers, one can occasionally catch glimpses of Iturbide's design. This was not

[21] Iturbide, La Correspondencia de . . . después de la proclamación del Plan de Iguala, II, 241-242.

[22] Iturbide, Breve diseño crítico, pp. 147-150.

[23] Iturbide, II, which is a bound volume of pamphlets belonging to the Genaro García Collection of books in the University of Texas Library.

[24] Exposiciones dirigidas al soberano congreso general de la nación.

only to subvert the republican government of his native land but also to secure supreme power for himself. As the only political system which he considered suitable for the stage of development that his countrymen had attained was monarchical, one is forced to the conclusion that he had visions of restoring the Mexican Empire.

The movements of the former Emperor were meanwhile being carefully watched in Mexico. News concerning his departure from Leghorn precipitated a discussion in Congress, which decided on March 15 that the remainder of his pension should not be paid until a satisfactory explanation of his flight from Italy was received.[25] On April 3 a committee headed by Deputy Marin laid before Congress a report which contained the following proposals. That whenever Iturbide might present himself in any Mexican port, he was to be considered a traitor. Any persons who might aid his return to Mexico were also to be considered traitors.

In the resulting discussion Carlos María de Bustamante maintained that Iturbide did not flee from Italy because of his fear of Ferdinand VII. Padre Mier urged that the first proposal should be modified so as to indicate that the exile ought to be considered as a traitor under whatever title he might present himself in Mexico. Two other deputies urged that under such circumstances he should be declared beyond the pale of the law. A proposal that instead of the phrase *fuera del ley* the word *proscripto* should be substituted was not approved. Barbosa expressed the opinion that the phrase outside the pale of the law signified that there would be no need to use legal formulas in order to apply the punishment. With respect to Article II another deputy expressed the opinion that it was simply a reaffirmation of the decree of April 16, 1823, which declared that those persons who favored Iturbide as Emperor were to be considered traitors.[26]

On April 28, 1824, Congress adopted a three-fold decree:

1. That, should Iturbide under any pretext whatever present himself in any Mexican port, he was to be considered outside the pale of the law, an enemy of the State, and a traitor to his country.

2. That those persons who might co-operate in his return to Mexico by laudatory writings or in any other manner were to be considered traitors to the Mexican Federation.

[25] Bustamante, *Continuacion del cuadro historico*, p. 246.

[26] *Diario de las sesiones del congreso constituyente de la Federación Mexicana*, pp. 39-47. The decree of April 16, 1823, is in *Coleccion de ordenes y decretos de la soberana junta provisional gubernativa y soberanos congresos generales de la nacion mexicana*, II, 95.

3. That the same treatment was to be prescribed for any person who might in any manner promote the designs of a foreign invader upon Mexico. All Mexican officials and tribunals, whether civil, ecclesiastical, or military, were ordered to carry out this decree.

"It is not a crime of the entire Mexican nation that Iturbide the Liberator was condemned to death, but it is a crime of all those persons who signed that decree and of those who carried it out."[27] Such is the comment of the former Emperor's most recent Mexican biographer. Had a motion prevailed in Congress that Iturbide was to be notified of the proscriptive edict, and if he had been given an opportunity to alter his course, the outcome might have been less tragic. But this is one of the might-have-beens that are found in the pages of history.

On May 7, after Iturbide's exposition dated February 13 had been read to Congress, it voted that the appeal should be published along with its punitive decree of April 28.[28] Motions which proposed that the exile should be informed that congressmen had heard this plea "with displeasure" or "with indignation" failed to pass. One deputy hinted that the government should notify Iturbide of the ominous decree through its commissioners in London.[29] News of the proscription did not reach England, however, before the *Spring* unfurled her sails.[30] Before the vessel reached Mexican shores, another deputy had suggested in Congress that Iturbide might entertain designs upon Central America as well as upon Mexico.[31]

According to Malo's printed account of the return voyage, on July 1 the passengers on the *Spring* caught sight of the shores of Nuevo Santander which had recently been designated the state of Tamaulipas.[32] Accompanied by some sailors, Beneski landed in order to search for Colonel José Trespalacios, whom Iturbide expected to meet near this coast. As the Pole did not find the colonel, he soon returned

---

[27] The fatal decree of proscription is printed in Dublán y Lozana, *Legislacion Mexicana*, I, 705, under date of April 23, 1824; on the exact date, see Alamán, *Historia*, V, 801; the comment quoted is from Cuevas, *El Libertador*, p. 106, where the author erroneously gives March 16, 1824, as the date when the decree was enacted.

[28] *Gaceta del gobierno supremo de la Federación Mexicana*, May 8, 1824, pp. 241-242.

[29] *Diario de las sesiones del congreso constituyente de la Federación Mexicana*, pp. 423-428.

[30] Beneski, *A Narrative of the Last Moments of the Life of Don Agustin de Iturbide*, p. 4; Castillo Negrete (*Mexico en el siglo xix*, XVI, 37-38), basing his view upon misgivings expressed in a letter, maintained that Iturbide was aware of his proscription before he landed on the Mexican coast.

[31] *Diario de las sesiones del congreso constituyente de la Federación Mexicana*, p. 595.

[32] Malo, *Apuntes historicos*, pp. 35-36. Alamán states that the Bay of San Bernardo was reached on June 29 (*Historia de Mexico*, V, 601).

to the ship which then set sail for Tampico. Contrary winds, however, forced the captain to cast anchor near the town of Soto la Marina. It so happened that not far from the town there was stationed General Felipe de la Garza, who after the downfall of Agustín I had displaced Gaspar López as the commander of the Eastern Interior Provinces.

At that anchorage Beneski was again sent ashore. This time he bore a letter from Treviño, who seems to have been a relative of Garza, to that General commending to his good offices the Polish colonel as well as a companion who was said to be interested in Mexican colonization. Apparently suspecting that the companion might be the proscribed exile, Garza intimated to Beneski that he was one of the former Emperor's adherents. Eventually the Pole indiscreetly admitted that this personage was actually on board the *Spring*. Though Beneski alleged that Garza then wrote a note to Iturbide criticizing the government and suggesting that the expatriate should return to Mexico, this seems unlikely.[33] That Iturbide was not certain of a favorable reception by his countrymen after thirteen months of absence is indicated by his letter to Matthew Fletcher containing advice about his children in case misfortune should befall him.[34]

Whatever may have been Garza's real intentions, on the forenoon of July 17 Beneski and Iturbide disembarked near the town of Soto la Marina. There they secured horses. A tale is told that when a certain Mexican who had served in the Army of the Three Guarantees caught sight of Beneski's comrade mounting a horse with remarkable agility, he exclaimed, "That person who has just mounted is either Iturbide or the devil in his figure."[35]

It is not easy to imagine what feelings stirred Garza's breast when he met the disguised voyager whom he speedily recognized as his former sovereign. The general promptly informed Iturbide that he had been proscribed.[36] Garza soon undertook to escort him to the legislature of Tamaulipas, which was in session at Padilla in order that it might reach a decision concerning the action to be taken with respect to the national decree of proscription. A Mexican scholar has taken the view that instead of detaining Iturbide, his captor should have allowed him to re-embark on the *Spring* with the understanding that he was to depart from the Mexican coast.[37] It is by no means

[33] Beneski, *op. cit.*, p. 7.
[34] Iturbide, *Breve diseño crítico*, pp. 174-175.
[35] Malo, *op. cit.*, p. 40.
[36] *Ibid.*, pp. 40-41; *Gaceta extraordinaria del gobierno supremo de la Federación Mexicana*, July 26, 1824, pp. 52-53.
[37] Iguíniz, "Iturbide en el destierro y en el cadalso," *El Universal*, September, 1921.

certain, however, that the former Emperor would have welcomed that solution which might have saved his life. At the very time when Garza was meditating about the dilemma in which he found himself, Iturbide's consort, accompanied by servants, two priests, her two youngest sons, and the luggage of the party, was landed at Soto la Marina.[38]

When Garza submitted the fate of the former Emperor to the judgment of the Tamaulipas Congress, that body, which had already committed itself concerning the treatment to be accorded him, refused to consider certain documents that he wished to submit in justification of his conduct. By an almost unanimous vote it decided on July 18 that the national law of April 28, which condemned him to death as a traitor, should be observed and that in consequence he should at once be punished as stipulated in that edict. On the next day the President of the legislature ordered Garza to execute the sentence at once.[39]

The condemned man penned a protest against that decision. He justified his actions, both as the Liberator and as the Emperor of Mexico. He explained that he had returned to his country in order to defend it against an attack by the Holy Alliance. He asserted that, after a scrupulous examination of his conduct, he had not discovered the crimes for which presumably the national Congress had condemned him to death. Was it a crime, he asked, to risk the threats of the Holy Allies and to return to his native land? He avowed, however, that, if his blood was destined to fertilize the tree of liberty, he would willingly offer it as a sacrifice.[40]

A cleric named José Bernardo Gutiérrez de Lara, who was serving as the president of the Tamaulipas legislature, administered the last sacraments to the unfortunate prisoner. "Three times," said that priest, "did the condemned man confess his sins." Upon leaving his prison for the place of execution on July 19, he entrusted to Gutiérrez de Lara certain documents which elucidated his political views. According to tradition, he asked his confessor to forward a letter to his wife, to send the rosary from his neck to his eldest son, and to distribute some small gold coins among the soldiers who were to serve as his executioners.[41] He walked steadfastly to the place of execution, de-

---

[38] Iturbide, La Correspondencia de . . . después de la proclamación del Plan de Iguala, II, 220.

[39] Castillo Negrete, Mexico en el siglo xix, XIV, 287-288; Cuevas, El Libertador, p. 453.

[40] Breve diseño crítico, pp. 163-167.

[41] The quotation is from "Papeles de Iturbide entregados antes de ser fusilado," Boletin del archivo general de la nacion, vol. II, no. 2, p. 168; see also Alamán, Historia, V, 604.

clared that it was not necessary to bind his arms or to bandage his eyes, but quietly allowed this to be done. Facing the firing squad, he bade farewell to his countrymen. He exhorted them to love peace and to preserve their holy religion. "Mexicans," he exclaimed, "I die with honor, and not as a traitor! . . . That ignominy I shall not leave to my children nor to their posterity. No—I am not a traitor—No!"[42] In the words of his confessor, "then he sank to his knees, facing the soldiers; and, without anyone advising him, in a distinct voice he pardoned his enemies; he met his death . . . his blood flowed. . . ."[43]

In a letter addressed to *"Anna Santa,—muger de mi alma,"* Iturbide had besought his wife to convey a last farewell to his children. He asked her to flee with them to a foreign land where they could safely be educated in the faith of their forefathers. On July 20, 1824, in the forty-first year of his age, shrouded in the habit of a humble priest, the body of the Liberator of Mexico was interred in the cemetery of the parish church at Padilla.[44]

The chief actor in the drama which culminated in the execution had some pangs of conscience. In a letter addressed to Manuel de Mier y Terán, who was the Secretary of War and the Navy, declining to accept an advancement in grade which had been offered him, Garza expressed remorse at his part in the doleful tragedy. He avowed that there was gratitude and sympathy in his heart for the man who on a critical occasion had treated him with magnanimity. "In his favor," wrote Garza, "your Excellency will find powerful reasons in his writings as well as in his actions and words prior to his execution."[45] The Mexican government apparently wished to avoid an exposé of the conspiracy to restore Iturbide to power; for, according to Bustamante, it ordered that all the papers which he had brought with him should be burned.[46] Whatever may be the truth in that allegation, fortunately some of them escaped the flames as well as the ravages of years.

When Secretary Alamán wrote to José Mariano de Michelena and described the circumstances attendant upon the tragedy in order that the envoy might inform the English government, he justified the

[42] Iturbide, *Breve diseño crítico*, pp. 171, 188-189. Another account of the execution is found in Beneski, *A Narrative of the Last Moments*, pp. 17-18.

[43] Letter of Gutiérrez de Lara to J. M. Saavedra, July 30, 1824, in *La Voz de México*, September 27, 1878.

[44] Cuevas, *El Libertador*, pp. 110, 455; Pacheco, *Descripcion de la solemnidad fúnebre con que se honraron . . . Agustin de Iturbide*, p. 63.

[45] Iturbide, *op. cit.*, p. 192. Two years later Carlos Bustamante undertook to defend Garza; see *El General D. Felipe de la Garza vindicado de las notas de traidor é ingrato con que se le ofende en un papel . . .* , pp. ii-iv.

[46] Bustamante, *Continuacion del cuadro historico*, p. 261.

execution upon the ground that there could be no doubt that Iturbide intended to start a revolution and thus bring upon the Mexicans desolation and bloodshed. He believed that the fear of such a result was "a powerful motive which impelled the sovereign Congress to enact the particular law in the religious observance of which there were involved the decorum and the welfare of the nation."[47]

Four months later Michelena was informed that his government was pleased at the policy which had been followed by England toward Iturbide.[48] In a letter to Garza, after stating that the one-time Emperor now belonged to history, the ruling Triumvirate declared that not a single circumstance concerned with his tragic end should be ignored.[49] The legislature of the state of Vera Cruz decided that the names of the Tamaulipas legislators who had voted in favor of Iturbide's execution should be inscribed on the walls of its hall in letters of gold.[50] On July 29 *El Sol* published an editorial which declared in a conciliatory spirit that although it had received various communications concerning Iturbide's death, it would not publish them: "Humanity and policy both advise us not to disturb his ashes. His misfortunes should make us forget his previous conduct; for by his death he has paid for whatever offenses he may have committed against the laws of his country."

Upon printing documents from Mexico relating to Iturbide's execution, the *Times* criticized his return to Mexico as "a striking miscalculation of talent and means" and "the most nerveless of all efforts to recover a usurped throne."[51] In an editorial concerning his adventurous enterprise, another London newspaper, the *Morning Post*, compared him to General Murat, who returned to the country where he had reigned only to be executed. This newspaper reasoned plausibly that Iturbide's death could not be considered as anything else than a benefit to Mexico, for it had saved her from the danger of internecine strife "and prevented those contentions, which even if they had not amounted to civil war, would have impeded . . . the full establishment and recognition of Mexican independence."[52]

Consul Taylor reported to Washington from the Mexican town of Alvarado that a feeble attempt was made by public officials there to announce the execution of the Liberator by the ringing of bells and

---

[47] July 22, 1824, in A.G.R.E., 40-11-2.
[48] Castillo Negrete, *Mexico en el siglo xix*, XIV, 323.
[49] The Supreme Executive Power to Garza, July 27, 1824, in A.M.C., D/481.3/304.
[50] Alamán, *Historia*, V, 606, 810-811.
[51] September 18, 1824.
[52] September 18, 1824.

the discharge of cannon. "Yet none but Spaniards rejoiced in the event."[53] On September 30, 1824, the *Gaceta de Madrid* took notice of the death of a personage upon whom the attention of both the Old and the New World had been focused. It declared that, like O'Donojú of "the traitorous Treaty of Córdoba," he had fittingly met with a disastrous end. In a passage imbued with a servile spirit, it added that the views "of those persons who dreamed that Iturbide had acted in accord with the Spanish King were very strange. . . . Ferdinand VII has never made use of thievish methods; nor has he employed, in order to accomplish good, any person considered to be a criminal."

In an entry made in his diary during the latter part of July, 1823, Miguel Beruete began the vilification of the Liberator by a certain class of Mexicans which has lasted almost to the present day. He likened Iturbide's return to his native land unto Napoleon's return from Elba. He alleged that the deposed Emperor had acted in a most abject manner at Padilla, because he had crawled around his cell behind Garza beseeching that general to send him to the *Spring* with fetters on his ankles and promising that he would go to "the end of the world."[54] In a periodical which he had dedicated to the cause of independence, Carlos María de Bustamante wrote, *Quem deus vult perdere, prius dementat.* "The Lord Almighty," he said, "never does things by halves nor does he leave his dispensations incomplete."[55] Marchena wrote to Rocafuerte to exult over the tragedy at Padilla and to express regret that all the partisans of the knavish victim had not met the same fate. The one-time spy, who was still in the Mexican diplomatic service, expressed fear that imperialists would soon cast their eyes upon the Liberator's eldest son.[56]

High Mexican officials soon began to meditate about the future of the deceased's family. In a secret session of the national Congress on July 26 Alamán expressed the view that Iturbide's wife and children ought not to reside on the soil of the republic. He ventured the opinion that they might sojourn in Colombia with safety to Mexico. A committee headed by Ramos Arizpe was appointed to consider the suggestion. Certain congressmen then proposed not only that the committee should designate a place of residence for the Iturbide family outside of Mexican territory but also that the proscriptive decree of April 28, 1824, should be applicable to his namesake, the so-called

[53] W. Taylor to Adams, August 3, 1824, in D.S., Consular Letters, Vera Cruz, 1.

[54] Diario, f. 152 bis, in MSS, T.U.

[55] *La Abispa de Chilpancingo*, September 15, 1824.

[56] Copy, August 31, 1824, Hernández y Dávalos Collection, 17-4-4064, in MSS, U.T.

heir apparent to the throne of Mexico, who was still in England.[57]
On July 27 Congress authorized the government to transport the relatives of Iturbide who were at Soto la Marina to a convenient place
outside of Mexico.[58] Accordingly on the next day, the Supreme
Executive Power directed that the bereaved widow, her two youngest
sons, and the necessary servants should be transported in a government vessel to a Colombian port which she was to designate.[59] The
executive authority also decided that those foreigners who had accompanied Iturbide on his last voyage and who had had no part in Mexican revolutionary movements should not be allowed to disembark from
the *Spring*, but that the members of the ship's company who had
actually landed in Mexico or who were citizens of the country should
be placed under arrest.[60]

A month later Secretary Alamán addressed a letter to Miguel Santa
María, who was again serving in Mexico as the Colombian minister,
to inform him that the government had decided that Iturbide's widow
and her two sons who were in Mexico should reside at a place in
Colombia to be selected by her. Alamán asked that the government
at Bogotá should undertake to prevent any of those persons from returning to Mexico as long as her government might judge their absence
to be necessary.[61] In reply Santa María affirmed that he would inform
his government of this policy so that it might contribute fraternally
to the welfare and stability of the Mexican republic.[62] It appears,
however, that difficulties of transportation prevented the Mexican government from carrying out its design of exiling the family of the former Emperor to Colombia. Instead Señora Iturbide, who had become
the mother of another child, was allowed to sail to New Orleans.[63]
On June 25, 1825, *Niles' Weekly Register* printed the following item
of news: "Madam Iturbide with three of her children arrived at
Baltimore last week." A little later she took up her residence in
Philadelphia.[64]

[57] Copy by J. M. Lafragua of Sesión secreta ordinaria, July 26, 1824, in MSS,
B.N.M.

[58] Dublán y Lozano, *Legislacion mexicana*, I, 710.

[59] The Supreme Executive Power to F. Arillaga, July 28, 1824, in A.M.C.,
D/481.3/304.

[60] *Idem* to Garza, July 28, 1824, *ibid.*

[61] Alamán to Santa María, August 28, 1824, in A.G.R.E., 9-4-2.

[62] September 1, 1824, *ibid.*   [63] Alamán, *Historia*, V, 605.

[64] On the flyleaf of the writer's copy of *A Statement of Some of the Principal Events
in the Public Life of Agustin de Iturbide* there is the following inscription: "From
Ana María Huarte de Yturbide to her friend Mr. George Follin, March 23d, 1833.
Philadelphia." Romero de Terreros (*La Corte de Agustín I*, pp. 59-60 n. 2) furnishes
other details concerning the history of the Iturbide family.

Michelena had meanwhile become interested in the children whom Iturbide had left in educational institutions. Fearing that they might be in want, shortly after he heard of the execution of their father, this diplomat wrote to Matthew Fletcher, who was in charge of Iturbide's affairs in England, to inform him that the Mexican government had granted a pension to the widow of the personage "who had been shot because of his crimes, . . . thus fulfilling the law." Desirous that Iturbide's children who were in England should continue their education, in order that they might be inspired by ideas "of love and gratitude" toward their native land—so reasoned Michelena—he had undertaken temporarily to be responsible for the payment of their expenses to the extent of eighty pounds sterling per annum for each child.[65] Fletcher promptly responded that he was pleased to learn that the Mexican government was performing such an act of justice to the family of the worthy and unfortunate man.[66] Whereupon Michelena retorted that the proposal to be responsible for the expenditures involved was made by him personally. Further, he stated that he would expect to be reimbursed by Iturbide's widow or that a sum equal to the outlay would be withheld from her by order of the Mexican government.[67]

Other passengers on the *Spring* were treated with consideration. After the ship departed secretly from the Mexican coast, the Supreme Executive Power notified Garza that Malo, López, and Treviño were to be exiled from Mexico forever.[68] Upon returning from Padilla to Soto la Marina, Colonel Beneski was thrust into a dungeon and held for trial before a military court.[69] Alamán informed Secretary Mier y Terán that Beneski had brought to London letters from conspirators in Mexico which informed Iturbide that an extensive plan had been arranged to restore him to the throne. Hence the Pole was to be questioned about the ramifications of the conspiracy.[70] In response to a belated letter from the renowned scholar Alexander von Humboldt

[65] September 20, 1824, in A.G.R.E., 9-4-2.

[66] September 22, 1824, *ibid.*

[67] September 24, 1824, *ibid.*

[68] August 11, 1824, in A.M.C., D/481.3/304.

[69] Beneski, *A Narrative of the Last Moments of the Life*, pp. 19, 41.

[70] On August 21, 1824, Alamán wrote to Manuel de Mier y Terán as follows: "Segun noticias q. el Supremo Govierno ha recevido de Londres aparece q. aunq. D. Agustín de Iturbide tenia formado siempre el designio de venir á esta República con el objeto de apoderarse de la corona abrevió su marcha la circunstancia de haber llegado á Inglaterra Beneski con cartas de los complices de la conspiración q. devia haber installado aqui en favor de aquel, y le aseguraban estar formado un plan mui estenso y bien convenido en su apoyo" (Hernández y Dávalos Collection, 17-4-4053, in MSS, U.T.).

beseeching clemency for Beneski, one of his "compatriots from Prussian Poland,"[71] Alamán replied that this prisoner should have suffered the same fate as Iturbide, but that, because of the clemency of his judges and of the Mexican President, the Pole had been condemned to expulsion from Mexico under pain of death if he dared to return.[72]

Perhaps it was because of a premonition of death that on shipboard Iturbide had written his will. Affirming that he was of sound mind, sure of the inevitability of death, but uncertain of the hour and the circumstances in which this might take place, he declared that in simple fashion, without the customary legal formalities, and by virtue of a privilege enjoyed by military men, he wished to make known his last will and testament. He avowed that he was a Roman Catholic, that he desired to die in this faith for the salvation of his soul, and that he wished his body to be buried without any pomp. He stated that he was married in *facie eclesie* to Doña Ana María Huarte, from which union there had sprung eight children besides another child then unborn. He acknowledged that he was in debt in Mexico because of obligations mainly contracted for the welfare of his country when he was at the head of the State. He admitted that he had accounts pending with two firms in London. He declared that some thirty-two thousand pesos of the sum used by him to purchase the hacienda of Apeo came from his wife's dowry. He recorded that he had made improvements in the hacienda at Chalco and maintained that an allowance for this should be made in the arrangements concerning his estate. With regard to the reward of a million pesos and twenty square leagues of land which had been granted to him by the provisional government of Mexico upon the establishment of her independence, he desired that his executor should urge this claim upon the Mexican government.

It was his wish that one-fifth of the amount which was liquidated from his estate should be used for the support of two adopted daughters named Justa and Antonia, for the execution of various commissions entrusted to Gómez de Navarrete, for the support of his nephews, and for the benefit of "his beloved and venerated father." The remainder of his estate, of his rights, and of his claims he bequeathed to his children and to a child then unborn, share and share alike. His widow was to serve as the tutor of his children. As execu-

[71] Humboldt to Victoria, December 10, 1824, Hernández y Dávalos Collection, 17-7-4222, *ibid.*

[72] Alamán to Humboldt, March 15, 1825, Hernández y Dávalos Collection, 17-7-4223, *ibid.*

tors he named Gómez de Navarrete, Nicolás Carrillo, and José López, who were to act successively in that order. He charged them, as well as his wife, to allow his eldest children to remain in the educational institutions in which they had been placed until their courses of study were completed.[73] In accordance with a custom of the Spanish Indies, the testator thus provided that the bulk of his property was to be inherited by his children.

From the chancellery at Santiago de Chile, in July, 1825, Juan de Díos Vial del Río addressed to the Mexican Secretary of Foreign Relations a letter which furnishes an indication of contemporary Spanish-American sentiment concerning the execution of the one-time Emperor: "The tragic end of this unfortunate American is certainly deplorable, but when Iturbide, forgetting the most sacred duties to his country, dared to commit treason against it and to violate the proscription to which he had been condemned, he made himself liable to this terrible punishment which will probably serve as a warning to those persons who may in the future intend to disturb the tranquillity of a nation that is jealous of the preservation of her liberty and of her rights."[74]

[73] Castillo Negrete, Mexico en el siglo xix, XIV, 452-455. In a copy of a draft of Instrucciones para gobierno de los apoderados Don Juan Gómez Navarrete y Don Nicolás Carrillo, en el giro y manejo de mi casa en México, Iturbide mentions Justa and Antonia as "las dos hijas adoptuas" (Documentos relativos al Imperio de Iturbide, f. 254, Genaro García Collection, in MSS, U.T. Library). With an attested copy of Iturbide's will there is a memorandum by his widow dated at Soto la Marina, August 13, 1824, which states that he drew his will on board the Spring on July 12, 1824 (Testamento del exmo. Señor general Libertador Don Agustín de Iturbide, A.H.I.N.A.H., 48-2-5).

[74] July 9, 1825, A.G.R.E., 1-12-1171.

CHAPTER XV

Epilogue

AFTER Iturbide's body had been interred at Padilla, the government of Mexico repeatedly showed itself inclined to aid his family and to honor him. In September, 1832, it provided that his widow and children were to be paid a pension equal to that which had been granted to O'Donojú's widow, that is, 12,000 pesos per annum. In November, 1833, Congress passed a law which declared that, because of the proclamation of Iturbide's plan at Iguala and because of the establishment of the independence of Mexico by his prudence and valor, he was recognized as one of the chief founders of her independence. Further, it voted that his ashes were to be deposited in an urn in the capital city like those of other heroes of Mexican independence, that his widow and children could again reside on Mexican soil, and that they were to continue to enjoy the pension which had been assigned to them by law. A not inconsiderable part of the later history of the family was concerned with attempts to have its accounts with the Mexican government liquidated.

On April 18, 1835, Congress decreed that the grant of 1,000,000 pesos to Iturbide by the Junta in 1822 would be paid to his heirs when the condition of the national treasury permitted. With regard to the concession of twenty square leagues of land in Texas, that grant was to be carved out of the national domain in New Mexico, or in Upper and Lower California, or in a region satisfactory to the interested parties. A month later a decree passed Congress to the effect that the name of Don Agustín de Iturbide was to be inscribed in a prominent place in its hall. In August, 1838, while General Anastasio Bustamante was President, Congress decreed that the mortal remains of the Liberator should be brought to Mexico City. Soon afterward, with imposing ceremonies, his ashes were transferred from Padilla to the metropolitan cathedral where they were placed in a tomb in the chapel of San Felipe de Jesús. On the sepulcher there was carved a eulogistic epitaph.

As the agent of the Iturbide family, in 1841 Gómez de Navarrete

THE PROCESSION CONDUCTING ITURBIDE'S ASHES TO THE CATHEDRAL OF MEXICO CITY ON OCTOBER 28, 1838

From José R. Pacheco, *Descripción de la solemnidad fúnebre con que se honraron las cenizas del Héroe de Iguala Don Agustín de Iturbide*

A COAT OF ARMS OF THE SECOND MEXICAN EMPIRE
A Mexican painting in the San Jacinto Museum of History

petitioned the Mexican government for a definite assignment of land in Upper California. Yet no such allotment was made. Twelve years later, Congress decreed that, as part payment of the "sacred" grant of 1,000,000 pesos which had been awarded Iturbide for his distinguished service to the nation, his heirs were to be given land worth 200,000 pesos in Sonora and Sinaloa or in Lower California. Difficulties arose, however, which prevented the fresh grant from being surveyed. According to a printed testamentary memorandum preserved in the Iturbide Papers, on June 6, 1857, the treasury of Mexico paid the descendants of her first Emperor some 760,000 pesos for the final liquidation of the award of 1,000,000 pesos.[1]

Shortly after the war between the United States and Mexico had ended, the heirs of Agustín de Iturbide presented a claim against the United States on account of the land given to him in Texas by the Mexican government in 1822, a grant which in 1835 had been made by it applicable to New Mexico or Upper California. In July, 1852, a claim of those heirs for twenty square leagues of land in the state of California was submitted to the United States Board of Land Commissioners. As the board ruled against the claim in 1854 on the ground that the strip of land had never been located, the executors of the Iturbide estate appealed to the district court of the United States.[2] Though it affirmed the decision of the land commissioners, his heirs next presented a claim to the American Congress. Many years later the Mexican minister at Washington reported to his government that early action on this plea seemed unlikely.[3]

In September, 1863, after Mexican monarchists had decided to invite Archduke Maximilian of Austria to become their Emperor, the ephemeral Regency issued a decree which prescribed a new escutcheon for Mexico. This imperialistic escutcheon made additions to the coat of arms of the First Mexican Empire.[4] Shortly after the Archduke had accepted the phantom crown, a strange scene took place in the castle of Chapultepec. Expressing a desire to honor the memory of the Mexican Liberator, Emperor Maximilian made a secret agreement with members of the Iturbide family by which he not only bestowed the title of prince upon two grandsons of the Liberator named Agustín and Salvador but also promised them high positions

---

[1] Dublán y Lozano, *Legislacion mexicana*, VI, 760-761; *Testamentaría de Iturbide*, pp. 6-7. A copy of this pamphlet is in the I. MSS, 19.

[2] *In the District Court of the United States for the Northern District of California. On Appeal from the Decision from the United States Board of Land Commissioners.*

[3] M. Romero to I. Mariscal, May 3, 1888, in A.G.R.E., 12-2-29.

[4] Iguíniz, *El Escudo de armas nacionales*, pp. 29-31.

in the State. Moreover, Maximilian conferred the title of princess upon their aunt Josefa. He also undertook to liquidate the debt which was still owing to the Iturbide family by the Mexican government. The Emperor, who was childless, even contemplated making Prince Agustín, the son of Angel de Iturbide, who had married a citizen of the United States named Alice Green, the heir to the imperial dignity.[5]

After Maximilian was executed by the Mexicans at Querétaro, complications arose concerning the estate of the first Mexican Emperor. In May, 1878, Alice Green de Iturbide, the widow of Angel de Iturbide, brought a suit against José Malo. She not only denounced his acts as an agent of the expatriate, but also criticized his measures as the executor of the Iturbide estate from 1824 to 1830, especially because he had transferred the hacienda of Apeo to Mateos Echais. In her plea she asserted that during his campaign for the independence of Mexico the Liberator had given to the Army of the Three Guarantees more than 71,000 pesos of his salary, that he had loaned General Nicolás Bravo 6,000 pesos, and that shortly before he went into exile he had furnished the national army with fodder to the value of some 10,000 pesos. On September 2, 1878, a judge gave sentence to the effect that the Apeo hacienda was rightfully the property of Iturbide's heirs and that the correspondent was to pay the cost of the suit.[6]

The design later adopted for a monument to the heroes of the Mexican struggles for independence did not provide for the transfer of the ashes of the Liberator from the metropolitan cathedral to the massive mausoleum in the Paseo de la Reforma which now enshrines the remains of Hidalgo, Matamoros, Mina, Morelos, Bravo, and Guerrero. To an American visitor who was present at the ceremony accompanying the transfer of their remains to that monument in 1925, President Calles evidently remarked that he had left Iturbide in the cathedral "among his kind, where he belongs."[7]

Although many years have passed since the writer began to search for papers concerning Iturbide, there still is a lack of sources on certain phases of his meteoric career. In particular, relatively few documents have been found concerning his family life. Enough material is at hand, however, to show that he was devoted to his parents, to his children, and to the Roman Catholic Church. It is true that

[5] Convenio secreto que celebran con S.M.Y. los hijos del Libertador, D. Augustín de Iturbide, September 9, 1865, in H. H. u. S., Mexikanisches Archiv, 16; A. Dano to Drouyn de Lhuys, October 10, 1865, in A.A.E., Mexique, 65.

[6] Martínez, Testamentaría de Iturbide, pp. 10, 37-43. A copy of this pamphlet is in I. MSS, 21.

[7] Gruening, Mexico and Its Heritage, p. 80.

he was accused of being unfaithful to his wife, but marital infidelity was not uncommon in his age and country. Though allegations have been made that Iturbide was a Mason, yet no evidence has been presented which supports such a view.[8] Quite otherwise: at least during the later part of his career certain members of the Masonic Order were his bitter enemies.

Some uncertainty exists concerning the views of Iturbide because he occasionally employed a ghost writer to compose dispatches. In the archives of the Mexican Department of War there still are drafts of letters which he dictated to a clerk or to a secretary. It appears that at times, as when the Treaty of Córdoba was framed, an amanuensis undertook to put words into his mouth. Occasionally Iturbide disclaimed ideas thus attributed to him. Unfortunately no material has been found about his habits of composition similar to that which is at hand concerning the preparation of state papers by his great contemporary, Simón Bolívar, who even composed while lolling in a canoe on the bosom of the Orinoco River. It is clear, however, that, while the former Emperor was residing in a country house in Italy, his secretary wrote the draft of a representation which his master had at his elbow when he composed his *autobiografía*, the most important single document concerning his public career.[9] The repetition of certain phrases and the reiteration of particular ideas in his letters and state papers, as, for example, his assertion of willingness to sacrifice himself and his interests to the welfare of his country, indicate that he habitually viewed events concerning his activities in a light which was favorable to himself. Whether as a royalist officer, an insurgent generalissimo, or a deposed Emperor, Agustín de Iturbide was a confirmed poser. At times he strayed from the truth.

Although he spoke admiringly of General Washington, there is nothing to show that he ever studied the strategy of that general or of any other military commander. During Iturbide's career as a royalist officer his actions were marked by remarkable celerity, by wanton cruelty toward the insurgents, and by the manner in which he undertook to profit by his private mercantile transactions. These traits he evidently possessed to a greater degree than some other royalist officers of his time. The most distinctive trait of his military policy after he preclaimed the Plan of Iguala was his decision to follow a conciliatory and humane policy toward his opponents. It does not appear that, in

[8] McLeish, *High Lights of the Mexican Revolution*, p. 59.
[9] Robertson, "The Memorabilia of Agustín de Iturbide," *Hispanic American Historical Review*, XXVII, 440-442.

addition, he ever mapped out a strategic plan for military operations against the royalists. His movements during the campaign of liberation were to a large extent opportunistic. Cautiously did he aim to avoid taking such risks as might imperil the success of the revolutionary cause. One by one he and his lieutenants captured important forts and cities. Finally they converged upon the capital.

In 1850 a Mexican named Francisco Quintanilla, who had espoused the republican cause during the struggle for independence, expressed the opinion that during the revolutionary war Mexico imperatively needed a man of genius. "That man, that genius," said Quintanilla, "was Señor Iturbide. Nature had endowed him with many political gifts, but the men of his period did not appreciate these great qualities or did not wish to appreciate them."[10]   A score of years later a patriotic Spaniard named Carlos Navarro y Rodrigo, who composed a biography of Iturbide, praised his role in the final campaign for Mexican independence. Navarro y Rodrigo declared that it would be unjust not to recognize the singular skill and moderation which the Liberator displayed in that struggle, both as a military man and as a politician.[11]   Among other comments upon the Liberator-Emperor's public career, omitting the encomiums of blind adulators, let it suffice to mention here the opinion of Simón Bolívar. In extravagant words he declared in September, 1823, that Napoleon and Iturbide were the two most distinguished personages in modern history, "the leading benefactors of their respective countries and of national independence." He added, however, that both of those politico-military publicists had "profaned the temple of the laws and the sanctum of all the social rights."[12]

There is no doubt that Iturbide believed that a monarchical form of government was the system best suited for people who had just been released from the Spanish yoke. Not only did he frequently champion this view in letters and addresses, but, upon becoming the chief executive of Mexico, he persistently implemented it in practice. In a spirit resembling that assumed by Manuel Belgrano at the Congress of Tucumán and by José de San Martín in negotiations with Spanish agents at Punchauca in 1821, the author of the Plan of Iguala discredited the idea of establishing a republican form of government in Spanish America. His views concerning the best political system

[10] Quintanilla to L. Alamán, October 1, 1850, Alamán, Archivo relativo a su historia de México, 1808-1849, Genaro García Collection in MSS, U.T.
[11] Iturbide, p. 89.
[12] Cartas, III, 229.

for his native land remained substantially as he had formulated them in 1821. In a manifesto addressed to his countrymen during that year, he expressed the belief that they were satisfied with the device of liberty, independence, and union:

"Article III of the Iguala Plan declared that the government of the nation was to be a limited monarchy in harmony with the Constitution and suitable to the Kingdom. Article II of the Treaty of Córdoba provided that the government of the Empire was to be a limited constitutional monarchy. I adopted this basis not because I felt that it was the system of government which most honored a society, but because no one doubts that a limited constitutional government is the system most suitable to the imperfections and the passions of men. Only thus can they avoid a condition in which the people contend for their liberty, the nobles and the great men struggle for power, and the monarchs strive for arbitrary dominion."

He further explained that with respect to the choice of a monarch, he had decided that a member of the Spanish ruling dynasty should be selected and that the national Congress of Mexico should decide upon the conditions to be laid down for the advent of that personage to the throne or for the choice of another ruler. After mentioning that some persons wished to adorn him with the diadem of the Empire, he said: "In nothing did I question the right which all publicists and all civilized nations acknowledge belongs to the people to form, to maintain, to perfect, and to alter their constitution to suit their welfare and happiness." He explained that this was the sole object which he proposed in all his operations, "particularly in the establishment of the fundamental bases of the government which was to replace the Spanish system." The right to alter the form of government, he declared, belonged exclusively to the nation.[13] As shown in previous chapters, Iturbide frequently asserted that he did not wish to become the Emperor of Mexico. In May, 1822, however, he did not propose another candidate, but yielded to the insistence of the rabble.

Beyond the Atlantic, prominent European statesmen favored monarchical rule in Latin America. The role of Chateaubriand at this time involved the thwarting of democratic trends in Mexico and South America by the founding of Bourbon monarchies in that vast region.[14] Again, linked to Canning's idea of delaying an acknowledgment of the independence of the rising Spanish-American states was his thinly

---

[13] *Manifiesto que el Señor D. Agustín de Iturbide dirije á los habitantes de Méjico*, pp. 2-3; cf. p. 102b.

[14] Robertson, *France and Latin-American Independence*, pp. 261-294.

veiled notion of establishing monarchies there. This attitude was partly due to his desire to prevent the division of the world into two spheres: one republican, and the other monarchical. As he once explained his policy, he wished to "link once more America to Europe."[15]

In his attempt to establish monarchical rule in Mexico, however, Agustín I showed such a strong trend toward centralization that he became an almost absolute monarch. This tendency it was which in large part altered the attitude of certain influential Mexicans who had lauded his acceptance of the crown. Instead of remaining his adulators, they became his spiteful critics and antagonists. Nevertheless, even during the last phase of his rule, the Emperor not infrequently expressed himself as being in favor of a limited monarchy. History demonstrates that he was not the only Latin-American magistrate who was constrained to relinquish his political theory in practice. Indeed fate might have been kind to Iturbide, if, like some other Latin-American magistrates, he had been willing to exercise despotic power under cover of a republican form of government.

Persons interested in this critical period of Mexican history have sometimes alleged or implied that Iturbide was a tool of the Roman Catholic Church. Incidents occurring throughout his life in fact demonstrate that he was a devout Roman Catholic. Though it appears that he solicited the participation of certain bishops in the ceremony of his anointment as the Emperor of Mexico, and though he used the paraphernalia and machinery of the Church of Rome to add support and luster to his rule, yet he did not favor the retention of historic rights and privileges by the Church at the expense of the nascent state. The most convincing proof of that tendency was his attitude toward the *Patronato Real*. Agustín I was one of the earliest magistrates of independent Spanish America to maintain that upon the establishment of independence the right of nominating candidates for appointment to ecclesiastical positions in a given state had passed from the King of Spain to the new government. Indeed when commenting upon the attitude of the First Mexican Empire toward the re-establishment of the Society of Jesus, a Jesuit author went so far as to assert that it implied a declaration of the independence of the Mexican Church.[16] The first Emperor of Mexico did not go to Canossa.

Clio has not accorded to Agustín de Iturbide the place which he deserves. This neglect has been partly due to the fact that until our

[15] Temperley, *The Foreign Policy of Canning*, p. 159.

[16] Decorme, *Historia de la Compañía de Jesús en la República Mexicana durante el siglo xix*, I, 228.

own time no serious attempt was made to collect, to edit, and to publish his widely scattered papers. Although a Mexican historian has recently published a portly volume of Iturbide memorabilia, yet some unedited documents concerning him still gather dust among family papers or in archival repositories. Another reason for the neglect shown the Mexican Liberator was the intense prejudice which has prevailed against him in his native land. His cruelty as a royalist officer has at times overshadowed his service in proclaiming the Plan of Iguala. His skill in negotiating the Treaty of Córdoba has been belittled by some writers because of his mistakes as the Emperor. His supposed subservience to the Church of Rome has induced anti-clericals to cast suspicion upon his motives. Though historians in southern South America have lauded the military achievements of the self-abnegating San Martín, and though historians in the northern part of the continent have praised Bolívar as a warrior, a statesman, and a political thinker, some Mexican writers have utterly failed to appreciate Iturbide. Others have passionately taken sides as bitter critics or as impassioned champions of their Liberator.

A Masonic writer has alleged that as the result of a bitter quarrel between Iturbide and Pedro José de Fonte, the Archbishop actually placed the Liberator under the ban of the Church. No evidence has been adduced, however, to show that Fonte ever took such action. On the other side, in a letter from Teloloapan dated February 21, 1821, addressed to Juan Ruíz de Cabañas, the Bishop of Guadalajara, Iturbide wrote the following appreciation of his heritage:

"I cannot relinquish the ingrained ideas of my ancestors which my venerated and most dearly beloved parents transmitted to me by means of education. I do not believe that there is more than one true religion, namely, that which I profess. I know that it is more delicate than an immaculate mirror which the slightest breath of air will dim or sully. I believe that this most holy religion has been attacked in a thousand ways by impious decrees which foreshadow an actual schism in the Church. Moreover, I believe that Roman Catholicism would be destroyed if there were not strong spirits who openly and without subterfuge will undertake to protect it. I also believe that this vigor of decision and spirit is an obligation of a good Catholic. . . . In a few words, either I shall preserve pure and undefiled the sacrosanct religion in New Spain or I shall cease to exist. Thank Providence that for the greater glory of the Almighty, just as in other times some humble fishermen were the persons destined to propagate the

Holy Faith, so in the nineteenth century the most humble subject of New Spain will be the strongest supporter of the most holy doctrine."[17]

The neglect shown Iturbide by some students of history is due, in part, to the fact that there were no such dramatic scenes in the Mexican's life to attract attention as those which occurred in the lives of his great South American contemporaries. There was no march in Mexico like that of San Martín across the lofty Andes in 1817 from Mendoza to Chacabuco. There was no march like that by which Bolívar surmounted the Granadian Andes in 1819 on his way to Boyacá. Neither was there such a focal event as the momentous interview of Bolívar and San Martín at Guayaquil.

Yet Iturbide has a special claim to consideration by historians. He was not compelled like Bolívar to establish the liberty of his native land as the result of a series of devastating campaigns. In 1821 there was no war to the death in Mexico like that which took place in Venezuela from 1813 to 1816. Largely as a result of the cleverly devised Plan of Iguala, the last great champion of Mexican independence succeeded in winning the support of diverse classes in society. Although it is not correct to state that independence in this or that section of Mexico was won without the shedding of a single drop of blood, yet it is true that Iturbide brought about the separation of his native land from Spain by a movement which may be termed bloodless. Viewed in the lurid light of Spanish-American revolts, this was a remarkable achievement.

With regard to that part of Iturbide's public career when he was struggling to lay the foundations of an independent government, notice should be taken that the presence in the Mexican population of a large aboriginal class and of an influential mestizo caste rendered the twofold task of constructing and launching the Ship of State peculiarly difficult. In sharp contrast with the Mexican Liberator, when San Martín relinquished the position of Protector of Peru, he declined to take part in the reconstruction of society in his native land. The Argentine Liberator was right when in his interview with Iturbide he advised him not to return to the scene of his former triumphs. In his declining years Simón Bolívar lamented the chaotic political condition of northern South America. In a fit of despair he declared that as the result of the long struggle for liberty, independence was the only blessing which his country had gained at the expense of every-

[17] *Católicos sentimientos del Sr. Generalísimo Don Agustín de Iturbide expresados en su carta al Señor obispo de Guadalajara*, pp. 1-2.

thing else. Indeed long before his death Iturbide might well have voiced the sentiments which Bolívar expressed several years later when he exclaimed that those persons who had brought about the Great Revolution in Spanish America had plowed in the sea!

Once the independence of Mexico had been won, Iturbide took a keen interest in international affairs. He wished to see his country gain her rightful place among nations. He soon realized that Spanish publicists were opposed to the acknowledgment of Mexican independence—a view which was borne out by the long delay made by Spain before she recognized the independence of the Spanish-American republics. Iturbide was anxious to acknowledge the independent rank of neighboring countries. Especially was he interested in developing intercourse with England and the United States, in spite of their expansionist tendencies. It was partly due to his initiative that Mexico was the second Latin-American nation whose independence was recognized by the government at Washington. His desire to develop economic and political relations with England was illustrated by his significant interview with the English minister at Florence.

While in exile Iturbide displayed interest in the development of intercourse between Mexico and the Anglo-Saxon nations because he viewed those powers as constituting a great buttress against intervention by the Holy Alliance to restore the rule of Ferdinand VII over the revolted American colonies. A fear that the Allies might actually intervene for that purpose haunted the minds of liberal statesmen on both sides of the Atlantic. Although that fear was a chimera, and although Tsar Alexander I appears to have been the only Ally who seriously contemplated the use of force on behalf of Spain in America,[18] yet that apprehension influenced the thoughts and the actions of such publicists as Canning, Iturbide, and Monroe.

The first Emperor of Mexico had a prophetic vision. He foresaw the role which the liberated peoples of America were destined to play in world politics. He believed that the time would come when European powers would feel the impact upon their governments of the political communities that were springing into existence in the New World. Odd though it may seem, certain contemporary European statesmen were harboring similar thoughts about the international influence of the American nations. Prince Metternich and his adviser Friedrich von Gentz were seriously concerned about the future rela-

[18] Robertson, "Russia and the Emancipation of Spanish America, 1816-1826," *Hispanic American Historical Review*, XXI, 211-217.

tions between Europe and America.[19]   Indeed, Iturbide is entitled to a place among those public men of his age who were deeply interested in important reactions between the Old World and the New. The galaxy of contemporary personages who were concerned about inter-hemispherical relations includes John Quincy Adams, James Monroe, Prince Metternich, Simón Bolívar, José Bonifacio, Viscount Chateau-briand, George Canning, and Tsar Alexander I.

Mainly because of the unfortunate outcome of his essay at imperial rule, when he deprived of liberty the people whom he had emancipated from Spanish domination, Iturbide must be assigned a niche in the Pan American temple of historical fame inferior to that occupied by Bolívar or San Martín. Still, in recent decades some Mexican journalists and historians have shown an increasing tendency to acknowledge the genuine service which Iturbide performed for his country during the last struggle for independence from Spain.   In 1921, upon the occasion of the one hundredth anniversary of his triumphal entry into Mexico City, such leading journals as *Excelsior, El Universal,* and the *Revista de Revistas* paid tribute to him by publishing historical articles which commemorated his achievements as the Liberator of Middle America. It is a further pleasure to record that discerning Mexican writers have recently displayed a tendency to comment favorably upon the historic role of Iturbide in the emancipation of Mexico. Worthy of special mention is the article by Juan de Díos Robledo in *El Universal* for September, 1921, concerning Iturbide and the criterion of the Mexican nation. Díos Robledo concluded his judgment upon the Liberator and Emperor of Mexico with these words: "Iturbide paid for his faults and errors by the greatest price which a man can offer, his own life. We do not have to be more cruel than destiny itself by pursuing the person condemned at Padilla into his tomb."   At that time, when he anticipated a period of peace following revolutionary tempests, Robledo added sympathetically, "it is necessary that our words should be cordial with regard to all those men, who on the soil of Mexico and inspired by the ideal of their nation, have furnished their quota of life and blood."

[19] *Idem*, "The Monroe Doctrine Abroad in 1823-24," *American Political Science Review*, VI, 559, 560.

Selected Bibliography

A. Sources

A. MANUSCRIPTS

Note

Many gaps in the printed materials concerning Agustín de Iturbide have been filled by the use of unedited documents found at one time or another in various archival collections. Attention must here be confined to the main repositories. In 1907, while I was engaged in research concerning Miranda in the Archivo General de la Nación in Mexico City, Director Justino Rubio allowed me to have access to volumes of the correspondence of various royalist commanders who served Ferdinand VII during the Mexican struggle for independence. Among the papers stored in the attic of that vast repository were bound volumes of Iturbide's military correspondence during the years when he was serving as a royalist officer. Upon returning to the Mexican capital many years later, I greatly appreciated the efforts of Mr. Edward G. Trueblood, secretary of the American legation in Mexico, to facilitate anew my access to other Mexican archives, such as the Archivo General de la Secretaría de Relaciones Exteriores.

At various times I garnered supplementary materials from major repositories in continental Europe. I studied the attitude of Spain toward revolutionary struggles in Spanish America in the Archivo General de Indias in Seville, in the Archivo General de Simancas, and in the Archivo Histórico Nacional in Madrid. Citations of documents found in the Archivo General de Indias have been left in the same style as that used by the archive when the manuscripts were found, which was generally *estante—cajón—legajo*. While I was gathering materials about the policy of European nations toward Hispanic America, I came across widely scattered documents concerning important events in the life of Iturbide in other archives, namely, the Public Record Office in London, the Archives du Ministère des Affaires Étrangères in Paris, and the Haus-, Hof-, und Staats-Archiv in Vienna.

Important unedited documents concerning Iturbide's public life were found in various places in the United States. Of special importance was a large collection of papers of the Iturbide family which was secured by the Library of Congress from a descendant and namesake of Emperor Agustín I. Particularly useful regarding the last part of his career were manuscripts which fortunately had been gathered by a Mexican scholar named Juan Hernández y Dávalos, presumably with a view to the publication of a documentary collection. These papers were originally styled "Documentos inéditos para la historia de México," but are now designated the "Hernández y Dávalos Collection." That collection is kept in the Archives of the University of Texas with other valuable papers concerning Mexican history. Among these archives are also miscellaneous papers collected by the eminent Mexican scholar, Señor Genaro García. In a letter to the writer dated March 9, 1912, García wrote thus about his manuscripts: "Por último, conservo numerosas obras manuscritas e inéditas . . . e incontables copias tambien inéditas, tomadas de nuestros principales archivos públicos y particulares. . . ." There were also accessible to the writer certain of these García documents which were kept on the shelves of the University of Texas Library.

Among other useful collections were papers stored in the Middle American Research Institute of Tulane University, where scattered documents dealing with various phases of Iturbide's public career were found. Perhaps the most important of these was the manuscript "Diario" of one of Iturbide's contemporaries named Miguel Beruete. Of special assistance to me were the kind offices of the eminent Mexican historian and publicist Señor José C. Valadés, who secured my admission in 1941 to the Archivo General de Cancelados of the Department of National Defense of the Mexican Government. In that archive many letters and memoranda were found that were concerned particularly with the last campaign for the independence of Mexico.

The abbreviations used in the footnotes of the present work for the repositories in which useful manuscripts were found are given in the following list.

A.A.E.   Archives du Ministère des Affaires Étrangères, correspondance politique, Paris.
A.G.I.   Archivo General de Indias, Seville, Spain.
A.G.N.   Archivo General de la Nación, Mexico City.
A.G.R.E. Archivo General de la Secretaría de Relaciones Exteriores, Mexico City.
A.G.S.   Archivo General de Simancas, Simancas, Spain.

A.H.H.	Archivo Histórico de Hacienda, Mexico City.
A.H.N.	Archivo Histórico Nacional, Madrid, Spain.
A.M.C.	Dirección General de Archivo Militar: Archivo Central de Cancelados, Secretaría de la Defensa Nacional, Mexico City.
A.N.M.	Archives of New Mexico, Museum of New Mexico, Santa Fe, New Mexico.
	Some useful manuscripts found in the Archives of New Mexico when they were in the custody of the Library of Congress retain the footnote citations designated in that library, because they could not be located in the Museum of New Mexico after those archives were transferred to that state. Manuscripts relocated in New Mexico are cited in the footnotes of the text thus, A.N.M. . . , Santa Fe.
A.P.C.	Archivo Parroquial de la Catedral, Morelia, Mexico.
A.E.E.S.S.	Archivo de la Embajada de España cerca de la Santa Sede, Rome, Italy.
A.H.I.N.A.H.	Archivo Histórico del Institute Nacional de Antropología é Historia, Mexico City.
A.S.M.	Archivo de San Martín, Museo Mitre, Buenos Aires, Argentina.
D.S.	Department of State, National Archives, R G 59, Washington, D. C.
F.O.	Foreign Office, Public Record Office, London, England.
H.H. u. S.	Haus-, Hof-, und Staats-Archiv, Vienna, Austria.
I. MSS	Iturbide Papers, Library of Congress, Washington, D. C.
M. MSS	Monroe Papers, Library of Congress, Washington, D. C.
MSS, B.N.M.	Manuscritos de la Biblioteca Nacional de México, Mexico City.
MSS, C.	Manuscripts of Mr. G. H. G. Conway, Mexico City.
MSS, L.M.C.	Manuscritos del Lic. Leopoldo Martínez Cosio, Mexico City.
MSS, L.	Manuscritos de Señor Carlos A. Lira, San Luis Potosí, Mexico.
MSS, O.L.	Manuscripts in the Oliveira Lima Collection of the Catholic University of America, Washington, D. C.
MSS, P.	Manuscripts of Mr. E. T. Parks, Washington, D. C.
MSS, S.J.M.H.	Manuscripts in the San Jacinto Museum of History, San Jacinto Monument, Texas.
MSS, T.U.	Manuscripts of Tulane University, Middle American Research Institute, New Orleans, Louisiana.
MSS, U.T.	Archives Collection of the University of Texas, Austin, Texas.

MSS, Y.   Manuscripts of Mrs. Louise de Yturbide, Washington,
                 D. C.
MSS, Y.U.   Manuscripts of Yale University, New Haven, Connecti-
                 cut: Papeles que tienen relación al período de 1800
                 á 1821.

B. PUBLISHED MATERIAL

I. Books, Pamphlets, and Broadsides

Note

Important collections of printed materials were consulted from time to time in great libraries of America and Europe. Years ago I studied a multitude of pamphlets concerning the struggles for Mexican independence which were preserved in the British Museum. Books and periodicals were used in the Biblioteca Nacional of Spain. In the Biblioteca Nacional of Mexico the Vice-Director, Señor Juan B. Iguíniz, courteously gave me access to books, magazines, and other materials. Rare books in the Library of Congress were drawn upon for aid. In the Library of the University of Texas many publications which had been purchased with the Library of Señor Genaro García were most useful. Books assembled by the literary industry of Hubert Howe Bancroft were used in the famed Bancroft Library of the University of California. Rare Mexican imprints were found in the valuable collection of books, brochures, and broadsides which were gathered years ago by the enterprising mining engineer and bibliophile Adolph Sutro, who dreamed of founding a monumental library on the California shores of the Pacific. In 1946 a precious portion of that collection was stored in the gloomy basement of the Library of the City of San Francisco. Issues of rare periodicals such as *El Mexicano Independiente* were occasionally found in the Hernández y Dávalos Collection in the Archives of the University of Texas and in the Sutro Branch, California State Library.

A.A.A.   *La Nulidad de los tratados de Córdoba resuelta por la España.*
         Mexico, 1822.
Á. *la coronación de nuestro augusto Emperador Agustín Primero. Marcha
         imperial que deberá cantarse en la noche del 21 de Julio de 1822 en
         el coliseo de esta corte en tan justa celebridad por la compañia de opera.*
         Mexico, 1822.
*Acta de instalación de la junta national instituyente conforme al decreto
         imperial de 31 del último Octubre.* Mexico, 1822.
Acta de la junta de Puebla sobre la reinstalacion del congreso mexicano.
         Mexico, 1823.

Actas del congreso constituyente mexicano (vol. IV has the title *Diario de las sesiones del congreso constituyente de México*), vols. I-IV. Mexico, 1822-1823.

Al Feliz cumple años de S.A.I., el Principe Heredero. Marcha que deberá cantarse en el coliseo de esta corte la noche del 30 del presente por la compañia de opera del mismo con tan fausto motivo. Mexico, 1822.

ALAMÁN, JUAN B. *Apuntes para la biografía del exmo. Sr. D. Lucas Alamán, secretario de estado y del despacho de relaciones exteriores.* Mexico, 1852.

ALAMÁN, LUCAS. *Historia de Mexico con una noticia preliminar del sistema de gobierno que regia en 1808 y del estado en que se hallaba el pais en el mismo año,* 5 vols. Mexico, 1883-1885.

———. *Liquidación general de la deuda esterior de la república mexicana hasta fin de Diciembre de 1841.* Mexico, 1845.

[ALAMÁN, LUCAS]. *Noticias biográficas del licenciado Don Carlos María de Bustamante y juicio crítico de sus obras escritas por un amigo de D. Carlos y mas amigo de la verdad.* Mexico, 1849.

ÁLVAREZ, FRANCISCO DE PAULA. *Santa-Anna hasta 1822.* Guadalajara, 1822.

———. *Lista de la familia imperial.* [Mexico], 1823.

El Amante de la humanidad. Sentencia de Pío Marcha dirigida al soberano congreso. Mexico, 1823.

American State Papers, Foreign Relations, vol. IV. Washington, 1834.

ANAYA, JUAN P., AND OTHERS. *Representación de los diputados y otros presos por opinion que se hallan en el carcel público dirigida al exmo. Sr. capitán general de esta provincia.* Mexico, 1823.

ANDRADE, JOSÉ A. DE. *Aviso al público,* March 1, 1823. Mexico, 1823.

Aniversario de las sangrientas victimas de Salvatierra sacrificiados por el memorable Iturbide. [Mexico], 1823.

APODACA, JUAN RUÍZ DE. *Apuntes para la historia. Consulta que ha hecho el excmo. Sr. virey, gefe político superior á la excma. diputación provincial, audiencia territorial y otros tribunales y córporaciones.* Mexico, 1821.

Ardiente patriotismo de los señores brigadieres D. Antonio López de Santana y D. José María Lobato en la proclamación del Emperador Agustín I. Mexico, 1822.

Armisticio celebrado entre los señores Don Agustín de Iturbide, primer gefe del ejército imperial mejicano trigarante, y Don Francisco Nobella, mariscal de campo y comandante accidental de la guarnición española de Méjico. Mexico, 1821.

ARRANGOIZ, FRANCISCO DE PAULA DE. *Méjico desde 1808 hasta 1867,* 2 vols. Madrid, 1871-1872.

Aviso al público, July 12, 1821. Mexico, 1821.

BARCA, CALDERON DE. *Life in Mexico during a Residence of Two Years in That Country.* London, 1843.

BÁRCENA, MANUEL DE LA. *Manifiesto al mundo. La Justicia y la necesidad de la independencia de la Nueva España.* Puebla, 1821.

———. *Oración gratulatoria a Dios que por la independencia mejicano dijó en la catedral de Valladolid de Michoacán . . . el día 6 de Septiembre del año de 1821.* Mexico, 1821.

BARKER, EUGENE C. (ed.). *The Austin Papers* (American Historical Association Report, 1919, vol. II, part I). Washington, 1924.

BELTRAMI, J. C. [GIACOMO C.]. *Le Mexique,* 2 vols. Paris, 1830.

Benedición que nuestra madre la santa iglesia da al nuevo Rey ó Emperador en el día de su coronación sacada del pontifical romano y traducida del Latin al Castellano. Mexico, 1822.

BENESKI, CHARLES DE. *A Narrative of the Last Moments of the Life of Don Agustin de Iturbide, ex-Emperor of Mexico.* New York, 1825.

BOCANEGRA, JOSÉ M. *Memorias pora la historia de México independiente, 1822-1848,* 2 vols. Mexico, 1892.

Boleras cantadas en el teatro de la imperial ciudad de México la noche del 21 de Mayo de 1822 para solemnizar en lo pronto la gloriosa proclamación de Agustín Primero, Emperador del Orbe Mexicano á quien prospere muchos años el cielo. Mexico, 1822.

BOLÍVAR, SIMÓN. *Cartas del libertador, corrigidas conforme a los originales,* edited by Vicente Lecuna, vols. II and III. Caracas, 1929.

BRAVO, NICOLÁS. *Manifiesto a la nación mexicana del ciudadano Nicolás Bravo, benemérito de la pátria, por declaración del soberano congreso constituyente.* Mexico, 1823.

BULLOCK, WILLIAM. *Six Months' Residence and Travels in Mexico, containing Remarks on the Present State of New Spain, Its Natural Productions, State of Society, Manufactures, Trade, Agriculture, and Antiquities.* London, 1824.

BUSTAMANTE, ANASTASIO. *Habitantes de las provincias internas de oriente y occidente.* Mexico, 1822.

BUSTAMANTE, CARLOS M. DE. *Apuntes para la historia del gobierno del general D. Antonio López de Santa-Anna desde principios de Octubre de 1841 hasta 6 de Diciembre de 1844 en que fue depuesto del mando por uniforme voluntad de la nación.* Mexico, 1845.

———. *Campañas del general D. Félix María Calleja, commandante en gefe del ejército real de operaciones llamado del centro.* Mexico, 1828.

———. *Continuacion del cuadro historico. Historia del Emperador D. Agustin de Iturbide hasta su muerte y sus consecuencias y establecimiento de la república popular federal.* Mexico, 1846.

———. *Cuadro historico de la revolucion de la América Mexicana, comenzada en quince de Setiembre de mil ochocientos diez por el ciudadano Miguel Hidalgo y Costilla,* vol. V. Mexico, 1827.

——. *Continuacion del cuadro historico de la revolución mexicana,* vol. VI. Mexico, 1832.

——. *Cuadro historico de la revolucion mexicana . . . ,* 5 vols. Mexico, 1843-1846.

——. *Diario historico de Mexico,* vol. I. Zacatecas, 1896.

——. *Exposición que el lic. D. Carlos María de Bustamante, preso en el convento de S. Francisco como diputado de la provincia de Oajaca en el congreso constituyente, hizó al Emperador por medio del exmo. Sr. ministro de relaciones.* Mexico, 1823.

——. *El General D. Felipe de la Garza vindicado de las notas de traidor é ingrato con que se le ofende en un papel intitulado: "Catástrofe de D. Agustín de Iturbide aclamado Emperador de México el 18 de Mayo 1822."* Mexico, 1826.

——. *El Honor y patriotismo del general D. Nicolas Bravo demostrado en los ultimos dias del fugaz imperio de Iturbide ó sea memoria formada sobre los apuntes existentes en la secretaría de dicho general Bravo.* Mexico, 1828.

——. *Manifiesto histórico á las naciones y pueblos del Anáhuac. Leido en la sesión pública del soberano congreso del 15 de Abril de 1823.* Mexico, 1823.

CABRERA DE NEVARES, MIGUEL. *Memoria sobre el estado actual de las Américas y medio de pacificarlas.* Madrid, 1821.

CADENA, PEDRO I. *Anales diplomáticos de Colombia.* Bogotá, 1878.

CAMPOS Y RIVAS, MANUEL. *Adición al proyecto del ceremonial impreso en 17 del corriente para la inauguración de SS. MM. II.* Mexico, 1822.

Capitulación acordada para la evacuación de la ciudad de Puebla, entre los dos señores coroneles D. Juan Horbegoso y D. Saturnino Samaniego por parte del exmo. Sr. D. Ciriaco de Llano, gobernador y comandante general de la provincia, y los tenientes coroneles D. Luis Cortazár y el Sr. Conde de S. Pedro del Alamo, por parte del Sr. D. Agustín de Iturbide, primer gefe del egército imperial mejicano de las Tres Garantías. Cholula, 1821.

Capitulación hecha entre el Señor D. Agustín de Iturbide, primer gefe del ejército imperial mejicano de las Tres Garantías, y el comandante de la plaza de Valladolid D. Manuel Rodríguez de Cela, teniente coronel del regimiento de Barcelona. Puebla, 1821.

Cartas de los Sres. generalísimo D. Agustín de Iturbide y teniente general Don José Dávila. Mexico, 1822.

Cartas que han mediado entre los señores coroneles Don José Joaquín del Calvo, comandante de la vanguardia de este ejército, y D. Francisco de Paula Álvarez, secretario del Emperador. Puebla, 1823.

Cartas que S. M. I. con motivo de su exaltación al trono dirigió al excmo. Sr. capitán general del sur. Mexico, 1822.

Case of de Yturbide Heirs against the United States. House Report No. 724, 50th Congress, 1st Session. Washington, 1888.

CASTALDO, ANDRÉS. *Ceremonías de la iglesia en la unción y coronación del nuevo Rey ó Emperador escritas en Latin por D. Andrés Castaldo y traducidas al Castellano.* Mexico, 1822.

Catástrofe de Don Agustín de Yturbide, aclamado Emperador de Méjico el 18 de Mayo del año 1822, ó relación exacta de las circunstancias que han acompañado el desembarco y la muerte de este hombre célebre. Paris, 1825.

CAVO, ANDRÉS. *Los Tres siglos de México durante el gobierno español hasta la entrada del Ejército Trigarante . . . publicada con notas y suplemento el lic. Carlos María de Bustamante,* 4 vols. Mexico, 1836-1838.

CHATEAUBRIAND, F. R. VICOMTE DE. *Correspondance générale de Chateaubriand,* edited by L. Thomas, vol. V. Paris, 1924.

El Clamor de la justicia de los antiguos patriotas titulados insurgentes. Mexico, 1822.

CLAY, HENRY. *The Private Correspondence of Henry Clay,* edited by C. Colton. New York, 1856.

CLEMENTE VÁZQUEZ, ANDRÉS (ed.). *Bosquejo histórico de la agregación á Mexico de Chiapas y Soconusco y de las negociaciones sobre limites entablados por México con Centro América y Guatemala* (Archivo histórico diplomático mexicano, no. 36). Mexico, 1932.

Colección de los decretos y ordenes del soberano congreso constituyente mexicano desde su instalación en 5 de Noviembre de 1823 hasta 24 de Diciembre de 1824 en que cesó, 2 vols. Mexico, 1825.

Colección de los decretos y ordenes que han expedido las cortes generales y extraordinarias [and with a different title], 10 vols. Madrid, 1813-1822.

Colección de documentos históricos, inéditos ó muy raros referentes al arzobispado de Guadalajara publicados por el ilmo. y rmo. Sr. dr. y mtro. Don Francisco Orozco y Jiménez, vol. IV. Guadalajara, 1925.

Coleccion eclesiastica mejicana, 4 vols. Mexico, 1834.

Colección de los leyes fundamentales que han regido en la República Mexicana y de los planos que han tenido el mismo carácter desde el año de 1821 hasta el de 1857. Mexico, 1857.

Coleccion de ordenes y decretos de la soberana junta provisional gubernativa y soberanas congresos generales de la nacion mexicana, 4 vols. Mexico, 1829.

La Constitución de 1812 en la Nueva España (Publicaciones del archivo general de la nacion, vols. IV and V). Mexico, 1912.

Constitución del imperio ó proyecto de organización del poder legislativo presentado á la comisión actual de constitución por el Sr. Valdés como individuo de dicha comisión. Mexico, 1822.

Constituciones de la Imperial Orden de Guadalupe instituida por la junta provisional gubernativa del imperio á propuesta del serenísimo señor generalíssimo almirante Don Agustín de Iturbide en 18 de Febrero de 1822. Mexico [1822].

Contestaciones que precedieron á la capitulación de la ciudad de Valladolid entre los señores coroneles D. Agustín de Iturbide y D. Luis Quintanar. Mexico, 1821.

Convenio del Sr. Chávarri con el ayuntamiento de Veracruz. Mexico, 1823.

Correspondencia entre el general D. Juan O'Donojú y el brigadier D. Francisco Lemaur y las últimas cartas de aquel al General Dávila con las respuestas de éste. Habana, 1821.

CUEVAS, MARIANO (ed.). *El Libertador. Documentos selectos de D. Agustín de Iturbide.* Mexico, 1947.

Decretos del rey Don Fernando VII, vols. I-VII. Madrid, 1818-1824.

Defensa de su magestad imperial contra sus declarados enemigos. Mexico, 1823.

Diario de las actas y discusiones de las cortes, legislatura de los años de 1820 y 1821, vols. XV-XXIII. Madrid, 1820-1821.

Diario de las discusiones y actas de las cortes, diputación general de los años 1822 y 1823, legislatura de 1822, 11 vols. Madrid, 1822.

Diario de la junta nacional instituyente del Imperio Mexicano, vol. I. Mexico, 1822.

Diario de las sesiones del congreso constituyente de la Federación Mexicana. Mexico, 1824.

Diario de las sesiones de cortes, legislatura extraordinaria (esta legislatura dió principio el día 22 de Setiembre de 1821 y terminó el 14 de Febrero de 1822), 3 vols. Madrid, 1871.

Diario de las sesiones de la soberana junta provisional gubernativa del Imperio Mexicano instalada según previenen el Plan de Iguala y Tratados de la villa de Córdova. Mexico, 1821.

DÍAZ NORIEGA, JOSÉ M. *Funestos recuerdos del libertador de México. Exhumación y autenticidad de sus respetables restos conducidos desde Padilla y depositados actualmente en la santa iglesia catedral.* Mexico, 1860.

Dictamen de la comisión especial de convocatoria para un nuevo congreso. Mexico, 1823.

Dictamen de la comisión de patronato leido en sesión pública del soberano congreso mexicano. Mexico, 1823.

Dictamen de la comisión de patronato del soberano congreso sobre la jurisdicción eclesiastico-castrense. Mexico, 1823.

Dictamen de la comisión de relaciones sobre las instrucciones que debe llevar el embiado á Roma con el objeto de establecer las correspondientes á esta república con la Silla Apostólica. Mexico [1824].

La Diplomacia mexicana, 3 vols. Mexico, 1910-1913.

In the District Court of the United States for the Northern District of

324　　　　　BIBLIOGRAPHY

California. On Appeal from the Decision from the United States Board of Land Commissioners. San Francisco, 1856.

Documentos citados en la contestación de la Sra. Da. Alicia G. de Iturbide al representante del ministerio público. Mexico, 1853.

Domínguez, José. *Justicia y negocios eclesiásticos, sección eclesiástica.* Mexico, 1822.

————. *Memoria presentada al soberano congreso mexicano por el secretario de estado y del despacho de justicia y negocios eclesiásticos.* Mexico, 1822.

Dublán, Manuel, and José M. Lozano (eds.). *Legislacion mexicana ó coleccion completa de las disposiciones legislativas expedidas desde la independencia de la republica,* vols. I-VI. Mexico, 1876-1877.

Echávarri, José A. *Proclama del Sr. Echávarri á los habitantes de Puebla y Veracruz.* Mexico, 1823.

Elogio de los excmos. Señores D. Agustín de Iturbide y D. Juan O'Donojú, individuos de la regencia del Nuevo Imperio Mejicano, que en los siguientes sonetos hizó el editor de la Abeja Poblana, D. José María Moreno, por encargo de un eclesiástico el cual le dió la idea en los Textos Sagrados que respectivamente preceden. Puebla, 1821.

Entrada pública en Valladolid de la Señora Doña Ana Huarte de Iturbide, digna esposa del inmortal caudillo y primer gefe del egército de las Tres Garantías. Valladolid, 1821.

Espinosa de los Monteros, Juan J. *Aviso al público.* Mexico, 1821.

Estatutos para la sociedad económica mexicana de amigos del pais. Mexico, 1822.

Expenditures on Account of Private Land Claims in California. Executive Document No. 84, House of Representatives, 36th Congress, 1st Session. Washington, 1860.

Fernández, León. *Colección de documentos para la historia de Costa Rica,* vol. X. Barcelona, 1907.

Fernández de Lizardi, José J. de. *Cincuenta preguntas del Pensador á quien quiera responderlas.* Mexico, 1821.

————. *Defensa de la libertad de la imprenta.* Mexico, 1821.

————. *Ideas políticas y liberales por el Pensador Mejicano.* Mexico, 1821.

————. *Oración de los crillos hecha por un Gachupin.* Mexico, 1822.

————. *El Pensador Mejicano al excmo. Señor general del ejército imperial americano, D. Agustín de Iturbide.* Mexico, 1821.

————. *Pésame que el Pensador Mejicano da al excelentísimo Señor generalísimo de las armas de América Don Agustín de Iturbide en la muerte del. excmo. Sr. Don Juan de O'Donojú.* Mexico, 1821.

————. *Por la salud de la patria se desprecia una corona.* Mexico, 1823.

————. *Sentencia contra el Emperador propuesta en el soberano congreso.* Mexico, 1823.

————. *El Sueño del Pensador no vaya á salir verdad, dedicado al soberano congreso de cortes.* Mexico, 1822.

————. *El Unipersonal de Don Agustín de Iturbide, Emperador que fue de México.* Mexico, 1823.

FILISOLA, VICENTE. *La Cooperación de México en la independencia de Centro América* (Documentos inéditos o muy raros para la historia de México, vols. XXXV and XXXVI). Mexico, 1911.

————. *Memorias para la historia de la guerra de Téjas,* vol. I. Mexico, 1848.

FONTE, PEDRO J. *Impugnación de algunos impíos, blasfemos, sacrílegios y sediciosos artículos del codigó de anarquía cujo título es: decreto constitucional para la libertad de la América sancionada en Apatzingán a 22 de Octubre de 1814.* Mexico, 1816.

GAMMELL, HANS P. N. (ed.). *The Laws of Texas, 1822-1897,* vol. I. Austin, 1898.

GARCÍA, GENARO (ed.) *Documentos historicos mexicanos,* 7 vols. Mexico, 1910.

————. *El Plan de independencia en la Nueva España en 1808.* Mexico, 1903.

GARCÍA DE TORRES, JOSÉ J. *Oración fúnebre de la Señora Doña María Josefa de Arámburu, Carrillo y Figueroa, Villaseñor y Cervantes, digna esposa del excmo. Señor D. José Joaquín de Iturbide y Arreguí, regente honorario, y madre tambien digna del serenísimo señor almirante y generalísimo de las armas del imperió Don Agustín de Arámburu.* Mexico, 1822.

————. *Solemnes exequias de la Señora Doña María Josefa Arámburu de Iturbide, digna madre del serenísimo Señor . . . Don Agustín de Iturbide y Arámburu celebradas en México . . . año de 1821.* Mexico, 1822.

GARZA, FELIPE DE LA. *Representación del brigadier D. Felipe de la Garza al Emperador.* Mexico, 1822.

GÓMEZ FARÍAS, VALENTÍN. *El Ministro es responsable á la prison de las ss. diputados. Voto particular del Señor Gómez Farías sobre el mismo asunto.* Mexico, 1822.

GÓMEZ DE NAVARRETE, JUAN. *Exposición que dirige al congreso general el ciudadano Juan Gómez Navarrete, como albacea del ecsmo. Sr. D. Agustín de Iturbide, promoviendo el cumplimiento del decreto de la junta soberana gubernativa de 21 de Febrero de 1822.* Mexico, 1832.

GÓMEZ PEDRAZA, MANUEL. *El Chantre Ramos Arizpe. Biografía la mas completa de este personaje.* Ramos Arizpe, 1935.

————. *Manifiesto del ciudadano Manuel Gómez Pedraza.* Mexico, 1823.

————. *Manifiesto que Manuel Gómez Pedraza, ciudadano de la república de Méjico, dedica á sus compatriotas ó sea una reseña de su vida pública.* New Orleans, 1831.

326   BIBLIOGRAPHY

Grito de república en Veracruz por el general Don Antonio López Santana.
Mexico, 1823.

GUERRERO, VICENTE. *Carta del general en gefe del sur, Vicente Guerrero,
Tixtla y Marzo de 1823.* Mexico, 1823.

———. *El Ciudadano Guerrero á la nación mexicana.* Mexico, 1823.

———. *Felicitación del exmo. Señor D. Vicente Guerrero á S. M. I.* Tixtla,
1822.

———. *Manifiesto del cuidadano Vicente Guerrero á sus compatriotas.*
Mexico, 1823.

———. *Manifiesto patriótico que hizó siendo comandante general de la
división del ejército de las Tres Garantías, D. Vicente Guerrero, para
desvanecer las imposturas y calumnias con que el conde del Venadito
pensaba alucinar á los ciudadanos y dividir las opiniones de los defensores
de la Patria.* Mexico, 1821.

GUERRERO, VICENTE, AND NICOLÁS BRAVO. *Plan ó indicaciones para reintegrar á la nación en sus naturales é imprescriptibles derechos y verdadera libertad de todo lo que se halla con escándalo de los pueblos cultos
violentamente despojada por D. Agustín de Iturbide, siendo esta medida
de tan extrema necesidad que sin ella es imposible el que la América
del Septentrion pueda disfrutar en lo venidero una paz solida y
permanente.* Mexico, 1823.

GUTIÉRREZ DEL MAZO, RAMÓN. *Aviso al público,* September 17, 1821; and
September 26, 1821. Mexico, 1821.

HALL, BASIL. *Extracts from a Journal Written on the Coasts of Chili, Peru,
and Mexico in the Years 1820, 1821, 1822,* vol. II. Edinburgh, 1824.

———. *Extracts from a Journal Written on the Coasts of Chili, Peru,
and Mexico in the Years 1820, 1821, 1822,* parts I and II. London,
1840.

HARDY, ROBERT W. H. *Travels in the Interior of Mexico in 1825, 1826,
1827, & 1828.* London, 1829.

HERNÁNDEZ Y DÁVALOS, JUAN E. (ed.). *Coleccion de documentos para la
historia de la guerra de independencia de Mexico de 1808 a 1821,* 6
vols. Mexico, 1877.

HERRERA, JOSÉ M. DE. *Lista de los señores diputados designados por
S. M. I. para que compongan la junta que ha de substituir al extinguido
congreso conforme al decreto imperial de 31 del último Octubre.* Mexico,
1822.

———. *Memoria presentada al soberano congreso mexicano por el secretario de estado y del despacho de relaciones interiores y exteriores.*
Mexico, 1822.

HUMBOLDT, ALEXANDER VON. *Atlas geographique et physique du Royaume
de la Nouvelle-Espagne, fondé sur des observations astronomique, des
mesures trigonometriques et des nivellements barométriques.* Paris,
1811.

————. *Essai politique sur le Royaume de la Nouvelle-Espagne*, 5 vols. Paris, 1811.

————. *Vues des cordillères et monumens des peuples indigènes de l'Amérique*. Paris, 1810.

I. N. T. *Carta al Dr. Monteagudo sobre las juntas secretas de la Profesa*. Mexico, 1826.

Idea de la conspiración descubierta en la capital del Imperio Mexicano en 26 de Agosto de este año publícase de orden de su gobierno. Mexico, 1822.

Indicación del origen de los extravios del congreso Mexicano que han motivado su disolución publícase de orden del gobierno. Mexico, 1822.

Instrucciones que los vireyes de Nueva España dejaron a sus sucesores. Añádense algunas que los mismos trajeron de la corte y otros documentos semejantes a las instrucciones. Mexico, 1867.

ITURBIDE, AGUSTÍN DE. *A la guarnición de esta capital el generalísimo de las armas*. Mexico, 1821.

————. *Agustín a sus conciudadanos*. Mexico, 1822.

———— [?]. *Arenga de S. M. á las tropas de su mando*. Mexico, 1823.

————. *Breve diseño crítico de la emancipacion y libertad de la nacion mexicana y de las causas que influyeron en sus mas ruidosos sucesos acaecidos desde el grito de Iguala hasta la espantosa muerte del libertador en la villa de Padilla*. Mexico, 1827.

————. *Breve manifiesto del exmo. Sr. D. Agustín de Iturbide, generalísimo del egército imperial megicano*. Mexico, 1821.

————. *Breve manifiesto del que subscribe*. Mexico, 1821.

————. *Carrera militar y politica de Don Agustin de Iturbide, ó sea memoria que escribió en Liorna antes de haber hecho la malhadada espedicion á su pátrio suelo donde terminó sus glorias perdiendo su vida en un cadalso á manos de los violentos Tamaulipas en la villa de Padilla el mes de Julio de 1824*. Mexico, 1827.

————. *Carta y despedida del Señor Iturbide á su hijo el mayor*. Mexico, 1838.

————. *Cartas que S. M. I. con motivo de su exaltación al trono dirigió al excmo. Sr. capitán general del sur y contestaciones que se dieron a S. M*. Tixtla, 1822.

————. *Católicos sentimientos del Sr. Generalísimo Don Agustín de Iturbide expresados en su carta al Señor obispo de Guadalajara*. Teloloapan, 1821.

————. *Comunicación oficial del primer gefe del ejército imperial de las Tres Garantías*. Mexico, 1821.

————. *. . . La Correspondencia de Agustín de Iturbide después de la proclamación del Plan de Iguala con una advertencia y una introduccion por Vito Alessio Robles* (Archivo historico militar mexicano, no. 1), 2 vols. Mexico, 1945.

328 BIBLIOGRAPHY

——. *Correspondencia y diario militar de Don Agustin de Iturbide,* 1810-1821 (Publicaciones del archivo general de la nacion, vols. IX, XI, XVI). Mexico, 1923-30.

——. *Correspondencia privada de Don Agustin de Iturbide y otros documentos de la epoca del archivo del teniente coronel Don Manuel de Iruela y Zamora* (Publicaciones del archivo general de la nacion, vol. XXIII). Mexico, 1933.

——. *Discurso al congreso,* February 24, 1822. Mexico, 1822.

——. *Don Agustín de Iturbide y Arámburu, Arreguí, Carrillo y Villaseñor, primer gefe del ejército imperial mejicano de las Tres Garantías.* Queretaro, 1821.

——. *El Emperador.* Mexico, 1823.

——. *El Emperador al ejército.* Mexico, 1822.

——. *Exposiciones dirigidas al soberano congreso general de la nación.* [On board the *Spring*], 1824.

——. *El Generalísimo almirante á sus conciudadanos.* Mexico, 1822.

——. *El Generalísimo almirante á los habitantes del Imperio.* Puebla, 1822.

——. *El Generalísimo al público.* Mexico, 1822.

——. *Legítima contestación de nuestro augusto Emperador al soberano congreso sobre la causa de los diputados presos.* Mexico, 1822.

——. *Manifiesto del general D. Agustín de Iturbide.* Mexico, 1871.

——. *Manifiesto de s.m. el Emperador.* Mexico, 1823.

——. *Manifiesto que el Señor D. Agustín de Iturbide dirije á los habitantes de Méjico.* Habana, 1821.

——. *Noticias plausibles comunicadas por las Provincias Internas del Oriente.* Mexico, 1821.

——. *Oficio y cartas del serenísimo sr. generalísimo almirante Don Agustín de Iturbide y otra en respuesta del general del castillo de S. Juan de Ulúa, Don José Dávila.* Mexico, 1822.

——. *Papel de S. M. Imperial dirigido al supremo consejo de regencia en 15 del corriente mes de Mayo.* Mexico, 1822.

——. *Pensamiento que en grande ha propuesto el que subscribe como un particular para la pronta convocatoria de las proximas cortes bajo el concepto de que se podrá aumentar ó disminuir el número de representantes de cada clase conforme acuerde la junta soberana con el supremo congreso de regencia.* Mexico, 1821.

——. *Poblanos ilustres.* Puebla, 1821.

——. *El Primer gefe del ejército imperial á la guarnición de Méjico.* Mexico, 1821.

——. *El Primer gefe del ejército imperial a los habitantes de México.* Tacubaya, 1821.

——. *El Primer gefe del exército imperial mexicano de las Tres Garantías á los habitantes de Puebla.* Puebla, 1821.

——. *El Primer gefe del ejército imperial mejicano de las Tres Garantías a los hijos y habitantes de la ciudad de Valladolid.* Huaniqueo, 1821.

——. *Proclama del generalísimo a sus conciudadanos para la convocatoría del congreso.* Mexico, 1821.

——. *Proclama del excmo. Señor Don Agustín de Iturbide.* Mexico, 1821.

——. *Proclama de s. m. el Emperador al ejército trigarante.* Mexico, 1823.

——. *Proclama del primer gefe del ejército imperial de las Tres Garantías a sus individuos.* Tacubaya, 1821.

——. *Proclama: El Primer gefe del ejército imperial de las Tres Garantías a los Españoles Europeos habitantes en esta América.* Puebla, 1821.

——. *S. M. el Emperador después de haber jurado en el congreso pronunció el discurso siguiente.* Mexico, 1822.

——. *A Statement of Some of the Principal Events in the Public Life of Agustin de Iturbide Written by Himself.* Translated by M. J. Quin. London, 1824.

——, AND JOSÉ DÁVILA. *Cartas de los Sres. generalísimo D. Agustín de Iturbide y teniente general Don José Dávila.* Mexico, 1822.

——, AND LUIS QUINTANAR. *Contestaciones que precedieron a la capitulación de la ciudad de Valladolid entre los señores coroneles D. Agustín de Iturbide y D. Luis Quintanar.* Mexico, 1821.

——, AND VICENTE GUERRERO. *Cartas de los Señores generales D. Agustín de Iturbide y D. Vicente Guerrero.* Mexico, 1821.

ITURBIDE, ALICIA G. DE. *Contestación de la señora albacea del general Don Agustín de Iturbide al pedimiento del represante del ministerio público en el incidente sobre aprobación de inventarios.* Mexico, 1878.

——, AND MIGUEL MARTÍNEZ. *Alegato de bien probado sobre la responsibilidad pecuniaria del lic. D. Juan N. Gómez Navarrete, apoderado y albacea del general D. Agustín de Iturbide y el abuso de su encargo cometido en haber donado la hacienda de San José Apeo á D. Mateo Echaiz.* [Mexico, 1878.]

ITURBIDE, ANA MARÍA HUARTE DE. *Representaciones que la viuda del exelentísimo Señor Don Agustín de Iturbide ha dirigido al supremo poder legislativo de los Estados-Unidos Mexicanos.* Mexico, 1833.

Iturbide caza Garzas sin disparar el fusil. Breve diseño de la desastrosa escena de cuatro de Julio en Madrid para escarmiento de México y sus revolucionarios. Mexico, 1822.

J. A. M. *México peligra, si Agustín I no se corona.* Mexico, 1822.

J. I. V. *Agustín y Ana María triunfaron en algun día de todos sus enemigos.* Mexico, 1823.

J. M. V. *Desahogo del sentimiento de un Americano en la sensible muerte*

330 BIBLIOGRAPHY

del exmo Sr. D. Juan de O'Donojú, caballero gran-cruz de las ordenes de Carlos III y San Hermenegildo, teniente general de los ejércitos nacionales de España. Mexico, 1821.

LABARRIETA, ANTONIO. *Informe del Dr. Don Antonio Labarrieta, cura de la ciudad de Guanajuato, sobre la conducta que observó Iturbide siendo comandante general del Bajío.* Mexico, 1821.

LAFRAGUA, JOSÉ M. *Composición leida el 27 de Setiembre de 1841 en honor del libertador Don Agustín de Iturbide.* Lagos, 1883.

LAGRANDA, FRANCISCO. *Consejo prudente sobre una de las garantías.* Mexico, 1821.

LEAL, CASIMIRO. *Refutación con notas interesantes al parte que dirigió al superior gobierno el teniente general Don Juan O'Donojú sobre el tratado que firmó en Córdoba.* Habana, 1822.

LECUNA, VICENTE (COMPILER), AND BIERCK, HAROLD A., JR. *Selected Writings of Bolivar,* 2 vols. New York, 1951.

Legitimidad de la elección de nuestro Emperador. Mexico, 1822.

LEMAUR, FRANCISCO. *Habitantes del reino de Méjico.* San Juan de Ulúa, 1822.

——. *Proclama que el general de San Juan de Ulúa dirija á los habitantes de este imperio conforme a las instrucciones que tiene del gobierno español.* Mexico, 1823.

EL LIBERAL JUICIOSO [pseudonym]. *Respuesta al sangriento papel conducta del Señor Iturbide.* Mexico, 1823.

LICEAGA, JOSÉ M. DE. *Adiciones y rectificaciones a la historia de Mexico que escribió D. Lucas Alaman.* Guanajuato, 1868.

Lista de los presos que fueron remitidos desde Tulancingo a Perote el día 10 de Abril por órden del ciudadano Nicolás Bravo. Mexico, 1823.

LLAVE, PABLO DE LA. *Memoria que el secretario de estado y del despacho universal de justicia y negocios eclesiásticos presenta al soberano congreso constituyente sobre los ramos del ministerio de su cargo leidó en la sesión de 8 de Noviembre de 1823.* Mexico [1823].

LUACES, DOMINGO. *Manifiesto.* Querétaro, 1821.

LULI [pseudonym]. *Refutación contra la memoria presentada por Don Miguel Cabrera Nevares sobre las Américas.* Madrid, 1821.

M. M. *Acta celebrada en Iguala el primero de Marzo y juramento que al día siguiente prestó el Sr. Iturbide con la oficialidad y tropa de su mando.* Mexico, 1821.

——. *Verdadera noticia del embarque de Sr. Iturbide y cargamento que lleva.* Mexico, 1823.

MALO, JOSÉ R. *Apuntes historicos sobre el destierro, vuelta al territorio mexicano y muerte del libertador D. Agustin de Iturbide.* Mexico, 1869.

——. *Funestos recuerdos del libertador de México. Exhumación y*

BIBLIOGRAPHY 331

autenticidad de sus respetables restos conducidos desde Padilla y depositados actualmente en la santa iglesia catedral. . . . Mexico, 1860.

Manda nuestro Emperador que ninguno le obedezca. Mexico, 1822.

Manifiesto del Emperador á los Mexicanos ó sea sueño de Iturbide. Mexico, 1823.

Manifiesto á los Mexicanos del regimiento infantería de línea número 1. Mexico, 1822.

Manifiesto a la nación mexicana de la junta de Puebla sobre la sesion del siete del corriente. Mexico, 1823.

Manifiesto de la suprema junta provisional gubernativa con el testimonio de su disolución. Mexico, 1822.

MANNING, WILLIAM R. (ed.). *Diplomatic Correspondence of the United States concerning the Independence of the Latin-American Nations,* 3 vols. New York, 1925.

MARCHA, PÍO. *Carta del capitán Don Pío Marcha á Don Guadalupe Victoria ó sea contestación á su proclama.* Mexico, 1843.

MARTÍNEZ, MIGUEL. *Testamentaría de Iturbide. Alegato de bien probado por el lic. D. Miguel Martínez en el juicio que sigue la albacea del general D. Agustín de Iturbide con D. José Ramón Malo sobre pesos.* Mexico, 1878.

MATEOS, JUAN A. (ed.). *Historia parlamentaría de los congresos mexicanos de 1821 á 1857,* vols. I-III. Mexico, 1877-1882.

MEDINA, ANTONIO DE. *Memoria presentada al soberano congreso mexicano por el secretario de estado y del despacho de la guerra.* Mexico, 1822.

Memoria presentada á s. a. s. la regencia del Imperio Mexicano sobre los principios en que debe fundarse un justo y razonable sistema de hacienda pública y los medios de arreglar la administración de este ramo para cubrir la falta que hay entre las rentas y gastos de estado. Mexico, 1822.

MENDIBIL, PABLO DE. *Resúmen histórico de la revolución de los Estados Unidos Mejicanos sacado del "Cuadro histórico"* . . . *que en forma de cartas escribió el lic. D. Carlos María Bustamante.* London, 1828.

MIER NORIEGA Y GUERRA, JOSÉ S. T. DE. *Diez cartas hasta hoy inéditas de Fray Servando Teresa de Mier se publican por iniciativa del c. alcalde primero Prof. Manuel Flores.* Monterrey, 1940.

———. *Historia de la revolución de Nueva España, antiguamente Anáhuac.* Mexico, 1922.

———. *Memoria política-instructiva enviada desde Filadelfia en Agusto de 1821 á los gefes independientes de Anáhuac llamados por los Españoles Nueva España.* Philadelphia, 1821.

MOLINOS, FRANCISCO. *Declaraciones de los derechos del hombre en sociedad.* Mexico, 1822.

[MONTÚFAR, MANUEL]. *Memorias para la historia de la revolución de Centro-América.* Jalapa, 1832.

Mora, José M. L. *Obras sueltas,* 2 vols. Paris, 1837.

Moreno y Jove, Manuel. *Oración funebre del Sr. D. Agustín de Iturbide pronunciada en la santa iglesia metropolitana de México en el día 28 de Septiembre del año de 1849.* Mexico, 1850.

Navarro y Noriega, Fernández. *Memoria sobre la población del reino de Nueva España.* Mexico, 1820.

Negrete, Pedro C. *Aviso patriótico.* Guadalajara, 1821.

———. *El General Negrete á sus compatriotas.* Puebla, 1823.

———. *Parrafo segundo de carta escrita por el Sr. brigadier D. Pedro Celestino Negrete al gefe primero del ejército imperial con fecha 31 de Agosto antes de la capitulación de Durango.* Mexico, 1821.

———, and Others. *El Supremo Poder Ejecutivo de la nación á sus compatriotas.* Querétaro, 1823.

[Nepomuzeno Cabrera, Juan]. *Notas al manifiesto publicado en Nueva-Orleans por el general D. Manuel Gómez Pedraza.* Mexico, 1831.

Ni Borbones ni Iturbide sino el congreso de la ley, exposición de D. Agustín Iturbide á Fernando VII. Mexico, 1824.

Noticia documentada de las últimas occurrencias con el Sr. D. Francisco Novella, mariscal de campo, sub-inspector de artillería y comandante general interino de la plaza de Méjico mandadas publicar por el Sr. D. Agustín de Iturbide, primer gefe de la nación, para conocimiento y satisfacción de las provincias. Puebla, 1821.

Noticia extraordinaria sobre la rendición de la capital. Mexico, 1823.

Noticias biográficas del exmo. Sr. D. Lucas Alamán, secretario de estado y del despacho de relaciones esteriores. Mexico, 1853.

Noticias circunstanciadas de la muerte de Iturbide para los que no la creen. Mexico, 1824.

Noticias plausibles comunicadas por las Provincias Internas del Oriente. Puebla, 1821.

Noticias de Goatemala favorables á Iturbide. Mexico, 1823.

Novella, Francisco. *Aviso.* Mexico, 1821.

———. *El Nuevo virey á los mexicanos.* Mexico, 1821.

———. *Proclama* (August 12, 1821). Mexico, 1821.

Obsequio poetico a los excelentísimos Señores D. Agustín Iturbide, primer gefe del egército trigarante y. D. Juan O'Donojú, precursor de la felicidad de este imperio. Mexico, 1821.

Observaciones á la carta que en 25 del último Julio dirigió el excmo. Sr. D. Pedro Celestino Negrete al ciudadano gobernador del estado libre de Jalisco, Luis Quintanar. Guadalajara, 1823.

Observaciones sobre algunos periódicos de la Habana. Mexico, 1822.

O'Donojú, Juan. *Habitantes de Nueva España.* Mexico, 1821.

———. *Manifiesto.* Vera Cruz, 1821.

———. *Manifiesto que por conducto del Señor gobernador intendente y gefe político de esta provincia hace á sus moradores el excmo. Señor capitán general y gefe superior político D. Juan O'Donojú.* Puebla, 1821.

———. *Modelo de virtud y filantropía: loor eterno al exmo. Señor capitán general Don Juan O'Donojú, carta de remisión al gobierno español del tratado celebrado en la villa de Córdova por el exmo. Señor Don Juan O'Donojú.* Mexico, 1822.

———. *Oficio del excmo. Señor Don Juan O'Donojú dirigido al Señor gobernador de la plaza de Vera Cruz.* Puebla, 1821.

———. *Segunda proclama del Señor O'Donojú á los dignos militares y heróicos habitantes de Vera Cruz.* Puebla, 1821.

Oficio de la junta de Puebla a los diputados de México. Mexico, 1823.

El Oficio que la comisión del soberano congreso presentó a S. M. I. y su contestación. Mexico, 1822.

O'Gorman, Edmundo (ed.). *Fray Servando Teresa de Mier, selección, notas y prólogo.* Mexico, 1945.

Olagaray, Roberto (ed.). *Coleccion de documentos historicos mexicanos,* vol. II. Mexico, 1924.

O'Leary, Daniel F. *Memorias del general O'Leary publicados por su hijo Simón B. O'Leary,* vols. XI and XIX. Caracas, 1880, 1882.

Orden de la función fúnebre en la traslación de las cenizas del Héroe de Iguala el día 26 del presente. Mexico, 1838.

Origen y destrucción del trono de Agustín Primero ó declamaciones de un buen patriota. Mexico, 1823.

Ortigosa, José. *Sermon que con motivo de la jura de independencia dijó en la iglesia parroquial de N. S. de la Asunción y N. P. S. Francisco de Toluca el día 13 de Mayo de 1822 el . . . lector jubilado.* Mexico, 1822.

Osés, Blas. *Oración inaugural en la apertura de la cátedra de constitución de la universidad literario de Méjico pronunciada el día 28 de Diciembre de 1820.* Mexico, 1821.

Pérez Lugo, J. [pseudonym] (ed.). *Le Cuestión religiosa en México: recopilación de leyes, disposiciones legales y documentos para el estudio de este problema politico.* Mexico, 1926.

Pérez Maldonado, Rafael. *Memoria que el ministro de hacienda presenta al soberano congreso sobre el estado del erario.* Mexico, 1822.

Pérez Martínez, Antonio J. *Discurso pronunciado por el Sr. Dr. D. Antonio Joaquín Pérez Martínez, obispo de la Puebla de los Angeles, entre las solemnidades de la misma que se cantó en la catedral de la misma el día 5 de Agosto de 1821.* Puebla, 1821.

———. *Sermon predicado en la santa iglesia metropolitana de Mégico el día 21 de julio de 1822 por el exmo. é illmo. Dr. D. Antonio Joaquín Pérez Martínez, dignísimo obispo de la Puebla de los Angeles, con motivo de la solemne coronación del Señor D. Agustín de Iturbide, primer emperador constitucional de Mégico.* Puebla, 1839.

El Plan republicano del triunvirato de Veracruz, Santana, Victoria y Lemaur, refutado por un amigo de la verdad. Mexico, 1823.

Planos del Sr. Iturbide para la nueva reconquista de América. Mexico, 1824.

[POINSETT, JOEL R.]. *Notes on Mexico, made in the autumn of 1822, accompanied by an Historical Sketch of the Revolution.* Philadelphia, 1824.

Posiciones que ha de contestar D. José Ramón Malo como albacea de Doña Nicolasa Iturbide en el juicio seguido por la testamentaría del general D. Agustín de Iturbide. Mexico, 1876.

Posiciones que se articulan á D. José Ramón Malo en el juicio sobre devolución de $20,000 y sus reditos legales que le ha promovido la albacea del general D. Agustín de Iturbide. Mexico, 1878.

PRADT, DOMINIQUE G. F. DE. *L'Europe et l'Amérique en 1822 et 1823,* 2 vols. Paris, 1824.

———. *Examen du plan présenté aux cortès, pour l'independance de l'Amérique Espagnol.* Paris, 1822.

Los Precursores idealógicos de la guerra de independencia (Publicaciones del archivo general de la nacion, vols. XIII and XXI). Mexico, 1929, 1932.

PRESAS, JOSÉ. *Juicio imparcial sobre las principales causas de la revolucion de la América Española y acerca de las poderosas razones que tiene la metropoli para reconocer su absoluta independencia.* Bordeaux, 1828.

———. *Memoria sobre el estado y situacion politica en que se hallaba el reino de Nueva España en Agosto de 1823 escrita en 20 de Febrero de 1824.* Madrid, 1824.

Primer centenario de la constitución de 1824 . . . dirigida por el Dr. D. Pedro de Alba y el Professor D. Nicolás Rangel. Mexico, 1924.

La Prison del Sr. Bravo por S.M.I. Mexico, 1823.

Proclamación de la libertad en las Provincias Internas del Oriente. [Monterrey, 1823.]

Proyecto del ceremonial que para la inauguración, consagración y coronación de su magestad el Emperador Agustín Primero se presentó por la comisión encargada de formarlo al soberano congreso en 17 de Junio de 1822. Mexico, 1822.

Proyecto de reglamento politico de gobierno del Imperio Mexicano presentado a la junta nacional instituyente y leido en sesión ordinaria de 31 de Diciembre de 1822. Mexico, 1823.

Proyecto de reglamento provisional de la regencia del imperio leido en la sesión pública del soberano congreso constituyente mexicana el dia 13 de Abril de 1822. Mexico, 1822.

Proyecto de la república federal de México, ó sea discurso importante a la nación. Mexico, 1823.

Publicaciones del Archivo General de la Nación, vol. XXIII. Mexico, 1933.

R.M., *Conducta de Don Agustín Iturbide.* Mexico, 1823.

RAMÍREZ Y SESMA, JOAQUÍN (ed.). *Coleccion de decretos, ordenes y circulares espedidas por los gobiernos nacionales de la Federación Mexicana desde el año de 1821 hasta el de 1826 para el arreglo del ejercito de los Estados-Unidos Mexicanos.* Mexico, 1827.

Un Regalo de año nuevo para el Señor Rocafuerte ó consideraciones sobre sus consideraciones. Escritas por uno que lo conoce. Mexico, 1832.

Reglamento para formar el ceremonial con que deben ser trasladados y colocados en la catedral de México los restos del Héroe de Iguala D. Agustín de Iturbide. Mexico, 1838.

Reglamento para el gobierno interior de la soberana junta provisional gubernativa del Imperio Mexicano. Mexico, 1821.

Reglamento de la Orden de San Fernando y de la de San Hermenegildo. Madrid, 1815.

Reglamento que han de observar la camerara mayor, damas y camaristas de s. m. la Emperatriz en los vestidos y adornos . . . qdo. se hallen en servicio. Mexico, 1822.

Representación que los generales y gefes del ejército reunidos la noche del 11 del corriente en junta presidida por el capitán general de la provincia dirigieron al serenísimo señor generalísimo almirante para que s. a. tomose las providencias oportunas á fin de proceder legalmente contra el autor del papel intitulado: Consejo prudente sobre una de las garantías y evitar los males que pudiese producir la circulación de tan escandaloso folleto. Mexico, 1821.

REVILLAGIGEDO, JUAN V. *Instruccion reservada que el conde de Revilla Gigedo dio a su succesor en el mando, Marqués de Branciforte, sobre el gobierno de este continente en el tiempo que fue su virey.* Mexico, 1831.

[ROCAFUERTE, VICENTE]. *Bosquejo ligerísimo de la revolución de Mégico desde el grito de Iguala hasta la proclamación imperial de Iturbide. Por un verdadero Americano.* Philadelphia, 1822.

———. *Ideas necesarias á todo pueblo independiente que quiera ser libre.* Mexico, 1861.

ROMERO, MATÍAS (ed.). *Bosquejo histórico de la agregación á México de Chiapas y Soconusco . . . Colección de documentos oficiales que sirve de respuesta al opusculo de D. Andrés Dardon intitulado "La cuestión de límites entre México y Guatemala,"* vol. I. Mexico, 1877.

SAN MARTÍN, JOSÉ DE. *San Martín, su correspondencia. 1823-1850.* Buenos Aires, 1911.

SANTA ANNA, ANTONIO LÓPEZ DE. *Mi Historia militar y politica, 1810-1874. Memorias ineditas.* (Documentos para la historia de México, vol. II). Mexico, 1905.

———. *Manifiesto de Antonio López de Santana á sus conciudadanos.* Mexico, 1823.

————. *Manifiesto á sus compatriotas.* Vera Cruz, 1823.

————. *Manifiesto del brigadier Santana á los habitantes y tropa de Veracruz.* Mexico, 1822.

————. *Manifiesto que hace á la nación americana el teniente coronel D. Antonio López de Santa Anna.* . . . Puebla, 1821.

————. *Muerte del Señor Concha.* Mexico, 1821.

————. *Proclamas del brigadier Santana á los habitantes y tropa de Veracruz.* Mexico, 1822.

————, AND GUADALUPE VICTORIA. *Plan ó indicaciones para reintegrar á la nación en sus naturales é inprescriptibles derechos y verdadera libertad, de todo lo que se halla con escándalo de los pueblos cultos violentamente despoida por D. Agustín de Iturbide, siendo esta medida de tan extrema necesidad que sin ella es imposible el que la América del Septentrion pueda disfrutar en lo venidero una paz sólida y permanente.* Mexico, 1823.

SANTA MARÍA, MANUEL. *Despedida del ministro plenipotenciario de la República de Colombia cerca del gobierno de México.* Mexico, 1822.

Segunda parte de la conducta de Iturbide. Mexico, 1823.

Señores consejeros de estado nombrados por S.M.I. a consequencia de la propuesta hecha por el soberano congreso constituyente. Mexico, 1822.

Sentencia contra el Emperador propuesta en el soberano congreso. Mexico, 1823.

Sesiones extraordinarias del congreso constituyente con motivo del arresto de algunos señores diputados. Mexico, 1822.

Solemnes exequias de la Señora Doña María Josefa Arámburu de Iturbide, digna madre del serenísimo señor generalísimo almiranto de este imperio Don Agustín de Iturbide y Arámburu, celebradas en la parroquia de San Pablo por su imperial congregación del santísimo sacramento. Mexico, 1822.

SOTA RIVA, MANUEL DE LA. *Ministerio de guerra y marina,* December 21, 1822. Mexico, 1822.

Tercer trueno de la libertad en México ó sea nombramiento del excmo. Señor Marqués de Vivanco de general en gefe del Ejército Libertador. Mexico, 1823.

Testamentaría de Iturbide. Memorandum sobre los sueldos, la pensión, los terrenos y el millión de pesos decretados en favor del libertador D. Agustín de Iturbide. Mexico, 1878.

Testamento de Iturbide que otorgó antes de embarcarse. Mexico, 1823.

TORNEL, JOSÉ M. *Manifiesto del origen, causas, progresos y estado de la revolución del Imperio Mexicano con relación á la antigua España.* Mexico, 1821.

TORRENTE, MARIANO. *Historia de la revolucion hispano-americana,* 3 vols. Madrid, 1829-1830.

Tres palabrítas á Victoria y Santana por varios amantes de S. M. Mexico, 1823.

Triunfo de la libertad de la imprenta, no. 3. Puebla, 1821.

Triunfo de la libertad mejicana ó sea resumen oficial de los progresos de la independencia de Nueva España bajo el plan que en los días 1 y 2 de Marzo del presente año de 1821 proclamó y juró en Iguala Sr. D. Agustín de Iturbide entonces comandante general de las tropas del sur y hoy primer gefe del ejército imperial mejicana de las Tres Garantías. Guadalajara, 1821.

VALDÉS, ANTONIO J. *Constitución del imperio ó proyecto de organización del poder legislativo presentado á la comisión actual de constitución por el Sr. Valdés como individuo de dicha comisión. Publicado con el fin de excitar el partiotismo de los hombres ilustrados en asunto tan interesante.* Mexico, 1822.

VALLE, RAFAEL HELIODORO (ed.). *La Anexión de Centro América á México. Documentos y escritos* (Archivo histórico diplomático mexicano, First Series, nos. 11, 24, 40; Second Series, nos. 3, 4, 7), vols. I-VI. Mexico, 1926-1949.

———. *Valle, prólogo y selección.* Mexico, 1943.

VERA, FORTINO H. (ed.). *Colección de documentos eclesiasticos de Mexico o sea antigua y moderna legislación de la iglesia mexicano,* 3 vols. Amecameca, 1887.

VICTORIA, GUADALUPE. *Proclama de Don Guadalupe Victoria á las provincias de oriente y occidente.* Mexico, 1823.

VILLAVICENCIO, PABLO DE. *Manifiesto del Payo del Rosario á sus compatriotas ó sea suplemento á la memoria del Sr. Iturbide.* Mexico, 1827.

———. *El Payo del Rosario á la grata memoria de Iturbide.* Mexico, 1826.

——— (ed.). *Representaciones de D. Agustín de Iturbide para venir á México.* Mexico, 1827.

———. *Tristes recuerdos del hombre de Iguala.* [Toluca], 1827.

VIVANCO, MARQUÉS DE. *El Marqués de Vivanco á los militares.* Mexico, 1823.

WASHINGTON NAPOLEON [pseudonym]. *Retrato vivo del hombre que se llamo Emperador.* Mexico, 1823.

WEBSTER, CHARLES K. (ed.). *Britain and the Independence of Latin America, 1812-1830,* 2 vols. London, 1938.

Ya se va Agustín Primero desterrado y sin corona. Mexico, 1823.

ZAVALA, LORENZO DE. *Ensayo histórico de las revoluciones de México desde 1808 hasta 1830.* 2 vols. Mexico, 1918.

———. *Proyecto de reforma del congreso.* Mexico, 1822.

———, AND OTHERS. *Proyecto del plan de hacienda para el año económico de 1823 presentado por su comisión y leidó en la sesión extraordinaria del 6 del presente mes.* Mexico, 1822.

ZÉRECERO, ANASTASIO. *Memorias para la historia de las revoluciones en México.* Mexico, 1869.

ZOZAYA, JOSÉ M. B. *Oración cívica pronunciada en la Alameda el 27 de Octubre de 1841.* Mexico, 1841.

ZÚÑIGA Y ONTIVEROS, MARIANO J. DE. *Calendario manual y guía de forasteros en México.* Mexico, 1817, 1821.

II. Newspapers, Periodicals, and Other Publications

1. Newspapers and Periodicals

In some cases the sets used were not complete for the periods here specified.

La Abeja Poblana. Puebla, 1820.

La Abispa de Chilpancingo escrita para perpetuar la memoria del primer congreso instalado allí el día 12 de Septiembre de 1813 por el Señor D. José María Morelos. Mexico, 1821-1824.

La Aguila Mexicana. Periódico quotidiano político y literario. Mexico, 1823-1825.

The Annual Register or a View of the History, Politics, and Literature. London, 1810-1825.

Annuaire historique universel, 1821-1824, ed. C. L. Lesure. Paris, 1822-1825.

Aurora, Philadelphia, 1820-1824.

The Chicago Times, Chicago, January 17, 1887.

The Courier, London, 1824.

Diario Político Militar Mejicano. San Nicolás Tolentino, 1821; Puebla, 1821.

Diario de Vera Cruz, Vera Cruz, 1822-1823.

El Farol, periódico semanario de la Puebla de los Angeles en el Imperio Mejicano, Puebla, 1821-1822.

Ejército imperial mejicano de las Tres Garantías, papel volante, 1821.

Gaceta del gobierno de Guadalajara, Guadalajara, 1821-1822.

Gaceta de Madrid, Madrid, 1821-1824.

Gazeta de Mexico (with varying title indicated in footnotes), Mexico, 1784-1825.

Journal de Paris, Paris, 1824.

El Mejicano Independiente, 1821.

El Monitor Ultramarino, Madrid, 1822.

Le Moniteur universal, Paris, 1821.

The National Intelligencer, Washington, 1860.

Niles' Weekly Register, vols. XXI-XXV, Baltimore, 1821-1824.

Noticioso General, Mexico, 1821-1823.

El Precursor, Mexico, August 10, 1841.

La Sabatina Universal, periódico político y literario, vol. I. Mexico, 1822.

Semanario Político y Literario de México, 4 vols. Mexico, 1820-1822.

El Sol. Mexico, 1821-1825.

The Times. London, 1822-1825.

El Universal, . . . *Edición conmemorativa del primer centenario de la independencia mexicana.* Mexico, 1921.

La Voz de México. Mexico, September 27, 1881.

Voz de la Patria, vol. II. Mexico, 1830.

2. Articles in Newspapers, Periodicals, and Other Publications

"El acta original de la independencia de Centro América," *Anales de la sociedad de geografía é historia de Guatemala,* XI, 3-11. Guatemala, 1934.

"Bolívar y Iturbide," *Boletin del archivo general de la nacion,* vol. II, no. 1, pp. 3-24. Mexico, 1931.

BOLTON, HERBERT E. "General James Wilkinson as Advisor to Emperor Iturbide," *Hispanic American Historical Review,* I, 163-180. Durham, N. C., 1918.

———. "The Iturbide Revolution in the Californias," *ibid.,* II, 188-242. Durham, N. C., 1919.

"Cartas confidenciales de D. Agustín de Iturbide durante su expatriación," *La Voz de México,* September 27, 28, and 29, 1879. Mexico.

"Una correspondencia desconocida de Don Agustín de Iturbide," *El Universal,* September, 1921. Mexico.

"Descripción de la entrada del ejército trigarante en México," *Boletin del archivo general de la nacion,* vol. X, no. 3, pp. 481-497. Mexico, 1939.

"Examen de la memoria del ministro de ultramar leido en las córtes el día 6 de Marzo de 1822," *El Mercurio Ultramarino* (May 15, 1822), pp. 81-103. Madrid, 1822.

GONZÁLEZ OBREGÓN, LUIS. "Un manifiesto de Iturbide," *Revista de Revistas,* September 25, 1921. Mexico.

"La independencia y el Pensador Mexicano," *Boletin del archivo general de la nacion,* vol. VI, no. 4, pp. 621-628. Mexico, 1935.

ITURBIDE, AGUSTÍN DE. "Political Life of the Ex-Emperor of Mexico, Don Agustín de Iturbide, Written by Himself during His Residence at Leghorn, and Dated September 27, 1823." *The Pamphleteer,* XXVIII, 395-435. London, 1827.

"James Wilkinson on the Mexican Revolution, 1823," *Bulletin of the New York Public Library,* vol. III, no. 9, pp. 361-364. New York, 1899.

LECUNA, VICENTE. "La Conferencia de Guayaquil. Documentos referentes a la conferencia," *Boletin de la academia nacional de la historia,* vol. XXVI, no. 101, pp. 3-80. Caracas, 1943.

"Las Mulas de Iturbide," *Boletin del archivo general de la nacion,* vol. II, no. 1, pp. 71-93. Mexico, 1931.

"Notable carta del cura de Guanajuato, Dr. D. Antonio Lavarrieta," *ibid.,* vol. I, no. 1, pp. 89-97. Mexico, 1930.

340 BIBLIOGRAPHY

"Papeles de Iturbide entregados antes de ser fusilado," *ibid.*, vol. II, no. 2, pp. 161-180. Mexico, 1931.

B. SECONDARY ACCOUNTS

A. BOOKS AND PAMPHLETS

Note: Some secondary accounts contain useful source materials.

ALAMÁN, LUCAS, AND OTHERS. *Episodios históricos de la guerra de independencia*, 2 vols. Mexico, 1910.

ALESSIO ROBLES, VITO. *Coahuila y Texas desde la consumación de la independencia hasta el tratado de paz de Guadalupe Hidalgo*, vol. I. Mexico, 1945.

———. *Miguel Ramos Arizpe. Discursos, memorias y informes, notas biográficas y bibliográficas y acotaciones.* Mexico, 1942.

———. *Ramos Arizpe.* Mexico, 1937.

———. *Monterrey en la historia y en la leyenda.* Mexico, 1936.

ANCONA, ELIGIO. *Historia de Yucatán desde la época mas remota hasta nuestros días*, vol. III. Barcelona, 1889.

ANZURES, RAFAEL. *Los Heroes de la independencia, Colección de biografías de los principales heroes de la independencia de México.* Tlaxcala, 1909.

Apuntes biográficos del señor prebendado de la santa iglesia metropolitana de Méjico, lic. D. Epigmenio de la Piedra. Mexico, 1873.

Apuntes para una bibliografía militar de Mexico, 1536-1936. Mexico, 1937.

BANCROFT, HUBERT H. *History of Central America*, vol. III (*Works*, vol. VIII). San Francisco, 1887.

———. *History of Mexico*, vol. IV (*Works*, vol. XII). San Francisco, 1885.

BANEGAS GALVÁN, FRANCISCO. *Historia de Mexico*, vol. I. Mexico, 1938; vol. II. Morelia, 1923.

BARKER, EUGENE C. *The Life of Stephen F. Austin.* Nashville, 1925.

BETTS, BENJAMIN. *Mexican Imperial Coinage. The Medals and Coins of Augustine I (Iturbide), Maximilian, the French Invasion, and of the Republic during the French Intervention.* Boston, 1899.

BOLTON, HERBERT E. *Guide to Materials for the History of the United States in the Principal Archives of Mexico.* Washington, 1913.

BUITRON, JUAN B. *El Seminario de Michoacán.* Morelia, 1940.

BULNES, FRANCISCO. *La Guerra de independencia, Hidalgo, Iturbide.* Mexico, 1910.

CALLCOTT, WILFRED H. *Santa Anna. The Story of an Enigma Who Once Was Mexico.* Norman, Oklahoma, 1936.

CASTAÑEDA, CARLOS E., AND JACK A. DABBS. *Guide to the Latin-American Manuscripts in the University of Texas Library.* Cambridge, 1939.

CASTILLO LEDÓN, LUIS. *Hidalgo, La Vida del Héroe*, 2 vols. Mexico, 1948-1949.

CASTILLO NEGRETE, EMILIO DEL. *Mexico en el siglo xix o sea su historia desde 1800 hasta la epoca presente.* Vols. IX-XVII. Mexico, 1884-1889.

CHÁVEZ OROZCO, LUIS. *Historia de México, 1808-1836.* Mexico [1947].

CORTI, COUNT EGON CAESAR. *Maximilian und Charlotte von Mexiko,* vol. II. Zurich, 1923.

COSSIO, DAVID A. *Historia de Nuevo León,* vol. V. Monterrey, 1925.

COTNER, THOMAS E. *The Military and Political Career of José Joaquín de Herrera* (University of Texas Latin-American Studies, vol. VII). Austin, 1949.

CUEVAS GONZAGA, LUIS. *Porvenir de México ó juicio sobre su estado político en 1821 y 1851.* Mexico, 1851.

CUEVAS, MARIANO. *Historia de la iglesia en Mexico,* vol. V. El Paso, 1928.

———. *Historia de la nacion mexicana.* Mexico, 1940.

DECORME, GERARD. *Historia de la Compañía de Jesús en la República Mexicana durante el siglo xix,* vol. I. Guadalajara, 1914.

FISHER, LILIAN E. *The Background of the Revolution for Mexican Independence.* Boston, 1934.

FONSECA, FABIAN DE, AND CARLOS DE URRUTIA. *Historia general de la real hacienda,* 6 vols. Mexico, 1845-1853.

FUENTE, JOSÉ M. DE LA. *Hidalgo íntimo, apuntes y documentos para una biografía del benemérito cura de Dolores D. Miguel Hidalgo y Costilla.* Mexico, 1910.

GALARZA, ERNEST. *The Roman Catholic Church as a Factor in the Political and Social History of Mexico.* Sacramento, 1928.

GALLO, EDUARDO L. (ed.). *Hombres ilustres mexicanos. Biografías de los personajes notables desde antes de la conquista hasta nuestros días,* 4 vols. Mexico, 1873-1874.

GANS, A. I. (ed.). *Catalogue of Mexican Pamphlets in the Sutro Collection,* 1623-1828 (Sutro Branch, California State Library). San Francisco, 1941. [Mimeographed.]

———. *Supplement to the Catalogue of Mexican Pamphlets in the Sutro Collection,* 1605-1828 (Sutro Branch, California State Library). San Francisco, 1941. [Mimeographed.]

GARCÍA CARRAFFA, ALBERTO AND ARTURO. *Diccionario heráldico y genealógico de apellidos españoles y americanos,* vol. XLVI. Salamanca, 1932.

GATES, WILLIAM. *The William Gates Collection: Manuscripts, Documents, Printed Literature relating to Mexico and Central America.* [New York, 1924.]

GILLIAM, ALBERT M. *Travels over the Table Lands and Cordilleras of Mexico during the Years 1843 and 44; including a Description of California, the principal Cities and Mining Districts of that Republic, and the Biographies of Iturbide and Santa Anna.* Philadelphia, 1846.

342 BIBLIOGRAPHY

Gómez, Marte R. *Iturbide. El Movimiento de independencia de México en sus relaciones con la causa de la libertad en México y en España.* Mexico, 1939.

González, José E. *Biografía del benemérito mexicano D. Servando Teresa de Mier Noriega y Guerra.* Monterrey, 1876.

González Obregón, Luis. *Don José Joaquin Fernández de Lizardi (El Pensador Mexicano), apuntes biográficos y bibliográficos.* Mexico, 1888.

——. *México en 1810.* Mexico, 1943.

——. *México viejo, 1521-1821.* Paris, 1900.

——, and Juan P. Baz. *Fray Melchor de Talamantes. Biografía y escritos póstumos.* Mexico, 1909.

Gropp, Arthur E. *Manuscripts in the Department of Middle American Research* (Middle American Pamphlets, no. 5). New Orleans, 1933.

Gruening, Ernest H. *Mexico and Its Heritage.* Mexico, 1928.

Guía del archivo histórico de hacienda, siglos xvi a xix. Mexico, 1940.

Guzmán y Raz Guzmán, Jesús. *Bibliografía de la independencia de México* (Bibliografías mexicanas, nos. 4, 5, 6). Mexico, 1937-1939.

Haggard, J. Villasana. *Handbook for Translators of Spanish Historical Documents.* Oklahoma City, 1941.

Hernández, Agustín. *El Archivo historico de hacienda.* Mexico, 1946.

Historia de la vida y reinado de Fernando VII de España, 3 vols. Madrid, 1842.

Iconografía de los gobernantes de la Nueva España tomada de la colección que se conserva en el salón de cabildos del palació municipal de la ciudad de México. Mexico, 1921.

Iguíniz, Juan B. *Bibliografía biográfica mexicana,* vol. I, *Repertorios biográficos* (Monografías bibliográficas mexicanas, no. 18). Mexico, 1930.

——. *El Escudo de armas nacionales.* Paris, 1920.

Iturbide, Eduardo. *Mi Paso por la vida.* Mexico, 1941.

Ker, Anita M. *Mexican Government Publications. A Guide to the Most Important Publications of the National Government of Mexico. . . .* Washington, 1940.

Kératry, Ernesto de. *El Drama de Padilla, una rectificación histórica.* Victoria, 1892.

Lafuente, Modesto, and Juan Valera. *Historia general de España desde los tiempos primitivos hasta la muerte de Fernando VII,* vols. XVI-XIX. Barcelona, 1889-1890.

Lafuente Ferrari, Enrique. *El Virrey Iturrigaray y los orígenes de la independencia de Méjico.* Madrid, 1941.

Lerdo de Tejada, Miguel M. *Apuntes históricos de la heroica ciudad de Vera-Cruz,* vol. II. Mexico, 1940.

Leturia, Pedro. *La Acción diplomática de Bolívar ante Pío VII.* Madrid, 1925.

Lista de documentos inéditos para la historia de México. [Typewritten.]

Mc Leish, John L. *High Lights of the Mexican Revolution.* Cincinnati, 1918.

Maggs Bros. *Bibliotheca Americana et Philippina, Catalogue No. 429,* part I; *Catalogue No. 465,* part IV. London, 1922, 1925.

Marure, Alejandro. *Bosquejo historico de las revoluciones de Centro-America desde 1811 hasta 1834,* vol. I. Guatemala, 1877.

Mateos, José M. *Historia de la masonería en México desde 1806 hasta 1884.* Mexico, 1884.

Medina Ascensio, Luis. *La Santa Sede y la emancipacion mexicana.* Guadalajara, 1946.

Miquel i Vergés, Josep M. *La Independencia mexicana y la prensa insurgente.* Mexico, 1941.

Mora, José M. L. *Méjico y sus revoluciones,* 3 vols. Paris, 1856.

Moreno, Landelino, . . . *Historia de las relaciones interestatuales de Centroamérica.* Madrid, 1928.

Navarro y Rodrigo, Carlos. *Iturbide.* Madrid, 1869.

——. *Agustin de Iturbide. Vida y memorias.* Mexico, 1906.

——. *Vida de Agustín de Iturbide, Memorias de . . .* (Biblioteca Ayacucho, vol. XXXVII). Madrid, 1919.

O'Gorman, Edmundo. *Breve historia de las divisiones territoriales* (Trabajos juridicos de homenaje a la escuela libre de derecho en su xxv aniversario, vol. II). Mexico, 1937.

Olavarría y Ferrari, Enrique. *México independiente, 1821-1855* (*México a través de los siglos,* vol. IV). Barcelona [c. 1880].

Osorno Castro, Fernando. *El Insurgente Albino Garcia.* Mexico, 1940.

Ortega y Pérez Gallardo, Ricardo. *Historia genealógica de las familias mas antiguas de México, segunda parte,* vol. III. Mexico, 1910.

Pacheco, José R. *Descripcion de la solemnidad fúnebre con que se honraron las cenizas del Héroe de Iguala Don Agustin de Iturbide en Octubre de 1838.* Mexico, 1849.

Páez Brotchie, Luis. *La Nueva Galicia a través de su viejo archivo judicial.* Mexico, 1939.

Paxson, Frederic L. *The Independence of the South-American Republics: A Study in Recognition and Foreign Policy.* Philadelphia, 1903.

Payno, Manuel. *Bosquejo biográfico de los generales Iturbide y Terán.* Mexico, 1843.

Peral, Miguel A. *Diccionario biográfico mexicano,* vols. I-III. Mexico [1944].

Peralta, Hernan G. *Agustín de Iturbide y Costa Rica.* San José de Costa Rica, 1944.

Pérez Verdia, Luis. *Compendio de la historia de México.* Guadalajara, 1935.

344 BIBLIOGRAPHY

———. *Historia particular del estado de Jalisco*, vol. II. Guadalajara, 1910.

PESADO, JOSÉ J. *El Libertador de México, D. Agustín de Iturbide.* Mexico, 1872.

PI Y MARGALL, FRANCISCO, AND F. PI Y ARSUAGA. *Historia de España en el siglo xix*, vol. II. Barcelona, 1903.

PRIESTLEY, HERBERT I. *José de Gálvez, Visitor-General of New Spain* (University of California Publications in History, vol. V). Berkeley, 1916.

PUTNAM, HERBERT. *Report of the Librarian of Congress . . . for the fiscal year ending June 30, 1912.* Washington, 1912.

RADIN, PAUL (ed.). *Catalogue of Mexican Pamphlets in the Sutro Collection, 1623-1826* (Sutro Branch, California State Library). San Francisco, 1939-1940. [Mimeographed.]

———. *The Opponents and Friends of Lizardi* (*Occasional Papers, Mexican History Series*, no. 2, part II, Sutro Branch, California State Library). San Francisco, 1939. [Mimeographed.]

RAMÍREZ CABAÑAS, JOAQUÍN. *Las Relaciones entre Mexico y el Vaticano* (Archivo historico diplomatico mexicano, no. 27). Mexico, 1928.

RAMOS, ROBERTO. *Bibliografía de la revolución mexicana* (Monografías bibliográficas mexicanas, nos. 21 and 30), vols. I and II: vol. III published in *Bibliografías mexicanas*, no. 9. Mexico, 1931-1935.

RAMOS PEDRUEZA, ANTONIO. *El Plan de Iguala. Sus orígines y su importancia.* Mexico, 1921.

RICHMAN, IRVING B. *California under Spain and Mexico, 1535-1847.* Boston, 1911.

RIPPY, JAMES F. *Joel R. Poinsett, Versatile American.* Durham, N. C., 1935.

RIVERA CAMBAS, MANUEL. *Historia antigua y moderna de Jalapa y de las revoluciones en el estado de Veracruz*, vol. II. Mexico, 1869.

———. *Los Gobernantes de México. Galería de biografías y retratos de los vireyes, emperadores, presidentes y otros gobernantes que han tenido México desde Don Hernando Cortes hasta el C. Benito Juarez*, 2 vols. Mexico, 1872-1873.

ROBERTSON, WILLIAM S. *France and Latin-American Independence.* Baltimore, 1938.

———. *The Life of Miranda*, 2 vols. Chapel Hill, 1929.

———. *Rise of the Spanish-American Republics as Told in the Lives of Their Liberators.* New York, 1918.

ROBINSON, FAY. *Mexico and Her Military Chieftains from the Revolution of Hidalgo to the Present Time.* Philadelphia, 1847.

ROMERO FLORES, JESÚS. *Iconografía colonial; retratos de personajes notables en la historia colonial de México existentes en el museo nacional.* Mexico, 1940.

BIBLIOGRAPHY

345

Romero de Terreros, Manuel. *La Corte de Agustín I, Emperador de México.* Mexico, 1921.

Rosa, Ramón. *Biografía de Don José Cecilio del Valle.* Tegucigalpa, 1943.

Rydjord, John. *Foreign Interest in the Independence of New Spain.* Durham, N. C., 1935.

Salado Álvarez, Victoriano. *La Vida azarosa y romántica de Don Carlos María de Bustamante.* Madrid, 1933.

Salgado, Bernardo. *El Abrazo de Acatempan.* Mexico, 1937.

Santibáñez, Enrique. *El Plan de Iguala ó de las Tres Garantías.* Mexico, 1921.

Serrano de Wilson, Emilia (Baronesa de). *México y sus gobernantes de 1519 a 1910; biografías, retratos y autógrafos (iconografía completa),* 2 vols. Barcelona, 1910.

Sierra, Justo (ed.). *México, su evolución social,* 3 vols. in 2. Mexico, 1900-1902.

Spell, Jefferson R. *The Life and Works of José Joaquín Fernández de Lizardi.* Philadelphia, 1931.

Sprague, William F. *Vicente Guerrero, Mexican Liberator: A Study in Patriotism.* Chicago, 1939.

Suarez y Navarro, Juan. *Historia de México y del general Antonio Lopez de Santa-Anna.* Mexico, 1850.

Temperley, Harold. *The Foreign Policy of Canning, 1822-1827.* London, 1925.

Toro, Alfonso. *Biografía del ilustre coahuilense D. Miguel Ramos Arizpe.* Saltillo, 1919.

———. *Compendio de historia de Mexico: la revolucion de independencia y Mexico independiente.* Mexico, 1943.

———. *Dos Constituyentes del año de 1824. Biografías de Don Miguel Ramos Arizpe y Don Lorenzo Zavala.* Mexico, 1925.

———. *La Iglesia y el estado en México.* Mexico, 1927.

Torre, Antonio Rivera de la. *Francisco Javier Mina y Pedro Moreno.* Mexico, 1917.

Torres Lanzas, Pedro (ed.). *Independencia de América, fuentes para su estudio,* primera serie, 6 vols. Madrid, 1912; segunda serie, Seville, 1924.

Twitchell, Ralph E. *The Spanish Archives of New Mexico,* 2 vols. Cedar Rapids, 1914.

Urbina, Luis G., Pedro H. Ureña, and Nicolás Rangel. *Antología del centenario, estudio documentado de la literatura mexicana durante el primer siglo de independencia,* 2 vols. Mexico, 1910.

Valadés, José C. *Alamán, estadista e historiador.* Mexico, 1938.

Valle, Rafael Heliodoro. *Bibliografía de Don José Cecilio del Valle.* Mexico, 1934.

———. *Como era Iturbide.* Mexico, 1922.

———. *Iturbide, hombre de Díos* (vol. XII, Vidas mexicanas). Mexico, 1944.

VALLEJO, ANTONIO R. *Compendio de la historia social y política de Honduras aumentada con los principales acontecimientos de Centro América,* vol. I. Tegucigalpa, 1926.

VARIOS JACOBINOS. *El Libertador de México, D. Agustín de Iturbide.* Mexico, 1908.

VILLANUEVA, CARLOS A. *La Monarquía en América: Bolívar y el general San Martín.* Paris [1911].

———. *La Monarquía en América: Fernando VII y los nuevos estados.* Paris, n.d.

WEBSTER, CHARLES K. *The Foreign Policy of Castlereagh, 1815-1822.* London, 1925.

YOAKUM, HENDERSON K. *History of Texas from Its First Settlement in 1685 to Its Annexation to the United States in 1846,* vol. I. New York, 1856.

ZAMACOIS, NICETO DE. *Historia de Méjico desde sus tiempos mas remotos hasta nuestros dias,* vols. VIII-XI. Mexico, 1877-1879.

ZÁRATE, JULIO. *La Guerra de independencia* (México a través de los siglos, vol. III). Barcelona, c. 1880.

ZUBIETA, PEDRO A. *Apuntaciones sobre las primeras misiones diplomáticas de Colombia.* Bogotá, 1924.

B. ARTICLES IN NEWSPAPERS, PERIODICALS, AND OTHER PUBLICATIONS

ARRIAGA, ANTONIO. "¿Traicionó Iturbide a los conspiradores de Valladolid?" *Universidad Michoacana,* vol. XI, nos. 8 and 9, pp. 20-24. Morelia, 1938.

BENSON, NETTIE L. "The Plan of Casa Mata," *Hispanic American Historical Review,* XXV, 45-56. Durham, N. C., 1945.

[BIGELOW, JOHN]. "The Heir Presumptive to the Imperial Crown of Mexico, Don Agustín de Iturbide," *Harper's Magazine,* LXVI, 735-749. New York, 1883.

CAMACHO, ANGEL M. "Don Félix Ma. Calleja, virrey de Nueva España," *Boletín del instituto de estudios americanistas de Sevilla,* vol. I, no. 1, pp. 51-54. Seville, 1913.

COELLAR, JOSÉ M. "Iturbide, soldado realista," *El Universal,* September, 1921. Mexico.

"Controversía entre el obispo de Puebla y el virrey Calleja," *Boletin del archivo general de la nacion,* vol. IV, no. 5, pp. 654-696. Mexico, 1933.

DALEVUELTA, JACOBO. "Como juró la independencia en Iguala D. Agustín de Iturbide," *El Universal,* September, 1921. Mexico.

DÁVILA GARÍBI, JOSÉ I. "Apuntes biográficos del Exmo. é Ilmo. Sr. Dr. D. Juan Cruz Ruíz de Cabañas y Crespo," *Anales del museo nacional de arqueología, historia y etnología,* 4th series, IV, 1-39. Mexico, 1912.

DOWNEY, THOMAS E. "Central America under Mexico, 1821-1823," *Greater America: Essays in Honor of Herbert Eugene Bolton*, pp. 362-378. Berkeley, 1945.

"El Ejército de Nueva España a fines del siglo XVIII," *Boletin del archivo general de la nacion*, vol. IX, no. 2, pp. 236-275. Mexico, 1938.

FLORES, JENARO M. "D. Epigmenio de la Piedra," *Divulgación histórica*, vol. I, no. 1, pp. 15-18. Mexico, 1939.

"Fr. Vicente Santa María y la conjuración de Valladolid," *Boletin del archivo general de la nacion*, vol. II, no. 5, pp. 707-769. Mexico, 1931.

FRÍAS, JOSÉ D. "Iturbide fue el autor del Plan de Iguala," *Excelsior*, September 27, 1921. Mexico.

FUENTE, JOSÉ M. DE LA. "El Sargento Pío Marcha," *Boletín de la sociedad de geografía y estadística de la república mexicana*, 5th series, I, 25-27. Mexico, 1900.

IGUÍNIZ, JUAN B. "Iturbide en el destierro y en el cadalso," *El Universal*, September, 1921. Mexico.

ITURBIDE, AGUSTÍN DE. "Don Agustín de Iturbide," *Records of the American Catholic Historical Society of Philadelphia*, XXVI, 289-310; XXVII, 16-44. Philadelphia, 1918.

MORENO, LANDELINO. "Independencia de la capitanía general de Guatemala . . . ," *Anales de la sociedad de geografía é historia de Guatemala*, VI, 3-32. Guatemala, 1929.

PALACIOS, ENRIQUE J. "La Revindicación de Iturbide," *Anales del museo nacional de arqueología, historia y etnografía*, series 5, I, 189-199. Mexico, 1934.

[PÉREZ, FRANCISCO]. "El Memorable abrazo de Acatempan," *Excelsior*, September 27, 1921. Mexico.

PEZA, JOSÉ MIGUEL DE LA. "La bella 'Güera' Rodríguez. Un episodio romántico de la agitado vida del Libertador de nuestro pais, el Generalísimo Don Agustín de Iturbide," *ibid*.

REVILLA, DOMINGO. "Estudios históricos, 27 de Setiembre de 1821," *El Museo Mexicano*, II, 231-236. Mexico, 1843.

ROA BÁRCENA, JOSÉ M. "El Templo de la Profesa," *La Cruz*, I, 574-577. Mexico, 1856.

ROBERTSON, WILLIAM S. "The Juntas of 1808 and the Spanish Colonies," *English Historical Review*, XXI, 573-585. London, 1916.

———. "The Memorabilia of Agustín de Iturbide," *Hispanic American Historical Review*, XXVII, 436-455. Durham, N. C., 1947.

———. "Metternich's Attitude toward Revolutions in Latin America," *ibid*., XXI, 838-858. Durham, N. C., 1941.

———. "The Monroe Doctrine Abroad in 1823-24," *American Political Science Review*, VI, 546-563. Baltimore, 1912.

———. "The Policy of Spain toward Its Revolted Colonies, 1820-1823,"

348 BIBLIOGRAPHY

Hispanic American Historical Review, VI, 21-46. Durham, N. C., 1926.

——. "The Recognition of the Hispanic American Nations by the United States," *ibid.*, I, 239-269. Baltimore, 1918.

——. "Russia and the Emancipation of Spanish America, 1816-1826," *ibid.*, XXI, 196-221. Durham, N. C., 1941.

——. "The United States and Spain in 1822," *American Historical Review*, XX, 781-800. New York, 1915.

ROBLEDO, JUAN DE DÍOS. "Don Agustín de Iturbide y el criterio nacional," *El Universal*, September, 1921. Mexico.

——. "Los Historiadores insurgentes: Don Carlos María de Bustamante," *El Universal*, September 18, 1921. Mexico.

ROMERO DE TERREROS, MANUEL. "La bella mujer que amó Iturbide," *Révista de Revistas*, September 25, 1921. Mexico.

SOTO HALL, MAXIMO. "Independencia del reino de Guatemala hoy Centro América," Ricardo Levene, *Historia de América*, VII, 97-266. Buenos Aires, 1940.

TORRE, JUAN DE LA. "Datos históricos de Morelia," *El Tiempo Ilustrado*, pp. 646-656. Mexico, October 2, 1904.

VALLE, RAFAEL HELIODORO. "Iturbide no es Autor Único y Exclusivo del Plan de Iguala. Una placa descubierto en Tasco y de Gran Interés Histórico," *Excelsior*, September 17, 1942. Mexico.

——. "Numismática iturbidiana," *El Universal Ilustrado*, November 24, 1921. Mexico.

VILLACORTA, C. J. A. "Bibliografía é iconografía de la independencia," *Anales de la sociedad de geografía é historia de Guatemala*, XIV, 1-17. Guatemala, 1937.

WINKLER, ERNEST W. "The Cherokee Indians in Texas," *Quarterly of the Texas State Historical Association*, VII, 95-105. Austin, 1903.

ZAVALA, SILVIO. "México: La Revolución, la Índependencia, la Constitución de 1824," Ricardo Levene, *Historia de América*, VII, 3-96. Buenos Aires, 1940.

Index

[349]

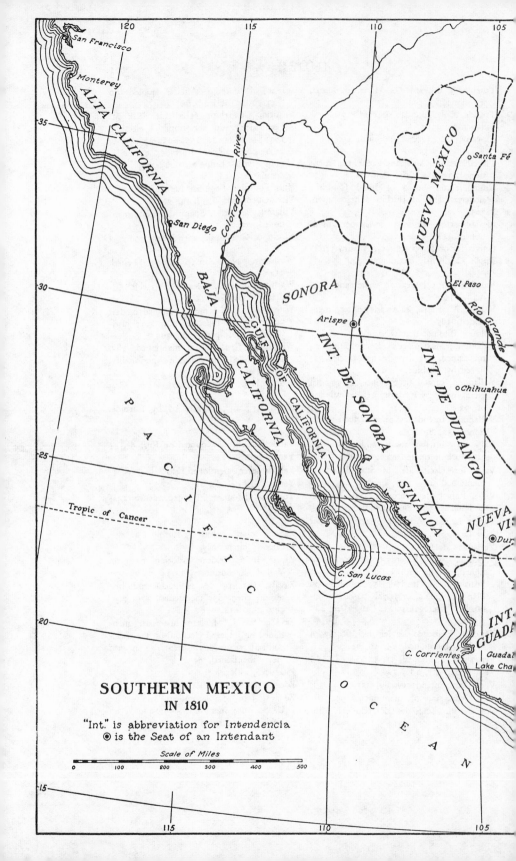

San Francisco

Monterey

ALTA CALIFORNIA

35

30

25

20

15

NUEVO MÉXICO

Santa Fé

River

Colorado

San Diego

BAJA

GULF OF CALIFORNIA

CALIFORNIA

C. San Lucas

SONORA

Arispe

INT. DE SONORA

SINALOA

El Paso

Río Grande

INT. DE DURANGO

Chihuahua

NUEVA VI:

Dur

PACIFIC

Tropic of Cancer

OCEAN

C. Corrientes

INT. GUADA

Guadal

Lake Cha

120

115

110

105

SOUTHERN MEXICO
IN 1810

"Int." is abbreviation for Intendencia
◉ is the Seat of an Intendant

Scale of Miles

0   100   200   300   400   500

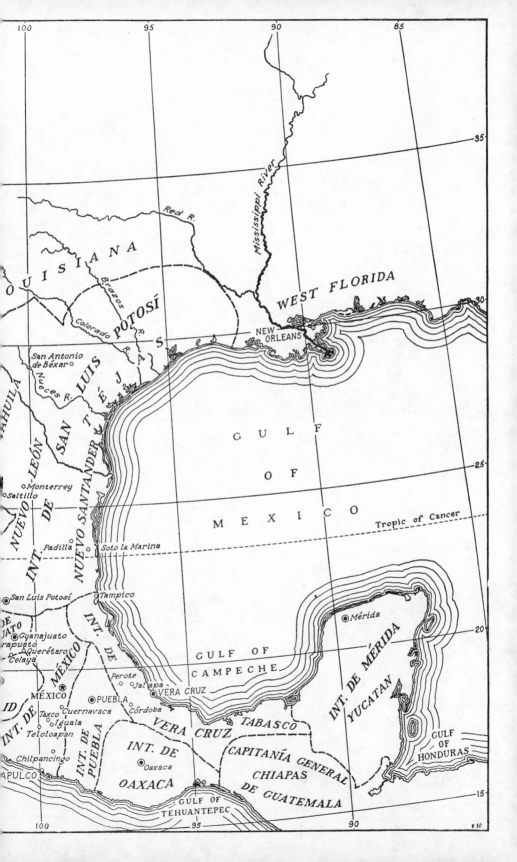